Aylesbury Bolton Wolverhampton Hove:

A Little Man and 101 Cardiacs Gigs

by
Adrian Bell

First published in 2011 by
Iron Bell Publishing
Phone: 07788 610305
Email: adrian_bell1889@hotmail.com

© Adrian Bell 2011

ISBN 978-0-9568795-0-9

Printed by
People For Print
Unit 10, Riverside Park, Sheaf Gardens,
Sheffield, South Yorkshire S2 4BB
0114 272 0915
juma@btconnect.com
Cover design:
Images Design For Print

Front cover photo by Anuli Photography
70 Frith Road, London E11 4EY
www.anuli.co.uk

Executive Producer: Clive Hutton

This book is dedicated to the one and only Tim Smith.
For the years, nay, DECADES of listening pleasure,
I am most truly, humbly, grateful.
Get well soon buddy.

And for Sarah Hailey - if it hadn't been for Cardiacs
we'd never have had such brilliant nights as that
Jesus Underground Band gig in a barn in Evenley.

*Steven -
This is the last one
I've got to sell, ever!
Enjoy.*

Acknowledgements

First of all, thanks to all those members of Cardiacs in my gig-going existence, providing the soundtrack to my life since 1988, largely, Tim Smith, Jim Smith, Tim Quy, William D Drake, Sarah Smith, Dominic Luckman, Bic Hayes, Jon Poole, Bob Leith, Clare Lemmon, Mel Woods, Steve Gilchrist, Dawn Torabi, Cathy Harabaras, and Kavus Torabi, with Sharron Fortnam and Oceansize hijacking the stage now 'n' again; roadcrew and ex-members who have found me in their way a few times, including Mark Cawthra, Little Hicky, Matthew Cutts, Dave Murder, Graham Simmonds, Clive Giblin, Captain John Hook, ordinary shop girls Lucy Cooke, Jane Kyprianidis and Bill Hiles; the best fixer of guest-list entries ever, John Daniel; for the dubious privilege of attending gigs with me, firstly John Atkinson and Peter Shoobridge, then frequently Simon "Sewer" Wright, Liz Nichols née Barton, Richard Jackson, Claire Thomas, and most of all, Ian Skinner; for answering my questionnaires, providing lifts, sofas and floors, Karen and Paul "Helocolin" Johnson, Paul Ashby, Malcolm Crosby, Dave "Diggy" Dawson, Andy Hossain, Pete Davis, Clare Kelly, Mike "Livo" Livesey, Al Gittens, Andy Thompson, Max Crowe, Jesse Vecchione, Stephen "Schlep" Wilson, Jill and Paul Howard, and Graeme and Carli Dogstand; those lucky ladies to whom I introduced Cardiacs into their lives, most lovingly Sarah Hailey, Annie Hall, Annette Zenk, Katrina Corry, Serena Clark, and Jitka Malkova; Gemma Ryan for having to listen to my worries and panics about the book (and other stuff that we won't go into) night-shift after night-shift (sorry love, this one goes past Chapter 6 too); everyone who has had to work with me past, present and future, whether it be GT News Sandygate Road, GT Leisuretime H****borough, GT Leisureworld Rotherham, Turners Wholsesale News Barnsley, Circle K Flitwick, Stormark Banbury, Tesco Pinner Green, Tesco Hackney Well Street, but especially and most fondly (yes, really), everyone who has had to put up with my lacklustre shifts after hitchhiking through the night post Cardiacs-gig or Sheffield United-disaster at Circle K/Neighbours/Spar/Alldays Brackley, Tesco Brackley, Tesco Bishopsgate, Tesco King's Cross, and Tesco Ashford (Middlesex); the whole of Cardiacs Chatlist, especially those who subscribed (see gig list at the back - them there names are those lucky subscribers who wanted to see their name next to a special gig and have been rewarded with a nice hardback limited edition which the rest of you can't get hold of, unless any of them fall on hard times and flog it on eBay - I'll be watching! (Fever Hitch for 23p indeed!)); Martin Lacey at People For Print for having to contend with my ever-increasingly fussy demands; Dan Wooding and Dan Hedges, from whom I borrowed a few ideas on writing (check out Rick Wakeman: The Caped Crusader and Yes: The Authorised Biography and you'll see what I mean); Dan and Cat Evans for sustenance and some rather fine dinners; Dave Roker for having to wait while I finished on his computer; Andy Bonell aka Musical Blade who actually took the cover photo for Fever Hitch you know; Dawn Skinner for a rather splendid Sunday Sport story; Michael Tyack, Will Summers and Circulus for putting the Crum back into Horn and letting me get in their way when Cardiacs stopped; Yes, Gong, Genesis, King Crimson and every other Prog band in my collection for providing inspiration, happiness, hope and entertainment; Sheffield United for ruining many a great day out; England's cricketers for winning The Ashes twice during the making of this book (and that's why it's two years late, folks); Dominic Lawson and Classic Rock Presents Prog (where were you in 1983 when I really needed you?).

Special thanks to a musical family, Rennie Bell, Helen Bell, Fiona Lau, Julian Bell, Alex Bell, and Deborah Woodhouse - I was the youngest so they all had their say.

Making life easier, Pete Davis and his fabulous Cardiacs gig list, http://www.death.plus.com/cardiacs/cdxgiglist.htm

Honourable and deserved second mention for Ian Skinner, for companionship often beyond the call of duty.

And finally, the "without whom" extra special mentions: Clive "Big Ship Iron" Hutton for making a dream a reality, and Sean and Marina at The Organ for being part of the story throughout.

Photo Credits

The vast majority of the photos/records/CDs/tapes/items of memorabilia presented herein are taken from my personal collection; here are the ones that aren't:

The front cover photograph was taken one dangerous Friday evening at the foot of the M1 at Staples Corner by Annelie Rosencrantz; Special Garage gig photo on the title page of Chapter 1 donated by Max Crowe; the two photos at the end of Chapter 2 "borrowed" from my Mum's collection; the photo of myself and Ian Skinner at Stonehenge at the end of Chapter 6 taken by Dan Evans; the title page photo of Cardiacs from on high, Chapter 7, taken by Clare Kelly with my camera; the photo of myself and Paul Helocolin dressed rather strangely at Tutbury Castle at the end of Chapter 8 was taken by Sarah Maher; the title page photo from Chapter 16 and the one at the end of Cardiacs Bear were provided by Pete Davis; the main photo of me being glowsticked on the title page of Chapter 23 is reproduced with the kind permission of Mei Lewis from Mission Photographic Ltd, www.missionphotographic.com, all the other photos from that chapter are thanks to Andrew Duffy; the photo at the end of Chapter 24 is from Carli Dogstand's collection; as was the one from the title page of Chapter 25; the lovely photo of Tim Smith before the Epilogue was taken at that last gig in Leeds and was lovingly donated by Pete Davis; the rear cover photo was taken by Andrew Duffy; all the photos in the middle bit are from me.

Contents

Introduction 7

Prologue 13

1. "Hope Day" The Special Garage Concerts, October 17th, 18th, 19th 2003 19

2. "Buds and Spawn" My Musical Journey 37

3. "Heaven Born and Ever Brighton" The Old Market, Brighton, November 12th 2007 53

4. "Plane Plane Against the Grain" The Organ 67

5. "Victory Egg" The Carling Academy, Oxford, November 13th 2007 79

6. "Look in the Back, See Who's Gayer, Birthday Boy or Leo Sayer" Ian Skinner 87

7. "Big Ship" The Thekla, Bristol, November 14th 2007 103

8. "The Obvious Identity" My Tattoo and the Helocolins 113

9. "A Pay-as-you-exit Bus for a Bus on the Bus"
   Rescue Rooms, Nottingham, November 15th 2007 129

10. "Odd Even" Paul Ashby 141

11. "In A City Lining" The Astoria, London, November 16th 2007 153

12. "Baby Heart Dirt" Those Long Suffering Girlfriends 169

    Illustrations 195

13. "Affectionate Friends" Little Trophy at Notting Hill Arts Centre and
    North Sea Radio Orchestra at Chalk Farm Roundhouse, November 17th 2007 211

14. "As Cold As Can Be In an English Sea" Those Overseas Enthusiasts 233

15. "There's Too Many Irons In the Fire" The Boardwalk, Sheffield, November 19th 2007 245

16. "Pip As Uncle Dick But Peter Spoiled It" Pete "Thrupty" Davis and Clare Kelly 257

17. "Two Civilians Scrap" The Sugarmill, Stoke-on-Trent, November 20th 2007 269

18. "If You Wanted to Catch One You Would Have to Take a Car"
    Andy Hossain, Diggy, Lil Malc 279

19. "Hopeless" Academy 3, Manchester, November 21st 2007 291

20. "Wind And Rains Is Cold" Al "Little Squirrel Feet" Gittens, Andy Thompson, and Livo 303

21. "The Seaside" Wedgewood Rooms, Portsmouth, November 22nd 2007 317

22. "Ideal" The Dogstands and the Howards 329

23. "A Time For Rejoicing" Clwb Ifor Bach, Cardiff, November 23rd 2007 345

24. "Look Out Everybody…" Clive "Big Ship Iron" Hutton 361

25. "Will Bleed Amen" Woodhouse Liberal Club, Leeds, November 24th 2007 379

    Epilogue Gong Live At The Forum, Kentish Town, June 15th 2008 393

    Appendices 397

    The Belch Cardiacs Gigs List 403

Introduction

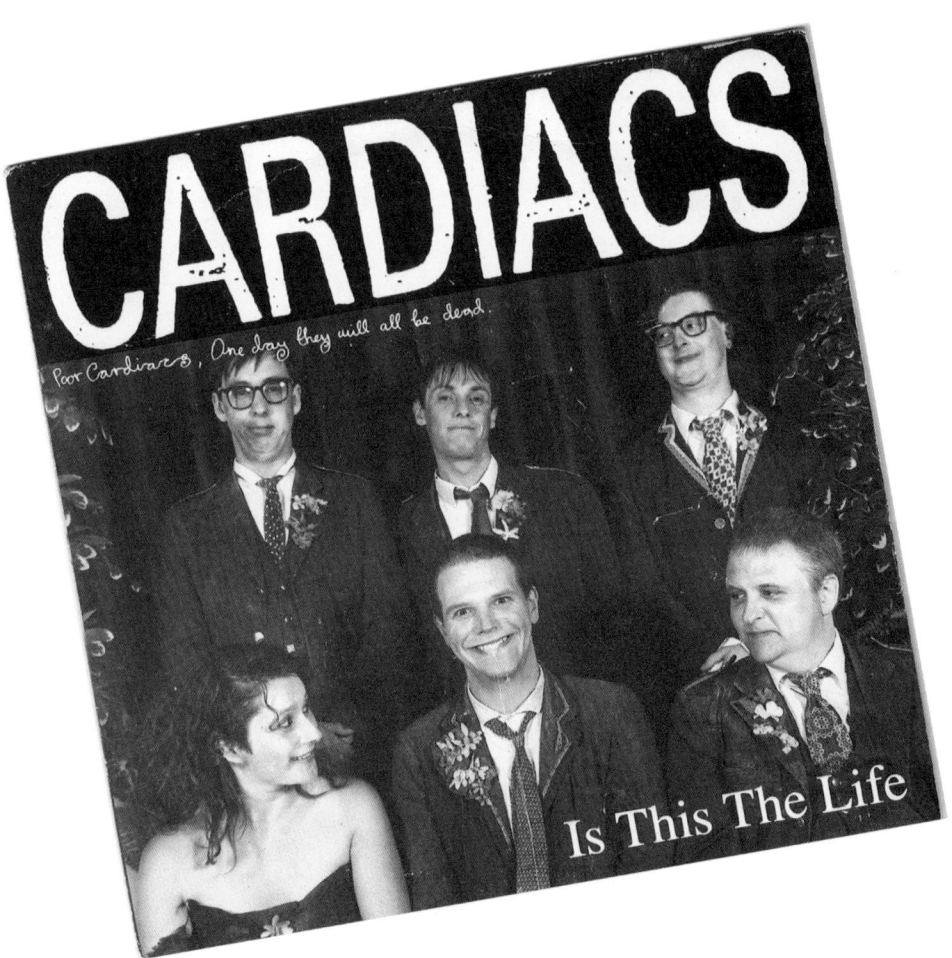

Introduction

The Power of Music

This is a book about passion. People are passionate about many things (in fact, some have suggested that I'm passionate about too many things, which may explain why I have so many sleepless nights trying to fit everything in): some people are passionate about football, some about cricket, some about golf; some people are passionate about work (heaven forbid), some about avoiding work, some about being off sick; then there are some people who are passionate about music. And that is where this book comes in. For not only is this book about people who love their music, this book deals specifically with fans of one band in particular - Cardiacs; wonderful, beautiful Cardiacs, a band who first crossed my radar in 1986, and by 1988 had become an obsession, an obsession that has lasted right up to the present day.

In the research and writing of this book, it has been fascinating to see how many other bands the individuals featured herein are passionate about, leading me to conclude that not only are we all passionate about our music, but that music in itself is a pretty powerful thing…

For example, when driving to Stonehenge with the beautiful Claire (formerly Clayre) in 2004 for the Summer Solstice, we were listening to "Ritual" by Yes, a 21-minute masterwork if ever there was one, a song that builds and rumbles and crashes and fights and shines and culminates in the most EPIC guitar solo Steve Howe ever conjured. As we came over the brow of the A303 from Amesbury and saw Stonehenge resplendent in all its majesty, this very guitar solo kicked in at that exact second and I went all gooey in the tummy, a huge shiver running down my spine whilst all the hairs on my arm stood on end. That's what music does for me, and it most likely does it for the most of you I imagine will get something out of this book.

Cardiacs: Who They?

Cardiacs don't have exclusive rights to fans going all dizzy with passion, but it *does* seem that a hefty percentage of their fan-base are rather more enthusiastic than may seem reasonable to outsiders (tattoos, following them around to every gig on a particular tour, that sort of thing);

you don't come across many people who say, "Oh, I *quite* like Cardiacs, I've got one of their albums." Their fans have all got every album (and more), and they've all been to at least 50 of their gigs (or so it seems). And I'm assuming that they've all thus bought this book and know who Cardiacs are. But there might be the odd stranger who has picked this up at a jumble sale, so I'd better just say a little bit…

Cardiacs haven't sold millions of records or ever sold out Wembley Arena, and they are not famous as such, but a lot of people think they may have heard about them or seen their name in *Sounds* back in the day. Well, Cardiacs *have* been around for a while, so their name may have drifted across the odd radar or two, and they nearly had a hit single in 1988 when "Is This the Life?" got a ton of airplay, but nowhere near enough discs were pressed up so it didn't get into Woolworths and the like. But no, you won't have seen them at the Brits (thank goodness) or on *Top of the Pops*.

When Ian Skinner (long-term Cardiacs buddy) and I were hitchhiking to Cardiacs gigs and Ian was in the front seat having to do most of the talking whilst I desperately leaned forward trying to stick my nose in, once he'd told the driver who we were going to see, they would invariably ask Ian who Cardiacs were. At that point Ian always used to turn round to me and say, 'Do your bit.' So I used to reel off a well-rehearsed gambit, and it went something a bit like this:

Cardiacs grew up in the 1970s listening to Progressive Rock (hereon-in more often than not referred to as Prog Rock, or sometimes Prog-Rock depending how grammatically correct I'm feeling) like Genesis and Yes and Gong, but were inspired to form a band at the height of the Punk explosion in 1976/1977, so they ended up sounding like a bizarre cross between the two. Still do to be honest, with a bit of Indie and Alternative thrown in. Basically they have all the complexity of Prog played with the passion of Punk. They do in four minutes what Yes do in twenty; they s-l-o-w down, they *speed* up, they stop. They start… And they are the best live band you will ever see. When listening to their albums, it is hard to believe they can pass it off in concert, but they do, with interest. (Can I just state this is NOT Gospel, just my own take on things.)

And there you have it. How they came into my life, and into the lives of others, is dealt with elsewhere in the book, so that will do for now. When we were hitching the odd driver expressed an interest, but I don't think we ever persuaded any of them to join us at a gig. But then it is fair to say that Cardiacs aren't to everyone's taste - in fact, some people are pretty passionate about hating them, which would be quite funny if I myself didn't find it so puzzling. As it is, I reckon it is they who are missing out, because I've right enjoyed it myself...

"Wots It All Abowt, Mate?"

I always had this idea that I'd do a trilogy of books, with the first being the most marketable (in that some people might actually want to buy it), the one about football and my ridiculous devotion to Sheffield United and all that silly hitchhiking. That came into being with the publication of *Fever Hitch* in 2001. The other two books would be about my Summer Solstice experiences at Stonehenge from 1984 up to the present day, and then my adventures traipsing around the country in order to catch Cardiacs live in concert. I actually started the Stonehenge book too, not long after *Fever Hitch* came out, but for some reason only got as far as Chapter 4. Trust me though (don't), it *will* be a good read, and it might get done one day (although I reckon there's more mileage to be gained from my tales of a lively career with a certain well-known retailer). However, the book I always told people I was really looking forward to writing was the one about my Cardiacs frolics. But how on earth would I structure it...?

Much like *Fever Hitch* came about through encouragement and enthusiasm garnered from spending a ridiculous amount of time on the Sheffield United Independent Shareholders Association message-board, the now-sadly-defunct *Viewpoints* site, this book was the result of mixing with another online community, that of the Cardiacs Email Chatlist, or The List as it is known to most.

For years I couldn't get on The List due to either lack of computer, or The List not accepting my email address for some reason. Ian, being much more technologically advanced than myself, was on it pretty much from the start though (sometime in the 1990s), so he was always telling me how good it was, and if ever I needed to get a message across, he'd do it on my behalf. Eventually, late on in 2006 I got in, and at last I was able to bore people rigid with tales of hitchhiking to Leeds in 1996 and what-have-you.

Not long after, I discovered the joys of MySpace and built a nice profile, sticking hundreds (and I mean HUNDREDS) of photos on there that I'd taken of Cardiacs and at Stonehenge, amongst others. Also, back in the early days I blogged like crazy, relating just about every gig and football match I attended (I'm a lazy blogger now, of course). So when the dates for Cardiacs' 2007 tour were announced (eleven of them eventually), with my Cardiacs Gig Tally standing at 90, I was delighted that this jaunt was going to take me to my century and beyond, although I was somewhat daunted by the amount of blogging I was going to have to do. But then it came to me, whilst dragging cages of stock around in the warehouse at work (sometimes a bland job can get you thinking quite creatively): from 90 to 101 gigs over the course of two weeks with plenty of flashbacks *á la Fever Hitch*, rather than blogging it make this your Cardiacs book... I excitedly told colleagues my plan, and they backed me 100% by getting on with their work. So I raced home and reported to The List community instead, their response being a little more enthusiastic.

I developed the initial idea to include hitchhiking to every gig (the best laid plans and all that), and put out a plea via The List for places to kip the night after each live extravaganza, with the promise that those who let Belch (that's me in case you don't know) doss on their sofa would get a chapter all about themselves in the book (and I pretty much came through with that one). You see, I soon realised that not only did I have a lot to say about My Life With Cardiacs In It, so did many others. As it turned out, this was the most fascinating aspect for me (and the hardest to write, because I've always been good at going on about myself, but trying to profile others, well, it would be a real test of my writing skills), fascinating because I doubt there has ever been a band that have drawn fans from such diverse genres; you've got your Proggers, your Punks, your Folkies, your Metal Heads, your Indie Kids... Fascinating also to see what other things these people had been brought up on; all *Wombles* and fairy tales and Classical

Music - great stuff! The one thing all had in common though; Cardiacs had featured prominently along the way, a fact making me both proud and very, very happy. I also hope it makes for a pretty good book.

Who's In It?

Well for a start I am in it, and I make no excuses or apologies for the odd indulgence. It's my book, and it's about how Cardiacs and music have affected my life, so if that involves a jolly funny story about sleeping in a hedge in Birmingham, then so be it. Much like Cardiacs put on their *Sampler* album, "This is not a best-of compilation," this book is not, I repeat NOT, a history of the band. I repeat repeat repeat, this is my own personal (largely musical) history, with Cardiacs chunks in it.

Except it's not just about me. There are also big bits about some of their wonderful fans, like I mentioned up there somewhere, and those featured are those that helped me out on the 2007 tour by either driving me around when I was feeling too grotty to hitch (most of the time) or by letting me kip on their floor etc. There are also mentions for enthusiasts from across the sea, with a bit of a nod towards bands who sound like they may possess a few Cardiacs albums, or have actually sprung from the loins of Cardiacs themselves. Not forgetting a chapter on the lovely (most of them) ladies in my life and how I tried to force a bit of Cardiacs on them. And because I know all these people and all these bands, I've managed to stick more bits about myself in each chapter too, just in case you were worried...

Of course, the members of the band all get a mention or two as well, so let's hear it for those current Cardiacs: Tim Smith, Jim Smith, Bob Leith, Kavus Torabi, Melanie Woods and Cathy Harabaras, as well as the past members I've seen performing with the band: Jon Poole, Claire Lemmon, Dawn Staple, Sharron Fortnam, Steve Gilchrist, Dominic Luckman, William D Drake, Tim Quy, Christian "Bic" Hayes and Sarah Smith.

In addition we also have an excess of roadcrew and a whole plethora of other fans who surface along the way, and heck, there was much to write about. In fact, it's over 125,000 words, so make yourself a drink, put on a very long concept album, and get stuck in...

Prologue

There now follows an announcement from
THE ALPHABET BUSINESS CONCERN

As some of you have no doubt become aware, Tim Smith, the stalwart front man of your beloved CARDIACS has fallen foul of ill health.

In order to quash any rumours and idle tittle-tattle amongst the faithful we find it appropriate at this time to furnish you with the necessary information to perhaps remove the worried furrows from the brows of the more hysterical amongst you..

On 25th June Tim collapsed and found himself the unfortunate victim of, ironically, a cardiac arrest. Thanks to the skill and dedication of those heroes of the streets, the paramedic service, he was speedily ensconced within the caring hands of the National Health Service where he was treated by expert medical staff and thankfully he is now making a recovery. There is no longer any danger to his life and he is improving every day though we must caution that there is a long road ahead.

Needless to say we are sure you all wish him a speedy recovery and in keeping with our reputation as the caring concern, THE ALPHABET BUSINESS CONCERN will soon be facilitating a method of sending him your personal messages of goodwill on our Web site which is sure to cheer him and his fellow CARDIACS no end.

Needless to say, all further information will be generously furnished by THE ALPHABET BUSINESS CONCERN as and when we see fit and we hasten to add that YOUR LOYALTY DEMANDS the utmost respect for his nearest and dearest and that no attempts to gather any more information be made during this most fretful of times.

With respect
THE ALPHABET BUSINESS CONCERN

Posted July 23rd 2008

There now follows an announcement from
THE ALPHABET BUSINESS CONCERN

Due to the extenuating circumstances we find ourselves in following the health issues pertaining to CARDIACS very own Tim Smith we have deemed it appropriate at this time to officially call to a halt all activities concerning CARDIACS for the foreseeable future. It therefore falls upon us to reluctantly cancel the forthcoming tour booked for November.

We apologise wholeheartedly for this unavoidable action and also for any delay in letting you know of our decision. Any delay has been necessary in order to assure all promoters and their hirelings have been made aware of this decision in advance to facilitate early redemption of any ticketing refunds as and when required.

On a more positive note, THE ALPHABET BUSINESS CONCERN has now provided a unique and encouragingly entitled special electronic code sequential address for the exclusive use of YOU the faithful to send your well wishes, uplifting verse or whatever you decide to encourage the earliest recovery of young Tim.

This is the facility you shall use and only this to ensure that your messages reach the sickly lad.

We will of course be certain to deliver to him those messages we deem appropriate at the appropriate time.
With respect
THE ALPHABET BUSINESS CONCERN

Posted: June 25th 2009
THERE NOW FOLLOWS AN ANNOUNCEMENT FROM THE ALPHABET BUSINESS CONCERN

A full year has now passed by silently and stealthily yet with ever an eye on promptitude and a passion for consistency it now falls upon THE ALPHABET BUSINESS CONCERN to provide this timely annual update to YOU our ever faithful family regarding the health and condition of Tim Smith.

One complete year on from Tim Smith's 'accident', THE AL-PHABET BUSINESS CONCERN is only too aware that since its previous gloomy news bulletin there have purposely been no further updates. In this time YOU have been both patient and respectful to the family of YOUR IDOL and to those so called friends with whom he keeps regular counsel. If rumour and tittle-tattle have reached the collective ear of THE ALPHABET BUSINESS CONCERN then we have seen fit neither to extinguish nor fan their ugly flames.

It is at this time, then, that THE ALPHABET BUSINESS CON-CERN has chosen to clarify the CURRENT situation At the time of his cardiac arrest Tim Smith effectively died. Resuscitation allowed his passage back from that world of mists and spirits to this one of foetid edges and filth, but upon re-entering this VALE OF TEARS it became apparent that he had suffered a terrible brain injury from the inability of his faltered heart to supply its regular goodness in the quantities required to sustain a healthy condition within his brainbox.

Quite what the sickly lad experienced over the course of the remaining months of 2008 remains largely unclear. He claims at one point to have been surrounded by 'cheap microphones' while at other times that he was visited by 'multiple cigarette smoking' friends whilst languishing in a 'cafe that served exquisite fruit juice' all set within a 'beautiful surreal landscape of rivers and curtains'. In keeping with our reputation as The HONEST Concern, THE ALPHABET BUSINESS CONCERN can state categorically that none of these constructs was of our making.

Since the accident Tim Smith's body has become his enemy. He is in a great deal of pain and is experiencing difficulty with the finer points of control with regard to his extremities so obviously perfected prior to the unhappy event, but Tim Smith, his family and those so called friends (with whom he keeps counsel) all assert that his mind, however, has been sharpened by the episode. THE AL-PHABET BUSINESS CONCERN can confirm that no part of YOUR favourite pop star's intellect or personality has been found to be absent WHATSOEVER.

So where does that leave CARDIACS and where does that leave YOU?

At this point Tim Smith can neither sing nor play his guitar. THE ALPHABET BUSINESS CONCERN, in keeping with its enviable reputation as THE REALISTIC CONCERN, can state that it is extremely unlikely that CARDIACS will perform live for the foreseeable future. THIS IS NOT, IT MUST BE NOTED, THE END OF CARDIACS. YOU must once again be patient before events can reveal themselves as foodstuffs for YOUR greedy little mouths.

Unlike the so-called prescient ways of that, at best, 'cosmic chancer' Nostradamus, THE ALPHABET BUSINESS CONCERN claim no 'second sight', therefore it would be mere folly to muse upon how future events may unfold. Tim Smith's condition permits no such speculation, but there is in his own words 'A glimmer of anticipation . . . Quite a glimmer.' And it is to give that glimmer the oxygen that it requires to become the roaring flame we all need to warm our clammy flesh, that he is participating in the trials and tribulations required within the system of neurological rehabilitation where he is making many small but positive inroads into his recovery. We are therefore left in no doubt that it is a long and arduous road beset with many trips and stumbles along the way that has yet to be travelled.

In respect of the awful events of last year, much of the machinery surrounding your favourite group, CARDIACS, had ground to a halt. In honour of YOUR patience, YOU will observe the cogs begin to turn and the pistons sputter to life once more. THE ALPHABET BUSINESS CONCERN will soon make available to YOU the goods and artefacts YOU so hungrily crave.

Tim Smith and it goes without saying, THE ALPHABET BUSINESS CONCERN, would like to thank all of YOU who have sent him YOUR kind thoughts and beautiful words and indeed in a few thankfully rare cases, your daubs and photos. They have all been gratefully received where appropriate and both Tim and ourselves would encourage you all to continue with your correspondence.

With Respect

from Cardiacs' website, www.cardiacs.com:

Chapter One
"Hope Day"
The Special Garage Concerts,
October 17th, 18th, 19th 2003

"Hope Day"
The Special Garage Concerts, October 17th, 18th, 19th 2003

The house lights go down and the Alphabet Business Concern chimes ring out through the PA. The atmosphere goes from idle chitchat amongst the crowd to a buzz of expectation. A cheer goes up before the chimes sound a second time, then a third, this time in the form of a keyboard fanfare. The buzz is now not only audible, but almost tangible as the most spine-tinglingly brilliant intro-tape begins. Starting from an almost inaudible rumble, it builds through industrial scrapes and hisses, doves cooing in amongst it all somewhere (actually they must be pigeons - doves are far too upper-class), growing louder and louder until a beautiful cacophony is tearing through the speakers.

Then there is a deep rumble and the drums start pounding in rapid unison. This time the crowd cheer wildly, because now they know they are but seconds away from the entrance of the band they are all gathered here to see - Cardiacs. Blessed, glorious Cardiacs, the finest band ever to have graced this beautiful old planet of ours.

First up is tiny Bob Leith, marching across the front of the stage, not even glancing once at the congregated masses. He must be shy, the poor lamb, so he just clambers up behind his drums, plonks his headphones on, then sits there waiting. Jim Smith is next, pausing for a brief bow, but the sight of Tim Smith striding on in his big menacing overcoat and pointy guitar soon stops that. Then there's new boy Kavus Torabi, all smiles and big hair, freshly promoted from Crew to Band Member.

And then, ooops - the tape seems to cut off a bit prematurely, but no panic; Tim just grins at everyone, then brings the boys in with an exaggerated dip of his guitar and they play a big chord. Then Bob bashes his sticks together cueing in the start of the instrumental "Leaf Scrapings", an unusual choice of opening piece, but then "unusual" is rather in keeping with the night, and indeed, the whole history of Cardiacs...

* * * *

By the time I returned to my flat in Walthamstow after the first of those three Special Garage Concerts in October 2003, I was still in a state of shock. This one had been Cardiacs gig number 76 for me, but it was very possible that I had never experienced one finer. It was certainly up there in the top five, that's for sure. I tried describing it to my flatmate but gave up and just sat there speechless (and anyone who knows me will tell you this NEVER happens). It is worth pointing out that my flatmate at the time hated Cardiacs with a passion. Every time I put them on, she used to close every door between my room and wherever she was, turning something else up very loud indeed. Oooh, them there Cardiacs - always ones for polarising opinion. But anyway, you can surely see the futility of trying to describe this most exceptional of gigs to a non-believer. Instead I just mumbled something about it being like seeing Cardiacs for the first time again, and left it at that.

So what was so "special" about these Special Garage Concerts? Well, it had been announced on cardiacs.com that at the forthcoming concerts they would only be playing songs from before 1983, some of which had never been recorded or even played live before. There was a suggestion that the band were hard at rehearsal, and that we should all make the effort to attend as these gigs were going to be something very SPECIAL indeed, so SPECIAL that they would be recorded and issued on two SPECIAL CD albums.

Upon reading all this, I worried that it was going to be awfully hard work for Cardiacs because the band was now a four-piece, and most of those old tunes were complex little masterpieces with large dollops of keyboard wizardry. But then whenever the band had played any old stuff since the loss of keyboard player William D. Drake in 1991 they'd pulled it off brilliantly, so why should this be any different? Well, in my mind they had an awful lot to do this time...

So there we all were squashed into the Garage in Islington, wondering if Cardiacs had bitten off more than they could chew. Would these gigs be brilliant, or would they be disastrous? The soothing brilliance of support band Stars In Battledress calmed us all down somewhat, to the point where I was nearly able to forget my earlier spat with the beast that was presumably the venue manager. A spat with a figure in authority? Why, of course... As she'd watched me pre-gig changing into my shorts, she'd insisted I put my mini-rucksack in the cloakroom.

'Oh, it's all right, I'll just stick it behind the speaker,' I said in a friendly manner.

'No you won't, you MUST put it in the cloakroom,' this harridan growled.

Didn't the daft cow realise I was on a tight budget? 'I can't really afford to go putting it in there; I haven't budgeted for that,' I explained helpfully.

She stood there watching as I shoved my trousers into my rucksack, but then as I made a beeline for the Cardiacs merchandise desk in the hope of stowing my gear behind there, she hauled me back telling me it was for my own safety. 'You'll only end up tripping over it and getting injured,' she insisted.

'Not if it's behind here,' I cheekily replied, but before I could even suggest to the Ordinary Shop Girls that they look after my stuff, this delightsome venue hostess gave me an ultimatum:

'Either you put it in the cloakroom, or you'll be watching the gig from out on the street, regardless of whether you hide it in there or not. The choice is yours.'

The moo. I tutted loudly, then marched off to the cloakroom muttering dark threats (such as, 'I will never bring a bag or a coat to this venue again. That'll show 'em!')

At least Stars In Battledress were helping me forget all this nastiness, and as ever with those wonderful Larcombe brothers, a real treat was being served up. Why, Richard even allowed me to get in Heckle of the Night when he was waxing lyrical about Cardiacs in between songs. Cardiacs had gained a reputation for doing annual gigs around the autumn-time, and so Richard was saying something along the lines of, 'Here we are again, all gathered at this time of year to see this most brilliant of bands. And we won't be gathered together again until this time next year...'

'Apart from tomorrow and Sunday!' shouted out a rather smug and clever me.

Everyone laughed (you know you shouldn't, it only encourages me), and Richard stuttered along, a little thrown off course, so much so that I apologised to him afterwards.

'Don't worry,' he replied, 'it was the perfect response, and so true.'

Just before Cardiacs took the stage, I was slightly concerned about the non-appearance of best-mate and long-term gig accomplice Ian, supposedly driving down from the wilds of Northamptonshire. I then received a text from him saying he was stuck in traffic so he was never going to make it. "Don't tell me how good it is," his text pleaded.

Al and Livo had made it down from Runcorn though. Sensible Al, always one for an early start when a classic gig was on offer; he'd even made it through the blizzards to see Magma at the Queen Elizabeth Hall when the rest of the country ground to halt and people couldn't even get there from parts of London (I got off the tube and walked that time).

Indeed, apart from Ian, it was the usual gathering of the faithful to witness this first Cardiacs Special Garage Concert. Andy Thompson was there with his long hair, doubtless on the look-out for Mellotron anecdotes. Pete "Thrupty" Davis was hovering innocently just off the front of the stage, ready to really let rip in the Pond. Purple Heather was there ready to update me on any unfamiliar song-titles. There were familiar faces whose names I didn't know, and a whole host of little fishes who would become valuable friends over the following years, such as Lil Malc and the Helocolins, Karen and Paul, as well as the mysterious Big Ship Iron. On top of all this, there were people who I didn't recognise (or remember) saying, 'Hello Belch.'

But now the acid test; would Cardiacs playing a load of really old stuff actually be any good?

"Leaf Scrapings" was but a short one to start things off, too short to determine anything. Blink and you'd miss the next two as well, "Aukomacic" and "Scratching Scrawling Crawling". But the eight-minutes or so of "As Cold As Can Be In An English Sea" left us in no doubt; this was going to be no ordinary Cardiacs gig - this was actually going to be stunning.

For me, the material off *Archive Cardiacs* was always special, but apart from the odd blast of "Icky Qualms" in 1992, 1995 and 1996, I never expected to hear any of those old relics performed live. Judging by the whoops of amazement and delight during the quieter passages of this epic meisterwork, I wasn't the only one in the audience who thought it was incredible to be hearing "As Cold As Can Be In An English Sea" in the flesh, so to speak.

From then on it just seemed to get better, even though much of the material was unfamiliar to me. You see, I'd been given tapes of Cardiacs' early stuff by Lee, guitarist with Katherine In A Cupboard, but as the sound was so murky and eighth-generation, I felt the material wasn't done justice to, so only listened to them once or twice. And at that point I hadn't managed to get my greasy little paws on 1979's "A Bus For A Bus On The Bus" EP, so that wasn't yet seared into my brain either.

But all this only added to the appeal. When I'd first seen Cardiacs at Reading Festival in 1986 I'd been too puzzled (and reserved) to really let myself go, but now as "An Ant", "A Bus For A Bus On The Bus", "Visiting Hours" and "Pip As Uncle Dick But Peter Spoiled It" ripped along, I danced wildly like anyone would do if they'd just discovered The Greatest Band In The World for the first time.

After "An Ant" Tim seemed a bit more relaxed too. 'How you gettin' on?' he asked us all. Kavus then got a bit of a chant when Tim introduced him, and we had a bit of panto with Tim asking us if this had been 'a good idea' (hooray) or 'a bad idea' (boo).

By the time Cardiacs played "Let Alone My Plastic Doll" I'd retreated to the edge of the Pond to get my breath back, but no matter where I'd have been in the room, I'd have been pinned to the back wall by the twin-guitar blitzkrieg that shattered on for nearly two minutes on pretty much one note. When Cardiacs do simple, they do it in their own way. Astonishing.

"Hope Day" was next up, Tim intense by the end as he laced

into those final vocal lines, so intense I thought he was going to burst.

Burst? That's appropriate; the set closer was "A Balloon For Bertie's Party", and after the impressive Prog-workout that forms the bulk of this song, as the end came gently plinky-plonking along, I watched a girl at the front waving her arms aloft in plinky-plonky time, and marvelled at what a wonderfully colourful bunch Cardiacs fans really could be.

Tim was almost apologetic about the first encore, "Is This the Life", Cardiacs' closest thing to a hit single, explaining that it *was* from the era. The last encore most definitely wasn't from the era, but then "Big Ship" can fit in anywhere it bloomin' well wants to with all that pomp and majesty, and as Tim said, it was the encore after all. That song was quite possibly the only one worthy enough to close such a wonderful night…

So, I sat on the tube home (only a few stops) and mused over it all, but I got in and still couldn't make any sense of it. And my flatmate was still none the wiser as to what all the fuss was about. At least I still had two more nights to sort it all out in my little head…

* * * *

The songs from *Archive Cardiacs* had been kicking around that little head of mine for over 14 years by the time the Special Garage Concerts took place, and those from *The Seaside* one year longer than that. *The Seaside* cassette had been bought by me in a bit of a spending frenzy at a Sheffield Leadmill gig in 1988, and in later years had been reissued (albeit in truncated form) on both vinyl and CD formats, but there didn't seem to be the same mystery surrounding those songs compared to the ones on *Archive Cardiacs*, probably because numbers like "RES" and "To Go Off and Things" from *The Seaside* had been regular staples of the live set over the years, as well as stuff like "It's a Lovely Day" and "Gina Lollabrigida" appearing sporadically. However, the material that formed *Archive Cardiacs* had a touch of the Holy Grails about it, certainly for me anyway, because the material seemed so buried in the past there never seemed any chance of hearing it exhumed and performed live.

Often I can like an album or song as much for the personal

circumstances I find myself in at the time as for their musical brilliance, hence for example I often cite *Starless and Bible Black* as my favourite King Crimson album, leaving me in a minority of one, I believe. And so it was that *Archive Cardiacs* always evoked special memories because of my situation just after the time of purchase…

It was the summer of 1989, and with over a year of procrastinating, I'd eventually sent a cheque off to the Alphabet Business Concern for some of the items that were only available to members of the *YOUsletter* Family, namely an "I AM IN IT" t-shirt and the *Archive Cardiacs* cassette. There was plenty of Cardiacs material available generally in 1989, all of which I had, thus the album *A Little Man and a House and the Whole World Window* had been played to death, along with the *Big Ship* mini-album, the "There's Too Many Irons In the Fire" twelve-inch EP, *The Seaside* cassette, the *Seaside Treats* EP, the "Susannah's Still Alive" single, the *Nighttracks* BBC session EP, and the *Rude Bootleg* and *Cardiacs Live* in-concert-extravaganza albums. What's more, Spring 1989 had seen the release of a brand new Cardiacs album, *On Land and in the Sea*, and this hadn't spent much time in its sleeve either, taking up residence on my turntable instead. So by the summer, I was craving some new Cardiacs material, and what better way to satisfy this craving than with a bit of stuff from before time began?

As usual, my goodies arrived in an envelope stuffed with confetti, and the *Archive Cardiacs* cassette began its rather protracted spell in my tape-player. What a joy it was too, being made up largely of complex keyboard/guitar-fuelled cyber-Punk explosions, alongside Prog-worthy instrumentals (mostly titled "Piffol") that sounded like a cross between a 1970s Henry Cow album and *The Clangers* soundtrack. Back in 1989, only the privileged had a CD player, so if you wanted something portable you either had to bung your bulky albums onto a C90, or carry around the few tape-albums in your possession. Thus it happened that *Archive Cardiacs* went everywhere with me for a year or so, thereby brightening up my office at work, threatening to get chewed up in my Walkman, or providing light relief on visits back to my parents' in Sheffield. I also used to blast it out of the PA speakers at work, but only after all the customers and staff had cleared off and left me to my own devices.

Ah yes, those circumstances I found myself in. That summer of 1989 was my first as manager of the Circle K convenience store in Brackley, Northants, and as I felt I had a lot of work to do to sort the shop out, I'd often work alone late into the night after I'd closed up, playing *Archive Cardiacs* at full blast through the shop-floor speakers whilst chatting to the ghost that supposedly haunted the place. My mood was nearly always tip-top due to being in a happy relationship with then-girlfriend Annie, and Sheffield United having just gained promotion from the old Division 3 to the old Division 2. So you see, there were many happy associations with those songs from *Archive Cardiacs*, happy, that is, up until the point when all that hard work at Circle K gave me glandular fever, an illness that still rates as the worst of all my many not-life-threatening-but-still-rather-bad ailments. Stuck at home for six weeks, I'm sure you can guess what provided the soundtrack to my moping about - yep, *Archive Cardiacs*, but only when I wasn't playing and replaying the *Sheffield United: 100 Years, 100 Goals* promotion video. Bizarrely, the memories were still happy, even with the added association of glandular fever; don't ask me how that works though - any psychologists reading this who wish to speculate on how I can get nostalgic for feeling so weak I couldn't even lift a spoon, all whilst sporting the worst-ever sore throat alongside a killer headache, just through listening to an old tape album?

The music was now well and truly seared into my brain alongside all the other Cardiacs material, but there never seemed much hope of hearing any of the old songs performed live in concert, largely because it seemed to be forbidden to even talk about them amongst polite Alphabet Business Concern company, as if they'd never existed. The sleeve notes to the *Archive Cardiacs* cassette hinted at this, bearing as they did a message from the Consultant that read: "ARCHIVE CARDIACS ENTIRELY FOR YOUR ENTERTAINMENT EXCLUSIVE only to our YOUsletter Family, purely to achieve the MAXIMUM ANNOYANCE to the Artists. Personally I find it IRKSOME and DISTASTEFUL, but play it if you must - although I would STRONGLY ADVISE that you DO NOT write or make comments to the Artists as they are TOTALLY UN-AWARE of the release of these recordings, which were made between the years of 1977 and 1979."

Not allowed to "write or make comments to the Artists"? I obeyed of course, although I did once hear John Daniel, Tour Manager and Accountant to the Alphabet Business Concern, and the finest fixer of Guest List additions you could ever wish to meet, talking about the "Bertie…" trilogy, but only after he'd ensured all of the Artists were out of earshot.

I still craved hearing this collection of songs live myself, however. At least they got a decent burial when in 1995 the Alphabet Business Concern put *Archive Cardiacs* out as a CD, meaning that at last my tape could be retired, lessening the chances of it snapping or getting caught up in the cassette player's mechanism. But up until that announcement on cardiacs.com in 2003 about the Special Garage Concerts only featuring songs from 1977-1983, there was no hint of hearing any of them performed at a gig, apart from those brief flashes of "Icky Qualms" in the 1990s, the first being at Northampton Irish Centre in 1992 when my enthusiasm was laid bare for all to see as I headbanged energetically, much to Annie's disapproval.

At last, it now looked like we were in for something of a treat, such a big treat that I even started to dream about the forthcoming gigs in advance. One such dream saw me watching Cardiacs performing "Piffol One Time", although on waking up I knew that this was unlikely to happen as there was a fair amount of woodwind in the piece, so much so that my dream featured Sarah Smith honking on a saxophone, alongside old Cardiacs stalwarts Tim Quy on percussion and William D. Drake on keyboards, none of whom would be appearing in 2003. Worryingly though, if I was dreaming about the songs they might play, it really was starting to get to me.

Goodness me, what a long winded way of explaining why I'd nervously anticipated the first gig, and was now wildly excited about the second.

* * * *

I may have been looking forward to the second of the Special Garage Concerts, but I was not relishing the next instalment of my confrontation with that beast of a venue manager. You see, the one downside of the previous night had been that at some point in the evening's proceedings, I'd lost my Sheffield United woolly hat, and there was only one person I'd be able to ask to see if it had been found...

To calm myself before the terror of that ordeal though, I went through what was seemingly becoming my pre-gig routine for these events, except that I modified it slightly; instead of spending the day leading up to the gig by working, this time I wasted more of my strict budget by going to watch Sheffield United at Millwall. Heck, when the football fixture list computer works in your favour by providing an away match in London on the same day as a gig, you expect luck to be on your side all the way, but I seem to have a thing about never seeing Sheffield United win on the same day as attending a Cardiacs gig, and this was no exception, the Blades turning in a woeful performance that resulted in a 2-0 defeat.

But the rest of the routine was intact, the bit that involved racing home, rapidly changing into my gig-wear, then boarding a bus (forgoing the tube this time for some reason) to Islington, before sitting down for cod and chips in the chippy down the road from the Garage, prior to venturing in to lock horns with The Beast. As it happened it wasn't much of a confrontation; I tracked her down and asked her if anyone had handed in a woolly hat the night before, and she gave me a smile and a look that suggested that even if they had, she was putting it straight in the bin.

'It's quite distinctive,' I persisted, 'it's a Sheffield United one, like my shorts.' Still she refused to say a word, just repeating that dismissive look before flouncing off. At least I had the last laugh in that I had no bag, coat or trousers to put in her rotten cloakroom.

As the crowd started to build it was evident that there were many of the same faces as the previous night, which was hardly surprising really as the Alphabet Business Concern pre-gig propaganda had stated that Cardiacs would be playing two completely different sets for the first two nights, and being such a keen bunch, none of us wanted to miss a thing. One face from the previous night was there in a professional capacity this time - due to a missing Crew member, Andy Thompson had been hastily promoted to Guitar Tech for one night only. There was one new attendee however in the form of Ian who had set off at something like dawn just to make sure he arrived this time. He thanked me for sending him a text the previous night saying, "Okay, I won't tell you how good that was…" before we settled down to watch Claire Lemmon and Mel Woods of Sidi Bou Said providing the support this time.

Sarah, my ex-girlfriend but still my best buddy, was also there that second night, adding a touch of glamour to proceedings. It is always brilliant to see Sarah, and not just because of her incredible beauty, but also because we always have a ton of stuff to catch up on - we have quite a lot in common you see, not least our love of Cardiacs, having met at one of their gigs in Milton Keynes in 1995. Just before Claire and Mel took to the stage, we indulged in a conversation typical for the two of us, the subject matter leading to one chap in front turning round and asking us what on earth we were talking about (he was right by the way).

No matter how good Claire Lemmon was (and Sarah in particular has always been a massive fan), once again it was Cardiacs we were all waiting for, and once again they didn't disappoint. The difference this time was that I had no nerves about whether or not this was going to be any good - I still had the warm glow and ringing ears from the night before to remind me. And this time things got off to a far more conventional start after the intro when the band hurtled straight into "Jibber and Twitch", a song that I'd often thought must have been their set-opener from around the time of the original recording and release of *The Seaside* in 1983/1984, a theory that I put to Ian as we moshed in a stoppy-starty way in the Pond.

Not only did I have no nerves, it seemed that the band had banished them too as they motored straight into "My Trade Mark", followed by a very early Tim-chat with the audience, a sure sign that he was relaxed and happy. He even proved my theory that the majority of the audience had been in the building the night before when he asked who'd been here last night (big cheer), and who'd not been here last night (smaller cheer). There then followed a nugget of Tim gold when he said, 'If one of these tunes because they're shy…if they land in your arms by accident, hold them, take care of them, stroke their little heads really gently, and if no-one's looking you can pat it a bit harder, then when someone looks you can pretend you didn't do it and stroke it soft again.'

There was not much evidence of stroking gently from the Pond as they whipped themselves into a frenzy with the fast and furious tunes firing forth from the stage; "Hello Mr Sparrow", "Pilf", "It's a Lovely Day" ('from the era' we were told)… The gig ripped on in a way that suggested it was at least going to be the equal of Concert Number One. One of those missing-from-any-CD songs from *The Seaside*, 'Dinner Time' rattled out giving us all hope that when, as promised, these gigs made it onto the market, we'd all finally have hard-copies of the song to save our wearing-thin tapes.

There was water-spraying, a regulated-and-timed-by-Tim one-minute 'Jim Jim Jim' chant, and all manner of musical mayhem, the set seemingly more *Seaside* than *Archive*, as well as plenty of those unknown-to-Belch songs that Purple Heather had to name for me afterwards, and all were met with the same response - frantic moshing. We even got a blast of Jim-vocals on "Food On the Wall". But if we were tired, there was to be no let up in "RES" as we all knew every twist and turn, and so felt compelled to show off by demonstrating this in dance. Well, we thought we knew every stop and start, but we all had to stop-and-not-start-but-admire for a minute or so as that incredibly complex instrumental bit towards the end was elongated beyond all reasonability and made ultra-complex; as Cardiacs passed this off with a nonchalance bordering on arrogance you could hear the audience laughing out loud with a combination of incredulity and respect, and when the vocals came back in to mark the end of that section, there was a burst of spontaneous applause - absolutely gob-smackingly brilliant.

By now, checking my Cardiacs watch, I deduced that we were

approaching the end of the set, and just as I was wondering what had happened to "A Game For Bertie's Party" from *Archive Cardiacs*, the vocal microphone swung round to Bob and he started singing it from behind his kit, as if things needed to get any better. As for Bob, sometimes he seems to think he's Phil Collins on "Los Endos" up there crashing away, but now he was even singing a song; "Supper's Ready" anyone? "A Game for Bertie's Party" thundered to its grandiose climax, providing a fitting end to an amazing set.

But we weren't done yet. For the encore, two extra microphone stands were brought out, Claire Lemmon and Mel Woods positioning themselves behind them, prompting the audience to switch from a 'Jim Jim Jim' chant to a 'Mel Mel Mel' chant, making her smile. And once again, just when you thought it couldn't get any better, Cardiacs cut a swathe through "Dirty Boy", a song even less from the era, but like "Big Ship" the night before, one of the few songs that could do justice to an incredible night by rounding it all off nicely.

As the dust settled and we all drank pints of water to rehydrate ourselves, Andy Thompson (taking a break from greasing guitar strings), Ian and I compared notes on the evening's entertainment. Ian asked sheepishly, 'Was it better than last night?'

I looked at Andy and his look suggested that like me, he couldn't be sure: 'Heck,' I said, 'that's a tough one - last night was the first, so that had the element of surprise, but tonight had the energy…call it a draw.'

And so once again on my journey home I pondered and puzzled and reached the conclusion that yep, everything was equal - two of the best gigs I'd ever experienced in my life. And all I could say to my flatmate on arriving home once more was, 'It was just like seeing them for the first time again for, erm, a second time…'

* * * *

Originally Cardiacs had only planned to do the two nights at the Garage, but late in the day the gig that was to take place on Sunday 19th October was pulled for whatever reasons, so Cardiacs were asked to do a third night. Sadly there wasn't time to rehearse a totally new set, instead it being rumoured that Kavus had been asked by the Alphabet Business Concern to select his highlights from the previous two sets and come up with the running order for this third and final night. Not everyone could make it, Ian and Sarah included, but I'd got nothing planned so there was no way I was missing out on a Cardiacs hat-trick, and as was now traditional I sat on the bus before sitting in the chippy. Well fed I entered the Garage for one last time, giving my friend the Beast a knowing smile as I did so (I really hope she enjoyed binning my Sheffield United woolly hat).

As well as the perennial Andy Thompson (back in the ranks again after his brief promotion to Guitar Tech), there was another Andy present, in the shape of the former-drummer with Mint 400, a rather splendidly dark band who had pinned Ian and I to the back of the wall at more than one venue, especially when they played "White Cadillac Man". Mint-400-Andy had been there every night for Cardiacs, and each time he'd taken up residence at the front of the stage by the right speaker, my favoured spot too, and each night we'd indulged in much chatter about Prog-Rock. When we strayed on to Rush he asked me if I was a musician 'because you like musician's music - Cardiacs, Rush, Prog in general.' Alas no, Andy, I'm just a frustrated musical snob...

Another attendee was Jon Poole, still then the current Cardiacs guitarist, but unable to make the first two gigs due to commitments with the Silver Ginger Band, hence Kavus Torabi's promotion, at the time considered temporary. Anyway, with no Silver Ginger Band gig that night, Jon was in the audience, presumably looking to enjoy himself.

As this was an extra performance, the vibe seemed even more relaxed, helped by William D. Drake providing the support. But again, Cardiacs were the star turn, and after two goes at it, by this third night Cardiacs were really on song. However, the promise that all songs would be ones that had been played on the first two nights was immediately blown out of the water when straight from the intro they launched headlong into "The Obvious Identity", serving to remind me that I'd been wondering where this had gone on the Saturday when I'd also been searching for "A Game For Bertie's Party".

Well, here it was, and a gloriously lively old start to the gig it was too.

After that curve ball, from then on the set was a romp through the best bits of the first two nights, and have a guess - yes, it was absolutely stunning. Again. A slightly different high from the previous two nights though, it being the last night of the run it gained something of a joyous, celebratory mood, a mood not uncommon at Cardiacs Concert Performances, but on the back of three of the best gigs ever attended, everything seemed magnified. We were even treated to a conversation between Timmy on the stage and Jonny in the audience prior to "An Ant", Jonny doing the 'It must be an ants' nest' bit before following it up with an enquiry as to whether Timmy had seen '*Superman 2* on the television, about three weeks ago,' leading in turn to Timmy remembering that he'd received a phone call from someone who thought he was phoning Jonny and, and… 'It doesn't really matter, does it…' - wonderful entertainment, believe me (but it helped if you were there).

Highlights of the set for me were "Visiting Hours" (with that wonderful circular guitar figure winding it up at the end) and "As Cold As Can Be In An English Sea" which really did see some frenzied action in the Pond, especially that fast reggae/thrashy bit at the end. And if Tim had been so intense that I thought he was going to burst at the end of "Hope Day" the first time, I really think he did burst at the end of it this time.

But for me, absolute top marks went again to "Let Alone My Plastic Doll", a terrifying slab of Gothic grandeur, once again that blitzkrieg of a guitar duet pinning me to the back where I could get a better view of all the paint and wallpaper shredding - thank-you Kavus for picking that one.

By the end, just prior to main-set-closer "My Trade Mark", Tim really did seem quite touched by the audience's enthusiasm: 'We DO actually love you!' he beamed from on high.

The encores were slightly different, in that Cardiacs allowed themselves to race through two more favourites from the previous nights, an astonishingly good "Jibber and Twitch" and a perky "Gina Lollabrigida". Eventually they allowed themselves to follow the pattern of Friday and Saturday by winding everything up with a classic from after the 1983 cut-off period, and once again it was a majestic epic that sent us all home with warm hearts and fuzzy tummies, "Stoneage Dinosaurs", the kind of song that brings everybody down to a nice relaxed high after the frenzied activity of all that's gone before. A perfect ending if ever there was one, and if you don't believe me, just remember the tears of those in the audience.

So, there I was again trying to explain to my flatmate what it had all been about. Once again, words failed me pretty much, so I resorted instead to something of a repeat; 'It was quite possibly the best gig I've ever seen them do, again. And erm, well, it was like seeing them for the first time again, for, erm, a third time. Ah heck, I'm off to bed…'

* * * *

Exactly two years after those Special Garage Concerts of October 2003, the Alphabet Business Concern finally put out two monumental CDs of the shows, and if ever a recorded disc or two could accurately put across the sights, smells and sounds of a live Cardiacs performance, then these were they. Turned up full blast, they provide two hours of sonic brilliance that take the breath away. Why, when listening to *Volume I* on the bus once, the bloke sitting opposite me had to give me a nudge and ask me to stop tapping (well, banging actually) my foot in time to that fast, thrashy reggae bit at the end of "As Cold As Can Be In An English Sea". What a miserable git - if I'd not had my headphones on I could have understood it, but what's wrong with a bit of enthusiastic foot-banging when Cardiacs are in your ear…?

It's hard to say whether any of those gigs *were* actually the best ever, because there are a great many wonderful Cardiacs gigs from my 101 attended, but all three are in THE list of the greatest ever, and I think as a *series* of three consecutive gigs, they have never been bettered, by anyone. Cardiacs, it really was a privilege to be there every single night…

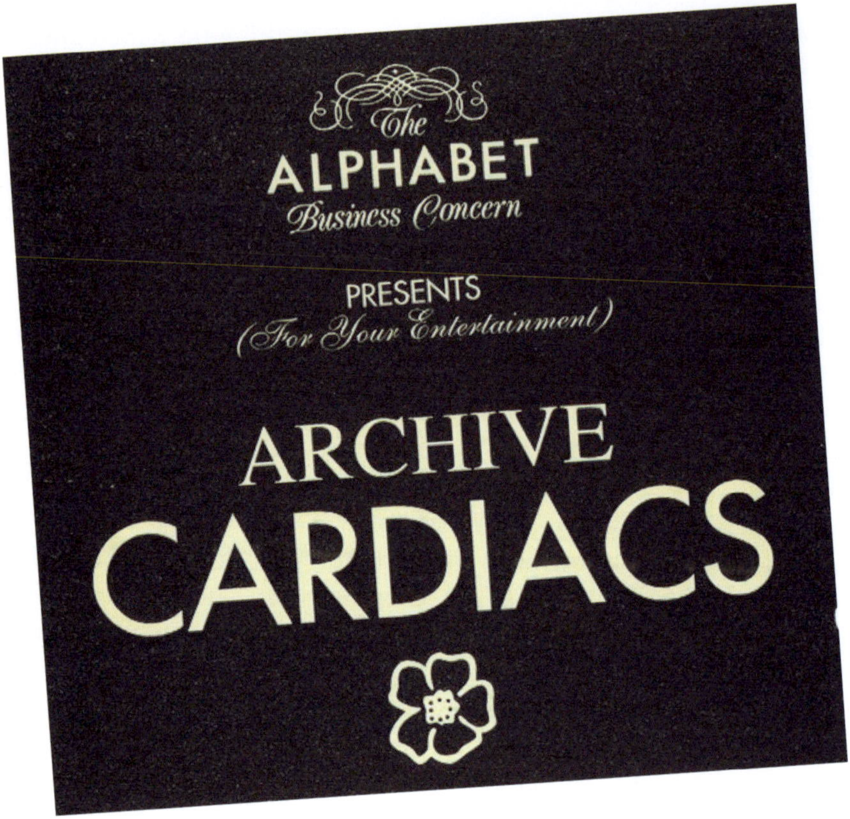
The
ALPHABET
Business Concern
PRESENTS
(For Your Entertainment)
ARCHIVE
CARDIACS

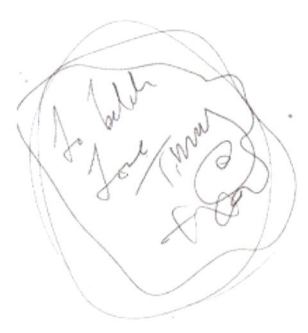

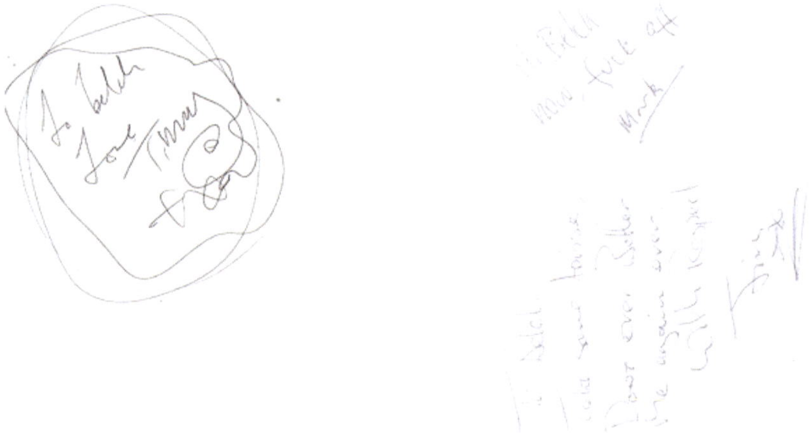

Chapter Two
"Buds and Spawn"
My Musical Journey

"Buds and Spawn"
My Musical Journey

Stonehenge Free Festival 1984 was the start of many things in the life of Adrian Thomas Bell (Belch to some, Greenwich Blade to others, me to myself), and yes, I know I've written this before in other places, but for the purposes of this massive undertaking of a book, there is no harm in mentioning it again whilst delving further back and then flying on forward, all in an effort to establish just when and where this love affair with music in general and Cardiacs in particular began.

Yes indeed, Stonehenge Free Festival 1984, that great pivotal moment in my life, was the first time I'd hitchhiked anywhere, and as some people may know, I've clocked up a fair few thousand (or even a few hundred thousand?) miles via this mode of transportation, whether it be to see Sheffield United struggle, witness Cardiacs or a number of other bands in concert, or just to get to and from work sometimes.

Stonehenge Free Festival 1984 was the first time I'd ever even seen the Stonehenge Monument itself, and I found it both mysterious and exciting, with the Floating Free Anarchy that surrounded the free festival itself adding to both sensations, so much so that when my Mum told me in January 1985 (as I lay in my sick bed with some vomiting bug) she'd just heard on the news that they were banning that year's festival, I announced straight away that no-one could stop us and that I'd still be attending. And so I did, although the Powers That Unrighteously Be did stop us to a certain extent - even so, this little Belch was in attendance in or around Stonehenge every year from then on (with the exceptions of 1992 and 1997) protesting and making a general nuisance in order to try and spread the police net a little further and weaken their efforts to stop people doing what they had a perfect right to do. These protests continued right up until 1999, and then miracle of miracles, in 2000 free access to the Stones was finally granted, and don't you just know it, I've gone every year since then too.

Stonehenge Free Festival 1984 also provided me with first

viewings of a number of bands and solo artistes who have gone on to become firm favourites of mine, and are still right up there in my album collection, notably Roy Harper and Here & Now. It was also the second time I'd seen Hawkwind, but anyone who knew me from back then will tell you that those Hawk Experiences on Solstice Eve and Solstice Morn triggered an obsession with the Sonic Assassins, in particular Nik Turner, that lasted, well, pretty much up to now, only overtaken when a certain band called Cardiacs came along...

Ah yes, Cardiacs. You see, unbeknownst to me, Stonehenge Free Festival 1984 also provided me with my first Cardiacs contact. I say unbeknownst because at the time Cardiacs entered the stage (rather inconsiderately in the middle of the night, between The Enid and Hawkwind who were on again at dawn), I was trying to grab a bit of sleep in my tent in order to be refreshed for sunrise which I intended to take in from within the Stone Circle. It was altogether an unsuccessful attempt because that tent was both right next door to a Free Jam marquee, and within earshot of the main stage. The Free Jam area was basically an excuse for people to get up and make as much racket as possible, and it never seemed to stop. Meanwhile, the music I could hear through the din, coming from the main stage, didn't sound much better to me. I had it down as nasty Punk, and as I lay awake in my tent I was mighty glad I'd opted to give it a miss, although I was rather narked that they were keeping me up all night.

It was a whole two years before I found out that the band who had helped me to my first sleepless Solstice Night were in fact Cardiacs, a band I'd just seen for the first time at Reading Festival 1986. So just how did I find out that information, and how did that band go on to influence my life so massively from then on? And just as importantly, what had influenced me to attend festivals such as Reading in 1986 and Stonehenge in 1984? It was the music, of course, and it is perhaps worth exploring how music came to be such a big thing in my existence, and how it all led to a life with Cardiacs at almost every turn.

* * * *

It's hard to avoid the influence of music when you come from a family such as ours (although one big brother seems to have avoided the musical gene altogether). My Dad is hugely into his choral music (Handel's *Messiah* is where it's at for him), still singing tenor with the Hallam Choral Society to this day. He even got most upset when he heard that I'd chosen to sing bass in the Britannia Ward Ensemble - sorry Dad, but I'm just not a tenor; bass is much more my range. My Mum meanwhile is more into her symphonies, so much so that she bought busts of Beethoven and Tchaikovsky from Wilson Peck in Sheffield and proudly displayed them in the living room. And so it was perhaps because in those pre-school years I was at home with my Mum, she had the biggest influence on my formative years. When I wasn't forming a strange addiction to *Waggoner's Walk* on Radio 2, I was picking up on Rolf Harris's "Two Little Boys" which my Mum seemed to like because it reminded her of me and John, my best friend next door who was the same age as me. I liked "Two Little Boys" so much, I received it for Christmas 1970 (and yes, we've had the debate on Cardiacs Chat about "Two Little Boys" being number one for Christmas 1969, but I'm absolutely certain I got it for Christmas 1970).

When we weren't glued to Radio 2, my favourite record coaxed out of our battered old mono player for our own version of *Listen With Mother* was *Peter and the Wolf* by Prokofiev (I never could hear the duck at the end), and the "Peter…" signature tune still pops into my head to this day, usually when I'm in a good mood (you know, like when Sheffield United win or I've just finished work), but I also loved the big old twelve-inch long-players my Mum had of Hans Christian Andersen's fairy tales.

Now, even though my parents had no liking for pop music (Rolf Harris excepted), our Mormon upbringing meant they allowed all us five kids a certain amount of free-agency, and so if we wanted to watch *Top of the Pops* on a Thursday night (and later, a Friday), so be it. Big brother Julian seemed to be the one most into his pop tunes, particularly T.Rex, and as he was everything I aspired to be at the time (he bought albums and went to see Sheffield United away from home), I became something of a Marc Bolan devotee too, doing a particularly nifty impression of him doing "Hot Love" in our old playroom at Rustlings Road, Sheffield. Meanwhile, eldest sister Fiona read *Jackie* and took piano lessons, so a strange mixture of 70s pop culture was battling it out with classical over in the girls' corner.

Me being me, though, whilst always happy to let older-sibling influences in through the door, there was forever a part of me wanting to discover things for myself, and at the age of six a viewing of The Sweet on *Top of the Pops* performing "Blockbuster" made a huge impression on me, so much so that I got it for my seventh birthday, February 1973. I don't know what it was, whether it was the sirens at the start, the timpani in the middle, or just the fact that they looked so freaky-yet-cool with all that make-up, glitter and long hair, but I was totally obsessed with this song, and didn't my family know it.

Still, not put off from encouraging me, one year later a kind sibling bought me "Tiger Feet" by Mud, again the current number one at the time of my birthday, presumably because I was showing signs of obsession with this tune too, having perfected the "Tiger Feet" dance-routine accompanied by John from next door, complete with tennis rackets for guitars.

From the ages of six to eleven, I was an avid *Top of the Pops* viewer and listener of the chart countdown of a Sunday evening. My liking for epics emerged with the release of Queen's "Bohemian Rhapsody" at the end of 1975, and I was highly delighted when Julian brought it home one day. It's also worth mentioning that at the age of eight I took up violin, and whilst I obviously wasn't a natural, I could squeeze a tune out of it eventually (although I know it was a painful experience for my family having to listen to my early efforts), and by the age of eleven I'd passed my Grade Two with merit.

Also by the age of eleven I'd been exposed to some serious rock music. It was one evening in autumn 1977 when I first heard Yes whilst listening to the chart countdown. "Wonderous Stories" had by some miracle entered the charts, and I remember thinking how beautiful it sounded compared to everything else. Even so, I wasn't quite ready for Yes full-on yet, but I was moving forward, and the name lodged somewhere in my subconscious.

By this time, brother Julian had a job driving a delivery van for Fletcher's Bakeries in Sheffield, and on payday he always used to buy an album. The first one of these to really grab my attention was *Even In The Quietest Moments* by Supertramp, not least because I spotted it had a ten-minute track on it called "Fool's Overture". I was fascinated by the possibility of a song lasting so long, and with repeated listenings I grew to love this epic masterpiece, along with the whole accompanying album.

However, when Julian brought home *Going For The One* by Yes, I was positively agog because this had a track on it that was *fifteen* minutes long! I pointed this out to my brother, and he said, 'Yes I know, but you won't like it.'

He was right too; I just could not get my head around it, but then I was only eleven-years-old after all. He got into it though and soon went on to buy *Close To The Edge* and *Tales From Topographic Oceans*, both of which I detested. 'Boring' was my verdict. Ten minutes was fine for a song, I felt, but stretching something out to twenty was too much, and with ...*Topographic Oceans* opting for one song per side of a double album, well, I was out of there. No, I was much more at home with Electric Light Orchestra and "Mr Blue Sky" which was my current favourite, once again a single that turned up amongst my presents, this time for my 12th birthday, February 1978...

Not long after this, my hard-earned paper-round money started going on albums of my own, namely *Out Of The Blue* by the Electric Light Orchestra, and *News Of The World* by Queen, as well as a bunch of singles such as Elvis Costello's "Oliver's Army" and "She's So Modern" by the Boomtown Rats. But Progressive Rock was about to take over, thanks to that increasingly influential big brother Julian and his employment of saturation tactics (now you know where I got it from, folks), even when I was suffering from great illness.

I shared a room with Julian by now (other brother Alex had a room of his own because it had a sink in it, and as he was asthmatic it was deemed an advantage because he could get up in the middle of the night and cough his guts up into it - I was jealous because from his window you could see the floodlights at Bramall Lane in the distance), and Julian took full advantage of this arrangement by ramming his new-found love of Progressive Rock down my neck. On one stand-out occasion I was bed-ridden with flu so he proceeded to force me to listen to all four sides of Yes' ...*Topographic Oceans*, knowing I was a helpless victim. These days that might just prompt a visit from Social Services; however, on this occasion my defences started to come down, even if I did have one eye on the clock throughout, always feeling a sense of relief as the twenty-minute mark was approaching on each song.

Eventually I had to cave in and admit that the title track of *Close To The Edge* (taking up the whole of side one) had got me, seeing as I'd spent all day humming it. I particularly liked the church organ bit in the middle, but also found myself fixated with Roger Dean's inner-gatefold painting.

'Right,' said Julian, 'now you can listen to side two, because if anything, the two songs from there are just as good.'

'Okay,' said Steve Howe at the start of "And You And I", and I had to agree; horror of horrors, I was a twelve-year-old Yes fan.

Julian and I used to listen to *Tales From Topographic Oceans* together, and he would actually explain the lyrics to me, probably better than Jon Anderson could. I clearly remember the excitement I felt the day he bought *Relayer* by Yes. We listened to "The Gates of Delirium" for the first time in stunned silence, a silence only broken when I pointed out that the hissing sounds at the end of the battle sequence were the snakes from Roger Dean's album cover. As "Soon oh soon the light" faded away at the end, Julian exclaimed, 'That was absolutely brilliant.' Who was I to disagree? Even to this day, thirty years on, when someone asks me what my favourite song of all time is, I always say "The Gates of Delirium" (and bless my little heart, I cried when Yes played it during their 2001 Yessymphonic tour).

I also remember that in September 1978, when Yes released *Tormato* and Julian brought it home on the day of release, after perusing the sleeve I voiced my disappointment upon seeing that there were as many as nine tracks on the album with the words, 'There are no long songs on it!' Ah yes, a true Progger, and at such a tender age.

Mine and Julian's voyage of musical discovery progressed at the same pace throughout that Spring and Summer of 1978. Contrary to popular opinion we Mormons are quite an adventurous bunch, and so it should come as no surprise to learn that there were a few Prog-Rock fans at church. Firstly, a gentleman called Keith Allen, upon hearing of Julian's new-found love of Yes, told him, 'If you like Yes, you'll like Genesis,' and promptly loaned him his entire Genesis collection, apart from *Selling England By The Pound* and *Seconds Out* which Julian went out and bought himself.

And so it came to pass that when Julian and I weren't translating Jon Anderson's words into Sheffieldish, we were poring over Genesis albums, marvelling at the Biblical connotations of "Supper's Ready" with all its apocalyptical visions, and revelling in the fantastical fairy-tales of *Nursery Cryme*. I was still only twelve.

Then another friend from church, Ian Cooper, told Julian to buy Pink Floyd's *Dark Side Of The Moon* because 'it's the best album ever.' I remember Julian saying, 'It's not the best album ever, but it's still brilliant,' and so the free posters adorned our bedroom wall and the stickers our door, never to be removed.

This same Ian Cooper also loaned Julian *Shamal* by Gong with the words, 'If you can get into this, you can get into anything.' We listened, we admired, but we didn't quite get, and so moved it to the A-Bit-Weird-but-Maybe-One-Day file…

Now there was a big conflict going on in my head because my Mum used to take me to the Sheffield Philharmonic concerts around this time at Sheffield City Hall, normally featuring the Hallé Orchestra, and I was leader of the Greystones Middle School Orchestra on account of me gaining a Merit for my Grade 2 Violin. But there was no competition really, because I used to sit there in those classical concerts thinking about how good Yes would look on that City Hall stage, even dreaming up Rick Wakeman keyboard parts to go with Elgar compositions. Besides, when I started at High Storrs Comprehensive School in September 1978 I was soon disillusioned with orchestra life, largely because I was no longer Top Dog as there were so many more pupils, and indeed I found myself relegated to Second Violins in the High Storrs School Junior Orchestra (I eventually clambered up to First Violins, thankfully). Even worse, the leader of the orchestra, one Peter Shoobridge, was way ahead of me. He'd passed his Grade 6 Violin, and just to rub it in he told me that violin wasn't even his first instrument, having achieved Grade 7 Piano and Grade 8 Flute. Pah!

But then, joy of joys, I discovered that he too had a liking for Yes thanks to some older cousins, and so from my position directly behind him in the orchestra pit we could talk Progressive Rock. I mentioned Gong to him once, so he only went out and bought one of their albums, *Camembert Electrique,* inviting me round to his house for a listen. So now both of us were Gong fans as well as Yes fans, and with the addition of things Planet Gong to my collection, I felt I was starting to branch out into the unknown.

By 1979 Julian had done what all good Mormon boys should do and gone off on a mission, so I gleefully inherited his record collection, but never one to be satisfied with only owning a fraction of a band's output, over the next few years my paper-round money was spent on Yes albums that Julian didn't have, and then all the solo albums I could lay my hands on (I remember feeling particular elation upon finding Patrick Moraz's *i* at Sheffield's Moorfoot Market).

By Autumn 1980, aged 14, I'd yet again worked my influence on John Atkinson (no longer next door since we'd moved, but still my best mate), but now rather than making him dance to "Tiger Feet", I was forcing him to listen to Yes, and the response was positive, so much so that in September 1980 John, Peter Shoobridge and myself went to our first ever gig, Rick Wakeman in concert at Sheffield City Hall. By this time I'd suffered the taunts of schoolfriends as Wakeman and Jon Anderson had left Yes only to be replaced by the Buggles, but at least this gave us the opportunity to witness Rick on his own. The whole performance left me mesmerised, but even better was to follow in December 1980 when the three of us (at fourteen years of age, quite possibly the youngest Yes fans in town) went to see Jon Anderson, again at the City Hall. This really was it for me, although this time my Mum had banned me from hanging around the stage-door at the end as John and I had done after the Rick Wakeman gig (we arrived home very late but it was worth all the grief though, as we met Rick Wakeman himself and got his autograph), and so my Dad picked us after the Anderson gig, thus denying me the opportunity to meet my number one hero, old Jon-Boy (I made up for it over 17 years later when I chatted up Jon Anderson's daughter Jade on the *Open Your Eyes* tour by the stage-door at the Hammersmith Apollo - check out forgottenyesterdays.com if they've not deleted the story by now).

Goodness me, where is all this going? Ah yes, towards Stonehenge 1984, and them there Cardiacs. I'll try and be a bit more brief now that we've established that by the ages of 14 and 15 I was a massive Yes fan who simply had to possess everything they'd ever released (and that included singles, most of them featuring tracks that I already had - my obsession with this side of collecting has continued in fits and starts over the years, leading to bonkers items in my collection such as a seven-inch $33\frac{1}{3}$ from New Zealand featuring "Yours Is No Disgrace" in its entirety on one side, and the full unedited "America" on the other).

Much like Julian taking on the recommendations of friends, I was prepared to do likewise, thanks largely to Peter Shoobridge who was hearing about bands via his older cousins, thus on his say-so I bought albums by King Crimson, Emerson Lake and Palmer and Gentle Giant as I progressed through the ages of 14-to-16. Also, Tommy Vance's *Friday Rock Show* on BBC Radio 1 was essential listening, as was Winton Cooper's *Something Else* on BBC Radio Sheffield, both providing new sounds and new names to look out for.

By 1982, aged 16-going-on-17, I was in the sixth form at High Storrs School and had made a new friend, Sewer (also known as Simon Wright, but what a double act Sewer and Belch were). Upon discovering that he liked the Electric Light Orchestra during triple Geography (no Ian, that doesn't mean he only liked ELO in Geography lessons), I proceeded to turn him on to a bit of Prog. Before long he was as obsessed with Yes, Gong, Genesis and King

Crimson as me, and we were seen at almost every Prog-worthy gig in Sheffield in the mid-80s, once we'd discovered that live music existed outside of the City Hall upon seeing Solstice with local heroes Haze in support at the Leadmill. Oh yes, the New Wave of British Prog-Rock was upon us, and we took advantage of the fact that decent music was back in vogue by going to Glastonbury to see Marillion in June 1983, before taking in IQ at Sheffield University later the same year.

As 1983 became 1984, and sixth form and bad 'A' Level results became unemployment, I reckoned I'd got every Prog-Rock album that was well known, so I now scoured record fairs around Sheffield for albums by the more obscure bands I'd read about or heard mentioned in the same breath as better-known heroes like Yes and King Crimson; hence Gryphon, Quintessence, Premiata Forneria Marconi and Greenslade all turned up in my collection. And on it went…

What I've probably not emphasised enough is that throughout all this I was probably as obsessive about Gong as I was Yes, seeking out all solo and offshoot projects spawned by the luminous green planet, and with this I really did feel like I was showing the true spirit of musical adventure. Tim Blake was synth player in Gong, and so as a completist I'd felt compelled to purchase *Levitation* by Hawkwind as he was on it (I was also tempted by the fact that it was on lovely blue vinyl), and around three years after that purchase, in February 1984, Sewer and I went to see them at Sheffield City Hall. I was immediately struck by Nik Turner's stage presence, and he was elevated to Belch Hero status from that day on. At the same time I was always fascinated by reviews of the Stonehenge Free Festival in *Sounds*, and after my Glastonbury experience of 1983, I was up for more, especially as I felt I was a bit of a hippy.

And so it was upon finishing my 'A' levels, in June 1984, I set off in search of new music combined with a totally wild and free experience. Stonehenge Free Festival 1984 provided it all right, that event proving to be quite possibly the defining moment of my life…

* * * *

Over the years I've had a few twinges of regret over not-quite-sleeping through Cardiacs at Stonehenge Free Festival in 1984, but then when I get all philosophical about it I think to myself that maybe it was for the best because, who knows, even though I was filled with the spirit of adventure back in 1984, I still may not have been ready for Cardiacs back then. And so I'm prepared to go with the natural order of things and reflect on what was, not what might have been... What *was* was that I missed Cardiacs in 1984, but developed an obsession with Hawkwind and a huge liking for the Enid (on before Cardiacs at Stonehenge, remember) which led to me travelling down to see both of them on the Sunday at Reading Festival in 1986.

I only went for the one day because quite frankly, none of the bands on the other days really appealed to me, and anyway, a three-day ticket was way too expensive. So I found myself strolling onto the festival site one sunny Sunday morning, clutching a programme which demanded a good study before proceedings began at midday, just to see what I could expect.

According to that programme, first band up were Cardiacs, and judging by the two awful, even disturbing, pictures on display, I was prepared to hate them - all garish make-up and polo-necked jumpers, complete with wacky smiles. Ugh. Not even the mention that Fish of Marillion liked them swayed me; I'd long-since decided that even though he liked Yes, Genesis and Pink Floyd, his taste in more-modern music could be somewhat dodgy. But as I had nothing else to do, I was prepared to stick around and watch Cardiacs, and from the off I was intrigued. The intro tape was weird enough for me to take notice, and the band themselves really attracted me with their look, all dressed in dusty bandsman uniforms, faces smeared with that make-up, most of them banging big bass drums as the set slowly thumped to a start.

As the set progressed, the music also captivated me as it seemed complicated beyond the wildest dreams of any Progressive Rock fan, and yet it maintained the power and energy of a Punk band, the type of music I'd allowed myself to like upon seeing Nik Turner's Inner City Unit. Could it be that they were playing the perfect music for Belch 1986?

I remember starting the gig positioned over to the left of the stage, but as the performance progressed I moved slowly but surely towards the centre, remaining about halfway back so I could take it all in.

Quite a sight Cardiacs were too; they had a miserable looking bass player, a clockwork keyboard player, a beautiful female sax player, and a manic guitarist/singer whose mental state apparent from his onstage persona gave me serious cause for concern. Mind you, he seemed to have one thing right; he seemed as transfixed as I was with that sax player, periodically going over to her and giving her a right good snog. Goodness me, I was almost jealous. Meanwhile, his between-song rants seemed to get more and more deranged, and yet I found myself chuckling out loud at such gems as, 'This is called "Tarred and Feathered" because Jim's too fat and he's going to die probably.'

By the end of final song "The Whole World Window" I was cheering wildly as a consequence of the onstage spectacle of balloons, flowers and popping champagne corks. Timmy (who I'd now established was the manic singer) looking bewildered whilst being led from the stage by the strange lady and gentleman who had entered with the balloons whilst the band played on amidst the swathes of confetti was a scene I actually found incredibly moving, and a huge imprint was left on my brain.

Not long after they'd finished, a Hawkwind-fan friend of mine approached, and we got chatting about all things Hawk-related. He then asked if Cardiacs had been on.

'Yep - you just missed them,' I replied.

'What were they like?' he asked.

'Pretty good actually,' I said.

'Yes, well, they were good at Stonehenge in 1984...' he muttered.

Stonehenge 1984 did he say? I was there, and I'm sure I'd have remembered a band as visual as this lot. 'When did they play at 'Henge?' I asked, slightly annoyed with myself.

'In the middle of the night, between the Enid and Hawkwind,' he answered.

Well, that solved a few mysteries, simultaneously starting those feelings of regret as well.

From then on I kept an eye out for Cardiacs' name in *Sounds*, but there never seemed to be any gigs in Sheffield, although I made mental notes of the release of mini-album *Big Ship* and twelve-inch single "There's Too Many Irons in the Fire". But most memorable of all was when I was working a rare Sunday shift for my then-employers GT News in March 1987. I noticed on the front of the *Sunday Sport* a reference to a shocking pop music story inside, so in between customers I looked it up, feeling both repulsed and pleasantly surprised to see that the "POP SEX SHOCKER" was actually about Cardiacs, specifically singer Tim and sax player Sarah being brother and sister and having an incestuous relationship. Blimey, I thought, they DID seem a bit friendly onstage. But then the article was telling me that they were husband and wife too. I was as confused as Tim's Mum appeared to be in the article, but one thing was for sure; they'd left yet another big impression on me, and maybe now I could understand why the music was so odd (don't worry folks, like most things you read in the newspaper, it wasn't really true).

One year on, and my career with GT News had led me to their wholesale news department in Barnsley where they had Radio 1 belting out dirge all day. One day, as I bundled magazines together I was struck by the brilliance of an atmospheric, effects-laden guitar solo blaring out of the radio. Much too good for Radio 1, thought I, I must catch what it is at the end. I was gob smacked to hear Garry Davies say, 'And that's the new single by Cardiacs…' Gob smacked and thrilled.

And what do you know, Garry Davies played it every single day for three weeks, not just the edited version, but the full-whack twelve-inch affair, complete with that mesmeric guitar solo at the end. Even the likes of Simon Bates played it, and one of my colleagues gleefully informed me that they'd heard it on Radio Hallam. Goodness me, it seemed Cardiacs were about to take over the world

- if only they'd realised and pressed up a few more thousand copies of that new single, "Is This the Life"…

So now I had to make up for lost time, picking up their newly-released album *A Little Man And A House And The Whole World Window* from an independent record shop in Barnsley one lunchtime, and both seven-inch and twelve-inch formats of "Is This The Life" along with, a little later, that twelve-inch of "There's Too Many Irons In the Fire" and the *Big Ship* mini-album from the ever-reliable Record Collector in Sheffield.

What's more, I saw a poster around town that told me Cardiacs were playing at the Leadmill, so as I knew the woman that was helping plug "Is This the Life", for the first of many times I secured my place on a Cardiacs guest-list.

That gig (April 23rd 1988), I went a bit mad with my money, buying *The Seaside* cassette album along with the vinyl album *Rude Bootleg* which the bloke serving on the merchandise desk told me was a recording of their appearance at Reading Festival in 1986.

'That was the first time I saw them,' I exclaimed excitedly, 'I've got to have that.'

I also had to have a cassette album entitled *Mr and Mrs Smith and Mr Drake*, and my first-of-many Big Flower t-shirts, proudly displaying the just-released album name from which it came on the back. The bloke on the desk (one Bill Hiles as it turned out) chucked in a few free badges for my expense, and I was the happiest person alive. Cardiacs Fever had truly taken hold of me…

That first indoor-gig was every bit as memorable as Reading, although I was slightly disappointed that they didn't end with "The Whole World Window", although "Big Ship" did a rather good job of making up for it. At the time I wasn't familiar with this song, but I was struck by its grand epic feel, and by the way the whole audience raised their arms above their heads and danced in a way that perfectly illustrated the music I was hearing.

I came away from that gig a changed man, and every man, woman and child that crossed my path either had to listen to me raving about Cardiacs or had to view the photos I'd taken at the gig.

Doubtless those victims were concerned for my mental stability, a concern most likely shared by everyone else I've come into contact with since, but they've all gone away certainly knowing of Cardiacs existence.

It was the culmination of one musical journey, but in a lovely clichéd way, it was the start of another one, one that was set to run and run…

Chapter Three
"Heaven Born and Ever Brighton"
The Old Market, Brighton,
November 12th 2007

"Heaven Born and Ever Brighton"
The Old Market, Brighton, November 12th 2007

This was not the way I'd envisaged starting off the latest Cardiacs tour, lying on my side on a treatment table in St. Peter's Hospital near Chertsey, trousers and boxers round my knees and something cold and metal shoved up my bum (I really hope none of you are reading this over breakfast, or any meal for that matter). It felt like the thin metal torch I had at home, not that I'd ever shoved that up there you understand. I just assumed that if I did, it would feel like this mini-telescope thing that the proctologist had just eased in. Whatever, I wasn't about to go home and have a bash with the torch because trust me, this was not a pleasant experience.

'What a way to spend a Monday morning, eh?' said the proctologist.

'Well, it beats work,' I replied, showing a level of wit quite surprising considering the situation.

'This *is* work for me,' countered the proctologist displaying even more wit, I thought. 'What do you do for work?' he continued.

'Oh, I work for Tesco,' I sighed wearily.

'In Ashford? Opposite Ashford Hospital?' he asked.

'That's the one.'

'And have you got to go back there after this?' he probed (excuse the pun).

'No, I'm on holiday for two weeks starting today. Great start to the holiday, this.'

Sounding like a barber now he asked, 'Are you doing anything interesting for the two weeks?'

'Actually I am,' I responded, warming to my theme, 'I'm going on tour following my favourite band Cardiacs, and I'm going to be writing a book about it because by the end of the tour I'll have seen them 101 times.'

'Goodness, that *is* interesting,' he marvelled. 'Are they famous? Because I've never heard of them.'

'Neither have I,' added his until-now-silent lady assistant.

'Not famous, no, but to those of us that like 'em, they matter.

Sort of a cult thing really,' I explained.

'And you're writing a book about it? Fantastic. Are you a bit of writer then?' he enquired further.

'I like to think so. I've written one book and had it published already - *Fever Hitch*, about me hitchhiking to see Sheffield United,' I semi-boasted.

This was the sort of conversation I usually had with people who'd been good enough to pick me up whilst hitchhiking, but this one took place whilst a proctologist examined my rectal passage on a small screen. Fairly unusual I'd say.

Much to my relief it was all done now, and the proctologist was dictating a letter to my GP into a voice recorder. After going on about what he'd observed up my passage, he added at the end, 'He is a music lover and is going on tour with the band the Cardiacs (I thought it churlish to pull him up on the addition of that "the" which irritates all those who love Cardiacs) for the next two weeks, so he will not be around until after then.' Rather cool that he mentioned them in the letter I thought.

Well, I was no wiser as to what was up with my rear passage, but at least we'd got things under way and all would surely become clearer over the course of the next few months. However, the consultant had now suggested that I go for a blood test in another part of the hospital, and trust me, no matter how unpleasant having a metal thing stuck up your bum might be, I knew this was going to be worse. I've had plenty of blood tests in my time but it never gets any easier and I really dread the things. But needs must, so off I trooped in search of the right area of the hospital.

For someone who hitchhikes plenty and therefore relies on his wits a fair amount, I have a rubbish sense of direction, one not always aided by signposts. Yes indeed, although there were plenty of signs pointing me in the direction of the blood tests, I still managed to get hopelessly lost, instead finding myself in an area that announced "CARDIAC RECOVERY UNIT". Not now, I'll need that in two weeks time, I thought, allowing myself an ironic chuckle.

At last all examinations and blood tests were done and I could head home on the bus and ready myself for the first gig of the tour, Brighton.

* * * *

The original plan for this here book was that I'd attend all eleven gigs on the tour, bringing me up to the magic century in Cardiff and 101 by the end of the next night in Leeds. Just to add a bit of spice I'd be hitch-hiking to as many of the gigs as possible, if not all. However, it was at the back of my mind that even though I'd hitched all over the country for years on end, I'd never quite undertaken such an intensive spell of hitchhiking as this, and I already had half a mind that in the end I'd probably get to at least half of them by other means. As far as I was concerned the important thing was getting there. Besides, with most of the fun to be had before, during and after the gigs, and with 90 other Cardiacs gigs to draw on, I wasn't going to be relying on hitchhiking tales to fill the book out.

So of course, I got off to a really good start by deciding not to hitchhike to Brighton because after my little visit to St. Peter's Hospital I was feeling somewhat groggy and just a little bit sore, so the train it was to be. I felt fully justified in this by remembering that I'd seen Cardiacs three times before in Brighton and not once had I hitched there (come to think of it, whenever I've been to see Sheffield United there I haven't hitched either, although on one occasion I got there in a very expensive taxi from Dover having just landed on a ferry, only to find there were no trains - for the record Hammersmith Blade and I had just returned from seeing England beat Slovakia 2-1 in Bratislava in 2002, going on afterwards to visit Prague and Berlin; Sheffield United beat Brighton 4-2 despite playing rubbish and trailing 2-0 for most of the match).

My first Cardiacs gig in Brighton at the Concorde on November 8th 1996 nearly didn't happen when the reports filtered through that the band were having van troubles crossing London. The promoter, an angry man pacing up and down the pavement outside the venue, issued Cardiacs an ultimatum over the phone; either they were here by 7pm or the gig was off. He was pretty strict too: 'Even if you're a minute after, the gig's off,' he barked. With ten seconds to spare Cardiacs' lovely minibus appeared around the corner, a line of fans already patiently waiting outside the venue, Mr Angry Promoter with his arms folded looking like he'd rather call the whole thing off.

As it was, the whole queue of Cardiacs devotees was commandeered to load the gear into the venue and a jolly good time was had by all, except that after a rather stupendous gig the venue seemed somewhat keen to get Cardiacs' crowd out and the clubbing crowd in - think the Astoria but even ruder (hard to imagine, I know). So there we all were, fans, band and equipment alike all out on the pavement. In the end everyone cheered themselves up by running on to Brighton Beach and playing dare with the waves whilst skimming stones - a glorious frenzy of Big-Flower-shirted happiness in the dark.

For the Brighton Pressure Point on October 24th 1999 I was going to hitch but got lazy and opted for National Express instead, and for the Brighton Concorde 2 on November 6th 2005 I'd had to go straight from a dreaded Sunday Duty Manager shift at Tesco King's Cross, so in order to make it on time the train was the only option (and quite by chance there was a lovely locomotive that went from King's Cross itself all the way to Brighton - how considerate).

That most recent gig in Brighton had also been the first of a tour and was one of my least favourite Cardiacs gigs. It was great to see many old friends, and indeed it started out as wild as ever (my mobile phone jumping out of my pocket at one point and getting a good old scratching as the Pond unknowingly leapt all over it - it survived remarkably well considering), but for some reason as the gig progressed the sound got louder and louder until it got to a point where it was actually incredibly distorted out there and almost impossible to make out what was being played through the white noise (having since seen videos on YouTube from this gig the sound seems all perfectly balanced and reasonable so I can only assume that either whoever filmed it had a magic sound-balancer on his equipment, or my ears were totally out to lunch). Sometimes I demand perfection, especially where music is concerned, so I got a right grump on and spent the last twenty minutes of the gig standing well back in the middle with my arms folded, a stance that was noted by more than one person from a vantage point most privileged.

* * * *

So here we were again at Brighton for the start of a tour and once more I was going on the train, so chances were the gig would be crap. Fearing this might be the case I'd decided to liven things up by inviting two young ladies along, Gemma from Tesco Ashford (Middlesex) and Marzena from Poland who lived in nearby Rye, a crazy chick I'd met at a Circulus gig near Mile End just a couple of weeks earlier. I didn't hold out much hope for either to be honest, but as Marzena was close by and Gemma was always going on about how much she liked random nights out in Brighton you just never knew.

In fact many an ex-girlfriend and potential "just good friend" had been dragged along to see Cardiacs. Mine and Annie's first date had been Cardiacs at the Marquee Club in 1988, which must have been a success as we were together for nearly five years afterwards and she clocked up many more Cardiacs gigs. As for Sarah, I actually met her at a Cardiacs gig in Milton Keynes in 1995, so naturally she was at my side for many gigs over the years, Cardiacs and otherwise. Then there was Annette from Germany and Katrina from Tottenham who saw them but never quite got the point, and Debbie who refused point blank to go anywhere near any of their gigs. At least Jitka from Czech Republic was a successful convert, but then she *did* like Yes to start with (more on all these lovely ladies in a future chapter). But I digress (it's a bad habit). Two girls invited, neither of whom would probably show up.

I wanted to be organised so I tried to print out directions from Brighton Station to the venue, The Old Market, which as it happened was more Hove than Brighton (but then if they can share a football team…by the way, when did AFC Bournemouth ditch Boscombe?), but my printer was playing up so I had to write out the directions which was always going to be a bit tricky (well, annoying really). As I wanted to leave nothing to chance I set off very early (well mid afternoon, early for a gig) and arrived sometime like about 5pm. Numerous texts were sent, no replies were received, so I set off following my silly directions and after making very slow, deliberate progress I suddenly realised that indeed there it was, the venue, a big grand white looking thing. There seemed to be nobody around and I was starving hungry, so I was about to set off in search of food when the texts started to flood in.

Uh-huh, Gemma wasn't coming because she'd only just finished work; eeh dear, Marzena wasn't coming because she couldn't afford to get over from Rye and she'd had a really busy day at work "and really you only tell me about concert very late" (it's true, but then I've dropped everything with three hours of notice before); but a-ha, what was this? Malc was in town wondering where I was. One quick call later and I was meeting him by a café called Belchers, comedy photo opportunity taken…

And so then it all started to come together after a very desolate-feeling hour or so (this is what happens, Belch, when you turn up to a gig about four hours before the start). Even at this stage it was a slow start as Malc and I headed to KFC, feeling that carbs would be necessary for a night of Cardiacs Frenzy, but the texts were going so we knew people were in town. It was just finding them - however did we cope before the days of mobile phones and texting? Carli and Graeme, otherwise known as the Dogstands, were in a bar somewhere. Finding them was an exercise we managed to make difficult even with the use of modern technology, but eventually both parties managed to locate each other at the top of a street somewhere, so then it was back to the bar.

Along the way we'd picked up Andrew Hossain, and Marina from *The Organ*, who'd appeared in a car together, as well as spotting a representative of the Alphabet Business Concern looking a bit lost and trying to top up his mobile via a cash-point. We'd also spotted one or two Big Flower and Little Man and a House t-shirts on people we didn't recognise, but then even after 90 Cardiacs gigs even I couldn't say that I knew *everyone*. Anyway, the Dogstands took us back to Barney's Bar and a quiet time was had by all.

It was now that I told them who my financial benefactor for this 'ere book was, a certain Mr. Big Ship Iron, aka Clive Hutton. I know he won't mind me saying that for reasons I'll go into in a later chapter, Clive wasn't the most popular person on Cardiacs Email Chatlist, and I'm sure the Dogstands won't mind me saying that when I told them about Clive's book offer, they were less than impressed, the vibe I got from them being that I'd teamed up in league with the Devil. I explained that Big Ship Iron was actually a very generous person and was somewhat misunderstood, largely because he was just a little shy of all us so-called raging intellectuals on The List, and therefore didn't feel comfortable blowing his own trumpet on-list. Not like me - I'll blow my trumpet at every available opportunity, and to whichever daft berk wants to listen. But I'll also blow trumpets for other people when it's deserved, and I felt it was worthy of laudation that many items from Clive's incredible Cardiacs collection had been donated to other less fortunate Cardiacs fans on request. What's more, he'd told some lucky fishies to hold back on bidding on eBay for certain items, leaving the way open for him to purchase the item for them.

I could see the Dogstands were a little cynical. 'Oh okay, maybe he's not all bad,' said Carli.

'Well, everyone'll get the chance to see for themselves tomorrow 'cos he'll be in Oxford, but he can't make it tonight 'cos he's stuck in Switzerland,' I cheerfully announced. By the time we got to the pub across the road from the venue, it was packed with Cardiacs t-shirts of all designs and various stages of tattyness. It was in here that I met Dave "Diggy" Dawson for the first time. It's a wonderful thing to have conversed with someone on the Internet for a year or so before meeting them in person for the first time, especially when that person happens to have emailed you once to tell you that having studied your MySpace profile he's never come across anyone whose taste in music, films and television programmes mirrors his own so closely.

Meeting Diggy also provided us with a rather splendid spontaneous comedy moment when a group of us headed out into the street. A Listee heading into the pub wanted to know if any of us knew what Diggy looked like as he planned to meet up with him pre-gig.

'He's still in the pub,' I said helpfully, 'in fact that's Diggy there in the window,' at which point three of us (me, Malc and Skitzo Pete, otherwise known as Thrupty) struck up an impromptu chorus of, 'How much is that Diggy in the window?' (insert orange triangle here) to much laughter all round.

After this fabulous comedy interlude it was into the venue and on with the night's entertainment, once everyone had purchased the obligatory new tour t-shirt (long-sleeved grey with large black Little Man and a House logo).

* * * *

What can I say? After all the build up and excitement, and the joy of meeting friends old and new, the gig itself was actually a bit of a letdown. There, and you all thought this book was just going to be an exercise in me showering nothing but praise on Cardiacs... For a start, support for the whole tour was from the God Damn Whores. They'd supported Cardiacs at the Astoria the previous year, and due to a certain Ian Skinner arriving late to collect the ticket I'd got for him I'd missed them, although the feedback I'd received suggested I'd not missed much.

It seemed their main saving grace was the presence in the ranks of Jon Poole, former guitar hero of Cardiacs. Well, on the evidence of the final twenty minutes of the set this seemed fairly accurate as it had to be said that the music they performed wasn't exactly up my street, but watching Jon is always entertaining, what with his leaps and axe-hero poses, and his between-song banter is consistently amusing. In fairness though, they were good at what they did, and word from those that had seen them the year before was that they'd improved vastly, and I must say as the tour wore on I grew to appreciate them a whole bunch more.

But for now, here in Brighton, I just wanted them to get a move on so we could proceed on with the main act. As we waited patiently for Cardiacs the beautiful music of the Gasman filled the hall, a most appropriate aperitif, and one set for the rest of the tour. And then, after all that waiting, like I said, a bit of a letdown...

For a start, the hall had terrible acoustics with the sound bouncing and echoing all around. Then there was the Peter Crouch look-alike who I kept bumping into. Not only did he look like him, he had his physique as well. Like the real thing, he was pretty difficult to knock off the ball too. At such close quarters I wasn't about to call him 'Freak' like those cruel Sheffield United fans had done to Mr Crouch, and I couldn't get him substituted or booked by employing Keith Curle tactics of pinching, sly kicking and unseen hair pulling, so I just had to try and avoid him in the Pond as regular bumping and bashing against him was proving quite painful.

Then there was the odour. I couldn't understand why this was the smelliest gig I'd ever been to, and not just by a short distance. No, actually I'd never noticed foul whiffs at a gig ever before, and it really was puzzling me as to why I'd only just noticed it now. It was Pete who came to the rescue by pointing out that it was the smoking ban. In the past there'd always been tobacco smoke (and other more sweet-smelling vapours) to mask the odour of sweat and breaking wind, but now there was nothing to chase those smells away, and heck, was it awful.

The thing was, the poor quality of the sound seemed to be rubbing off on the band and none of them looked the happiest I'd ever seen up there onstage. The choice of songs was, of course, brilliant because even with my ridiculously easy-going policy of liking everything any of my favourite bands have ever done, Cardiacs show incredible consistency by not having any songs that I think I might not like quite as much (and hence I am always mystified when discussions crank up on Cardiacs Email Chatlist about songs they don't like - come on people, love them all!). So basically, Cardiacs can play anything in their set and Mr Unfussy here will be happy. Of course, I'm even happier when they play a song I haven't heard them do very often, and there are some songs that hit right at the top of the Belch Appreciometer, but by and large I'm always very happy (and sometimes ecstatic).

You see, with Cardiacs the thing that makes a gig so special is that such complex tunes are played as well live as they are on record, but there is the added bonus of the *energy* of the live performance, both musically and physically, if you know what I mean. But on this night in Brighton, even though the band were playing perfectly well, the sound was so awful there was no way it sounded as good as listening to the CDs at home. And the usual safety net of the energetic performance was negated by the slightly dispirited look and feel of the band. But…there *was* a highlight; during "The Breakfast Line" the band broke…no, not broke, that's the wrong word; the band DOOMED into a slow-grind version of the most Glorious Riff of them all, Gong's "Master Builder", also known as "The Om Riff" (8 out of 10 Listees stated it as their favourite riff ever). It took me a few seconds to work out what it was, but once I was there I was gripped with excitement. Everyone already knew that Tim was a serious Gong-Head, and indeed it wasn't the first time we'd heard him play it during a gig, but before it had always been a case of doodling between songs - this time it was a bona-fide part of the show, so deliberate was the slow-down, shimmer and move into that thump-thump-thump of the drums from Cath and Mel with the rest slinking alongside to perfection.

The Gong moment was THE highlight, closely followed by hearing the two b-sides from the recently released single, "Gen" and "Made All Up". And was this another one coming up? Cardiacs gently started the title track of that single, "Ditzy Scene", for all those already in possession a well known steady-builder of a rip-roarer. But no, it was not to be. The quiet beginning may sound simple, but Cardiacs don't really do simple, and once Tim lost his way there was no way back, so with a very annoyed expression he waved his arms and abandoned ship.

A bit of a Cardiacs tradition is the last chord elongated beyond all reasonability, and this night was no exception, but just in case there was to be a bit of atmosphere, the venue completely ruined it by putting the house lights up as that last chord plundered on. Ah well…we were all here and we were all quite happy, even though we were all being harassed by a crusty couple who seemed to be in a 90s Brew Crew time warp (we later saw them being questioned by the police outside). In keeping with many venues though, there seemed to be an indecent haste in shooing everybody out of the building. I'd barely got my bag from the cloakroom than I was being hustled outside. Still, we were a goodly gathering out in the street, all happy and smiling in the cold night air; but oh no, hang on, we weren't safe from the security woman yet - she was out on the street with us, herding us even further away. 'She won't be happy until we're out of Brighton,' I grumbled. What's more, I seemed to have developed a sore ear at some point in the evening, although still with some way to go to beat the perforated eardrum Cardiacs gave me on the 2005 tour. Still, another ten nights to go...

* * * *

I'd been unsure what to do after this gig. I'd put out a bit of a plea on the Internet for places to stay in every town that Cardiacs were playing in, and by and large I'd come up trumps, but for Brighton no-one was forthcoming. Big Ship Iron had told me he'd get me put up in the same hotel as him (I quite fancied a night in The Grand), but he'd only gone and got stuck in Switzerland. It wouldn't usually be too much of a problem because trains run quite late back to London, but this wasn't enough nowadays, because I was now living in the charisma-and-character-free-zone of Ashford in Middlesex (don't bother checking it out to see if I'm right, just trust me on this one) and the last train from Waterloo to there leaves before midnight, which if you ask me just proves what a grim and dreadfully dull place it really is. Of course, there was always the option of hitchhiking, which was after all what I and this book were supposed to be all about. But actually I didn't fancy it. Much better to do a bit of negotiating. Andrew was giving Marina a lift back to London, so I tagged along. It soon became evident that Andrew didn't fancy going via Ashford (can't blame him), so a night spent on *The Organ* sofa was suggested. It may not be the same *Organ* house of old in Walthamstow where on more than one occasion I'd found myself crashing after Cardiacs gigs in the mid-90s, most times with Ian, and one memorably funny night with the whole of trance-rockers Timeshard in the room after Cardiacs at King's Cross Water Rats Splash Club, but a night at Organ Towers was a bit of a tradition, so it all sounded good to me.

Before any of that though, we had to find Andrew's car parked up in Brighton. As we wandered down a side street a block or two away from the venue, I was doing that thing that you do when you're not particularly paying attention to anything close to midnight - you see a light on in a window three-or-so storeys up, you notice that the curtains are open, and then you notice that there's a Sheffield United plaque displayed on the wall. Oh yeah, that happens a lot, especially when the plaque is barely visible to the human eye. Come off it - this wouldn't even get spotted in Sheffield, not so randomly and distant and small (but is anything related to Sheffield United invisible to the Belch eye?). And in Brighton? No way.

But there it was, and it was worthy of shouting down the road to Andrew (an Arsenal fan) and Marina (not a particularly big football fan to the best of my knowledge): 'Hey, there's a Sheffield United badge up there!' I even dragged them back up the road to have a look, by which time I'd noticed the window was slightly open, so the occupant may have been able to hear me. In my best Sheffield accent I bellowed, 'Nah den Blade!' I only had to repeat it once before someone appeared at the window. Instead of telling me to shut up and throwing a saucepan at me, he obviously spotted my Sheffield United woolly hat and waved instead. Just to make sure he'd got the message I showed him my Sheffield United rucksack, then rummaged around in it and produced my just-in-case-I-have-to-hitch bright yellow away shirt, waving it at him like a lunatic. He held up his hand as if to say, 'Wait a minute,' and then came back holding an old white Sheffield United away shirt up to the window (when we were sponsored by Wards, Blades fans, the one that saw us losing in the play-off final to that last-kick-of-the-game David Hopkin goal against Palace at Wembley in 1997). Of course, this got the thumbs up from me.

He then obviously decided to get to the bottom of this and opened the window fully. 'Are you really a Blade?' he asked. Hmmm, let's see - woolly hat, rucksack, yellow away shirt; yep, I think so.

'He's not just any Sheffield United fan though,' chipped in Marina, allowing me to be modest for once.

'Have you read the book *Fever Hitch*?' I asked (the modesty didn't last long).

'No,' he replied. Ah, right...

'Have you ever seen *Football's Hardest Away Days* on the telly?' probed Marina.

'Yes, I saw that, the one with the Sheffield United fan hitching to Plymouth,' he remarked.

'That was me!' I trilled gleefully.

'It wasn't was it?' (Leans out of window, looks more closely) 'F*** me, it IS you! I'm coming down!'

And down onto the street he came where hands were shaken and photos taken. It's always nice to meet a fellow Blade, but in such random circumstances and so far from Sheffield it was a truly wonderful and bizarre moment, far and away the highlight of the day (even outstripping Cardiacs' Gong moment). As Marina took our photo a neighbour came out onto the street and told us to keep the noise down because 'it's after midnight you know.' We risked her wrath by ignoring her whilst exchanging email addresses and mobile numbers as well as names. He was called Pascal, and I really should contact him sometime soon.

* * * *

Night buses home can be quite fun, but the trek across town from Brixton where Andrew dropped us off to Kensal Rise where the Organs now live was anything but. Both Marina and I were knackered, and with both of us planning on doing Oxford the next day, a good night's sleep wouldn't go amiss, but goodness me, those night buses can crawl sometimes. It may have been nearly 4am when we got to Organ Towers, but admirably Sean was still up when we got in, and even more admirably he didn't seem at all put out by the news that I'd be staying the night. In fact he seemed rather concerned that I'd be sleeping in a room with so much Manchester United memorabilia around (maybe he thought I'd trash it), but actually I always feel comfortable on a sofa, especially when from said sofa I can see a copy of that seminal Cardiacs video *Seaside Treats* on a shelf. Ah yes, Cardiacs, that's what we're all about here in Organland, as they might say. Brighton may not have been the best gig, but tomorrow was Oxford, and Cardiacs have never done a duff one in Oxford. As I drifted off to sleep surrounded by stacks of CDs and tapes and boxes of Org Records releases, I started to get all excited about the forthcoming trip to Oxford. I'd started the day on a treatment table and finished it on a sofa. Things were on the up, and tomorrow I was sure it would get even better.

Chapter Four
"Plane Plane Against the Grain"
The Organ

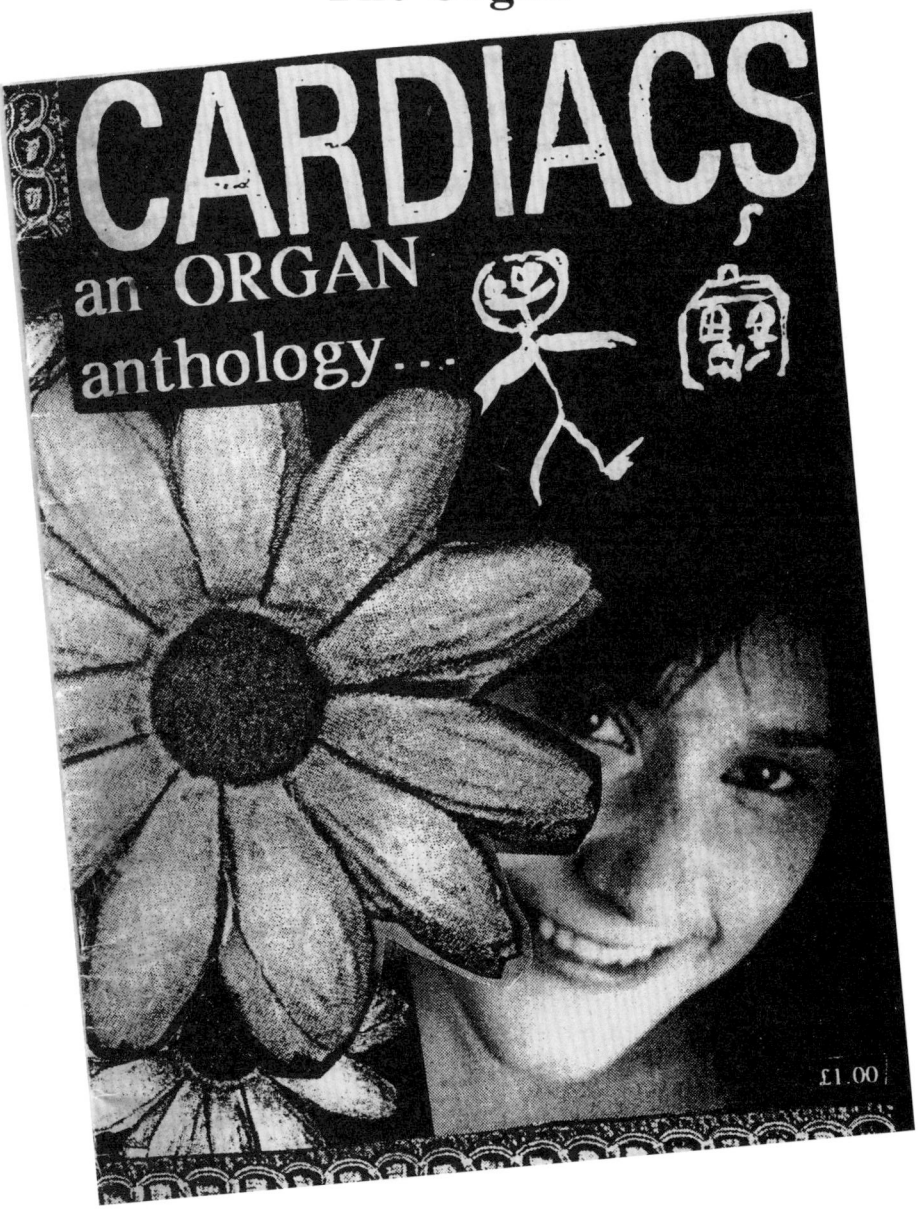

"Plane Plane Against the Grain"
The Organ

I'm not sure when it was that I first encountered *The Organ* as a fanzine, or indeed when I first met the Organs themselves, but I have it in my head that it was around mid-1988; in fact I may be able to pinpoint it to a benefit gig to Save the Black Rhino at the Town and Country Club in Kentish Town, London, on Spring Bank Holiday Monday, 1988. I'm pretty sure that as I queued outside for what seemed like an age, worrying about the fact that Ozric Tentacles were already onstage, in order to calm myself down I purchased a copy of *The Organ* from a pavement-up-and-down-the-queue vender, and was delighted to find that not only did they appear to love Progressive Rock, they raved about Cardiacs, making them out to be the best band in the world ever ever ever...

The fact that Sean or Marina, possibly both, were slogging up and down the pavement outside the venue should come as no surprise to anyone, not least because the bill that day was a very *Organ*-friendly line-up of Hawkwind, Here & Now, Doctor & the Medics, Nik Turner's Fantastic Allstars, Larry Wallis & the Love Pirates of Doom and Robert Calvert & the Starfighters, on top of the aforementioned Ozrics. But also it should come as no surprise because, well, over twenty years on they're still out there doing it now; that is when they're not putting on gigs themselves, releasing records, or writing reviews for the still-going-strong *Organ*.

I definitely know that I had a good chat to Marina in the foyer of the Charing Cross Road version of the Marquee on December 21st 1988, following on from a rather stupendously brilliant Cardiacs gig, because I dug deep into my pocket and left the venue with a number of *Organ* compilation tapes as well as the latest issue of everyone's favourite fanzine. At that point they had only been "kissing big ugly sharks" for just over two years (although they didn't realise it back then because Tim was still two years off coining that particular phrase), but now they've been doing it for over twenty, an impressive run for any magazine, never mind one that has always operated around the dangerous edges of alternative musical culture. I'm pretty sure that most of you reading this will be familiar with *The Organ* and Org Records, but at the same time you may well wonder at the incredible staying power of this determined little organisation and may even feel a little mystified. By the same token, if you're reading this and you have no idea who or what I'm talking about, you will be *totally* mystified. Either way, a history lesson is doubtless in order…

* * * *

As I couldn't put it better myself, here's a bit of *Organ* history from their MySpace page: "*ORGAN* started out as an old-school handmade hand-painted fractured DIY zine back in the last century - November '86 if you really want to know. Somewhere along the line, instead of folding after a couple of issues like most zines back then did, *Organ* evolved in to a full-on magazine, a record label called ORG…and then, later on, a website, a weekly FM radio show, a TV show and more…

"We started a tape label that became a full-on record label called ORG - loads of bands have emerged via ORG since the first bit of 7" vinyl in '94…albums, singles and a whole load of releases from bands and such…

"We're still messy and DIY in spirit, and still rather defiant… It all comes rather naturally, we're still shouting, we're still not going to toe the line…

"We've been doing this *Organ* thing longer than most and we'll probably be here doing it long after most others have given up or worse still, have allowed themselves to be sucked up in to the mainstream music business rather than building a real alternative.

"*ORGAN MAGAZINE* is currently weekly at organart.com, a new issue goes on line every Thursday afternoon. There's also a daily alternative music news on this site…

"*ORGAN MAGAZINE* is about throwing up signposts and pointing you towards all the good exciting music being made by good people all over the world; you'll find new signposts going up every day over on the website at organart.com - signposts and links at the end of reviews, news stories and radio playlists that point you towards all the wholesome earfood, art and creativity, all the alternatives that are out there waiting for you.

"We like to avoid pigeon holes, our musical tastes are all over the place - that's what real Punk Rock should be - for far too many now just see everything as an MTV fashion parade - time to take it back! Music and the associated culture that evolves around the music should not be under the thumb of the corporations, there is a different way…first you need to communicate. To us Punk Rock is a way of thinking, a state of mind, not a sound, a fashion or a free sticker."

* * * *

And so it was that in 1988, whether it be in May or in December, *The Organ* crossed the Belch Radar, and it has been on there pretty much ever since. Over the first five years I bought all my copies of *The Organ* from Cardiacs gigs, and as these have always been attended regularly by myself, I doubt there were many copies that I missed. There then came a time around 1995 when I'm certain I must have been subscribing to *The Organ* because I seem to remember copies of the fanzine flopping onto my doormat, along with the tons of merchandise I mail-ordered from them, whether it be t-shirts, or records, tapes and CDs.

Ah yes, recordings… By now *The Organ* were releasing things that they liked on their own record label, Org Records, but on top of that they also provided a vital outlet for bands that weren't on their label but provided ear-music worthy of *Organ*-laudation. Thus Org-releases by Huge Baby and Angel Cage (amongst many others) arrived at my address along with delights from Sleepy People and Flyscreen (except they didn't flop onto my doormat, rather postie had to ring on the doorbell as even a wonderfully-sized 10" by Map was too wide to squeeze through the letter-box).

Whether my method of payment was at a gig or via subscription, my method of exploration and discovery was constant: I'd read the whole fanzine from cover to cover and put a big asterisk next to anything that appealed. The good thing about *The Organ* was their reviewing policy; they'd only review something if they liked it, because why review something that was rubbish and take up valuable page-space when you could tell the world about something that was really adventurous or challenging instead? The other thing was that you could always get around the worry that they might like something whilst you may not by their simple method of describing things and comparing bands to either peers or heroes. Hardly groundbreaking you wouldn't have thought, but anyone who has read the *NME* may wonder why their reviewers don't follow a similar format. As it was, in *The Organ*, if something was Prog-Rock, they would shamelessly describe it as Prog-Rock, and if it was Punk, it would be described thus. And if it was a cross between the two (like Cardiacs), they'd use their own term, "Super Bendy Pronk", a term that technically didn't make much sense, but upon reading it, you knew exactly what they meant. Thus I was therefore able to avoid buying anything that appealed to Sean's thrashier tastes in Metal due to *The Organ*'s admirable honesty. And just in case I was in any doubt at all, there would be a band name chucked in here and there, just as a guideline you understand (one relatively recent example, Pure Reason Revolution compared to Yes).

Now, all this would come to fruition in a number of ways, the most obvious being the one already mentioned - reading about a band in *The Organ* then sending a cheque to either the band or *The Organ* in exchange for a plastic disc or two. Another way was to read about a band, lodge the name in my brain, then whilst trawling through the racks in HMV or similar I'd have my memory jogged by a recording jumping out at me, one example being how an album by Osmium worked its way into my collection. There were also incidences of *The Organ* merely confirming what I already knew or suspected. Thus I was not surprised to see Poisoned Electrick Head and Ring mentioned within their pages as I'd already seen them live and had described them myself as "Cardiacs crossed with Gong" and "Cardiacs crossed with Hawkwind" respectively. There was also once a rather rare moment when the music press got something right in a review of the Wizards of Twiddly. I'd seen the name at the top of a piece and was immediately attracted, even more so when it went on to describe them in a way that sounded very favourable to this Belch. But there was some inkling of my mistrust of the music press when I had to seek confirmation via *The Organ*, confirmation duly provided. Indeed, not only were *The Organ* raving about them, it seemed they were putting on gigs with them on the bill…

Did I say *The Organ* were putting on gigs? Why yes, not just satisfied with putting out a fanzine and founding a record label, they were now promoting gigs too, regular *Organ* nights becoming a feature at the Monarch in Chalk Farm. Living in Brackley at the time, I couldn't make it to every gig, but if work and time allowed Ian and I would either hitch down or, when flushed with cash, train-it or Oxford-Tube-it. The Monarch staged some incredible gigs, one of the main attractions being that *The Organ* would always put together a line-up of bands they felt complimented each other, hoping that fans of the headline act would therefore pick up on the supports. One incredible line-up saw the David Cross Band (ex-King Crimson violinist) headlining with Pop-a-cat-a-Petal (who eventually morphed into Ultrasound) and the Monsoon Bassoon (featuring a pre-Cardiacs-even-in-his-guitar-tech-days Kavus) as the supporting cast. Ian and I were suitably impressed by the whole evening, all three bands playing variations on Super-Bendy-Pronk and Prog-Rock. One wonders why more gig promoters didn't adopt this rather obvious policy of billing bands together with a similar appeal and a common target audience…

Organ nights at the Monarch also provided Ian and me with a rare Sea Nymphs performance, featuring Jon Poole on keyboards in place of William D. Drake (I think Bunty Chunks supported that night), but perhaps my favourite night at the Monarch saw Wizards of Twiddly supported by Old Fruit…

It was one of those nights where Ian and I had an absolute hitchhiking nightmare. Via a bewildering zigzag of lifts we'd gone down the M40, anti-clockwise on the M25, ended up near Reading, then gone M4 and back clockwise round the M25, all in the pouring rain, eventually coming to rest in Enfield where we legged it to Turkey Street and boarded a train into London and finally onto the tube. Even with the eventual switch to public transport, we missed the first band Map, but blustered through the door just in time to see Old Fruit taking the stage.

It's safe to say that even in the realms of Super-Bendy-Pronk, Old Fruit were pretty unique. They were quite something to behold, having amongst their ranks a guitarist/vocalist dressed like a psychedelic Andy Pandy, as well as a flautist with a rectangular beard who at one point played vacuum cleaner in the ensemble. Their sound was something else too; if Cardiacs sped-up and condensed Prog-Rock by fitting into five minutes what Yes would do in twenty, Old Fruit took it one stage further by squeezing everything into one-minute-or-less bursts of musical-mayhem. Their "album" (it's hard to call it an album when the whole CD only lasts nineteen-minutes-and-thirty-six-seconds, but what else can you call it when it has 17 tracks on it?), *That's What I Call Now Music*, bears this out. Both on the album and live, songs such as "Mr and Mrs Spoonhandle", "The Friar", and "I Sense the Power of Moonlight and Magic Calling Me Through the Night" had me and Ian simultaneously in stitches and raptures. I even got a Satsuma thrown to me by the bassist…

The drummer from Wizards of Twiddly could be seen sat at the side of the stage looking on with a combination of bemusement and amusement. Someone (and I forget who it was) later told me that the Wizards could possibly have been a trifle miffed at Old Fruit's brand of Pronky-Jazz-With-a-Zany-Hue because the Twids themselves felt this element made them unique, but I'm sure they admired like-minded souls. I know for a fact that the audience did, and once again *The Organ*'s gig-bill policy came up trumps as a huge percentage of Wizards of Twiddly fans went home that night with Old Fruit's name tattooed on their brain.

Organ nights didn't just take place at the Monarch - indeed, I believe it was not long after this 1994 gig that they fell out with the venue (something to do with a rubber shark I think), so *Organ* nights moved about a bit, the problem being that Sean and Marina would be at just about every gig in London I felt moved to attend, so it can be a bit hard on the old memory remembering which ones they promoted and which ones they were present at out of enthusiasm. However, I'm 99% certain that those Huge Baby gigs scaring me to death at Barfly @ the Falcon, Camden, were *Organ*-ised, so presumably they took up residence there for a while. What is 100% clear is that for consecutive years they staged hugely-ambitious "Seven Day Itch" events where they put on a gig every night of the week, both years culminating in Cardiacs gigs at the Venue in New Cross (May 2nd 1993 and May 29th 1994 to be precise). In true *Organ* tradition, the accompanying bills were stunning, featuring as they did Poisoned Electrick Head both years, *and* the quite unbelievably gorgeous Miranda Sex Garden in 1994.

It was round-about this time that Ian and I, sometimes with Tom, sometimes without, would regularly crash at Organ Towers when it was situated in Walthamstow, usually after Cardiacs gigs. Why, we even turned up one afternoon unannounced just to say hello, and as ever were made hugely welcome. But perhaps my favourite Organ Towers crash was after witnessing Cardiacs headlining the Splash Club @ the Water Rats in King's Cross, May 11th 1995. I believe we got a lift home with someone and as we turned the corner, a white van was seen parked outside. 'Have we got anyone stopping tonight?' asked Marina.

'Oh yes,' remembered Sean, 'we've got Timeshard stopping over.'

So I ended up sharing some floor-space with Timeshard, a band from Merseyside who played a quite mind-blowing style of hippie-trance, not dissimilar to Astralasia. The conversation continued deep into the night, and I must say Timeshard provided marvellous company as we laughed and anecdoted long and hard.

That mid-90s period was something of a fertile one musically with a whole plethora of gigs worthy of a trek down to London. The Dublin Castle in Camden was a hot favourite - it seemed there was a wonderful gig taking place there almost weekly, and I always seemed to be in attendance (although I obviously can't have made all of them). Hence it was I witnessed such wonders as Huge Baby, the People's Friend, Katherine In A Cupboard, Nub, Podsdarapomuk (from Germany), the Monsoon Bassoon, and many, many more.

Whether these were *Organ* gigs or not was immaterial because all bands were championed by them, and most of them had been brought to my attention, as well as the attention of most present, through either reading *The Organ* or attending their gigs.

By 1997 *The Organ* had moved their regular nights to the Bull & Gate in Kentish Town, and it was one such night that led to a bit of a life-changing experience for me (and apologies to anyone who has read about this in *Fever Hitch*, but if truth be known it's probably more appropriate to this tome).

It was one of those nights where I was torn, torn between two gigs. *The Organ* were putting on Poisoned Electrick Head and Sleepy People at the Bull & Gate, whilst over at the Borderline, Sidi Bou Said were treading the boards. The conflict in my head wasn't helped by the fact that Sarah, by then my ex of just over a year, was planning to head down to London from Milton Keynes but hadn't decided which gig to attend. As a consequence, and because I was still a little bit in love with Sarah, I couldn't decide which one to go to either, and even as my train pulled into Paddington I was unsure, but as I headed to the tube, I decided to go to the gig that would double my musical pleasure - I really wanted to see Poisoned Electrick Head in their new form, and as yet I'd not seen Sleepy People, so really the Bull & Gate it had to be. Deep down I had a feeling Sarah would rather go to Sidi Bou Said, but in the days before we owned mobiles, the only way was to turn up to a gig and see who was there.

As suspected, the Bull & Gate was Sarah-less, although so early was I it's fair to assume Sarah probably wouldn't have reached anywhere near the Borderline either. I may have made my decision about the gig, but another conflict was now bouncing around my head - that old football/music thing again. That same night the Chesterfield/Middlesbrough FA Cup Semi-Final tie was to be replayed, and as the first match had provided one of THE great sporting occasions when the two teams drew 3-3 with Chesterfield equalising in the last minute, I didn't want to miss anything this time round.

As I entered the Bull & Gate, Sean was on the door so I asked him what time Poisoned Electrick Head were on. 'Oh, they've split up so they've cancelled,' he delivered, plunging a dagger right through my heart. I knew I should have gone to see the Sidis, I thought to myself. But then I remembered that I was desperate to see Sleepy People too, so I asked Sean what time they were on.

'About 10.30,' he replied.

'Oh good,' said I, 'that means I can watch the football in the bar.'

The door through to the main room was open and through it could be seen a band soundchecking, a band who sounded somewhat interesting, a bit like Industrial Hardcore Jazz if you like. 'Oh no,' said Sean, 'you MUST see this band.'

For some reason the first thing I felt the need to ask was the band's name, to which Sean replied, 'Jesus Underground Band.' Interesting name, interesting sound - perhaps Sean was right. So I decided to watch the gig whilst holding a radio earpiece in place which kept me updated on the football. However there was only ever going to be one winner…

Middlesbrough were making short work of Chesterfield this time and when they went three up, it really was pointless trying to listen to Radio 5Live whilst watching this mad bunch onstage. I was propping myself up by the mixing desk at the back and after a minute of Jesus Underground Band I decided I wasn't going a step closer. Most of the band were semi-naked, covered in what looked like green slime and mud. This totally insane-looking "singer" (more growls and screams than singing) was destroying microphone stands before picking up an audience member and banging him repeatedly against the stage. Nope, I was staying right where I was…

I was mesmerised by the music however; impossible to sing along to, but HEAVY, Jazzy and INDUSTRIAL, the trumpet duets between the singer/trumpeter and the sax-player/trumpeter proving to be their most breathtaking moments. Their daubed-cosmetics filled the air with an interesting smell too, whilst the onstage theatrics got madder and more violent, culminating in the frontman wrestling with the keyboard player, the keyboard player at half the singer's size obviously at something of a disadvantage, so much so I felt most concerned for the poor chap when the tussle climaxed with him being dropped from a great height onto his back.

At the end Andy Thompson and Dan Chinn were less enthusiastic than myself as I raved up to them with, 'Wow! What did you make of that lot then…?'

Andy paused for a minute before observing, 'They smelled wonderful…'

I then asked Sean where on earth he'd dug them up from. 'Slovakia I think,' he replied. When Sleepy People had also worked their magic, I headed to the merchandise desk and bought a Sleepy People t-shirt and a Jesus Underground Band CD. I was hooked…

Contact was made through *The Organ* due to my desire to put Jesus Underground Band on somewhere in Oxfordshire, even possibly Brackley, Sean including in his note a heartfelt, "Good luck - you'll need it with that lot."

He wasn't wrong, but heck was it a lively old time. Just over a year after that initial contact with Jesus Underground Band at the Bull & Gate in 1997, I was heading down to London in order to move into their communal madhouse in Canning Town and become the band's manager. We got banned from venues, upset PA hire companies everywhere (they seemed to object to their microphone stands coming back bent), and one evening I even found myself visiting the offices of the Royal Mail in Harrow wearing my best suit and tie fully expecting prosecution (skilfully avoided); for all that fun, and for the fact that I moved to London, I've got *The Organ* to thank…

* * * *

Of course, it didn't all end for me and *The Organ* with my arrival in London, summer 1998. They surged on with Org Records, carried on with the fanzine, embraced the Internet, promoted gigs (albeit less frequently, but they still manage to put on free shows at Notting Hall Arts Centre where Sean also doubles up as DJ), and even got their own radio show on Resonance FM, a show where I observed them in production once or twice just to see what went on in the studio. And what do you know, they're still introducing me to music via all these outlets, hence I discovered Battles thanks to the radio show and Rose

Kemp as a result of regular endorsements on MySpace. In the further past, those Organs introduced me personally to a mad Norwegian "Weird-Metal" band Cheese Cake Truck, and of course, before long I was on the road with them selling t-shirts and CDs from behind their merchandise desk…

The Organ also gave me my best review for *Fever Hitch*, but then when you're a music-loving football fan with a bit of hitchhiking history behind you (Sean), then you really are likely to see everything in the book that I'd hoped…

Throughout all this, *The Organ* have remained staunch supporters of Cardiacs, making one wonder if Cardiacs would ever have been able to keep going without them, because not only have Cardiacs featured at *Organ* gigs, Org Records holds the privilege of being the only other label to issue Cardiacs releases since the foundation of the Alphabet Business Concern, including the most recent single, "Ditzy Scene". It's only when you become aware how insular the Alphabet Business Concern is that you realise the high regard they must have for *The Organ*, and that really is quite an endorsement, I can tell you…

Chapter Five
"Victory Egg"
The Carling Academy,
Oxford, November 13th 2007

CARDIACS CONCERT PERFORMANCES

In an institution with the moral stature of the ALPHABET BUSINESS CONCERN wild rumours abound. Our dedicated hirelings try to ignore such tittle-tattle but unfortunately not all are as strong-willed as is preferred, and inaccuracies have been known to spread like evil tendrils. Contrary to any spurious suggestions you may have heard, it is with great pride that we, the ALPHABET BUSINESS CONCERN, present some gala live performances by CARDIACS. These are to take place at 'THE VENUE', Clifton rise, New Cross, London, The WOLVERHAMPTON POLYTECHNIC, and the 'VENUE',Co-op hall, Cowley rd, Oxford and are events which should be given the highest attendance priority, considering the gargantuan efforts made by all involved, the tale of which we have generously deemed appropriate to share with YOU our YOUsletter family.

As we all know and understand, William D Drake had been placed under a great deal of stress in the twilight months of the last year and as a result had been undergoing a rigidly enforced program of hypnotic regression, reccomended by our resident neuro-psychologist.
Needless to say, everything was going to plan and Drake was coming on in leaps and bounds when as luck, that fickle strumpet, would have it, an unforeseen tragic allergic reaction to a particular 'in house' brand of medication combined with the physical duress involved in wrist displacement therapy, resulted in a total de-stablising of the cerebral equilibrium and a near catastrophic coupling of the concious and sub-concious mind, leaving Drake without any means of discerning reality from his own self destructive fantasies.
Obviously no productive use of Drake could be made at this juncture until a suitable compromise could be arranged.This came in the form of a series of surgical incursions and the use of an experimental hormone implant. Preliminary results were incouraging and William returned to his normal duties, but a more recent assesment of his progress showed a deterioration in behavioural patterns and a projected forcast shows an accelerated decline.
Owing to the high cost of further medication and the allready substantial cost to the ALPHABET BUSINESS CONCERN we have decided to terminate the recovery program.
Unfortunately this will mean that May 16th is probably the last time that Drake will be permitted to be representative of the ALPHABET BUSINESS CONCERN in public.

MAY 2nd...... WOLVERHAMPTON POLYTECHNIC

MAY 3rd......'THE VENUE',CLIFTON RISE, NEW CROSS, LONDON.

MAY 16th.....'THE VENUE',CO-OP HALL,COWLEY RD, OXFORD.

ALPHABET, PO Box 202, Kingston-Upon-Thames, Surrey KT1 2QG

"Victory Egg"
The Carling Academy, Oxford, November 13th 2007

Cardiacs don't do bad gigs in Oxford. Fact. And just to make sure, without even looking at my trusty Cardiacs Gig List, I know that apart from London, Oxford is the city or town where I've seen Cardiacs the most. Hang on (*consults list*); yep, there we go - nine times, an awful lot of them during a curious little period between 1989 and 1991 when they didn't gig too much, apart from seemingly only ever playing at the Oxford Co-op Hall (which by 1991 had become the trendier-sounding Oxford Venue).

Oxford must have been held in high regard by Cardiacs themselves as it was at the Venue on May 16th 1991 that they chose to play their last gig with William D Drake behind his pile of keyboards. Now that really was a cracking night. It was a red hot day followed by a humid evening, and because all self-respecting followers of the Alphabet Business Concern desired to be there, the place was soon sold out. The thing about the Venue was that it was one floor up, and so it was probably considered safe to open a few windows and let some fresh air flow through to cool everyone down. However, so desperate were some to get in that they were scaling the walls and scrambling through those invitingly open windows, a sort of slightly scaled down version of the tales of Van der Graaf Generator's return to live concert performance in 1975 when legend has it that ticketless Italians were removing the tiles from the roof of London's Victoria Theatre in order to gatecrash this momentous occasion.

Oxford and its then-Co-op Hall also provided me with one of my most awe-inspiring moments as an audience member watching the band up on the stage. That was on June 17th 1989 and things were getting a little bit out of hand in the Pond (except I don't think we called it the Pond back then, it was just a good old fashioned moshpit). Elbows were flying and I remember one particular delicate girl being reduced to tears after taking one full in the face. During "Baby Heart Dirt" it really was getting wild, so Tim turned to the band mid-song and motioned for them to stop. And they did. All on the same note. At the same time, not a stray note in sight. Tim then turned back to the audience, crouched down and told everyone to 'calm down - keep those elbows in.' Once he felt he'd got his message across he stood up, turned back to the band, and like an eccentric orchestral conductor brought them all back in. And they resumed exactly at the point where they'd left off. Brilliant. Absolutely dumb-strikingly brilliant. Telepathy? Six musicians so well-rehearsed? Who knows, but I'm not sure that there's any other band in the world who could pull this one off with such aplomb. I was awestruck at the time, and I'm still awestruck now, evidenced by the amount of Cardiacs fans I've told about it since.

But perhaps my favourite Oxford gig was the first, Oxford Polytechnic November 10th 1988. This was at an interesting time of my life when I was training for a franchise of Circle K in Brackley, Northamptonshire. At the time I wasn't sure if I was going to be staying down there or moving back up to Sheffield, doubt brought about by the seeming collapse of the franchise's planned expansion into my home town.

Well whatever the future, I was living for the Now and taking advantage of my thoughtful employers often giving me two days off together by embarking on my first string of consecutive Cardiacs gigs. The fact that I still had contacts in Sheffield (parents) meant I could see Cardiacs in Leeds then Huddersfield, and the fact that I was working a mere twenty miles from Oxford, in Brackley, meant that I thought I could make it to that third gig in a row, even if I was working until fairly late in the evening.

The other problem was after Huddersfield I was going to have to hitch through the night in order to get back to Brackley, nab a few hours of sleep, then get into work close enough to the time I was supposed to start. The biggest advantage was that my gig-going companion at the time was Richard, a prodigiously talented drummer from Sheffield who was now living in Oxford, so at least I had someone to keep me company as we whizzed down the M1 before standing for ages in the fog on the A5 in Weedon. Not for the last time that misty November I found myself in this situation in the early hours, and rather than feeling thoroughly miserable about it like most people would, I was getting an enormous buzz from it all.

Eventually our hitch got me to Brackley, with Richard carrying on to Oxford. The trouble was, it was only 6am and at the time I was stopping in Bed and Breakfast at the Red Lion, and at that time in the morning if I'd tried to get in I'd most definitely have been locked out, so instead I headed for my already-open place of work and announced to the bewildered early-morning staff that I'd just hitched back and was in need of a bit of sleep upstairs in the stockroom.

After about an hour of broken kip I wandered back down to the manager's office and sat in a bit of a daze until Danielle, morning supervisor and dominatrix of the newspaper rounds, came in with a stack of mail. 'Your post's here,' she announced and plonked it on the table in front of me. I just looked at it through the haze, and the next thing I knew I was coming to with a very sore nose and my face buried in those letters. Not normally one for blacking out, I figured I must have been very tired indeed.

Most sensible people would have opted out of the next gig, reasoning that having seen them the previous two nights there was no need to do a third, so better to have a nice restful night, especially as there was an early start the next morning. But I was beginning to learn that I didn't operate this way, and as I worked away later on that day, I started to hatch an elaborate plan, the first of many when it came to attending Cardiacs gigs…

Now, considering I'd been unemployed for three months between May and August of 1988, by November I was still finding having money a bit of a novelty. Okay, hitchhiking was a great way to save money, and a great way to travel around, but it was also nice to now have the back-up of money if things went wrong. This Oxford gig was going to be one such time where money was going to bail me out, and I wasn't going to have time to even contemplate hitching.

During my day's work, which started around midday, I worked out a way in which I could get to that night's gig. Taxi, train, taxi should do it, and I spent the spare moments of my break (and a considerable amount of loose change) on the clunky pay-phone in the manager's office sorting it all out. I booked a taxi to pick me up from work sometime around 8.30, phoned up the railway timetable to find out what time there was a train from Banbury to Oxford (of course making sure my taxi got me there just in time), then when I'd confirmed what time the train would arrive in Oxford, got the number of an Oxford minicab firm and booked one to pick me up from Oxford Station and take me to the Polytechnic. I reckoned that I'd miss the start of the gig but as I'd secured a place on the guest list, entry would be swift and gig-loss would be kept to a minimum.

There's nothing I like more than when a plan comes together, and this was one plan that slotted together perfectly. All the relevant modes of transportation dovetailed neatly, and as predicted, I found myself wandering around the Oxford Poly campus at just gone 10pm. However, one thing I'd not been able to sort out in my masterplan was where exactly the gig was, but I trusted my gig-nose on this one and hoped. Sure enough, after only a few minutes of aimless wandering I heard the strains of "Everything Is Easy" coming from the bowels of one of the buildings. Third song in - not bad.

I ran round the front and said to the bloke on the door, 'I'm on the guest list.'

'What's your name?' he asked.

'Belch,' came the inevitable reply.

'Okay,' said Doorman, 'but where's Richard?'

No offence Richard, but I wasn't really too bothered whether you'd got there or not. I was just interested in joining the heaving mass at the front as soon as possible. Besides, I figured you'd probably done that thing of turning up early and hanging round in the building until showtime (he had).

As I sprinted through the door into the boiling cauldron of a Cardiacs gig, I heard a voice say, 'Hello!' and there on turning round I saw Rebecca, a girl who I'd been at school with in the 6th Form at High Storrs School in Sheffield. We'd been in the same Economics set (not my strongest subject) and to see her there in Oxford was rather random. We only had time for the briefest of chats before I finally dived into the happy throng, still wearing my suit and tie from work, a suit and tie that remained in place right the way through to the end of the gig.

The Alphabet Business Concern were so impressed with my efforts that night that they awarded me a free poster, which almost compensated for the fact that I ended up paying a small fortune to get all the way back to Brackley in another minicab. An early start at work the next morning meant that I was totally knackered for the whole day, but I had an inner glow knowing that I'd just completed my first ever Cardiacs Hat-trick.

* * * *

After all those wonderful gigs of bygone years, this latest Oxford gig on November 13th 2007 was going to have a lot to live up to, especially as Brighton the night before had been so disappointing, but I was confident yer know, not least because the venue was a tried and trusted old favourite. Yes indeed, since the days of the Co-op Hall and the Oxford Venue, it had changed its name twice more, firstly to the Oxford Zodiac (favourite gig under this name, Gong with Pierre Moerlen drumming in 1997 - jaw-droppingly brilliant), and now it was the Oxford Carling Academy. Okay, I wasn't too keen on the sponsorship, and the illuminated fascia had me yearning for the quaint open windows inviting the ticketless to clamber through on a hot summer's day, but you still felt that you could rely on this venue and this town.

I still had to get there of course, and after catching up with a bit of sleep at home following a night on the Organ sofa I was off again, meeting Andrew at Earl's Court. Marina was meeting us there but the fact that she was standing at the wrong gate for about half an hour meant I had plenty of time to reflect on one of my life's regrets - missing Pink Floyd there in 1994. Anyway, eventually she showed and off we went on our merry way. But ho hum, another gig not hitchhiked to…

Once there we had the small matter of a pre-gig Cardiacs Email Chat List pub meet in the Hobgoblin, and with many attendees missing from the previous night, it felt like this was the List in person - well, the most verbose on the list that is (except Lol who has lots of opinions on lots of things but couldn't get up from Devon). Nick had allowed himself to do an "away" gig, and the Luxford had done the Oxford Tube thing (you know, the Oxford Tube really is the best bus in the world - London to Oxford and back ALL THROUGH THE NIGHT). Jill the Zag WAG was there (subs please check!) (if this is still there when published it means I was updating things when my Internet connection was down - it happens a lot yer know) and of course, as Oxford is almost local, Kettering-resident Ian (and my bed for the night) HAD to attend. Roscoe, these days largely a silent observer on the list, did a pretty good virtual representation of this in sitting quietly by and listening to all that was going on around him. The Helocolins (Karen and Paul) were massively welcome, largely because they bought a copy of *Fever Hitch* off me, but also because they are both huge personalities and wonderful fun to be with. And Malc was there too, of course, determined to make it to the first ten gigs before having to declare on the final night and keep the peace with his other half.

And then there was Big Ship Iron, freshly returned from Switzerland and actually a little nervous about the reception he'd receive, so much so that he called me on his mobile in order to act as tugboat and guide him in. My preparation had been worthwhile though, because Mr Ship Iron was welcomed at the table, especially as he got the drinks in and then joined us in a bit of a nacho frenzy. Nachos consumed, glasses emptied, it was on and into the venue, excitement mounting...

From the very first notes of opener "Jibber and Twitch" it was obvious that the sound was going to be far superior to Brighton, and as a result the performance was leagues ahead. The sound was crystal clear throughout and so the decision to change into my Sheffield United combat shorts in the toilets just before the start was a sound one as I bopped the night away.

Another interesting development was the different set from the night before. Okay, there was some crossover, but apparently the purchase of new technology meant that it was possible to take many more songs out on the road with them, and so we were met with a smattering of numbers different from the previous night.

I wasn't the only one to respond to all this positive activity, and the Pond was indeed an energetic and happy frenzy. Energy levels were increased by an impressive amount of kids in the audience; you know, teenagers, some of them very young teenagers. Goodness me, youth to grab the baton from some of us old-timers - most brilliant and most welcome. No matter how much energy was expended though, Tim was giving no water out tonight.

Just one thing remained to be seen though - would they make it through "Ditzy Scene"? Well, they bravely started it and Tim seemed to be concentrating extra hard. However, he seemed to be losing it at exactly the same point as the night before, but just before it got to the point of no return the rest of the band carried on with determined smiles and hauled him back in, and we were off and running - magnificent. A bit like the gig actually.

Another good thing about this venue (not really happy to call it by any name these days in case it changes again) is the close-proximity of a late-opening Tesco Metro, ideal for a bit of post-gig rehydration, and a good opportunity for me to show off with my staff discount card. Then there was the small miracle of Andy having parked his car right behind Mr Skinner's thus making the transfer of my rucksack from one to the other a whole lot easier.

Ian was up early for work the next morning so he was in no mood to loiter on the way back to his place. However, he did take a wrong turning along the way (I was right! I was right!) which slowed him down a bit (and meant I lost about twenty minutes of future sleep-time). Along the way though we had time to discuss my guilt over thoughts I'd had as to what I'd do if a close family member of mine was inconsiderate enough to die during the tour, possibly robbing me of my 100th gig. When Ian was fed up of listening to my sick ramblings, he replaced me with his favourite recording of Victor Lewis-Smith, a choice which left me totally incapable of objection.

Once back in Kettering he gave me a brief viewing of the latest series of *The Mighty Boosh* on his computer, but as my ears were ringing so much I couldn't hear a thing, this was abandoned and sleep took over.

Once again it was sleep on a sofa, but this time it was accompanied by those ringing ears, which believe it or not actually act as a sleep-aid for me, which was probably why back in those mad early dates of Cardiacs hat-tricks and Oxford triumphs my sleep was always blissful - blissful but brief.

Chapter Six
"Look in the Back, See Who's Gayer, Birthday Boy or Leo Sayer"
Ian Skinner

"Look in the Back, See Who's Gayer,
Birthday Boy or Leo Sayer"
Ian Skinner

It was past midnight, meaning that we were now into June 25th 1996. The day before, a matter of hours earlier on June 24th, Cardiacs had played a blinding set at the Duchess of York in Leeds. Ian and I had hitched up, and then post-gig had been on the scrounge for a lift at least some of the way back. I used the fact that at midnight it was to become Ian's birthday in order to gain some sympathy, and as a result of this Captain John Hook, who was driving the van with all the gear in it, loaded us in the back and told us he could take us to the first services on the M1. It would be a start I suppose, and if you can get to a service station at any time of day or night, you stand a fighting chance of a) getting a lift and b) scuttling off somewhere warm if you don't get a lift.

Mind you, I didn't really need to tell anyone that it was Ian's birthday because all evening, unbeknownst to him, I'd gone around the whole band and entourage getting them all to sign a birthday card for him, a card which he still treasures to this day. Another thing that got brought up in conversation during the evening apart from Ian's birthday was me telling everyone that when I was 15 my curly mop had been not unlike a certain Leo Sayer, a fact that Jon Poole, Cardiacs then-guitarist, certainly found amusing, especially as he spent the first year that he'd been in the band referring to me as Curly (always said with a northern accent).

So anyway, there we were right at the back of the van, with Captain John driving and Jon Poole and Kavus (guitar tech back then) passengers. Mine and Ian's quick whispered conversation before getting in had been that we should keep quiet and hope that they forgot about us, suddenly starting to make noises when we neared Rothersthorpe Services, the turn off towards Brackley and home.

And so it was that we stowed away in the back and kept very very quiet, listening to those three talking largely rubbish (but funny rubbish) in the front. The van hit the M1 and we were keeping a careful watch out the back window for the first service station. And what do you know, we sailed straight past it thus prompting a silent fist-pumping celebration from the two of us. This little action was repeated with every passing service station, and before too long we were in danger of reaching our goal, Rothersthorpe…

About twenty miles short of there though, we noticed that the three of them had gone quiet. Jon and Kavus now appeared to be whispering to each other. Then the two of them turned their heads towards the back of the van and recited in unison, 'Look in the back, See who's gayer, Birthday Boy or Leo Sayer.' Genius.

So how did it get to this, where Ian felt such devotion to a band that he would hitchhike all the way to Leeds and back in very uncomfortable circumstances just to see them play the same set they'd done the day before in Northampton? Time to seek out some answers…

* * * *

Back in 1989, when I was slaving away at the franchise of Circle K, first as a deputy manager then as THE manager, I noticed that there was a youngster with long hair who used to come in shopping, presumably for his family, pushing his baby brother around in a pushchair. But not only did he have long hair, he also wore a Jethro Tull *Rock Island* t-shirt. Long hair and a Tull t-shirt? On one so young? Why, he couldn't be a day over 13 (of course, I completely forgot that at the age of 12 I was listening intently to Yes and Genesis, so it shouldn't have seemed so remarkable).

Well, it turned out his mum, Ann Skinner, worked at the other Circle K shop in town (the one that took no money, not even after they moved the Post Office into it) and on the occasions that I had to go down there she was always telling me about her talented musician son Ian and how he was in a band. Guitar and flute seemed to be his thing, although I later discovered that if you gave him a lump of metal and a rubber band he'd probably get a tune out of it. I'd not been far out with my age-estimate either – it turned out he hit 14 in June 1989.

For Ian Skinner, the musical path that led to him wearing a Jethro Tull t-shirt whilst shopping in Circle K and being in a band aged 14 began with hating recorder class at school at the age of six. The horrors of the recorder were not enough to put him off music altogether though, and by the age of eight he had undertaken guitar lessons. The first music he was aware of that made any kind of impression was listening to The Corries (Scottish folk) on the way to Wales aged about nine, but then two albums given to him as presents were what really started it all off. The first one was a Chieftains album courtesy of his Nan, and the second was Jethro Tull's *Minstrel In The Gallery*, bought for him by a hippy friend of his parents who thought he'd like it.

The hippy friend must have hit the spot somewhere along the line because Tull on their *Rock Island* tour in 1989 was the first indoor gig Mr Skinner attended, fortunate to have a Mum cool enough to go with him (I didn't even bother asking mine if she fancied going to see Rick Wakeman with me when I was 14). Before that, Ian's first experience of live music had been Fairport Convention's Cropredy Festival in 1987 where not only did his Mum attend, but the whole family as well.

Shortly after the Tull gig, just to prove he was striking out on his own, Ian ventured off solo to see Fields of the Nephilim, and prior to that the first recorded work he purchased under his own steam had been *Brain Salad Surgery* by Emerson Lake & Palmer 'because I liked the artwork.' However, it's fair to say that Jethro Tull were the first band he was passionate about, although REM were up there too for a while.

With musical taste taking in an interesting sweep of Folksiness, Prog-Rock and Gothic darkness, who knows where all this might have led. It may have led to where it arrived at naturally, but then, just to make sure, as Ian says, at the age of 16 'some fat northern bastard did me a tape...'

At the completion of this interview, Ian suggested that I'd probably be better at filling in the gaps than him. Not wrong there, Mr Skinner, so excuse me while I take over...

At some point Ian's Mum had started working in my shop,

and when Ian hit 16 in 1991 she told me that he was now available for employment. Before I could say anything she said, 'And he *will* tie back his hair!' (Just for the record, can I say that I had no problems with a long-haired youth working in my store, but my bosses were somewhat less liberal.) And so it was that I eventually found him a Saturday job.

At first I found him very quiet and difficult to get to know, with just the odd chat about music filling in the silences. And of course it was music that eventually proved to be the catalyst...

I can't honestly say how long it was into Ian's employment at Spar (for it was no longer Circle K), Brackley, when the sound of Cardiacs first passed his ears, but I remember exactly the occasion. My radio/cassette player was pretty much a fixture in my office, mainly to listen to football commentaries on days when Sheffield United were playing and I was working, but also as a means of listening to some decent music when the going got tough, but only if I remembered to bring my tapes in. On this occasion I was listening to the cassette version of *The Seaside* by Cardiacs when Ian popped into the office to pick up his wage envelope. I can even remember what track was playing: "Nurses Whispering Verses".

'What's this?' asked Ian.

'Cardiacs,' replied I. He didn't say anything, but instead just gave me a big thumbs-up, with a look of enthusiasm that suggested to me that I'd hit upon a winner.

So I did him a tape. (I wasn't that fat back then.)

I don't actually remember what I put on it, and in fact knowing me I probably did more than one tape, but if it was in 1992 there'd have been some Wizards of Twiddly on it and probably some Porcupine Tree, both bands I was listening to heavily at the time, and there'd have been tons of Cardiacs on it, on any tape I did. In fact I probably did a tape of nothing but Cardiacs. Of course, all this led to many many conversations about the wonders of music, and over the course of the year from 1992 to 1993 our friendship grew and strengthened over such journeys as Brackley to the Tufnell Park Dome in London to see Wizards of Twiddly, accompanied by Ian's bandmate Tom Colvin.

Tom also got into Cardiacs and it was with him that Ian attended his first Cardiacs gig, at ULU in London sometime in 1992 (Ian thought it might have been 1991, but I know it was 1992, and I'm never wrong on these things don't you know). My vagueness over the date suggests that I wasn't there myself, and I'm not sure now why that was – perhaps it was a work thing, maybe even football, or even heaven forbid, a family occasion. Whatever, I wasn't there, but at the time Ian wouldn't have known me well enough to realise that I'd be supremely envious of someone attending not just a gig, but ANY event I wanted to go to, but he certainly knows now, and whilst never gloating (much) he always manages to mention with a knowing smile how good something that I've missed has been. (After consultation with Pete's exhaustive Cardiacs gig list I can confirm the date of Ian's first Cardiacs gig as being November 27th 1992).

The first gig we attended together was one of those wonderful mid-90s Organ Specials at the New Cross Venue, on May 2nd 1993, with Poisoned Electrick Head as support. There were four of us going: Ian, the afore-mentioned Thomas Colvin, myself, and my then-girlfriend-Annie's step-brother Darren. As we had all decided to hitch we split into two, with ever-faithful Annie, even though not wanting to go to the gig herself, prepared to drop us at different points along the M40. Not wanting to set anyone at an unfair disadvantage in my position of Senior Hitchhiker, I let Tom and Ian get out at the best spot, junction 10 by Cherwell Valley Services, whilst Darren and I went on to junction 9 nearer Oxford (why oh why didn't we just all get out at the services?). (Actually, were the services there then? Regardless, junction 10 was still the top spot…)

Suffice to say, Ian and Tom had a dream hitch, Darren and I an absolute nightmare. We crawled through the doors of the Venue just as Poisoned Electrick Head were taking the stage, much to the amusement of the Junior Hitchers who'd had time to put their feet up and see all the other bands on before.

That was the first of many times we crashed on the floor of

Organ Towers (Walthamstow version), the highlight for me being when Marina showed me her *Magpie* Annual from the 70s with a picture of Gryphon in it.

That was the weekend that confirmed it for Ian as he came away from the gig with a clutch of merchandise, including vinyl albums and t-shirts, as well as introductions to the *Organ* and Poisoned Electrick Head (my first exposure to the Leckie Heads had been at Stonehenge Pilgrims Festival in Cholderton Woods at Summer Solstice 1988, but that's a story for another chapter).

The journey back home the following morning was also his first introduction to that wonderful thing The Dodgy Hitchhike, but not before he'd performed one of The Great Moments in History at Brent Cross tube station. After disembarking from the train Ian decided it was a good idea to run as fast as possible down the station stairs, three or four at a time. He saved his party-piece until he reached the bottom where he sent himself sprawling, landing facedown spread-eagled, all big German army boots (yes, that's who I took my fashion tip from), long hair and big black overcoat, much to the very audible amusement of fellow passengers and even more audibly his travelling companions. Of course, I was never cruel enough to remind Ian of this display by saying, 'Great Moments in History re-enacted!' then throwing myself to the floor at the bottom of the stairs every time we visited Brent Cross station after that, oh no.

As for the hitch back, those were the good old days when there would always be a queue of hitchhikers at the bottom of the M1 at Staples Corner no matter what time of day or night you got there, and this day was no exception. Again we split into two pairings, but it made very little difference as there was a massive hitchhiking queue in front of us. Of course (and I think I told this tale in *Fever Hitch*) the police decided to intervene when they stopped their patrol car and invited every single one of us down to the bottom of the slip road in order to lecture us on this being a motorway not a public footpath and if they came past again 'we'll nick the lot of you'. Naturally, we all stayed put, and by the time the same police car was spotted coming back onto the roundabout I was in pole position at the front of the constantly-being-topped-up queue.

'Pigs!' was my urgent cry, and so there was an unseemly scramble as about a dozen hitchhikers legged it down the slip road, vaulted the railings and hid underneath the footbridge, watching with amusement as the police car sat at the traffic lights probably wondering how on earth we'd all managed to disappear.

Anyway, the dodgy bit of the hitch for Ian came when we all got picked up within minutes of each other. Darren and I got our own back for earlier disasters by getting a nice easy lift with an old (ish – he was probably my age) hippy and his girlfriend who told us about their time in the Himalayas, whereas Ian and Tom got a lift with a bloke who pulled off the motorway at one point and shot up (yes, THAT shooting up) whilst his passengers looked uneasily at each other in silence…

The funny thing was, just over a year later on May 29th 1994, at another Organ do at the New Cross Venue with Cardiacs headlining, an almost identical scenario took place in that Ian and Tom hitched down trouble-free, whilst I had another nightmare, this time with returning-hero-travelling-companion Richard back from those early days. This time Annie (by now my ex, but still greatly put upon by me) bailed us out with a lift in to Oxford where we got the Oxford Tube. Not so lucky this time, we scrambled in just as Poisoned Electrick Head were doing their last song, "Pendulum". The good thing was we were in plenty of time to see Miranda Sex Garden who were absolutely stunning in every way imaginable (for Ian it was Donna McKevitt, for me Hepzibah Sessa – I know you're a happily married man now Ian, but you'll be glad to know that when I met Katharine Blake – with all her clothes on for once – at Faery Fest in 2007 where she was performing with Mediaeval Baebes, I put in a word for you regarding Donna McKevitt).

The reason I mention all this is because Miranda Sex Garden had been the first band Ian introduced *me* to; it makes sense when you think about it, as Miranda Sex Garden are probably about the only band in the world to straddle Gothic-Prog-Indie-Bendy-Folksiness.

Since that first New Cross Venue Organ event in 1993, Ian's been at so many gigs with me, not just Cardiacs but scores of others, it'd probably be impossible to remember them all (especially as I'm a bit lax and only seem to write down Cardiacs gigs these days), but just so you know, Ian, I reckon you're approaching 50 Cardiacs gigs, which I know is less than you estimated, but then I've studied my list and there's an awful lot of silly ones that I found myself at alone (like the Crown & Cushion, Bolton), plus don't forget I was already up to 27 before you'd attended your first. And you missed a load on the last tour.

But anyway, Ian's presence at a Cardiacs gig is always a comforting one, especially as he has a tendency to nip off to the gents and return with a pint-glass full of water which he pours over himself to cool down before offering it to me, whereby I do the same (except on one occasion where I took it and started to drink the water; Ian looking on horrified for a second before snatching it back off me and pouring the remaining contents all over me – how dare I break with tradition?).

Since those early explorations of the Alphabet Business Concern in 1992/93 it's fair to say that whenever asked who his favourite band are, Ian will always tell them Cardiacs, although having got into them just after the William D. Drake years, this is probably why his "favourites" list doesn't always match those of the battle-hardened 80s Cardiacs warriors (i.e. all those who say *A Little Man And A House And The Whole World Window* is their favourite album, although it *was* Ian's first purchased). Depending on which day it is, his favourite Cardiacs album is *Heaven Born And Ever Bright* from 1992, but then just to prove me and my theory wrong, on other days he'll go for *The Seaside* (and just to blow my theory even more his favourite song is "Leader Of The Starry Skies" from 1989's *On Land And In The Sea*, although live faves are 1996's "Dog Like Sparky" and "Fiery Gun Hand", the latter I suspect because of the way first Jon Poole and now Kavus sing the word "BOX!" – I can't describe it, just watch Kavus' mouth next time). As for his favourite Cardiacs gig moment, this is a little more obscure, and almost exclusive (except I was there sniffing around too); 'It's the RJG incident at the Toadbender,' he says. Let me explain…

The incident in question happened at the Roadmender (Toadbender, see?) in Northampton, June 23rd 1996. Robert John Godfrey of the Enid, being a resident of Northampton at the time, was present, and afterwards was saying to the chap tasked with keeping unwanted people out of the dressing room (he looked far too nice to be called security), 'Tell Tim RJG's here, he'll want to see me!' Minutes later Tim was witnessed (and only by me and Ian, which is what makes it so good) being let out of a hastily-unbolted back door, and running, nay *sprinting* off into the night. So, erm, maybe he didn't want to see RJG after all.

'Tim looked like the cartoon running from the cover of "Running Away" by Spookey Ruben,' says Ian.

If he's got a favourite piece of Cardiacs memorabilia, Ian would be hard pressed to better his copy of the *Sunday Sport* featuring Cardiacs, Tim and Sarah Smith claiming to be brother and sister rather than husband and wife – all very incestuous and mystifying for any Cardiacs fans back in March 1987, including this here Belch spotting the story when doing a rare overtime shift at GT News Sandygate Road, not a proper fan as yet, but still with the recent memory of Reading Festival in 1986. That famous newspaper became something of a Holy Grail to Cardiacs fans, especially as nobody I ever spoke to seemed to have it.

At some point in 1993-ish I'd loaned Ian my copy of the *Seaside Treats* video, and he'd been watching it round at his parents' house. At some point during this garish display, Ian's dad Donald (who now prefers to be called Dawn) had walked in and immediately recognised something familiar about the bandsmen uniforms and slap-dash face-paint. 'Were they in the *Sunday Sport* once?" he asked. Upon Ian answering in the affirmative, Donald announced that he had that very copy of the *Sunday Sport*. Excitement was slightly tempered when he went on to say he had no idea where it actually was.

I remember Donald taking up the story with me, saying that

he'd only bought the newspaper (in the loosest sense of the word) because he liked the front-page headline of "84 INCHES – SHE'S A NUN!", a heart-warming story about Tina Small, a lady with a supposedly quite spectacularly-sized chest, donning a super-sized habit and disappearing into a nunnery (all true – it must have been, it was in the *Sport*). As well as Tina, the centre-spread of Tim and Sarah making out that they were having an incestuous relationship must have made an impression, hence Donald's memory jogger six or so years later.

'It's probably in my garage somewhere, under a pile of other stuff,' Donald went on to tell me, 'so there's no point in me looking for it, but one day I'll come across it when looking for something else.'

And so it was about a year later, Ian gave me the triumphant news that a search for some modelling paint or some such had unearthed the legendary *Sunday Sport* itself. I was green with envy, whilst being highly delighted that at last a copy had come to light. Ian was determined not to let me get my hands on it (oh, he knows what I'm like), but one day in 1999 when we were both resident on Barking Road in Canning Town, east London, he allowed me to take it across the road to get it colour-photo-copied, and jolly splendid and authentic it looked too. I ended up scanning it and putting it up on the Internet as part of my University of Greenwich mature-student website, and much gratitude and praise was sent my way, all of which was passed on to Ian (possibly).

Like I said, it wasn't just Cardiacs gigs that saw the two of us in attendance. The mid-90s was a very fertile period for unusual and adventurous bands, some of them including members or ex-members of Cardiacs, some of them influenced by Cardiacs, some of them who'd perhaps never heard of Cardiacs, but nearly all of them seemingly having crossed the radar of the *Organ*, which subsequently meant they crossed the radar of me and Ian. There seemed to be a gig every week somewhere down in London between 1993 and 1998, some of them *Organ* nights, some of them not, but all of them worthy of attention, and many of them resulting in Ian and I travelling wn from either Brackley or Banbury in order to attend, usually by the old fashioned method of hitchhiking, sometimes on the Oxford Tube, sometimes on the train, and every now and again by persuading someone to give us a lift.

Ian's job at Record Savings in Banbury meant that he got friendly with tons of reps and thus discovered a whole host of adventurous Indie bands (at the time when all major record labels were forming Indie off-shoots in order to help bands keep their independent ideals, or something like that) (and not to fool the Indie kids, of course) and thus got us on the guest list for gigs such as Elkca, Pooka, and Ragga and the Jack Magic Orchestra.

Meanwhile, if there wasn't a Monsoons or Katherine In A Cupboard gig, there would be the People's Friend playing somewhere, or Huge Baby to be discovered (and to scare the living daylights out of us), with always the odd Porcupine Tree at the Astoria keeping us sane. No wonder we both ended up moving to London…

But that's getting a little ahead of the game. Between 1993 and 1994 I landed the job of managing Ian and Tom's band Strangeland, a band who blended Gothicness and Folkishness with a smudge of *Discipline*-era King Crimson (it was Ian and Tom's guitars intermingling you see) perfectly. Of course, the obligatory singer-falls-out-with-bassist thing led to the band's demise, but not before we'd done such blistering gigs as the Oxford Dolly (those posters we put up remained in place for years, so high were they; I had to climb on the bins) and the Blue Boar, Chipping Norton (no kidding, that really was a blinding night). I was rather proud of the fact that as well as converting Ian and Tom, I managed to get drummer Jonah and bassist Jeremy interested in Cardiacs, leading to one gig at the Dolly where one of the punters thought Strangeland were called Cardiacs, so many Alphabet Business Concern t-shirts were there being worn onstage.

The best thing to come out of Strangeland though was Ian's purchase of a smoke machine, nicknamed Walter. Walter's best moment for Strangeland was at the Red Lion in Kidlington when Jonah disappeared from view behind the mist, set up as he was in the bay window, it probably being a good thing anyway as he was having a legendary hissy due to the landlord telling us it was too loud so could we turn down (sticks across the chest, 'I take my cues from Tom and if I can't hear him then I'm not going to play!').

But really Walter's greatest moments of all were saved for grander occasions, like the time when Ian and I were renting that house on Church Road in Brackley and we decided it'd be a good idea to charge Walter up then take him down to the churchyard at midnight to squirt smoke all around the gravestones. The effect was stunning, as was the plume of smoke we pumped from out behind a tree just as a car was going past (and heck, did we run when the car screeched to a halt and the bloke got out to investigate).

Walter's finest moment of all though has a Cardiacs connection in that it was at a Monsoon Bassoon gig I put on myself at Brackley Cricket Club in 1997. I billed it as Belch's Birthday Binge (it was only a few days after my 31st), but really I just wanted to put on a decent gig in Brackley, and in order to ensure as many people benefited as possible, I invited everyone for free.

As well as having the Monsoon Bassoon as headline, I'd got Katherine In A Cupboard to play, along with Captain John's band Magnilda (also featuring Richard Larcombe, later of Stars In Battledress, and a certain Iain Lee on bass – now whatever happened to him?). Tim earned a decent crust by doing the sound for all three bands, which must have been why all three bands sounded magnificent, but the Monsoons were a cut above anybody else at the time, and so it proved that night. Their finale was the bone-crushing heaviness of "The Iceman's Back Garden", complete with feedback and all-round cacophony. As those final chords built up to their ear-splitting crescendo, Dan Chudley hit the foot-control button of the kindly-provided-by-Ian Walter, and kept his foot there for a good half a minute, maybe longer. I knew from experience that a five second squirt from Walter was enough to make a drummer disappear, so as I saw Dan's antics I had a feeling things might just get interesting

As the chords rang out and then fed back, first the band disappeared in the mist, then the front few rows, then the mixing desk, then the back of the room, and finally the bar. Meanwhile the feedback screeched and screeched and screeched and the crowd, although they couldn't see a thing, cheered wildly, and continued to do so as the cacophony started to fade a little and the stage began to clear of mist. The stage was bereft of musicians, with only their instruments propped up against their amps, still feeding back, and still the audience bayed for more. But just where were the band? As the smoke cleared from the front the mystery was solved – they were in the throng at the front cheering and clapping with the rest. Brilliant, and one of those gig moments for which you just had to be there. Even grizzled old gig veterans like Andy Thompson said it was one of the most amazing things he'd ever witnessed. And it was all because of Walter. I would say that only the birth of his son Rufus has made Ian more proud…

Over the years Ian and I shared houses at four different addresses; firstly Church Road, then Bannerman Drive in Brackley (where I was the home-owner and Ian paid his rent in CDs bought with staff discount at Record Savings), Barking Road in lovely old Canning Town, East London, and finally Portway, Stratford, also in East London. The memories and adventures are so many that it'd take a whole book to get them all down, but leaving the pub early on a Friday night in order to get home in time for *Beavis and Butthead* on Channel 4 springs to mind, as does many years being chased by the Wiltshire Constabulary at Summer Solstice. Add to that the fact that for a while Ian played bass in another band I managed, the Jesus Underground Band, and that apart from when I broke my rib on the checkouts at Tesco, I helped him every single time he went and moved house (actually, I somehow got out of the last move too) perhaps hints as to how much of our lives we've spent getting in each other's way, and that's without all the Cardiacs gigs and other musical mayhem. Why, we even managed to split up with girlfriends on the same day one time when we were living at different addresses – we cheered each other up by sitting round at Ian's flat in Banbury looking miserable then ordering a massive pizza each.

I'm not even sure that we're *that* similar (although we both stayed up all night to cheer the Labour Government home after the 1997 elections). He's a strict vegetarian whereas I will always make sure that something contains meat before eating it, and he can be way more sensible and level-headed than me. For example, when we were living at Church Road there was a Monsoon Bassoon gig to be attended at the Red Eye in Islington. I was going from home and Ian was going straight from work, but we both planned to hitch. Despite major disasters in the past when I've turned up to a gig only to find it cancelled (The Sea Nymphs in Norwich and Poisoned Electrick Head in Reading spring to mind), I never bothered to do that thing where you check with the venue before travelling long distances. Ian did on this occasion (back in the days when we both thought we were too cool to own a mobile phone).

I arrived at the Red Eye only to find a note stuck to the door saying, "Tonight's gig is cancelled!" so I turned round and went and hitched all the way back to Brackley. By the time I arrived home it was very late indeed, Ian having long since gone to bed, but stuck on the phone attached to the wall was a piece of paper that bore a simple message: "HA!"

Now married to Veronika (from the Czech Republic – yep, I had a slight hand in bringing those two together) with coming-up-for-two-years-old Rufus (at the time of writing – he'll be married with kids of his own by the time this gets published) and living in Kettering (well, he's in Long Eaton, Notts, now!), of course Ian and I don't get to anything like as many gigs together as we used to, but every now and then he'll get down to London and we'll do the right thing, whether it be the Wizards of Twiddly supported by Zag and the Coloured Beads at the Bull & Gate, or Man Man at Cargo in Shoreditch, and of course, it is always brilliant.

Analysing what Ian says he's listening to now (apart from all the old stuff of course), he says, 'Eastern European accordion music, speed brass band music, Alamaailman Vasarat, Bratko Bibic, and Bob Drake.' Ah yes, that'll be Bob Drake from Thinking Plague. Now, wasn't it me that started the whole Thinking Plague thing off by buying one of their albums in Pied Piper Records, Northampton, just because I liked the sleeve and then noticed Fred Frith guested on guitar? Yes, I think you'll find it was.

Maybe I have some influence on Ian Skinner still…

Chapter Seven
"Big Ship"
The Thekla, Bristol,
November 14th 2007

"Big Ship"
The Thekla, Bristol, November 14th 2007

So, the idea was for me to hitchhike to all these gigs on the tour, right? Thus far I'd made it to two gigs and not thumbed it to either, but this time I had no choice. I had spent the night on Ian's sofa in Kettering and the next gig was in Bristol – not exactly a straightforward journey. Ian wasn't planning on going to Bristol so I couldn't use a lift with him as back-up, and turning up at Kettering Station and asking for a single to Bristol just sounded ridiculously expensive. So a hitch cross-country then down-country it had to be, but at least I had all day to do it, and thanks to Ian and his early start at HMV in Northampton it really *was* all day.

The problem was, I like to take my time getting ready in the morning (just speak to anybody who's shared a flat with me) but also like to leave my getting-up time as late as possible – hardly an ideal combination. Added to a late night the night before, and factoring in Ian's desire to get a move on as he was going to drop me off somewhere decent to hitch before going to work, well, it all forced a bit of a rush, and most uncomfortable it felt too. In the end he was sat outside in the car with the engine running so I had to scoop everything up and stuff it in my rucksack whilst scrambling into the front seat, still getting dressed. As he slung me out on an A14 roundabout I was *still* getting dressed and there were still bits and bobs not shoved in my rucksack, so I took ten minutes at the side of the road to sort myself out, put on my bright yellow Sheffield United away shirt (the most recent model, not the old falling-to-bits one made famous by Richard Littlejohn on *6-0-6* and *Fever Hitch*) and tidy up a bit. There, I was ready to hitch and it was still only just 7.30am.

Well, it was a bit of a nightmare actually. One thing, I was still at my starting point two hours after being dropped off by Ian. Then after turning down countless lifts that would have taken me less than a mile but possibly to a better spot, I finally gave in to my instincts and took that lift that I could have walked in fifteen minutes (it turned out), and as if to rub it in, the next lift came along within three minutes and took me to Corley Services on the M6, a most decent place to stop for breakfast, a breakfast I could have had two hours earlier if only I'd not been so dense. That lift was made even more special by being in an Argos truck, the driver looking remarkably like my flatmate Dave, the only difference being a Manchester accent on the driver as opposed to a Hounslow accent on the bloke who has to wait an hour for me to emerge from the shower in the morning.

A very clearly defined sign ("M42 SOUTH") was necessary for the next stage of the journey in order to negotiate the rather sharp left turn from the M6 onto the 42, so I went off and bought a set of marker pens from WHSmith before carrying on. Hopwood Park Services was my next stop, a shame that it wasn't too far because the chap giving me a lift was into his Pink Floyd and remembered the good old days of *Tiswas* on a Saturday morning (the day I switched over from *Multi-Coloured Swap Shop* to *Tiswas* was a defining moment in my life, those late-70s/early-80s Saturdays of watching the anarchy and mayhem from ATVLand in the morning followed by watching Sheffield United lose in the afternoon surely helping to shape the person I am today).

Another well defined sign was also required ("M5 SOUTH") to negotiate yet another sharp left, and this time a gentleman called Simon was happy to oblige. Most impressive was the fact that he'd once had a knife pulled on him by a hitchhiker, and yet this hadn't put him off. 'You're safe with me – all I can pull on you is a set of marker pens,' I reassured.

The thing was, I broke one of my unwritten rules in accepting a lift from him because he couldn't get me to a service station, instead just to the Worcester North turn-off – never break your own rules Belch, as yet another two hour wait testified.

Now this really was a dull stretch. The only thing to brighten it up was a retro fire engine, but as it didn't pick me up I suppose it wasn't really that exciting. Eventually a Turkish guy came to my rescue by taking me to Strensham Services, just as I was beginning to worry I'd not make the gig as the afternoon was disappearing fast. The final piece in the jigsaw was a truck driver to Gordano Services on the M5 which looked pretty near Bristol to me. The trucker was fairly certain there was a bus from nearby into Bristol, and as it was now gone 5pm and dark, I was prepared to take that option rather than mess about on some silly 'A' road with my thumb out.

So, off for a wander I went, ignoring the nearby lay-by because surely that wasn't a bus-stop. As I wandered back I saw that it most definitely *was* a bus-stop judging by the bus that was stopped there, a bus destined for Bristol if its display was to be believed. My heroic sprint failed to impress the driver, even though he saw me all right. How could he NOT see me as he pulled away from the arm-waving maniac jumping out into the road trying to flag him down? But off he drove regardless. I hope that made his day, and I hope he looked in his mirror and spotted my less manic, more pronounced gesture. What if this was some West Country backwater where his bus was the last bus into Bristol?

Well, it wasn't, but I had to wait half an hour in the cold to be sure, all the while calming myself down with a blast of Chris Squire's majestic *Fish Out Of Water* on the iPod Nano. So, eventually my bus came, and a nice relaxing lift into Bristol was the order of the day, arriving in the city centre at 6.30pm. It is perhaps sobering to note that Max Crowe flew in from the States for the Bristol gig and it took him seven hours. I hitched it from Kettering in eleven…

* * * *

I may not have been to as many gigs in Bristol as I have Oxford, but its reputation is almost as good, in that I've not done a duff one in that city yet, and that doesn't just include Cardiacs gigs, not quite…

There is one other band I've been to see in Bristol – Inner City Unit at the Granary Club on August 27th 1985, worthy of a mention in here due to it being my first really big solo "away" gig hitch-hiking adventure, and also because it was the genesis of my getting-on-the-guest-list technique, as used many times in future years for Cardiacs gigs.

Back in 1985 my major obsession was still Hawkwind, despite having Yes, Gong, Genesis, King Crimson and even Marillion all above them on My Favourite Bands List. There was something about the Hawks you see. At that stage in my life I was relatively near the beginning of my love affair with Stonehenge, and of course Hawkwind were THE Stonehenge House Band, them being a major contributor to that life-defining event that was the Free Festival of 1984.

And as anyone who can remember me from those days will tell you, my favourite member of Hawkwind was Nik Turner, he of the sax, flute, vocals, orange hair-spike, outlandish costumes and bizarre face-paint. The problem was, earlier in the year Hawkwind had sacked him (again), but not to worry, because he had his other band, Inner City Unit, to entertain us all. Inner City Unit were always described in the music press as "Nik Turner's punk project", and their very existence gave me an excuse to appreciate something from that genre with none of the guilt that any Prog-Rock fan should feel for expressing admiration towards a style of music that had apparently killed off the likes of Yes *et al.* I'd already seen Inner City Unit earlier in the year at Sheffield University and had a couple of their albums, so I knew what to expect.

For some reason I felt the need for an adventure and now bitten by the hitchhiking bug, this trip to Bristol seemed ideal, especially with Haze, those Sheffield Prog-Rock heroes, playing their first Marquee headliner the night before in London. Indeed, I'd be able to take in both, even though Bristol wasn't exactly close to London; I had plenty of time, a brother's house in Ealing to crash at overnight, and a lust for doing something a bit different, so why not, eh?

Haze at the Marquee, supported by Twice Bitten, were splendid of course, but it was the unfamiliar nature of Inner City Unit at the Granary Club, Bristol, which had me filled with a thrill of anticipation, a feeling I would experience many more times in the future.

As often happens when hitching I arrived well in advance of doors-opening, so after finding the venue and seeing that the band hadn't arrived, I went for a wander around town, before returning to the venue to find that the band *had* now arrived. I was then invited in by a very friendly ICU guitarist Steve Pond and roadie John

Hughes.

There's something special about watching a band setting up their gear and sound-checking. Well okay, *I* find it special; it all adds to the overall gig experience for me, even the seemingly-endless sound-checking of the drum kit. What's even more special is getting to meet one of your heroes, and in line with what many Hawkwind fans have said about him over the years, Nik Turner was indeed charming and friendly, happy to chat about his recent impromptu appearance with Hawkwind at Summer Solstice on Westbury White Horse Hill, and prepared to have a little chuckle when I told him my name was Belch.

I must have made an impression on him because with all sound-checking duties complete, Nik came over and asked me if I was interested in a deal. 'We're off into town for a curry now, so if you look after our gear onstage, we'll let you stay in for free.' I was more than happy to take him up on this offer, so he gave me a bit of paper that passed for a ticket and departed with the band, one last instruction ringing in my ears: 'Don't let *anybody* get onstage!' Righto Nik… (I later learned that this little trip to a local curry-house was a celebration in aid of Nik's birthday.)

This was going to be soooo easy, I thought. After all, why on earth would anybody want to get onstage anyway? So, for a while I was just leaning up against the PA speakers looking bored, although the chat I had with the venue's DJ should perhaps have warned me things were going to liven up later when he told me tonight was Heavy Metal Disco Night…

The punters started to trickle in, and at first all was calm and quiet, but then as they drank more alcohol and the music got louder, the dance-floor started to liven up a bit. What's more, so did the front of the stage where I was still leaning looking bored. You see, even though there was no band up on that stage, for some Metal Kids the temptation to headbang in front of a stage is too much. Perhaps it was the presence of the monitors at the front, tantalising them with a chance to strike up the one-foot-on-the-monitor pose. Whatever, the fact that the stage area was raised up by all of about six inches meant

I was now having to work overtime to keep people away from Inner City Unit's gear, bearing in mind that back then I was half the width I am now, with a nice mop of friendly-looking curly hair (you'd be surprised how many times people mistake me for security these days, especially when I'm wearing my "Cardiacs World Tour 1995" jacket; in fact it happened the other week outside Gong at the Kentish Town Forum – I was only waiting for Andy Hossain to turn up).

One, shall we say, slightly overweight youth was my toughest opponent. Nothing was going to stop him from achieving his goal of getting up onstage and headbanging whilst facing his adoring audience. Trouble is, he was completely out of it, probably on numerous different substances, and my efforts to prevent him getting onstage led to him falling onto everything; sometimes onto the PA, sometimes onto the monitors, sometimes onto the stage, sometimes onto the floor, but most often onto me. Every time I pulled him off the stage he landed on me, and as he was a touch overweight, this was a most painful experience. His mates would heave him up off of me every time, always with an apology, followed by a plea for me to 'go easy on him – he's had a bit too much to drink.'

'I know,' I'd say, 'but I've been told to keep everyone off the stage...' Belch the Bouncer!

It was worth it of course, because it was a most wonderful gig that night. Having not witnessed Cardiacs up to that point, this was by far the wildest gig I'd ever experienced, and thanks to my deal with Nik, it was all for free. From then on, whenever I saw either Inner City Unit or a year or two later Nik Turner's Fantastic All-stars, I'd turn up as early as possible, help load in the gear, get on the guest list, then help reload the gear after the gig, a deal I regularly struck with Cardiacs in later years (at the Crown & Cushion in Bolton in 1996 as Kavus and I struggled down the stairs with umpteen flight-cases, Kavus said, 'You don't need to do this you know,' to which I replied, 'Well, you got me on the guest list, so I help with the gear,' leading Kavus to say, 'That's because you're a very fair person.').
On a few occasions my deals with Nik Turner went even further, including a lift for me back to the station after an Inner City Unit gig

at Manchester International, an announcement from the stage to get me somewhere to kip for the night at the Hammersmith Clarendon Hotel Ballroom at a Fantastic Allstars gig, and perhaps my personal favourite, a lift in their van (driven by Nik himself) to the M1 and somewhere decent to hitch after the Allstars played at the Retford Porterhouse, giving me the chance to chat to bass-player Glenda about Roy Harper (we both championed *Stormcock* as our favourite Harper album) in the back.

Hitchhiking to far-flung gigs, watching sound-checks, humping gear, getting on the guest-list, scavenging lifts – all very familiar in later years, and regular occurrences in my Cardiacs gig-history, but it all started with that Inner City Unit gig in Bristol 1985...

* * * *

If there's a cooler venue than the Thekla Social in Bristol, scene of my 93rd Cardiacs gig, then I want to know where it is. A club on a boat, a boat once owned by Viv Stanshall, and a boat with a fine restaurant on it – that takes some beating in my eyes, and well worth the eleven-hour nightmare hitch to get there.

Big Ship Iron was already there, and he took great delight in watching my struggles with a far-too-small-for-the-task rucksack (look, it was bought in a hurry – the big one was in bits). Whilst waiting for 'Spoon 5' to bring me my dinner delights, Max Crowe also took great delight, this time in telling me about his seven-hour trip from the States compared to my marathon. The Dogstands had also arrived early and were given the opportunity to see for themselves what a brilliant chap Mr Big Ship Iron was, and what do you know, by the end of the night they were best buddies, with Clive (Big Ship Iron remember) promising to sort them out with somewhere to sleep after the last gig of the tour in Leeds.

The bouncers at the entrance to the gig bit of the boat were eyeing up my rucksack in a less than friendly way despite my guest-list status. Maybe they thought the extra weight would sink the thing. Anyway, just as things were in danger of reaching an impasse, the interjection of one Tim Jackson, hitherto only met on the Cardiacs Chat List, and known to all as a close friend of the also-present-that-night

Lol, proved to be my saving grace as he offered the services of his car boot. 'I'm going to put my junk, In his trunk,' I told everyone poetically.

More celebrities arrived in the form of Lawrence all the way from Guernsey, a most interesting character, always ready to shake his fist at the photocopier at work, and quite possibly the only person present to find it interesting that my evening meal was identified by 'Spoon 5'. When we'd first met Lawrence at the Authority/Zag And The Coloured Beads gig earlier in the year he'd been most quiet and reserved. Not so this time, as he entertained and amused all that came within a mile or so of him.

A couple I was most grateful to see were the Helocolins, Karen and Paul, as I was kipping on their sofa back in Northamptonshire that night. It would appear they'd had a spot of SatNav trouble themselves and had ended up dumping the car somewhere in town and walking the rest of the way. Meanwhile, everyone was having fun with my new digital camera, especially Pete "Thrupty" and the Dogstands, and Clare, Pete's other half, took a couple of smashing photos of the gig from up above, including one of Lawrence facing the opposite way to everybody else.

And so, what of the gig itself? Of course, being on a boat they had to start with "Big Ship", and after the strangeness of starting with it in Brighton, it seemed more natural here – it must've been the undulations. Inspection of setlists ("setlist D", "setlist B" etc) suggested that over the course of the tour we'd be getting at least four different sets, and this one proved to be a right cracker. After Tim's reluctance to share his water at Brighton, this time he dished it out like it was Holy Communion, a good thing because after "As Cold As Can Be In An English Sea", a song that sends me over the edge every time with manic grooving, I needed rehydrating.

"Core" from *Heaven Born and Ever Bright* was played, quite possibly for the first time ever, and Jon Poole was humiliated from the stage by Tim, most definitely *not* for the first time ever.

All in all, it was a quite stunning and energetic gig, and by the end of the tour many of us would be looking back on it and saying it was the best of the lot (arguably). For me, it certainly was the best so far, eclipsing even the joys of Oxford the previous night. Not even being mistaken for Jim for the first of about four times over the fortnight could dampen my enthusiasm. Mind you, I was certainly cooled down as I ventured outside into the cold November night still wearing my shorts and sleeveless t-shirt in order to rescue my junk from Tim Jackson's trunk, an action I was to regret roughly nine hours later. At the time I wasn't worried though, I was just hyper as I bounced all the way off the boat, around the car-park, and all the way back onto the boat again.

Eventually Paul, Karen and myself bid everyone farewell and set off for their car, using the SatNav on its "pedestrian setting". The poor thing got confused though, and we were literally going round in circles, like a dog chasing its tail (Paul was the head, I was the tail). In the end we had to jump in a minicab, with the result being that the cab-driver took us a very short distance (once he'd stopped laughing), the fare so small that Paul paid him extra out of embarrassment. Well, at least we were back at the car, and a swift journey back to Northants was undertaken ("This car does feel exceedingly stable at 120mph!")…

Once back at the Helocolins abode I was fed veggie burgers (Ian would be so proud) with Reggae Reggae Sauce, and laid to rest on the sofa. I must say, as it was by now something like 2 o'clock in the morning, I was somewhat knackered. What's more, I was beginning to realise that my post-Bristol gig walk to Tim Jackson's car with too much naked flesh showing and whilst still all sweaty from the gig had been detrimental to my health. Maybe I'd feel better in the morning, ready for another hitch. However, as I drifted into sleep another get-out clause was being offered. The Helocolins were driving up to the next gig in Nottingham, stopping only to pick up Ian along the way. 'You're welcome to come with us if you want,' they said.

'Oooh, that really would be cheating,' I mumbled, 'but, erm, you never know. I'll see how I feel in the morning…' I think my mind was already made up.

Chapter Eight
"The Obvious Identity"
My Tattoo and the Helocolins

"The Obvious Identity"
My Tattoo and the Helocolins

For a while my tattoo was the talk of more than one Cardiacs Internet Forum. I'd had it done in 1998, a rather nice 'Little Man and a House' logo, and up until a Cardiacs gig at the Soundhaus in Northampton on November 9th 2005, I thought it set me apart as a rather uniquely disturbed case. But then, as a sparsely populated Pond tried their best to whip up a storm, I noticed the big bloke at the front with his missus had the exact same tattoo, the only difference being that his was on a muscle-bound, tanned arm as opposed to my rather unfit looking pasty-white affair. We gave each other a knowing nod, put our upper-arms together for a second or two of comparison, had a bit of a laugh, and then got back to being in the Pond. The feeling I think was relief, relief that there was another nutter as bad as me, but worryingly I couldn't be too sure.

So of course, there is an interesting story as to how my tattoo came about, and you may not be surprised to know that it came about because of a woman…

* * * *

So Mum, if you're reading this, erm, sorry about the tattoo thing and that I never quite got round to telling you about it. But you see, it's not my fault. No, it's all Sarah's fault, that ex-girlfriend of mine who you thought was so nice. Well, it was her that went and got me to have my ear pierced too. But really Mum, she's lovely – she just has a power over me that I can do nothing about…

Oh yes, Sarah. There will be much more about her later, but suffice to say that when we were in one of our many "best of buddies" phases in 1997, long after we split up, I would tell her anything and everything (still do, actually). One of the things I told her was that I'd always secretly fancied having my ear pierced. Now, Sarah really was the right person to tell this to because she had something like 15 or so piercings at the time, and they were expanding. Most of them were in her ears, but she had her nose pierced, and I think at that point she'd had her tongue done too (or was she one of many victims of Günter from the Jesus Underground Band? I suppose I could ask her) (there you go, one quick text later, and Sarah informs me that Günter was indeed the culprit, back in 1998 at the Jesus Underground Band communal madhouse in Canning Town; "I was 19 – he did it in the bathroom and it bled a lot…" she texts).

So of course, when I mentioned I'd always wanted my ear piercing, Sarah suggested we should go to a place in Milton Keynes where we could take advantage of a Tesco-style buy-one-get-one-free offer, as I only wanted my left ear pierced and she wanted to have a second nose-piercing. And because I'm so weak and feeble when a girl of indescribable beauty suggests I do something, I had to agree.

So one morning we met up in Milton Keynes, and I don't mind admitting I was incredibly nervous, so much so that as we walked towards the piercing place, Sarah kept saying, 'We don't have to go if you don't want to.'

'No, no, I agreed to do it, so we *will* go,' I said, trying to sound firm.

When we got there, Sarah said, 'I'll go first if you want,' but again, in a desperate attempt to re-affirm my manliness I insisted that I go first and 'get it over with.'

Mind you, the employees almost had to strap me into the chair, and I'm sure one of them was holding me down.

But then along came one of them with a big staple gun, kt-chhkkk, and it was done.

'Is that it?' I asked, surprised that I'd felt nothing.

'That's it,' they told me, so I got up from the chair wondering why on earth I'd made such a fuss.

So anyway, one year on and I'm telling Sarah, who'd just had a couple of tattoos done herself, that I'd always fancied having a Cardiacs tattoo, and there's Sarah telling me that the place where she'd gone in Milton Keynes (different to the piercing place) was really good, and she wanted to go back to get her belly-button pierced. 'We could go together,' she suggested all innocently. Once again, I meekly agreed…

Compared to my nervousness of the year before, because the

ear-piercing had been such a doddle, I was supremely relaxed about this tattoo here in 1998. Why, Sarah and I even settled down for a spot of breakfast in Burger King before strolling along to Bodyshock in Milton Keynes. I was keenly clutching an Alphabet Business Concern advertising pamphlet complete with a 'Little Man and a House' logo of what I thought would be just the right size to go on my upper-right-arm/shoulder.

The woman who was to perform the operation looked at it and immediately assessed, 'We can do that, no problem.' She quoted me £40 and I said that was fine.

She then warned me that because the lines on the logo were so thin it would all have to be done using outline, and because this went deeper, it'd be more painful. 'Go ahead,' I said.

Then one of the blokes also working there, who looked a bit like he should have been in the Ozric Tentacles, and sporting quite a few tattoos of his own, warned me that where I wanted it just off the shoulder, it would hurt. Ah, all these warnings; just get on with it…

So the tattoo artist did the bit with the dye and miraculously a perfect 'Little Man and a House' logo appeared off the shoulder in purple. Then she started to ink in the outline, and oooh heck, it hurt. Blimey, it HURT. And of course, I came to my senses and realised what she was doing – basically sticking needles in me at about a million miles an hour. I hate needles. Whenever I have an injection, trust me, it is the greatest act of bravery. Many is the time I've left a hospital or doctor's surgery and honked-up as soon as… Mind you, I never quite passed out (no, the only time I did that was when we dissected rats at school), but it must have been close a few times.

But here she was injecting me again and again (or so it felt). A short while in the fascination with what she was doing stopped and I started looking at the walls, and then I felt a light-headedness creeping up on me. My tattooist detected something was ailing me and asked, 'Is everything all right?'

'Erm, could I have a glass of water please?' I forced out.

'Right,' she said, 'I'm going to stop now for 15 minutes just while you relax a bit.'

I was sitting there feeling a bit other-worldly when the Ozric Tentacle bloke came in with a metal bowl and plonked it down in my lap. Why's he done that, I wondered, does he think I'm going to throw up? And of course, I immediately chucked, my aim good and true as my Burger King breakfast landed in the bowl with not a drop spilt.

'I knew that was coming,' said Tattoo Woman, evidenced by the fact that she'd stepped well back, 'as soon as you asked for the glass of water.'

'Don't worry,' said Ozric Tentacle Bloke, 'you're not the first and you won't be the last.' Sarah later said she'd never seen anyone looking as white as I did at that moment.

In the end it was more like half-an-hour before tattooing was recommenced. Ozric Tentacle Bloke said, 'It will still hurt, but you won't throw up again. That's now out of your system.' He also reassured me that my reaction was a good thing. 'It proves that in a life or death situation, your body's natural survival instincts will kick in,' he claimed. And so Tattoo Woman continued, as we all agreed half a logo would look pretty stupid, so there was no going back now.

Ozric Tentacle Bloke was indeed correct, it *did* still hurt, but I'd finished throwing up for the day. Tattoo Woman obviously now felt I was suitably relaxed to talk about the design going on my arm. 'It's one of the logos of my favourite band,' I told her.

'And what are they called?' she asked.

'Cardiacs,' I replied.

She stopped for a second then said, 'I thought I recognised it. I'm from Kingston and I used to see them playing squat parties and the like around the area back in the late-70s and early-80s, when they were known as Cardiac Arrest.' There was enough information in that second sentence for me to know that she really had been there at the time, and I have to say, a feeling of envy crept up inside me. But then what would a thirteen-year-old Belch have made of Cardiac Arrest in 1979? Not much probably – far too wrapped up in Yes and barely scratching the surface of Gong at the time…

When Tattoo Woman finally pulled back and said, 'Right,

that's it. You're done!' I felt a mighty surge of relief, but at the same time I was gloriously happy with the result and could not stop looking at it. I looked round to get Sarah's approval but she was laid out getting her belly-button done, so I just beamed with pleasure whilst Ozric Tentacle Bloke presented me with a badge which he said they gave to all people who reacted like I had done. And the legend on the badge? "I WAS A WUSS AT BODYSHOCK", a badge I still have to this day.

My first gigs with the new tattoo were the Garage in Islington, December 4th 1998, and a trio of gigs at the Camden Falcon January 29th, 30th, 31st 1999. For once I'm a little bit fuzzy on the following story in that I'm not really sure what venue it was, but Pete insists it was the Falcon, so that narrows it down to three possibles anyway. However, Pete was certain the t-shirt involved was a new one, whereas I know that it was an old one, a "Cardiacs Respectfully Remind You, All That Glitters Is a Mare's Nest" one to be precise, although Pete still doesn't think I'm right. Well Pete, all I can say is that there is no other Cardiacs t-shirt in my collection with the sleeves removed, so it IS that one. Let me explain…

As you'd expect, I was very proud of my new body art, but also dismayed that I wasn't brave enough to have it somewhere where it wouldn't be covered up by my short-sleeved t-shirts. I'd just bought a new t-shirt and was grumbling about how if I had an old t-shirt I could tear the sleeves off and show off my tattoo. Pete offered to remove the sleeves but I was having none of it, it being new and all that. But then I'm pretty sure I remembered that underneath I had on my old "…Mare's Nest" t-shirt, and really I wasn't that bothered if I lost the sleeves to this, so the new t-shirt came off and went in my new Cardiacs bag, me saying to Pete, 'Right, remove the sleeves from this…'

I had no idea how he was going to do it, so was marginally disturbed when he took out a cigarette lighter and set fire to the sleeve. No matter; it worked because after just a bit of flaming Pete was able to tear it right off. Quite impressive…

But the next sleeve moved things up a notch. It was the right sleeve I believe, the difference being that as this one flamed, Pete left it for a second or two longer whilst he produced from his pocket a cigarette which he then lit, from my flaming shoulder. I may not be a smoker, but *this* was cool...

As a result of this amputation, I've probably worn that t-shirt to more Cardiacs gigs than any other since, just to show off my rather special tattoo. Since then two other tattoos have come to light, one belonging to Pet Lamb, the Moderator and Administrator on the Cardiacs Mare's Nest Internet Forum (which I don't contribute to, for no other reason than I just don't have time, so it's nothing personal Pet Lamb and Pars Fu Man Chu, but I think I've told you that before), and the afore-mentioned tattoo belonging to Paul Helocolin. And of course, just like my tattoo, with Paul's there's a story involved, a story which in effect starts right at the beginning of Paul's musical journey, a journey made all the more fascinating by the fact that Paul, along with Karen, is part of a loving Cardiacs couple, made even more special by Paul being the first (we think) person to propose to his beloved at a Cardiacs gig, during "Ideal" no less. Romance is most definitely not dead...

* * * *

Where to start with the Helocolins, Paul and Karen? For not only are they a Cardiacs Couple, they have been to so many of the same gigs as me (especially Paul in his pre-Karen days) that it's incredible that we never really met properly until that Northampton Soundhaus gig in 2005 (although I'm sure we must have chatted at some point; it's just that people might not remember the Belch of old because they don't always associate the slim curly-headed chap pre-1998 with the slightly-more-bulky shaven-headed version of recent years). Perhaps the most likely gig when we may well have run into each other was Wolverhampton Civic Centre June 18th 1996, because there was hardly anybody else present due to England playing Holland in Euro '96 the same night. What's more, for some bizarre reason the venue left the house lights on for the whole gig meaning we got plenty of chance to eye up the whole audience (except I spent most of the night taking advantage of the light conditions by getting some brilliant photos).

Somehow we missed each other, but as I woke up on the Helocolins' sofa in a bleary, sore-throaty haze the morning after the Bristol Thekla gig in 2007, I felt like I'd known them for years…

So right, where to begin…? Maybe with an explanation of the nickname, or tag, or whatever they call them on the Internet these days… "Helocolin" dates back to when Paul was working on the installation of the prototype Internet at Warwick University back in the late-80s. It was his sign-on ID, derived from a rather funny 16-second Derek & Clive sketch. He missed one of the 'l's out because 'I wanted to make it easy to sign on when I was a bit the worse for wear.'

And so it remained as an email address for years afterwards, adding an 'xyz' somewhere along the line. The amusing (and sometimes confusing for us Listees) thing was that as Karen and Paul were a couple, they'd reply to emails on the Cardiacs List using the same email address, although eventually we all worked out that Karen's posts could be identified by a "love Karen x x" at the end. I think it may have been Ian who first referred to them as "the Helocolins", and, well yer know, it pretty much stuck.

And what of Paul's tattoo? Spookily in the same position as mine, there just had to be a story. So I asked him. I'll let him tell the tale…

Paul: 'I have a "birthmark" on my right arm, which I didn't have when I was born because it is pigment related, so not really a birthmark then. Anyway, it looks like a map of the world, and when I was little I could identify all the continents, the British Isles, China, Russia, the lot. When I became less little, the arm grew and every year in primary school I would proudly display my arm close to a globe of the "whole world". I would twizzle the globe around as I pointed at the continents on my biceps, and the class would all go "corr!" and "whoo!"

'When I was older it grew and looked less impressive, although I can still demonstrate all the continents on request. Anyway, my arm looked less and less like the "whole world" and my classroom trick was gone.

'In the late-80s I heard a noise which reminded me "appropriately" of all classroom excitement, and by 1998 having had a favourite band for ten years solid (them being Cardiacs of course), I firmly decided that I wanted that logo on my upper arm to restore all that pleasure and excitement of feeling special. It seemed..."appropriate".'

Blimey, it was done the same year as mine too.

Paul was a lot more careful about his than I'd been about mine though. For a start he photocopied an old t-shirt on "reduce" mode and spent an afternoon with cut-outs stuck with Selotape asking all the secretaries at work what size they felt worked best until it was perfect.

The tattoo shop was most impressed with Paul's range of templates and images of differing sizes. 'I pointed out the rest of my "whole world" bicep, and I think they were very thoughtful of it and artful in a beautiful replication of the logo. I had been to a different tattooist previously but the vibe was wrong. Good decision to wait. You know when it's right to make a decision.'

Yep, in 1998 seemingly...

* * * *

The fascinating thing about doing the research for this book has been to see where everyone arrived at Cardiacs from musically, not just from the music they were listening to in their teens, but going further back to childhood. Despite some unlikely-sounding links, the more you think about it, and the more you listen to Cardiacs, the more you can hear influences all over the place, subconsciously or otherwise, like Paul Helocolin's earliest musical recollections of Rolf Harris' "Tie Me Kangaroo Down Sport" and *Tobermory's Music Machine*. The Wombles and Cardiacs? You bet!

Even more likely was the first record Paul received as a present, it being "Zippedydoodah" by 'some Song of the South bloke accompanied by buzzing bees and random noises.' Random noises – very Cardiacs.

Moving on to buying his own discs, the bargain bin at WH-

Smith took a battering with either Deep Purple *Made in Japan* or the *24 Carat Purple* compilation being the first record Paul bought for himself. All this led to Deep Purple being his first passion, closely followed by Randy Rhoades-era Ozzy Osbourne. It seemed that he was destined to be a bit of a Metal-head, especially as Iron Maiden were kind enough to provide him with his first gig, 'The night they hit number 4 in the charts with "Run to the Hills",' he adds.

But other forces were at work, as is often the case when you come from a family of musicians, especially as Paul played drums from the age of nine in various bands with his Dad. 'My drum teacher took me to see Buddy Rich when I was about ten. I hated trumpets, but that coffin dodger with a bad cough could play.' A bit of Jazz chucked into the melting pot of Heavy Metal, it was no wonder that a splodge of Rush was just around the corner, Rush perhaps bridging the gap perfectly between Metal and Prog-Rock in my opinion, and we all know that a good many Proggers like a bit of Jazz.

Meanwhile, Karen Helocolin was coming at things from a different angle, starting with "Sugar Sugar" by The Archies, bought for her by the granddad who brought her up until he died when she was six-years-old. The first record she bought for herself was "Oliver's Army" by Elvis Costello, a most tuneful song. A fixation with Japan started moving things off in an interesting direction, leading to Karen's first gig attended circa 1981, Japan supported by Blancmange, closely followed by Duran Duran's first gig. Add to this melting pot the fact that 'George Galway, James the Golden Flute's brother, taught me clarinet – I still love it. Privately.' (Ooops, that's everyone told then.)

(Belch Note: whilst I'm at it, I must point out that I once attended a Circulus gig at Croydon Fairfields Hall as part of Witchfest where James Galway was playing in the main hall, so the foyer was full of witches, warlocks, protesting-Christians and ten-year-old flautists – and there was I, a Mormon with two Mormon chicks, both with pagan sympathies, one of whom used to practise Wicca – now that WAS a melting pot.)

Ah, you see, with these little developments in musical taste and influence, the two Helocolins were heading in the same direction. Paul admits that leading up to Cardiacs he went from mainstream Rock to Prog: 'I worked as a stage manager for a promoter at the time and thought I knew it all. I didn't,' he adds.

Meanwhile, Karen had arrived at a similar musical plateau with an obsession for *The Lamb Lies Down On Broadway* Gabriel-era Genesis, *The Lamb...* being her favourite album 'for so many reasons, and Genesis remain ultimately my best fave ever. What genre's that make me from then?' she asks. Oh I dunno, what with all the other stuff mixed in as well, but ultimately Gabriel-era Genesis is more Prog than Prog itself. I'm with Karen on this one – when I'm having a Genesis day there is absolutely nothing to beat *The Lamb Lies Down On Broadway*, "Supper's Ready" and in fact all of *Foxtrot*, along with most of *Nursery Cryme*. Rest assured, with Genesis, Rush and Prog-Rock as a whole, both the Helocolins were ready and receptive to Cardiacs when they came along.

Paul got the bug first. 'It was at Warwick University in 1989 (May 6th to be precise) when a flyer came round from a guy called "Andy Head" apparently. The flyer said, "If you have any appreciation for music whatsoever, get your arse to the Market Place. Free entry, but a whip-round for the band is requested."'

Suitably intrigued, Paul and a friend wandered along to see this not-to-be-missed band, Cardiacs: 'I stood watching, scared, and said, "What the **** is this?" to my friend. "Yes, really good aren't they," he replied. I wasn't too sure,' he confesses.

But intrigue normally leads to further investigation, and so Paul went out and bought *A Little Man And A House And The Whole World Window*, playing it incessantly whilst that prototype Internet was under construction. So that was him hauled in then.

When Paul met Karen he did that thing we've all done, deciding that a sure way to impress was to attend a Cardiacs gig together, it being the gig at the Splash Club @ the Water Rats in lovely old King's Cross, May 11th 1995. Karen wasn't sure she wanted to go: 'Paul made me go. I complained and squirmed and then met Timmy and was hooked...'

That one obviously made an impression on Karen, but it must've been the Woughton Centre gig in Milton Keynes a few weeks later that sealed the deal judging by the requests that keep coming my way from Paul for a copy of the video I have of that gig (you need to get that VHS player to me first, Paul). And if any deals still needed finalising, it was all tied up at a gig in Manchester a while later when Paul proposed to Karen during his favourite song "Ideal", just as Bob's pedal broke and he fell off his drum-stool.

Of course, Karen hadn't needed to buy any Cardiacs albums because Paul had them all, 'but he did say he would marry anyone, male or female, who would buy him *A Little Man And A House And The Whole World Window* on CD, so I complied.'

Now, not everyone is as meticulous in their gig-listing as me or Pete, and so when asked how many Cardiacs gigs they've attended, neither of the Helocolins are sure. 'I'd like to say, "This is number 100," at some stage, but then I might have done 100 already,' Paul ponders. 'I followed lots of tours without talking to anyone, in a lost-sheep, sad, reclusive, depressed-soul-kind-of-manner in the early days. By the way, I always say that I expect a gig to be rubbish before every one,' he goes on, 'but it never has been – yet. I expect the next one will be rubbish though...'

Karen says, 'I've maybe been about 40 or 50 times... It's not enough, anyhow.'

Some indication of just how many times Paul must've been to see them is illustrated by the sheer volume of memories he's amassed, such as meeting Thrupty (Pete) for the first time at Kidderminster Market Tavern in 1992, telling him he expected "Home Of Fadeless Splendour" to start things off, only to be blasted away by "Ideal" for the first time instead, thus establishing it as a favourite; or that Wolverhampton gig with very few people there. 'I sat in a pub before the gig playing drums with Dom Luckman (in the audience that night) using only teaspoons and pots of condiments for percussion, only to discover that you and Skinner were in the dressing room watching the England game, but we somehow never met. Small world,' he muses.

He has suffered for his fandom too: 'I had my front tooth knocked out at the Astoria 2 in the 90s, and at the Special Garage Concerts I shouted "_____" 'cos I'd had my tonsils out and had an open throat wound, in *that* sweaty, smoky, drippy place, all three nights running.'

Karen sometimes had to step in to help out: 'At the secret gigs at the Bull & Gate in 2005 I was being fiercely protected by Karen sitting on a box that claimed to contain Iron Maiden's drums, knowing that one false move and the bolts in my back (I've seen the x-rays, folks) would fall out meaning a certainty of permanent paralysis of the legs, only to recently see pictures of the gig showing that it was Malcy and Pies behind us.' (Pies is a legendary long-term Cardiacs fan, earning respect from all of us by having seen all the bands that mattered in the 70s, but why, oh why did she always fall asleep every time she went to see Gong? Oh, and the Piester was once mistook for Tim Smith's sister; not bad considering he hasn't got one.)

Not only does Karen protect fiercely, but there's competition there too. 'I knew all the words to "Fiery Gun Hand" before Paul did,' she announces proudly, 'and I know them all to "Ideal" too, 'cos no-one else ever knows them – it helps that the song is genius.'

And of course, with a successful relationship comes the pitter-patter of tiny feet, linking to an interesting choice of favourite Cardiacs song for Karen, "Arnald": 'It's for personal reasons,' she explains, 'our first child jigged about to it pre-birth through headphones, so was nicknamed Arnald because we thought *she* was a boy, pre-birth. She was listed on the maternity ward as "Child Formerly Known as Arnold". She is Sarah.'

Karen doesn't have a favourite album (although Paul still champions the first two albums "proper"), instead having 'compilations of everything I luurve, that moment which changes regularly but never ceases to have a bottom to the stuff I like.'

So you see, this thing called Cardiacs hasn't just grabbed me; there are others, and when I tell people that I'm merely a wee bairn in the bigger picture of Cardiacs fandom and that there are worse out there than me, I'm often thinking (in the nicest possible way) of

Karen and Paul.

'If I drop into "just Cardiacs listening", it is a sure sign a manic episode is nigh,' says Paul. 'This has proved to be immensely valuable to those around me over the last 20 years, knowing that tethering and removal of passport and/or ladders from the vicinity is most sensible…'

Karen has a more cheery line of closing thought: 'This last tour has been immense for camaraderie, where all the threads of our experiences met up and collided and had beautiful babies with a Cardiacs hue. I now have friends who I hope I will have for life. You included, Belchy Boy.' Awww, sweet…

* * * *

It really was an unusual experience waking up in the Helocolins' living room, on the sofa. The combination of gig-sweat and cold air had inevitably led to a snuffly nose, red eyes and a very sore throat. Every time I wearily opened my eyes there was a different Helocolins' kid coming in to say 'hello' to me. Then there was the dog, and I'm sure it said 'hello' to me too (some Lemsip, eh?).

The Helocolins had recently suffered a break-in, reported angrily on the List, and so I was able to confirm that indeed the window by the front door was boarded up, and yep, the carpet cleaners were coming to sort the living room out, because they were right there, hoovering around a rather sick Belch.

On Karen's advice I abandoned my plan to hitchhike (this thumbing-it plan was going really well) and opted instead to travel up with them (and Ian) to the next gig in Nottingham that evening. I was sent to bed (now all beds were vacant) with more Lemsip and a packet of Lockets, but my sleep was broken by people phoning me and texting me all day. And when I did get to sleep I had a most disturbing dream about a Cardiacs fan in a Big Flower t-shirt taking hostages with a gun. I tried to talk him round by going down the 'I'm a Cardiacs fan too…' route, but he was taking some talking round so I was quite glad to wake up from that one…

When I eventually abandoned sleep altogether I staggered downstairs just in time to catch the window-repairmen and the Helocolins' dog walker. There'd been a standing joke on the List about the Helocolins being way more affluent than the rest of us, so I was delighted to be able to report that they had their own dog walker, but then I could have got it all wrong in my Lemsip haze, and the dog walker may well have been a close relative...

A homemade hot curry had me feeling better, as did a trip into their garage to see the soon-to-be-erected Christmas decs (big-time snowman for the roof etc). And just because I needed cheering up a bit Paul told me about some of their bonkers former Eastern-European au-pairs, one of whom filled their shoes up with sweets and biscuits one morning but failed to tell anyone until they stood in marshmallow on what she referred to as "Booty Shoe Day", and another who filled up the toilet with something far less sweet...

What with Cardiacs' nod towards Gong on all three nights of the tour so far, we felt it only right and proper to accompany all this chatter with a lovely slice of Om Rock ourselves, and so with our souls recharged, and me croaking away in the back of the car complete with Sheffield-United-woolly-hat-and-scarf combo, we headed off to drag the Skinner-one from out of his nearby abode in Kettering.

Next stop Nottingham, and I was almost allowing excitement to get the better of my sore throat.

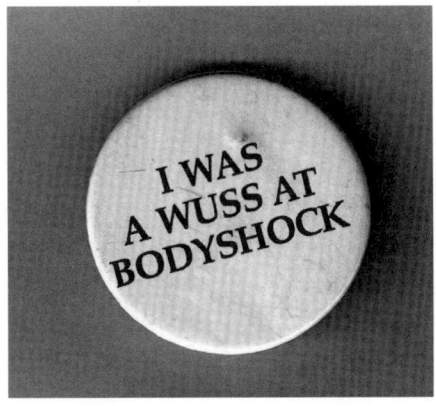

Chapter Nine
"A Pay-as-you-exit Bus for a Bus on the Bus"
Rescue Rooms, Nottingham, November 15th 2007

We hereby:-
Outlaw
on this day in the year 1190
at The Tales of Robin Hood
in the town of Nottingham

Adrian Bell.

This same has been
suspected of supporting
that infamous outlaw Robin Hood
and has failed to provide proper
answers to this charge.

So in the presence of the
coroner of the Lord King
for the said county of
Nottinghamshire they are
proclaimed Outlawed.

"A Pay-as-you-exit Bus for a Bus on the Bus"
Rescue Rooms, Nottingham, November 15th 2007

I did the thing about the miners' strike in the last book; you know, when Sheffield United played Nottingham Forest and I got two lifts, firstly with a Forest fan who wouldn't be going to the match because of all the unease that still pervaded around matches between the two teams brought about by the Nottinghamshire miners not striking back in 1984, and then a second lift with an ex-miner who'd been working in a Notts pit at the time and had gone on strike despite most of his colleagues continuing to work.

So no, I can't talk about that again. Luckily for me though, I've been to plenty of gigs in Nottingham in my time, some of them even involving Cardiacs or related bands (well, one Sea Nymphs gig, but not just any old Sea Nymphs gig – it was the *first ever* Sea Nymphs gig), so I can trip back in time to some of those fabulous events before moving on to more recent history.

You see when I was living in Sheffield, Nottingham was but a hop, skip and a jump away, whether it be by bus, train or hitch, and they had a couple of brilliant venues, Rock City and the Mardi Gras. Now admittedly, I didn't frequent these venues as much as, say, Sheffield's Leadmill, but it was rather handy for when one of my favourite bands didn't make it to my home town for whatever reason.

So, when Hawkwind (sadly shorn of Nik Turner, but still an entertaining proposition) did a short tour in June 1985, the nearest they came was Nottingham Rock City, so off I went. Then in 1986, IQ chose to do their first ever gig with new singer Paul Menel at the same venue, and with Haze as support, attending was a bit of a no-brainer (although IQ weren't as good as when Pete Nicholls was in them, oh no).

As one band did their first gig, another did their last; Twice Bitten, this time at the Mardi Gras, again in 1986 (well, I say their "last", they came out of retirement June 2008 to support Haze at their 30th anniversary gig at the Boardwalk in Sheffield, but as it was 22 years since that farewell gig, I don't think anyone felt cheated – as it happens Twice Bitten were immense at the Boardwalk). That Twice

Bitten night in 1986 really was rather special, and quite emotional. What's more, Haze came onstage for the encores and I recorded the whole thing myself (although for the second time in my life, my tape player went all wobbly during Twice Bitten's classic "Crocus Point").

Back to debut gigs, and in 1987 I was off to the Mardi Gras again, this time to see Nik Turner's Fantastic Allstars and their debut live performance. After the Punk of Inner City Unit, I was a little surprised by the Jazz/big-band-dance frolics of Uncle Nik's latest offering, but after about twenty seconds I realised that this was in fact great fun, and grooved the night away accordingly.

Motörhead at Rock City in 1987 gave me my noisiest Nottingham gig, if not my noisiest of any gig ever. I mean, can you imagine a band like Motörhead in a venue as small as Rock City? I couldn't hear a thing afterwards, especially after staying on for the Heavy Metal nightclub into the early hours. I ended up getting an early morning coach (like about 4am) from Nottingham back to Sheffield, and when I asked the driver how much the fare was, I saw his lips moving but could only hear the ringing in my ears. So I went, 'Eh?' and again, all I noticed was his lips moving, so I gave him a tenner and hoped for the best. He gave me change, so I must've been okay...

Once I moved to Brackley, the chances of going to gigs in Nottingham were lessened somewhat, especially as it was now easier to get to London, and let's face it, not many bands miss out London during a tour. In fact, it was probably a fairly safe bet that from now on, the only gigs I'd attend in Nottingham would be Cardiacs gigs, so determined was I to attend as many of their gigs as I could.

And so my first opportunity arose on June 6th 1992, on the *Heaven Born and Ever Bright* tour, only the second time I would have seen Cardiacs as a four-piece. It had been a strange period since the departure of Bill Drake in May 1991. All had been quiet for a while, although during that summer of 1991 I saw Dominic drumming for Here & Now/Planet Gong at a rather chaotic all-dayer at West Bromwich Town Hall (also on the bill, Poisoned Electrick Head), and he told me Cardiacs had got a new guitarist who 'looked like a mini version of Jim'. That intrigued me, but the news that they'd be using taped keyboards instead of a Bill replacement worried me a little. I wondered if it could ever be the same...

Well, my first viewing of the new line-up, at Northampton Irish Centre on February 28th 1992, allayed any fears. No, it wasn't the same, but actually it was... different. The new music seemed to reflect the change in circumstances; a little harder, a little stripped down, but if anything even more complicated than before and still wonderfully exciting and entertaining. In concert it came across just as vivid as ever, and they even did "Icky Qualms" as an encore... yep, Cardiacs were still the main draw for this Belch.

Annie accompanied me to that Northampton gig, and I'm not sure that she enjoyed it as much as me because when it came to the gig in Nottingham a few months later she decided she didn't want to go. She did, however, fancy a day out in Nottingham, and so it seemed did her step-sister, as she accompanied us all the way up from Brackley. The plan was for us all to do what we had to do in Nottingham, then for those two to drive back to Brackley, leaving me to gig it alone, me being expected to make my own way back afterwards.

Now, what the three of us basically had to do was visit Tales of Robin Hood in Nottingham, a rather nice little trip around a pretend forest indoors in cars a bit like the Jorvik Viking Museum in York (without the smells). Afterwards there was a little exhibition and shop upstairs where all the employees were dressed in period costume, including a rather tasty looking chick dressed as a jester. I remember thinking it'd be nice if she was at the gig that evening, hopefully wearing full jester regalia.

As we entered the room we were each given a question sheet to fill out, and it was here that I stoked up a little Yorkshire/Nottinghamshire rivalry with my answers. One of the questions was, "In what county was Robin Hood born? a) Yorkshire b) Nottinghamshire c) Derbyshire". I confidently told Annie it was Yorkshire because everyone knew Robin of Loxley was from, well, Loxley, and Loxley was part of Sheffield, and Sheffield was/is in Yorkshire.

When it came to having our answer-sheets marked by a bloke dressed as the Sheriff of Nottingham, he looked at my "Yorkshire" answer and said, 'Well, you've got that one wrong for a start.'

'No I haven't,' I replied, defiantly.

'Robin Hood was born in Nottinghamshire,' said the Sheriff.

'He was a Sheffield lad, like me, so he's from Yorkshire I'm afraid,' I persisted.

'You don't believe all that rubbish do you?' he said, and wielded the ultimate power by marking my answer as wrong.

When he looked at Annie's sheet he said, 'And did you listen to *him*?'

'Yes,' said Annie meekly.

'Well, you're outlawed too,' he smirked, and then gave us both certificates saying we were indeed outlawed from the county of Nottinghamshire, a certificate I accepted with pride, protesting Robin Hood's Yorkshireness to the end.

Annie and her step-sister took the outlaw notices to heart and drove back to Northamptonshire forthwith, but I had a gig to attend so was prepared to risk the wrath of the Sheriff of Nottingham by hanging around a bit. However, first I had to find the venue. Oh, but before that I had to find a Gents as I was in desperate need of a visit. Only I could make a mini-adventure out of a trip to the Gents, but you know me (in fact it happened to me in Staines yesterday too, when the tardis toilet stole my 20p and the door refused to open – an elderly Asian gentleman then approached the toilet and was about to part with his 20p too, but I forewarned him, and so we went on a trek together to raid the customer toilets in Debenhams).

So, there I was scouring the streets of Nottingham looking for a public toilet, desperate for some relief. There were no Gents to be found, and I wondered where to turn next. And then there it was, a building marked "TOILET", all glowing with angel music coming from it. Forget the smoke coming out of the window, I was going in. I'd barely taken two steps towards my goal when a fire engine screeched to a halt on the pavement and out poured half-a-dozen firemen. 'You can't go in there, it's on fire,' one of them said.

'I'm desperate – maybe I can help put it out?' I replied, quick witted as ever.

To much laughter they unravelled their hose and entered the public toilet, sadly turning down my offer of help. 'You'll have to find another toilet,' one of them grinned.

'Any idea where?' I pleaded.

'Sorry mate…'

As I walked away I noticed one of them coming out with a smouldering toilet roll, but I felt uneasy about going back in there so headed off in search of a public convenience that wasn't ablaze…

In that order, I found them; a public toilet, then Trent Polytechnic, Nottingham, and any lingering doubts I had about the four-piece Cardiacs were blown away that night. Before that though I was blown away by Levitation, the co-headliners on the tour. Levitation had also been on the bill at Northampton back in February, and I'd not been too sure. Now though, they were 'blinding', as Tim himself said from the stage that night.

Cardiacs were still in a different league however, good as Levitation were. Tons of energy, bags of confetti, just like Cardiacs of old. I sat around afterwards hoping to cadge a lift home, allowing myself a little chuckle as some poor female employee of the Students' Union had to hoover up all the confetti.

Somehow I managed to scavenge a lift back in Cardiacs' rather plush Band Width van, the deal being that I was barred from the comfy bit at the back, and I'd be dropped off at Rothersthorpe Services (junction 15a) where the long-suffering Annie would get a phone call requesting she drive the 20 miles to pick me up (at something like 2 o'clock in the morning – I really don't know how I got away with it). Anyway, as I was queuing to get on the tour bus (some things just come naturally to we English, even on a tour bus), Jim looked at me and growled, 'Have you paid yet?'

'It's pay as you exit, isn't it?' I answered with a nervous, weak smile.

'Whoever heard of a pay-as-you-exit bus?' muttered Jim as I got on board.

Jon Poole, that new guitarist who Dominic had described as a "mini-Jim", heard all this and was most concerned about my feelings. 'Don't worry Curly,' he said, 'Jim's always like that.'

Tim appeared from nowhere looking a bit flustered and said, 'It's all right Jon; Belch is from the old school. He knows all about Jim…'

I ended up sat in the front with Clive the roadie driving, and as the Band Width vehicle burned down the M1, coaches with students in them kept going past and capturing images of us with flash-photography, presumably because they thought the band inside were famous. I often wonder which poor now-adults have a photo of me and Clive-the-roadie sat in the front of a band-van/bus…

* * * *

Last time in Nottingham it had been burning conveniences and vanishing confetti, but now in 2007 in the pub just around the corner from the Rescue Rooms it was a magic trickster holding my attention. He was going from table to table earning an honest (well, maybe not that honest – he was an illusionist after all) living performing all manner of tricks with cards and bits and bobs; you know the sort of thing, where you are totally certain you have three cards in your pocket and you end up pulling out five, and they're the five that he tells you they will be. Something like that anyway. It's fair to say that he blew my mind, much to the amusement of my watching buddies, Malc, Ian, the Helocolins and Lawrence, amongst others. I watched him like a hawk, looking for clues, and was determined to prove him wrong with every trick, but he was right every time, and I had no idea how he did it. All I could think of was the episode of *Curb Your Enthusiasm* where Larry David can't work out how his wife's nephew does a certain card-trick, but then an inmate of a local mental institution who sees the trick gets it straight away and says, "Even an idiot can see how that's done…"

Well, they say a fool and his money are soon parted, and I guess the same goes for an idiot or a Belch, and so when our Card Trickster asked for a donation, I was only too happy to unload all my change into his magic moneybag. I couldn't help noticing nobody else seemed anything like as impressed as me – maybe they were all in on it together. Lawrence had seemed more obsessed (disturbingly so) with 'Spade 12' anyway, the spade that would signify my Supper was Ready (again).

In my wallet was my ticket for the next night's performance at London's Astoria (although I had to check in case Magic Trickster had had it away), along with a spare I'd bought just in case someone of female persuasion wanted to come with me. The person I had in mind was Julia, the Polish girl who worked in Tesco Ashford's coffee shop/staff restaurant. I'd once asked her what music she liked and she replied, 'Rock and Heavy Metal and thatz itt.' I detected a gap in the market and thought she might like Cardiacs, at least live in concert if not on disc, so invited her to the Astoria. I played her a bit on my iPod once, her response being, 'I no like – it izz crazy music,' but she kept an open mind on seeing them live (in that she didn't say 'no' straight off). For about two months she was saying she wasn't sure, she'd see etc etc, and now it was the day before the gig and still I had no answer. At the same time Ian was short of a ticket for that very same gig, and knowing how close-run it can be waiting for him to turn up to collect any spares, I figured we'd better get it sorted there and then in Nottingham.

So, as we walked to the venue I called Julia to enquire as to whether she was going to grace me with her presence the following night or not.

'Oh hello Adrianko,' she said in a tone of voice that suggested she already had her answer.

'You coming to this gig tomorrow night then?' I asked.

'I sorry, Adrianko, I no want to go,' she replied.

'Okay…'

'But you have nice time…'

'Okay – see you when I get back,' and with that I took out my spare ticket and without a word handed it to the approaching Ian…

Once inside the venue I felt a little happier; there's something about walking into a club and seeing all the gear set up on the stage, ready for that night's performance – all microphones and drum-kit and the majestic Alphabet Business Concern backdrop, not to mention the imposing Alphabet Business Concern bass-drums looking down from on high, ready for a thoroughly good beating from Mel and Cath. Mind you, I was still feeling rough despite polishing off the whole packet of Lockets the Helocolins had given me. The Sheffield United woolly hat and scarf were kept on right up until gig-kick-off.

The audience was an interesting one. As seemed to be happening more and more often (or maybe I just notice it more because I don't expect it), there were quite a number of youngsters in attendance, as well as Warren, sound engineer of Sheffield's Prog-Rock heroes Haze (he doesn't just engineer for Haze; if you look inside the CD booklet for the Arena live album, you'll see Warren proudly wearing his Big Flower t-shirt).

Not only were there plenty of youngsters there, many of them were attractive girls, and I was sorely grateful that Cardiacs seem to attract more members of the opposite sex than most bands I like (although I think Circulus hold the record for this). We were in for a good night...

That night's set provided the fourth different one of the tour, and from what we could all work out, this was the final piece of the jigsaw. It has to be said this one drew more on older material, and when I say older, I mean stuff from those pre-1984 days that they'd performed at the Special Garage Concerts in 2003, such marvellous Punky little anthems as "Dead Mouse" and "An Ant". And once again, Cardiacs proved my theory that their best gigs are in the smaller venues; Brighton – big hall, disappointing gig; Bristol and Nottingham – small club, sparkling gigs. Just like Nottingham in 1992 much energy was expended, the only difference being there was no confetti this time (I think Cardiacs must have got tired of promoters and venue owners always moaning about having to clear it all up).

When all was done and the cheers had died away, a chap with a greasy ponytail was seen attempting to nick Tim's special plectrums from his stand but a chant of, 'Thieving gypsy bastard! Thieving gypsy bastard!' shamed him into leaving them be. After that excitement, I decided to make the most of the presence of all these beautiful girls and the fact that everyone seemed to have spilled over into the late-night drinking establishment attached to the Rescue Rooms.

First on my list was the young lady with a Shaun-the-Sheep rucksack who I'd noticed singing along to a lot of the words. Her friend hadn't seemed quite so impressed, so I went along and made this observation to them. Shaun-the-Sheep Girl turned out to be called Cheryl, and her friend Natalie admitted that indeed Cheryl was the bigger fan. It also turned out that Cheryl wasn't as young as I thought, being 27-years-old (blimey Belch, it's a regular mistake, but you usually get it the other way round). When I asked how she'd discovered Cardiacs she said her friend Tim Jackson had introduced her to them.

'What, Tim Jackson who now lives in the South West?' I asked.

'That's him,' Cheryl replied with a touch of surprise, 'do you know him?'

'I put my junk in his trunk last night in Bristol,' I laughed, and was only too happy to show her the notes in my book.

'He's my perennial bassist,' Cheryl announced. 'He's in every band I ever have.'

My "junk in his trunk" scribbled notes seemed to allay Natalie's fears; 'I thought you might be a bit weird until I saw that, but you're obviously who you say you are,' she expressed.

'I probably am still a bit weird,' I reassured, 'but yep, I am who I say I am, doing what I say I'm doing, and now you'll be in the book.' They didn't seem to object, so here they are.

Cheryl then produced her mobile and said she was ringing Tim Jackson's number. She then handed the phone to me, and I went, 'Hello Tim, Belch here. Hello? Hello? I can't hear you. What's that Cheryl…? Voicemail…? Ah…'

Moving on I noticed that Pete was looking a bit worried as three incredibly beautiful girls were chatting to him, and as monogamous-Pete he needed someone to distract them, so in I heroically stepped, and with thanks Pete vanished. One of these very beautiful (and this time they really were very young) girls was called Hannah, and she wrote a note in my book that went, "I met Belch, he introduced me to the Cardiacs (we can forgive her the indiscretion of the "the"), they were soo good I stayed for the whole set. Belch is a legend." I didn't tell her to write any of this; she made her own mind up, and who was I to argue. She also wrote her email address in there – I just hope it's still active by the time this book finally makes it back from the printers.

The night was getting on and Paul Ashby, who was providing my bed for the night, was worrying a bit that we might miss the last bus home, so with Paul Helocolin found and my rucksack rescued from his boot, off we went into the cold November air to get that bus.

At least it wasn't a 4am bus this time with a deaf post-Motörhead Belch, or a pay-as-you-exit tour bus with a grumpy Jim, and this time either way the journey was going to be much shorter. The only problem I had once again was with the fare, not because I couldn't hear the driver for ringing ears, but because he insisted on the right change. I chucked money around a bit (difficult with a rucksack), pooled my resources with Paul of the Ashby variety, received my precious ticket, and then settled in for a trip around the neighbourhood.

As I settled down on Paul's thoughtfully-inflated airbed, mellowed by a bowl of proper soup (that's me mellowed, not the airbed), I sent a text to Julia telling her it was a shame she couldn't make it to the Astoria gig. She texted me back saying, "Yes but I decide I no want man in my life at this moment."

"Blimey," I replied, "I only wanted you to come to a gig with me – I wasn't expecting you to be my life-partner."

She wants to think herself lucky. If she'd have been Annie I'd have been texting her saying, "All right love; can you come and pick me up from the M1…?"

Chapter Ten
"Odd Even"
Paul Ashby

"Odd Even"
Paul Ashby

Back in 1978 when I was an impressionable 12-year-old (as opposed to the impressionable 40-something I am now), Wembley Stadium and the FA Cup Final, along with that lovely old trophy itself, were something of Holy Grails to me. Well maybe not Holy Grails, because I sense that when people think of Holy Grails, they are at least aiming for something that is just about feasible or findable, and anyone who cares to check Sheffield United's 1970s FA Cup record will see that it was nothing short of abysmal. So I never thought I'd ever get to an FA Cup Final to see my beloved Blades, but in 1978 one of my mates at Greystones Middle School, Sheffield, had a ticket for the final tie between Arsenal and Ipswich Town, and I was incredibly jealous.

The game itself wasn't exactly a classic, but Ipswich beating Arsenal 1-0 was considered something of a shock (after all, when they'd come to Bramall Lane in the 3rd Round and been 4-0 up after 15 minutes on the way to a comfortable 5-0 win, Arsenal had looked pretty good). Despite my envy, I was looking forward to getting a report on the Monday from my school chum. Why, he'd even have seen the Old Tinpot itself in the flesh, so to speak.

And then on that Monday, first thing in the morning in the school playground, my pal dropped the bombshell...

'How was the Cup Final?' was the first thing I obviously asked him.

'Oh, I didn't go – I had a bit of flu,' he replied.

What? He hadn't gone? Because of a bit of flu? I was horror struck. Despite the absence of any club that I actually liked, this was the FA Cup Final, and even with a limb or two hanging off I'd have struggled along. My feelings of jealousy were now replaced with anger, but instead of giving him a hard time, I just shook my head and walked away. Well, what did I expect? He was a Sheffield Wednesday fan after all.

Nearly thirty years on, and it was another event that took place at Wembley in 1978 that was invoking feelings of envy, although this event hadn't played itself out at the stadium itself, but rather at what was then known as the Empire Pool, now more simply referred to as Wembley Arena (or Wembley Cowshed when the soundman has an off day). It all came to light when regulars on Cardiacs Email Chatlist were discussing The First Gig I Ever Attended. I'm sure everybody knew mine already, but I repeated my "Rick Wakeman Sheffield City Hall September 1980" boast again. There were quite a few interesting ones in there, but one in particular trumped the lot; Paul Ashby went and told us all that his debut gig had been Yes at the Empire Pool, Wembley, October 1978.

I couldn't disguise my jealousy; this was better than some rubbishy Cup Final between two of Sheffield United's most disliked teams – this was the real deal. I pushed for further information, and yes, it turned out to be the one recorded and broadcast on Radio 1, considered by many to be one of the greatest Yes concerts ever, and comfortably the most bootlegged of the lot. Indeed, I'd had my copy of that gig on tape for something like 27 years, and even though when Tommy Vance first broadcast it in 1978 to launch *The Friday Rock Show* I was blithely unaware of any activity on the live front (I was after all a Yes fan of only about six-months standing), when he repeated it in 1979 I was right there by the dial, radio tucked away under the sheets, and it sounded absolutely mind-blowingly brilliant. And Paul was at the gig. Could I ever forgive him…?

The wonderful thing about Cardiacs Email Chatlist is that not only do you find out what people's first gigs were, you pick up all kinds of handy tips, like the recommendation that Oust air-freshener really does 'oust' the smell, not just mask it (thank-you the Helocolins for that one). You also find out what your fellow Listees are up to on those dull days when Cardiacs aren't on tour and don't have a new album coming out. It was from such a posting of mine that Paul Ashby (so many Pauls on this List) deduced that I may not be able to make it to the Premiership clash at Bramall Lane between Sheffield United and his beloved Tottenham Hotspur, so knowing I was a Sheffield United season ticket holder and that Spurs had already sold out their allocation, he sent me a hopeful email off-list.

Only too happy to oblige, a deal was struck that I felt couldn't be turned down. Indeed, so heavily stacked in my favour was the deal of a cheque *and* a rather hefty selection from Paul's extensive live recording collection, I felt the need to redress the balance somewhat (and I'm therefore really sorry Paul that for whatever reasons the signed photo of Martin Peters has still not winged its way over to you yet , the consolation being it does portray him in his Spurs heyday, and not the grey-haired version of the present day who looks slightly pensive when he realises the miffed looking bloke in front of him is a Sheffield United fan who clearly remembers the last day of the 1980/81 season).

What's more, Sheffield United only went and beat Spurs, so poor old Paul had to suffer the indignity of watching his heroes lose whilst surrounded by some of the Blades' finest. He was prepared to tell those sat nearby that he was a friend of mine, but wisely chose to keep his allegiance to Tottenham secret (the only "colours" he wore were a Cardiacs t-shirt).

A young fan of Yes when it was much more fashionable of kids our age to like Punk; a love of an under-achieving football team that leads to you sitting amongst fans of the opposition just to see your favourites; a desire to sport the apparel of your most-obsessed-about band...sounds familiar? I was already starting to believe that myself and Paul were indeed the same person before I entered his room after that Nottingham Rescue Rooms gig and saw that the wallpaper on his computer was exactly the same picture of Stonehenge I had on mine, but my painstaking research for this here book led to even more striking similarities...

* * * *

A year or two before I was listening to *Waggoner's Walk* with my Mum and soaking up the delights of Rolf Harris' "Two Little Boys" and Radio 2 in general, Paul Ashby was undergoing similar subliminal earworming, again courtesy of Radio 2, and as with me, it was thanks to a mum, this one with a 'ginormous Bakelite wireless, and yes, she still calls it that, even though it has thankfully shrunk in size and no longer has valves.' It wasn't bearded Aussies or people begging your pardon for never promising you a rose garden that seeped into Paul consciousness however, but rather "Cinderella Rockerfella" by the one-hit-wonders (in the UK anyway) Esther and Abi Ofarim, a song that he describes as 'an annoying piece of pap that works on the novelty earworm principle that it's so bad you can't stop it from in-habiting your head. Even then, I somehow knew it was wrong – maybe it was the non-contextual yodelling that was the clue. It's only good point was its brevity.' Not the best introduction to music then…

Indeed, musical salvation was a way off yet: 'The afore-men-tioned Bakelite monstrosity was just about the only source of musical gratification in our house for several years to come. We got a black and white telly in the early 70s, but they never let me stay up for *The Old Grey Whistle Test*, the occasional exposure to *The Black and White Minstrel Show* and my lunchtime appointments with *Camber-wick Green* and *Trumpton* being the closest I got to music.'

Ah yes, I had those very same lunchtime appointments in Trumptonshire (don't forget *Chigley* Paul; people always forget *Chigley*), and it has to be said the music was beguiling. Indeed, The Orb using the musical-box music from *Camberwick Green* is one of my most prized recordings. And just like Paul, my memories are all in black and white – so much so that if I were to see that trio of pro-grammes in colour now, I'd probably have to switch the telly to black and white in order to get all nostalgic. Our telly was such an old thing that it had a dial instead of buttons for changing channels and it could-n't pick up BBC2. It couldn't get ITV either, not because of any fault in the mechanism, but because my Mum wouldn't let us watch it (the irony is, my Mum now tapes *Coronation Street* and *Emmerdale*). Pre-sumably it was similarly strict parenting that led to Paul being banned from watching …*Whistle Test*.

If only our parents had known what they *were* exposing us to: 'On *Camberwick Green* I suspect they had to sing Mr Murphy's song very carefully,' points out Paul, before treating us to a recital; 'Mr Murphy is a master baker, Pudding pies and pastry maker, Biscuits buns or birthday cake, Everything is marvellous that Murphy makes…'

By about 1973, modern technology had finally entered the Ashby household in the form of a 1950s-style mono player that resembled a large powder-blue-and-cream make-up box. More similarities – our first spinner of discs was a similar mono contraption, suitably adjusted to enable it to play stereo records (I checked once, having worried that it may be ruining my Electric Light Orchestra singles). Ours was a grey-and-navy-blue affair, most notable for its ability to stack and play a ridiculous amount of consecutive seven-inch singles. For me, the other main attraction was the lovely smell of the valves as they heated up, but for Paul it was more a visual thing: 'My Mum told me not to watch the record going round and round or I'd make myself dizzy. It did. I overbalanced and fell onto it. This was the point when I should have realised that small pieces of black vinyl would have a serious effect upon my life for many years to come. A good job it wasn't an original copy of *Black Sabbath* (for the uninitiated, it's all to do with the Vertigo Records swirly label of the time), otherwise I would probably have regurgitated my Vesta dinner.' Oooh, another connection – Vesta, for years the only thing I could cook on my own in the school holidays when my Mum was at work...

The Ashby family's mono-record-player (happily still in existence, but now providing a handy home for Paul's Dad's drill and collection of rawl plugs, although sadly never for storing make-up) had been inherited from a Mancunian cousin, and just to prove what a generous lot those from that side of the Pennines are, he'd included a selection of seven-inch singles. 'Unfortunately, my cousin must have had quite shite taste, or just mainly given us crap ones, because the only one to catch my fertile imagination was a pre-health-and-safety-paranoia request for someone called James to hold a ladder steady. It was/is tosh, but it bounced along at a fair pace, and was better than the Kathy Kirby, although in retrospect not as good as the Big Bopper or Lord Rockingham's XI singles – I found out years later that Lord Rockingham accompanied himself by beating time on his head with a tea-tray, which gives it extra kudos. In fact I think I should give it another listen...'

Hmmm, I remember some old bloke on *Tiswas* in the late-70s

singing along whilst bashing himself over the head with a tray – one day I'll check to see who this genius was…

Paul's next stage along the musical journey came in the form of parentally-bought Disney storybook singles. 'The young reader followed the story as it was read, turning the page at the sound of a tinkling bell, thus developing Pavlovian responses and making the child more conducive to parental control.' Ooh, you old cynic Paul. Mind you, all I had of similar ilk were two LPs of fairy tales and a jigsaw puzzle of *The Aristocats*…

As 1973 moved into 1974, the black and white telly was doing its evil work, thanks to weekly exposure to *Top of the Pops*, and the record player would enable Paul to purchase then play the bands he was seeing. 'The leather-clad thighs of Ms Suzi Quatro ensured I was soon heading down "Devil Gate Drive". This must have been a post-Yule purchase as I'm fairly sure I was flush with Boots vouchers, and thus bought not just Suzi but also either Alvin (Stardust, not the bloke with them Chipmunks) and his "Coo Ca Choo", or maybe invested in Mud's "Tiger Feet." I still have these, waiting for the day that they somehow gain respectability.'

Yep, with weekly viewings of *Top of the Pops* and bopping to "Tiger Feet", Paul and I were more or less running parallel musically, but in our school-lives, things were about to diverge massively. In 1976 I was at Greystones Middle School, a school as representative of middle-class suburbia as it was ever possible to be, and my natural expected progression (later fulfilled) was to move on to High Storrs Comprehensive School, but Paul was going in an entirely different direction.

'You could say that I was schooled in rock, from experimental electronic to folk, encompassing all the big bands of the era,' says Paul, 'but in 1976 I wrapped my Slade and Wizzard singles in a spotty hankie and headed off to boarding school in deepest Kent.'

Initially ten-year-old Paul got to share a dorm with Terry 'who was mad about David Bowie, although strangely this often took the shape not of *Ziggy*…or *Diamond Dogs*, but of the much derided *Images*. A couple of years passed and I gradually swapped a bizarre passing penchant for Abba and the Barron Knights as the daily strains of Pink Floyd, Led Zeppelin, Dylan and Genesis interspersed with occasional doses of Fairport Convention, Deep Purple and Kraftwerk, took a hold on me. The school was divided into many dorms, and you could guarantee that you could walk down any corridor and hear a selection that would appeal to the average *Mojo* reader now.' That'll be me then...

Quite interesting this though. You see, in 1978 I was mainly exposed to what my brother was listening to, and to what I heard on Radio Hallam, whereas Paul had this whole host of different bands cascading around his ears thanks to the many residents at boarding school, hence he was exposed to a much wider variety of top-notch music than I was, and at a much earlier age. For me, the wider variety came about slightly later, like a year or two, by listening to *The Friday Rock Show* on Radio 1, and Winton Cooper's brilliant show on Radio Sheffield, *Something Else* (I can still hear the anguish and dismay in Winton's voice when he signed off on the occasion of his last show when Radio Sheffield scandalously dropped it). However, both paths led to us citing Yes as the first band we were obsessive about, in that 'they were the first band I really got into and treated as I would now,' explains Paul, and that's exactly how I feel about Yes too (although prior to that Paul was a Slade obsessive, whereas I was a T Rex man, followed by Electric Light Orchestra).

Fulfilling the "big brother" role for Paul at boarding school, in amongst the influences coming from all corners, there was one influence that was singly greater than all the others, an older boy called Mark who 'came from quite a well-off family, and subsequently had not only a decent stereo, but also a collection of LPs well in excess of 100.'

It was through Mark that Paul first heard Hawkwind properly and became acquainted with the Metal bands he read about every week in *Sounds*. 'We used to draw up lists of double and triple albums, like Santana's *Lotus*, and just listen to them in turn, actually immersing ourselves in the music rather than it just being background to whatever else we were doing.' Goodness, this sounds rather similar to John Atkinson having the nuances of *Tales From Topographic Oceans* pointed out to him by a very serious 12-to-13-year-old Belch, and the later super-serious Gong/Yes/King Crimson etc etc sessions Sewer and I would have.

Of course, with so many different influences around, Paul would always find it hard to settle on just one or two major ones, and in 1981/82 he had a room mate who insisted on nightly playings of Jeff Wayne's *War of the Worlds*, and this roomie Paul also considers to be hugely influential, even if he did eventually swap *War of the Worlds* with nightly playings of Pink Floyd's *The Wall*, an album Paul has never been able to listen to in its entirety since (oh go on Paul, it might be a tad depressing, but not half as much as *The Final Cut*) (and can I just put on record that this isn't a criticism – I must be one of the few Floyd fans who loves *The Final Cut*).

Of course, Prog-Rock was not exactly fashionable between 1978 and 1982, but maybe a boarding school existed outside the bounds of fashion? Besides, around 1979 we had the New Wave of British Heavy Metal, and Heavy Rock in general was thus in vogue, so if indeed Paul was worried about such things, there was always a bit of Blue Oyster Cult, UFO, and even Dio-era Sabbath to trendy things up. And then just when it looked like all long-haired music was to be consigned to the dustbin of history, the neo-Prog bands started to emerge in 1982-83, fronted by Marillion, and Paul, like me, was ensnared by their magic, playing their debut album *Script For A Jester's Tear* to death, as he put it. Unlike me though, with Paul Marillion was where Cardiacs appeared in his life, on the infamous Marillion-support tour towards the end of 1984. For me that tour was just another example of my spectacular talent for unknowingly missing Cardiacs that year – I'd slept through their set at Stonehenge Free Festival in June, and now for the first time since they'd hit the big time, Marillion were missing out Sheffield City Hall with that *Real To Reel* tour, so the fact that Fish liked a band called Cardiacs so much he invited them to act as support passed me by completely.

Paul meanwhile was ready to take in Marillion on this 1984 *Real To Reel* tour at the Hammersmith Odeon. 'I think by this time I had either just started college in London or was visiting friends,' he just about remembers. Having attended a number of gigs over the years, he knew that support bands weren't always great but was still expecting good things. However, nothing quite prepared him for Cardiacs who were, don't forget, at that time right in the middle of their garish-face-paint-and-bandsmen-uniforms phase.

'Like 99.9% of the audience I couldn't get my head around these Punky, Ska-ish, Proggy weirdoes with their bizarre time changes, shouty bits, and big pompy bits,' he relates. 'I didn't dismiss them totally, although I may have succumbed to peer pressure and declared them shit. If only I'd known where it would lead me...'

But just how did it lead Paul there? I had to press a little for the answer to this one.

'The truth is I can't properly remember,' he replies sheepishly. 'The gig with Marillion was December 1984, so sometime before Reading Festival in 1986, something must have happened to change my mind. I suspect that it might have been the *Seaside Treats* video.' Oh yes, a video guaranteed to stay in the memory, that's for sure, but then not exactly one that would turn everyone that saw it onto Cardiacs.

Another possible catalyst was a gentleman by the name of Grob, well known for his fanzines and his love of Hawkwind, and according to one interview I read with Cardiacs in *The Organ*, a gentleman who one day decided that Cardiacs were the best band ever.

Paul takes up the story: 'Around this time I was going to gigs at the Marquee on Wardour Street, as well as quite a few other venues around London. At a number of these gigs I, and most of the rest of the audience, were frequently harangued to buy a fanzine by Grob.' (Yep, I myself ended up in possession of one or two Grob fanzines, although I can't remember if I bought them from Grob himself – unlikely as they were all bought at gigs in Sheffield, although it's 100% certain that they were bought at gigs with a Hawkwind connection.)

'Having heard his sales spiel on many occasions,' Paul continues, 'and succumbing to buying his collection of rants, observations and gig listings, I think I may have succumbed further to his offer of a post-gig jazz Woodbine back at his palatial *pied-a-terre* in Kingston. I suspect this was where my brainwashing began…'

Before that Reading gig in 1986, Paul is almost certain that he must have seen them at the Marquee, 'otherwise I doubt I would have been so excited at catching their opening slot at Reading. So, if you're reading this Grob, wherever you are now, I blame you! And you still owe me £200…'

Ah yes, Reading Festival 1986, where Paul and I can be quite certain that our paths crossed without us realising it at the time. There was Paul, getting all excited about Cardiacs playing there having seen them before, and there was I, struggling down via the thumb and a night kipping in a farmer's field outside Marlow, just in time to catch them for the first time, although for me the main attractions on the bill were initially The Enid and Hawkwind.

And so it follows that our tastes in Cardiacs are very similar, but then again, many Cardiacs fanatics will cite the same favourite songs and albums whilst at the same time declaring an unconditional love for a huge percentage of Cardiacs pieces. 'So many bring a lump to the throat, or the feeling of euphoria that precedes throwing my 40-plus frame into the Pond in a desperate attempt to relive my 20-year-old self's energy and enjoyment,' Paul explains, sounding rather familiar.

"Big Ship" seems to especially hit the spot though 'for sheer unadulterated majestic OTT-ness, with "R.E.S." and "Nurses Whispering Verses" there for gurning, shape-pulling euphoric madness.'

Paul's favourite gigs are at either end of the timeline, with all the recent Astoria gigs rating highly 'probably partly due to the anticipation, apart from the one spent largely on the M1.' (Ah yes, I think Ian was with you on the M1 for that one.)

And at the early end of the timeline, there are any of the seven-or-six-piece gigs at the Marquee in the 80s: 'Several hundred people engaged in a stoppy-starty dance of madness, coming out covered in confetti and petals with sweat dripping off, torn clothes, and a big grin…'

That period also saw Paul's first purchase of a Cardiacs

recorded work in the form of *The Seaside* cassette. 'It sadly went AWOL along with my Ford Fiesta in about 1987. I was very happy to replace it with a CDR-ripped copy.' Hardly surprising really, because that version of "Nurses Whispering Verses" is far-and-away the best (another frequent topic on the List).

* * * *

The good thing about liking the kind of music Paul and I do is that even though you go on discovering new sounds and new bands, you still derive much enjoyment from all the old stuff, so the music in your head just builds up and up like a huge stacker-system on an old mono-player. And so whilst Paul may be currently listening to Siouxsie's latest solo album, The Kills, Midlake, Alabama 3, Gogol Bordello, Anti Product, Szeki Kurva (I once got my nose in on an interview that the singer of Szeki Kurva did with The Young Gods, but that's another story) and Sack Trick (I agree, you just have to love a concept album about moon bound penguins), it was refreshing to find that when we arrived back at Paul's house in Nottingham, November 2007, he put on that Yes-at-Wembley 1978 gig, and we both enjoyed it immensely.

Then the next morning I insisted that he put on *The Old Grey Whistle Test* DVD (probably so we could both see what we'd missed out on by not being allowed to stop up in the 70s) and fast-forward it to Yes doing "Yours Is No Disgrace", both of us marvelling at how young Rick Wakeman looked.

Then on the way down to London from Nottingham in Paul's car, we listened to mostly Hawkwind related stuff, and we both happily remembered that when it comes to Space Rock, the Hawks are in a league of their own…

Oh, did I say that we were in Paul's car? Erm, yes. You see, he was driving down to London for the Astoria gig, and to be honest I was still feeling a bit ropey from after the Bristol gig. Besides, it was a bit grey and cold and miserable. So that was another gig I wasn't hitching to.

Heck, it's a good job there was plenty of other stuff to write about…

Chapter Eleven
"In a City Lining"
The Astoria, London,
November 16th 2007

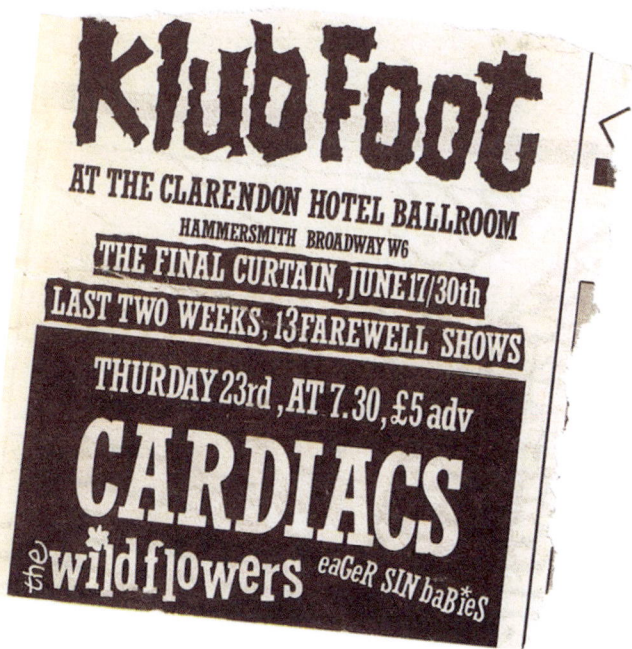

"In A City Lining"
The Astoria, London, November 16ᵗʰ 2007

For a Yorkshire bloke I quite like our capital city. In fact I'd go further than that and state that I love it. There, I've said it. Thank goodness it's in this Cardiacs book and not in the one about Sheffield United. Still probably get some flak for it though…

To me, back in the days before I lived in London a trip to the capital was always something to look forward to, and as these trips were usually for gigs or football matches, which have always featured strongly on my radar, there was always plenty to look forward to. Whilst I always eagerly anticipated Sheffield United matches no matter where they were, when it came to gigs the London ones were always that little bit more special. Maybe it was because for most gigs I stayed around in the city a bit longer (often overnight), and I was pacing the streets in the evening searching for the venue, the evening being when I found London to be at its most vibrant and exciting. Regardless of whether I was arriving on the bus, the train, or in a stranger's car, I'd always get a tremendous buzz as I entered town. Even now, having lived here for over ten years, I still get that buzz and will put down whatever I might be reading in order to soak up the atmosphere and just observe the life being lived out on those streets as I come into town.

My love affair with London started as long ago as 1977 when as an eleven-year-old pupil at Greystones Middle School, Sheffield, my place of learning organised a daytrip to the capital. This was something that I looked forward to for months, not least because at the time I used to count how many Rolls-Royces I'd see in one day, and I figured that there'd be plenty in London. Back then if you saw a car that appealed, you'd shout, 'Foggs that!' and if you got in before anyone else, it was yours (not that anyone ever put this right of ownership to the test by going up to a vehicle, tapping on the window and requesting the driver hand over the keys); I reckoned on plenty of "Foggsing" in London.

Not even the miserable wet day London presented us with could dampen my enthusiasm. I can still remember how awestruck I was by the sight of St Pancras station, and the excitement of using the Tube for the first time. The boat trip down the Thames was a revelation, even if I was sat right under a dripping tarpaulin that ensured I was soaked right through by the time we disembarked. Not that it mattered; our teachers made us watch a 40-odd gun salute in its entirety on the banks of the Thames, ensuring that by the time we moved on to Westminster Abbey all my friends were in the same state. Further trips on the Underground and a studious saunter around the Science and Natural History Museums meant that by the time we boarded the train home, I was suitably dried off. It was still raining when we got back to Sheffield…

Every time I heard a train after that day I thought of that trip to London, and any thoughts of London filled me with excitement and a desire to visit again…

By 1979 my eldest sister Fiona had got married and rather obligingly moved to North London, so more visits were on the cards. The first of these brought about a rather sad tale involving a Rick Wakeman picture disc that I'm not sure I can bring myself to tell you about; well, okay, I'd better, but please remember, I was only 13-years-old at the time…

I believe it was the morning before we set off for London and I'd popped into Impulse Records in Sheffield with the express intention of buying a picture disc, any picture disc, so taken was I with these latest gimmicks. I asked the girl behind the counter how much picture discs were, to which she replied, 'Which one?'

I almost panicked, but instead looked purposely around and much to my relief saw a Rick Wakeman seven-inch picture disc displayed above the counter. I pointed it out to the girl, parted with my cash, and went home feeling most pleased with my purchase, so pleased that I couldn't bring myself to be parted from it, so it travelled down the M1 clutched in my sweaty palms and spent the first weekend of its free life in a flat somewhere near Seven Sisters. Most kids had a teddy-bear; I had "Animal Showdown"/"Seahorses" by Rick Wakeman…

Anyway, I digress… That weekend, Scotland fans either on their way to or on their way from Wembley going bonkers in Trafalgar Square and a rifle through the "Yes" section in HMV Oxford Street (where I discovered hitherto unheard of Yes albums *Time And A Word* and *Yesterdays*) were the things that made the biggest impression on me (although I actually bought *Face The Music* by the Electric Light Orchestra).

Two years later, and my sister had inconsiderately moved to Chelmsford, but by the mid-80s I was almost blasé about visits to London, thanks to the many gigs I attended down that way. Haze provided me with my first London gig when Solstice kindly invited them to be their support at the Marquee on Wardour Street in January 1984. Haze hired a coach to take their fans down from Sheffield, and even though I was a bit slow off the mark, I managed to get a place on it thanks to a late cancellation. The thing that struck me most about the Marquee was how small it was considering its legendary status. I was still in awe though as I thought about all the times Yes and King Crimson had played there.

That following summer Haze were supporting Pendragon there, so off we all went on the coach again. Then one year later, June 1985, Sewer and I were hitching to what we hoped would be the Stonehenge Free Festival (of course, we ended up on Westbury White Horse Hill watching Hawkwind in the rain), and took a detour via London in order to see Patrick Moraz and Bill Bruford at Ronnie Scott's in Soho. Now, this really was a night, and a gig that many veteran Yes fans envy me for, especially as Sewer and I deliberately managed to position ourselves behind Bruford's drumset so we could study his technique; jaw-dropping I'd say (Pierre Moerlen, Bill Bruford, Christian Vander – my top three most-jaw-droppingest live-in-concert drummers). Afterwards we spent the night sleeping in deckchairs in Green Park.

Later that same summer we were back in London to witness the incredible Urban Sax in the grounds of GLC County Hall; sax-players on cherry pickers, sax-players abseiling down the sides of buildings, sax-players running amok amongst the audience – quite a night that one, but possibly most impressive for me was the sight of an illuminated Big Ben as we crossed Westminster Bridge late at night (still gets me, this one).

But perhaps my two favourite London gigs from that mid-to-late-80s period before I left Sheffield were both at the same venue, the Hammersmith Clarendon Hotel Ballroom. One was to see Nik Turner's Fantastic Allstars with Ring as support in November 1987, and the other was to see Cardiacs on June 23rd 1988. I know I've said Stonehenge Free Festival 1984 was the defining moment of my life, but when it comes to defining-gig-moments, these two are right up there, and both have a Cardiacs connection – hooray!

* * * *

The feelings I have for the Nik Turner's Fantastic Allstars gig at the Hammersmith Clarendon Hotel Ballroom in 1987 are somewhat similar to those for the Inner City Unit gig in Bristol back in 1985; a bit of a crazy solo adventure involving plenty of hitchhiking, two gigs, and a certain amount of blagging. This time the plan was to hitch down Friday during the day, see Nik Turner on the Friday night, scrounge somewhere to sleep, explore London on the Saturday, surprise big brother Julian by turning up almost unannounced Saturday evening, kip on his sofa, explore London a bit more, go to see Roger Waters at Wembley Arena Sunday evening, then hitchhike back to Sheffield through the night. A bit hopeful maybe, but of course, it worked perfectly…

It worked perfectly despite me not actually knowing exactly where the venue was, but then that was an old trick of mine; turn up at what I assumed was the nearest tube station then follow my nose. On this occasion I took the sensible option of asking a hippy-looking chap where the venue was as I exited Hammersmith tube station. It turned out to be about 20 yards away, so I hefted my rucksack through the door and started to mount the seemingly endless stairs. The way I remember it, I was about half-way up when I had to pay and opted to leave my rucksack behind the desk with the nice foreign girl stationed there. At the same time I heard someone from the venue talking about the support band and whether they'd be able to use their pyrotechnics; 'They've got some fire-jugglers and I'm not sure we'll be able to let them perform,' he was saying, proving that even in the 80s the health and safety people were having their say.

Well, to me fire-jugglers meant that support band Ring sounded jolly interesting, so I bounced up the stairs in order to catch the start of their set and was delighted to see (and hear) that they were something akin to a cross between Hawkwind and Cardiacs, what with the monotonous repetitive synths, poetry readings, clockwork guitars, slap-dash make-up and stoppy-starty rhythms. Not forgetting the health-and-safety-defying fire-jugglers and the crazy little bloke wearing a white coat running around amongst the audience with toilet roll and gaffer-tape.

My perceived Cardiacs influence was well-founded as it turned out, featuring as they did a certain Bic on guitar who two years later would be performing with Cardiacs, and also Bob White on keyboards, a future member of Levitation and Dark Star (both times alongside Bic). And their appreciation of Hawkwind became even more apparent when during Nik Turner's set the bloke in the white coat could be seen snapping away with his camera.

And what of Mr Turner himself? I think I'm right in believing this was the Allstars' first gig in London, so most of the Crusties, Hippies and Punks in the audience were probably expecting something more in line with Uncle Nik's recent past, but Nik soon put them right by announcing with a huge grin that if anyone was expecting any Hawkwind or Inner City Unit songs then they were going to be disappointed. Well, judging by the audience reaction any disappointment felt was short lived as they grooved the night away with the best of them.

Of course, I was having a groove-tastic time myself, but I still had one thing troubling me; where on earth was I going to spend the night? (And before you ask, for whatever reasons troubling my London-based brother Julian late on Friday wasn't an option – I'd just bother him late on the Saturday instead.) Well, I had a plan; use the fact that after various ligging sessions at Inner City Unit and Fantastic Allstars gigs, Nik Turner definitely knew who I was. So, as he came out for the encore I waved my arms about like an idiot to attract his attention. He spotted me and came over to see what I wanted. I explained my predicament and mentioned that I'd come all the way down from Sheffield. Nik nodded then strolled back to his microphone stand and made the following announcement, word for word: 'There's a mate of mine over here needs somewhere to stay tonight. He's here (points at me sitting on front of stage next to the PA speaker facing the audience, I wave like an idiot again). He's come all the way from Sheffield and he's a really good friend of mine, so if anyone's got anywhere he can stay I'd be most grateful and I'm sure he would too.' A really good friend of Nik's? That should do it...

It did. At the end of the gig this chap came over to me and said, 'You can stop at my place if you like,' so I stuck with him and all his mates. Before we left to trek across London I had to pick up my rucksack from behind the desk. Stuffed in there somewhere was an alarm clock which, as far as I could tell, had no "switch-off" time, in that it would just ring and ring (very loudly) until I got up and switched it off. I'd never actually tested it out to see how long it would go on for until it did stop...

'Is there an alarm clock in there?' asked the nice foreign girl behind the desk as she handed my rucksack over to me. The look on her face suggested she certainly knew how long it would go on for before stopping...

As I ventured out into the cold London night air with my new-found friends, I felt on top of the world. This was sort-of living life on the edge, but a safe edge (I reckoned) nevertheless. It got even more on the edge as we ventured across London. I should have guessed something about their lifestyle choices by the fact that we got all the way from Hammersmith to Bounds Green on the Tube without paying (no ticket barriers in those days), but then at least they paid for the fish and chips in North London (no mushy peas or curry sauce – what kind of a chippy was this?), so they obviously weren't such big anarchists after all. But wait, what was this? As we curved around the North Circular on foot they started to walk up the path of a house that was all boarded up. They needed a key to get in, but erm, well, this was a squat. Fantastic! I'm sure many people of my acquaintance would have been horrified by this, but I was intrigued and even excited. It was a terrible mess in there, and the toilet would only flush with the help of a bucket of water, but as we sat around listening to Hawkwind and Inner City Unit and talking about Stonehenge, I felt so at home that the fact that home was actually over 150 miles away mattered not one bit.

I ended up sleeping on a mattress in a room shared with three complete motorbikes (and many more in bits all over the floor and on the wall). Every time I woke up I briefly wondered where I was, saw the shadowy motorbikes looming, remembered, then went back to sleep all happy.

The rest of the weekend went well in that my brother was happy to put me up Saturday night and Roger Waters was stunning on the Sunday. I even managed an interesting hitch up the M1 through the night via Manchester (it was the only lift I could get) and a train (the car I was in broke down in Moss Side), but by far the biggest highlights of the weekend were the Nik Turner/Ring gig of the Friday evening and my first experience of a squat, alongside all the excitement the great city of London had to offer, and it was on these events that I looked back with most fondness over 20 years on from my great adventure.

By December 2006, I'd still not seen Ring again (and it's doubtful I ever will as they ceased to exist many many years ago), but Zag and the Coloured Beads, who had connections with Ring in that they shared a member or two, semi-rectified this sorry state of affairs by reforming and doing a gig at the Bull & Gate in Kentish Town, their first gig in something like 15 years. Of course, I sauntered along.

So impressed was I that I bought both their newly-transferred-to-CDR tape albums, tape albums that were originally flogged at all manner of underground gigs and squat parties in those mid-80s times. Having witnessed the gig and studied the artwork on *Loaf Of Legs* and *Sawtooth Gripmaster*, I really felt like I had been transported back in time to those dangerous-but-exciting days, back to an alternative scene that was heaving in London back then, a scene that I'd just about scratched the surface of with that night in London, November 20th 1987.

Of course, the Cardiacs List is wonderful for many things, but perhaps the most fascinating thing is reminiscing and discovering how many listees had been at particular non-Cardiacs gigs in the past. As it happened, I wasn't the only Listee in the Clarendon Hotel Ballroom that night. Jill, the original Zag WAG, had been manning the Ring t-shirt stall – if only I'd have given my alarming-rucksack to her for safe-keeping, eh? And Sneaky Pete Moltesen had not only been there, he'd recorded the gig. Sadly he'd lost the Ring recording, but he still had the Nik Turner one. On reading this I got very excited and told him to dig it out and listen out for Nik trying to get me a place to kip for the night. Pete duly reported back that it was all there, and what's more he even ran me off a CDR copy, bunging it in the post to me so I could relive the magic all over again.

Now, you really didn't think the reason I knew word-for-word what Nik Turner had said about me from the stage was that I'd been sad enough to memorise it all and store it in my head for 21 years did you? Well, did you…?

* * * *

Seven months later in June 1988 I was holed-up in Cholderton Woods along with several-thousand others, four miles from Stonehenge, freaking to Poisoned Electrick Head (amongst others) and plotting how we were all going to get into the ancient monument that year. Amongst all this activity, I bumped into my old mates from the Bounds Green squat. Hugs all round, we reminisced and briefly relived some great moments. I excitedly told them that just a few days after Summer Solstice I'd be back at the Hammersmith Clarendon Hotel Ballroom again, this time to see Cardiacs…

Yep, it was another of my mad adventures, this one being as follows; hitch from Sheffield to Stonehenge, find out where everyone was, hang out there until Solstice, retreat to the New Forest for a couple of nights, hitch to London, see Cardiacs at the Clarendon Hotel

Ballroom, sleep rough in London, hitch to Clare in Suffolk, spend three days or so in the company of The Enid at Lodge Farm, cadge lift home with friends. Quite a full week or so. Well, you'll be glad to know that the tales from Stonehenge that year will have to wait until I do a book on my Summer Solstice adventures (been talking about doing that for years), so all we'll concern ourselves with here is the bit about Cardiacs.

Suffice to say, after the mayhem of the early hours of June 21st I was ready for that rest in the Red Shoot Campsite, Linwood, in the New Forest. Trouble was, I didn't really get it thanks to extreme sunburn (not for the last time), and the fact that some party animals from Luton pitched-up their tent right next to mine having come straight off Salisbury Plain themselves. Lord Doom was the name of one of them, and one of his friends, Kate, was surely "the one"; these days I'd have got her mobile number and email address and would probably have married her by now – as it was, I just waved a sad farewell as they drove off in their bright orange VW Beetle.

I then walked to Ringwood and hitched it from there to London, making it to the Clarendon in such good time that I arrived before the band, and even before Richard who was hitching down from Sheffield. Knowing how steep the stairs were, when Cardiacs showed I did the decent thing and helped hump those flight cases all the way up, although Tim Quy warned me and Richard that as this was London, there wouldn't be a spot available on the guest list. The thing was, I was unemployed at the time and I was totally skint, Richard being in exactly the same situation. We *had* to blag our way in, or else miss the gig altogether. There was talk of the Alphabet Business Concern kidnapping us and holding us captive, and there was talk of us hiding in empty flight cases. In the end we settled on a compromise – we'd hide in Cardiacs' dressing room.

However, we reckoned without the officious security on duty that night. They chose the moment when every single representative of the Alphabet Business Concern was present in the dressing room before literally kicking the door open and demanding that everyone get their passes ready. Not a word was spoken as they went round the room, Richard and me observing silently as they checked some passes two, even three times. It was a bit like being on Death Row as we awaited the inevitable, us being sat nearest the door and so likely to be the last checked. However, having checked everyone else, one of them merely nodded vaguely in our direction before they both exited. The outpouring of relief from myself when they'd gone had the room in uproar. 'What's it like to be invisible?' said one voice. Mighty fine, I can tell you…

After that scare Richard and I decided to take no more risks, so whilst everyone else went off to the pub, we remained in the dressing room, the Clarendon employees obviously thinking we were part of the band judging by the way they asked us what time we were onstage and who our manager was. Even better, they brought in a big jug and a bucket or three of ice; 'Your drinks are here,' one of them announced, so as it was a hot day, Richard and I wiled away the two support bands' slots by drinking all Cardiacs' orange juice.

That night's gig was a total barnstormer, it being my first Cardiacs London gig and only my fifth ever. I was pressed right up against the front, and I got some smashing snaps on my bright green 110 instamatic camera (it got confetti stuck on it and it never came off). Tim was in a lively old mood and his face-pulling was in a class of its own. The set was a mad mixture of old stuff and the new material they'd played for the first time just a few weeks before at Scunthorpe Baths Hall, perhaps the most memorable song being "The Everso Closely Guarded Line". The set wound up with "Big Ship" and "Is This the Life" with what I described in my journal at the time as "a fantastic instrumental" in between (probably "Cameras"). But they saved the best for the encore. "R.E.S." was a song I'd not heard Cardiacs play over the previous four gigs I'd seen them perform; this I put down to the fact that it was an incredibly difficult tune to play. Indeed, every time I listened to *A Little Man And A House And The Whole World Window* I used to smile knowingly to myself when "R.E.S." came on knowing that it was too complicated to play live. Well, no more knowing smiles from now on as first up for the encore was "R.E.S.", and I stood there in dumbfounded silence as they played it note-perfect. I should have known better really – I'd soon learn that nothing was out of bounds with Cardiacs when it came to complexity.

Just as on the album, "R.E.S." was followed by "The Whole World Window", this being the first time I'd seen them play it since that first viewing at Reading Festival 1986, and in the crushed-up atmosphere of a hot, sweaty indoor gig it possibly came across even better as the Consultant and Miss Swift entered the stage at the end with balloons, champagne, flowers and buckets of confetti. The build-up to the last crescendo was topped off by one final loudest-of-them-all BANG on the confetti cannons, and as the confetti drifted down majestically from above, the devotees were in raptures.

I remember thinking as Richard and I walked out into the this-time-warm London air afterwards that I had probably never been to a better gig ever, surpassing even Yes at the NEC in 1984.

We headed for a kebab shop and Bill Drake was in there. He had a bit of confetti stuck to his head, so I told him he matched my camera. After that, Richard and I went for a walk to try and find somewhere to sleep. A combination of safety in numbers (well, two of us) and a warm night meant there was no need for the shelter of a squat this time. No, we found Shepherds Bush Green and promptly settled down for a night of broken slumber in a playground on a bed of woodchips, woodchips I'd be removing from my clothing and underwear for days to come.

The following morning, after a visit to the first Tardis toilet we'd ever seen, Richard and I went our separate ways. I believe he went down to Maidstone to see Cardiacs the following night at Kent Hall, but I tubed it up to the north of London and hitchhiked out of town in the direction of Clare in Suffolk for an appointment with The Enid at the Clare Carnival and a weekend of fun and frolics with Sewer and friends (and of course, this trip wasn't straightforward – this time it was big sister Fiona who got the unexpected visit as she tried to get on with family life in Chelmsford), but good as The Enid were, when I got home there was only one gig on my mind – Cardiacs at the Clarendon Hotel Ballroom in the vibrant city of London, up until that point quite possibly the best gig I'd ever been to in my whole life.

* * * *

So, Cardiacs at the Astoria, London on November 16th 2007, my 95th Cardiacs gig in all, had quite a lot to live up to, and to be perfectly honest it never really stood a chance. Not because I was expecting them to be rubbish, far from it, but probably more to do with the fact that London gigs had long-since lost that added excitement since I'd been living there for over nine years now. Add to that the fact that I always felt Cardiacs came across better in the more intimate settings (give me a Windsor Old Trout over an Astoria anytime), and that the staff at the Astoria could be, shall we say, a trifle brusque in their efforts to clear the building in order to get G-A-Y in after us, and you start to look more fondly on a cramped night in Bristol.

Having said that, the wonderful thing about all the recent preceding Astoria gigs had been that they were massive social events, largely due to them sometimes being the only gigs, or certainly amongst only a handful of gigs, Cardiacs would do in a year. But this time it was part of the biggest headlining tour for eight years, so every night was a social night. And one other thing – the Astoria gig to end all Astoria gigs had been in 2001 when they did "The Whole World Window" for the first time in yonks (and up until now, the last time), and as anyone who witnessed the anticipation and excitement and grown men in tears of that night will tell you, that was never likely to be surpassed this time round, if ever.

But of course, this was still a Cardiacs gig, and because it was in the capital city at the largest venue of the tour, this was still destined to be the biggest social occasion of the year, so we still had plenty to get excited about; I'm just being all contradictory and fussy…

Such a social occasion was it that Big Ship Iron had done his usual and brought a busload down from Doncaster, including family, friends and employees. He introduced me to his younger brother Keith ('Better looking than me, Belchy,' he announced), and his employees moaned good-naturedly that they'd be back home in the wee-small-hours, but Mr Big Ship Iron would still expect them in on time for work at 6am. 'Aye well, I've treated 'em all to their tickets, so it's to be expected,' he smiled in reply.

In the venue the employees manning the cloakroom were less understanding than their Clarendon counterpart from 1987 had been. They watched me tie my coat, trousers and long-sleeved t-shirt to my full-to-busting rucksack then told me I'd have to pay for each individual item.

'I tell yer what,' I spluttered, 'I'll unpack the whole lot and you can charge me for everything in there if that's the way yer going.'

'It's just policy,' said the jobsworth behind the counter, 'we can't accept items on the outside of a bag unless they are paid for individually, even if they are tied on.'

'Why not?' I asked, not unreasonably I felt.

He couldn't give me an answer, so after an uneasy silence he fell back on, 'It's just policy...'

Muttering dark threats, I withdrew my baggage-with-attachments and proceeded to put on quite a show as I tried to repack the whole bloomin' caboodle and squeeze everything inside. When security started telling me to hurry up I very nearly lost it good and proper, but then to my rescue came a rarity in that establishment, a Sensible Employee.

'What're you doing?' he asked.

I explained the whole sorry problem along with my unwillingness to hand over a whole wodge of wonga to the cloakroom.

'Well, don't waste time trying to cram all that lot in your rucksack,' he said, 'let me get you a couple of binliners.'

And so he came back with the promised rubbish-sacks and proceeded to lower my rucksack into one and put the other over the top. Now everything, including tied-on clothing, was safely tucked up inside. Impressed I most definitely was, and there may have been a hint of triumphalism as I handed over my now-legal baggage to the jobsworth in the cloakroom.

And so the social occasion continued. For the first time on the tour, Andy Thompson was there with the lovely lady in his life

Lisa, and there was Katherine In A Cupboard's Lee from Rotherham, latterly of Cambridge (and the person responsible for running me off copies of Ring tapes long after they'd become unavailable) looking like he'd been enjoying himself a bit too much, and Big Ship Iron had now ventured in with his whole entourage. Best of all though I spotted Sarah, the only one of my ex-girlfriends to have met me at a Cardiacs gig, twelve years on and still going strong on the Cardiacs front; still one of my best friends ever, it goes without saying that she was and still is totally gorgeous. Upon meeting her Big Ship Iron said, 'Belch, she is beautiful! Why ever did you split up with her…?'

'Ah, it wasn't that straight forward,' I smiled (sort of), 'but you're right, she IS beautiful…'

Michael from Circulus was spotted in the balcony and waved to, so he came down to say hello, telling us that Cath, Cardiacs percussion and vocals, had invited him as her guest, and that also his whole band, except for stalwart Will of the Crumhorns, had left him. 'Actually I'm quite relieved,' he said, 'I can rebuild the band now and just get on with it.'

There was one notable absentee though; where was Ian? After all, I'd donated the ticket originally earmarked for Julia to him and he'd still not paid me for it… As it turned out he'd set off driving down from Kettering, but was so tired he'd felt himself nodding off at the wheel, so figuring that it'd be better to survive to see a few more gigs in the future, he'd be better off turning around and heading back home. In my younger days I'd have called him a wuss, but that would probably have been a bit harsh…

Jon Poole's band, the God Damn Whores, were of course support again, and for the first time on the tour I got to see their whole set, and even though I still wouldn't rush out and buy their album, I have to say they were very entertaining.

As for Cardiacs, they were actually on top form and with the added bonus of the Astoria's massive lightshow it really was something of a spectacle. The Pond was absolutely bonkers, and there really did seem to be the most people I'd ever witnessed at the Astoria bumping around in there (and there are photos to prove it, what with me looking all breathless in my sleeveless t-shirt showing off my tat-too).

A brilliant night then, but then as we were all shooed out into the street by the happy staff, and as we all piled into the Angel, the debate raged; was it better than the Thekla? I reckoned not, but then I'm just a fussy old musical snob sometimes… In the Angel Michael presented the two Circulus albums to Big Ship Iron which triggered a whole chain of events still reverberating now (another story, I know). There was also much talk of who, how and where as regards the aftershow party.

It seemed to me that attempting entry to the aftershow was a whole load of hassle with no guarantee of much at the end anyhow. Besides, I'd seen most of Cardiacs slouched on the tour bus looking even less in the party mood than I was. After a week of much travel-ling, much gigging, and much feeling a bit grotty, I just fancied going home to bed, so I did, albeit after much debate in front of a new bunch of mates (made on MySpace) from the North West, including the cheerful Chippy who seemed most amused by my vague mutter-ings about the best route home (oh, how easy it was when I lived in Hackney). For the record, knowing that I'd miss the last train to Ash-ford from Waterloo if I tried the Cross London Dash, I opted for the tube to Hatton Cross, the bus to Feltham, and a conveniently-lost black cab home to Ashford.

My ears were ringing, my body was aching, my head was pounding, and I was nearly glad to be home. But as I observed the tranquillity and safeness of Ashford, Middlesex, quite possibly the dullest place on earth, I reckoned I'd much rather be in a squat in Bounds Green flushing the toilet with a bucket of water.

Chapter Twelve
"Baby Heart Dirt"
Those Long Suffering Girlfriends

"Baby Heart Dirt"
Those Long Suffering Girlfriends

Annie and I sat there watching Cardiacs' *Seaside Treats* video in silence. We were a few months into our relationship so I felt fairly comfortable letting her in on the secret delights of "The Consultant's Flower Garden". However, there wasn't much of a response from her thus far, nothing in fact but silence. Silence, that is, until the video was completely finished.

When it was done, Annie opened her mouth as if to speak, then paused briefly. And then it came: 'If you'd shown me that before we'd gone on our first date, I'd never have had anything to do with you ever again,' she pronounced. Blimey dear, was it the messy face-paint, or the rather off-putting eating habits on "To Go Off and Things"? Or maybe it was the bit when the Consultant found Bill "interfering with himself"? Whatever, she wasn't overly impressed. Good job I'd already won her over with that first date really, a first date that just happened to take in a trip from Brackley to London (via Banbury) to see Cardiacs at the Marquee Club (the Charing Cross Road version), December 21st 1988. Our relationship lasted near-on five years, so she must have been quite impressed…

* * * *

Fumbling around in the dark

Up until that point in December 1988 I'd always had difficulty in persuading girls that coming to a gig with me was a good way to spend an evening. Admittedly, Rick Wakeman or Jon Anderson at Sheffield City Hall may not have seemed attractive to members of the opposite sex, but then when I discovered the Leadmill I figured that here was a club that would surely make *me* seem attractive in their eyes. Sewer was my gig-going buddy by then, September 1983 being our first Leadmill visit, to see Solstice supported by local Prog-Rock heroes Haze. Eventually our rantings and ravings about Haze began to rub off, leading to a whole gang of us regularly turning up at their gigs whether they be at the Leadmill, the George IV, the Hallamshire, or Sheffield University. And what do you know, in amongst this gang were quite a number of girls from the High Storrs

School 6th Form (well Liz at least, and she'd probably dipped out of school by then anyway).

As 1984 progressed Sewer and I were almost in danger of becoming fashionable when Marillion carried on storming the charts, so when they played Sheffield City Hall on the *Fugazi* tour there was more than just Liz representing the fairer sex. However, they all had seats in the Circle whereas Sewer and I, well, we were hardcore so we were in the stalls pushing around at the front and harassing Fish by shouting for "Madcap's Embrace". Just before the gig started we heard 'Sewer! Belch!' (his name always came first for some reason, not that I'm bitter you understand), and we turned around to see Liz, Amanda and Jane all waving like mad in our direction. Still, regardless of Marillion's popularity, none of the ladies in our little gig-going group seemed to want to marry us as a result of this, and as the years advanced it felt like I was ploughing an ever more lonesome furrow (sniff).

Mind you, by the time of my second Cardiacs gig, at the Leadmill on April 23rd 1988 (my first being Reading Festival 1986 remember) I was perhaps beginning to have a little success. Barbara, a friend of mine from church, was working on behalf of Cardiacs trying to Push and Plug their "Is This The Life" single up the charts, so she managed to get me a spot on the guest list (the first of many); "Push and Plug Promotions plus 1," it said, and that "1" was Katey (I'm sure that's how she spelled it). Katey was glad to accept my invitation, and she seemed to quite enjoy the gig, but that potential relationship went nowhere, my interest subsiding when some male friend of the bloke she was with in Rebels Night Club one night told me to 'keep out of the way Belch'. I heeded that advice and moved to the South Midlands.

* * * *

Annie and the Whole World Window
So, there I was in Brackley, Northamptonshire, October/November 1988, aged 22, deputy-managing the Circle K convenience store there and flirting with Annie, a teenager who worked on the till Saturdays only. On days off I was madly hitchhiking all over the place

either to see Sheffield United or Cardiacs, more often than not travelling back through the night in order to get to work on time. Perhaps to Annie I appeared mysterious and attractive, or perhaps she just thought I was a nutter. Either way, when I got Nora (another till worker) to do my dirty work for me by asking Annie if she was interested in Cardiacs at the Marquee, the message passed back to me as I cowered in the Manager's Office was that she'd be up for it providing I didn't make her hitchhike. 'Tell her we can travel however she wants to,' I replied in a bit of a swoon if truth be known.

Well, we went on the train and once in London I wooed her with food in a greasy spoon just off Tottenham Court Road and a spot on the guest list for Cardiacs (goodness knows how I did this for a London gig). As for the gig itself (I still have the setlist for this one) I think she was intrigued rather than hugely impressed for the main part, but then "The Whole World Window" with the confetti cannons and such-like totally blew her away, just as it had done with me at Reading Festival in 1986. Years later she was still going on about it. Sealing the gig for me though was the not-even-on-the-setlist bonus of "Nurses Whispering Verses" as a final encore, complete with Mr Walmsley shovelling fake snow out of a bucket from up on the balcony (December 21st you see, Christmas), but for Annie "The Whole World Window" was the clincher. The relationship was sealed when we passed up the chance to crash the St Moritz Club with the band and headed back to Marylebone Station instead in an attempt to get home. We missed the last train but a friendly Night Station Manager told us what time the first one in the morning was, then pointed us in the direction of an empty room used when passengers fell ill. We spent the night snuggled up on a sick bed all happy and in love, and when we got on that first train to Banbury in the morning it seemed we were an item.

And so from then on Annie was my regular companion at most Cardiacs gigs attended up until we went our separate ways in 1993. She bought t-shirts and badges but never any albums ('I love them live but can't listen to them on record,' she said). Some of our happiest moments were at Cardiacs gigs, Aylesbury Civic Centre

June 23rd 1989 being one of my personal favourites…

I'd hitchhiked across the country after my latest attempt on
Stonehenge at Summer Solstice, picking up lots of dirt and sunburn
on the way so that when I met Annie on Aylesbury Station I was this
horrible mixture of red skin, muck, and blue aftersun soothing gel.

No room on the guest list meant we had to hide in the building for long periods, amusing ourselves by staging mock chariot
races on the stacks of chairs in the main (too large for Cardiacs) concert hall, all whilst being entertained by William D. Drake and Tim
Quy who both appeared (separately) up in the circle and started to
perform on the pipe organ until they were moved on by an officious
caretaker. He kept moving us on too but it was one of those lovely
big buildings where there was always somewhere to hide until the
gig started.

It was a ridiculously hot day, and after a fabulously energetic
gig we all needed cooling down, so as the Civic Centre staff cleared
everyone, band included, out of the dressing room and onto the
street, we were directed through a kitchen featuring a freezer full of
Cornettos, so everyone helped themselves, happily munching our
way across the famous Market Square as Heroes, speeding the beat
of the street pulse on into the night…

Annie's last Cardiacs gig was at St. Helen's Citadel on July
3rd 1993. By this time she'd learned to drive (something I never mas-
tered) and on this occasion had agreed to my madcap plan of driving up from Brackley on the Saturday evening after I finished work
at 5 o'clock. Well, we made pretty good time arriving just before
Cardiacs took to the stage, but unfortunately the gig was sold out, or
so the doorman said.

'Look, we just drove over 200 miles to get here,' I pleaded.

'Well, that'll be a fiver each then,' he replied. So I gave him
a tenner, which he put straight into his inside-jacket-pocket, then
looked the other way as we crept in.

Throughout those five years there was another Cardiacs Couple we always used to see whose ages seemed to match ours, and

we'd always have a chat in the Pond. I still see him now and again at Cardiacs gigs and we exchange nods, but like me his female companion is no longer by his side. Tim perhaps summed it up best when he said Annie's Big Flower t-shirts were probably all folded up neatly at the bottom of her wardrobe, never to be worn again…

* * * *

Sarah, the brightest spot in Milton Keynes

Sarah Hailey is unique in many ways, but perhaps most importantly in my life history for being the only one of my girlfriends to have met me at a Cardiacs gig. Indeed, so life-changing was that day I can remember pretty much everything that happened on May 24th 1995.

At the time I was a Night Manager at Tesco Brackley and was due a night off on the day of that Milton Keynes gig. However, I'd worked the night before and as the night progressed my sniffly cold got worse and worse. For my sins during that shift I'd had to fill produce (that's fruit and veg to the layman) and things got so bad I tied a toilet roll to a piece of string and hung it around my neck for convenience sake. I also attached a clear binliner to my belt and carried it around with me all night, so by the time the Duty Manager came in that following morning I had a bag full of snotty bog roll and looked a little worse for wear myself.

'Can we skip the walk-round 'cos I feel rough as a badger's arse?' I asked. The Duty Manager took one look at my sack full of nasties and hastily agreed, but only if I chucked all my snot rags down the compactor before I left.

So off home I went hoping that a day of sleep would make me feel better. It didn't really, but I had a night off and Cardiacs were playing fairly locally so there was no way I was missing out. Besides, Ian worked at Record Savings in Banbury, and through this had connections to the promoter, so we'd got ourselves on the guest list, and the Pitz at Milton Keynes Woughton Centre was one of those venues where they'd promised us sticky-on cloth patches; so I was going, right?

I met Ian at his place of work and we hitchhiked from Banbury to Milton Keynes, somehow finding the venue in amongst all the roundabouts and roads that looked exactly the same. As we sat in the bar prior to the gig it was obvious to all who saw me that I was not well as I snotted and sneezed over everything and everyone. This didn't stop people from coming over for a chat though, including numerous representatives of the Alphabet Business Concern, a bloke wearing a Peter Hammill jumper (a JUMPER! I trust his mum knitted it for him), and some chap who lived nearby called Malc who engaged me and the Skinner in a spot of King Crimson *Thrak* conversation.

As we sat there in the bar trying to work out if we were in a gig venue or a sports centre, in walked this most incredibly beautiful blonde girl wearing Doc Marten's boots and a *Heaven Born And Ever Bright* t-shirt.

'Close the betting! We have a winner!' I exclaimed to Ian, 'Chick of the Day is here! She won't be beaten...' I sighed wistfully (yes, I'm ashamed to announce that Ian and I used to regularly hold a Chick of the Day competition). Ian didn't have much to say, probably because he couldn't get a word in edgeways as I went on and on about how this girl was perfect in every way. But how to introduce myself?

I had a whole gig to think about it. Meanwhile, she almost had a rival with the arrival at the front of the stage of a homely looking girl in a Big Flower t-shirt. My judgement was that 'She (Homely Girl) is the type of girl you'd take home to meet your mum, whereas she (Stunning Blonde Girl) is the type of girl you'd just take home...'

Amongst the flashing strobes and pounding drums of Cardiacs' stage entrance (after a twenty-minute intro tape), Tim picked up a water bottle and crouched down in front of me as I was in pole position under his microphone stand.

'You've got a cold haven't you,' he said.

'Yes,' I replied, so Tim duly squirted the water full in my face. I must say, I wasn't too impressed with this, but you know what? It actually served to clear my head, nose, the lot (but folks, it's not a cure I'd recommend for home) so I was able to enjoy the rest of the night relatively snot and snuffle free.

Meanwhile, I kept Stunning Blonde Girl in my sights and was particularly impressed when she and her boots did a groovy little dance to "Arnald". At the end of the gig I was delighted to see that she was hanging around at the side of the stage leading to the backstage area, so Ian and I decided to make our passes look prominent (we'd stuck them on the thighs of our jeans, so thrusting our thighs forward seemed a perfectly natural thing to do). She was with a friend, so I came out with the stunningly original line of, 'Did you enjoy the gig then girls?'

In amongst the general Cardiacs-related chatter (it seemed her big brother had got her into them) I promised her and her mate that if they stuck close to us and our passes, we'd get them into the dressing room to meet the band. It would seem she'd already got them to sign her beer bottle or something, but hopefully my offer promised something more. Anyway, the two of them stuck close to the two of us and into the dressing room we all trooped (it's fair to say that Security didn't seem to give two hoots who went backstage by this time anyway).

I spent a good half hour chatting to Stunning Blonde Girl until someone came in shouting, 'Is there a Sarah Hailey here?'

'Yes, that's me,' said Stunning Blonde Girl.

'Your mum's waiting outside and she's not very happy,' came the reply.

'I've got to go,' she said to me.

Gulp. Make or break time, Belchy. As she didn't appear to be about to do a Cinderella and leave a Doc Marten boot behind, I whipped my Tesco Personal Organiser out of my pocket along with a pen and said to her, 'Before you go, stick your name and address in here.'

When she handed it back to me she said, 'I've put my phone number in there as well,' (phone numbers were much more important and difficult to get back in the days when none of us had mobiles) and then she was gone.

For the rest of the night as Ian and I ligged a bit more, and then as we hitched home, all I could do was alternate between exclaiming, 'She's called Sarah!' (it has always been a favourite name of mine) and, 'She gave me her phone number!'

Of course, I duly made that phone call a day or two later (and one can only speculate whether I'd have gone round and knocked on Sarah's door if she had only given me her address) and after a few nice little dates (can you believe I hitched over to Milton Keynes for our first date, was late, and she waited for me?) we became an item.

Unlike with Annie, mine and Sarah's relationship only lasted eight months, and in that time we only attended two Cardiacs gigs as a couple, including a rather memorable weekend at Long Marston Airfield for the Phoenix Festival of 1995. When Sarah had bought tickets for this one she'd still been with her ex and so he was there too, all of which led to a rather interesting few days, let's say (ho hum).

Well, I know I said mine and Sarah's relationship only lasted eight months, but that was just as boyfriend and girlfriend. In truth, our relationship has been ongoing ever since because out of all my ex-girlfriends she's the one I've stayed in touch with the most and remained the closest to. Back in 1995 when we first met there was a pretty hefty age gap between us, and you'll never guess, but there still is (well, I never), but it didn't seem to matter then and nobody seems to notice now (is it because I've always been a bit of a youth at heart, or is it because she's still jaw-droppingly beautiful?).

After we split up in 1996 we had a few dodgy spells, but by 1998 when I announced to all and sundry that I was moving to London to manage a rather insane Industrial Hardcore Jazz band from Slovakia, the Jesus Underground Band (worthy of a book all to themselves), Sarah and I were closer than ever, absolute best buddies. When I first hit London I was living in Canning Town with the band but working in Pinner Green for Tesco, whilst Sarah was at college in Amersham, not too far from Pinner, so many's the time she'd drive down to pick me up from work, after which we'd negotiate the London traffic to get to the madhouse that was the communal abode of the Jesus Underground Band, ticking off all the landmarks as we went (FLICK FASHIONS was a particular favourite).

I'd go so far as to say that at this time Sarah and I were almost inseparable (well, as inseparable as it's possible to be when one lives in East London and the other in Milton Keynes), and she was often there with me in the Pond at Cardiacs gigs, and still is of course, although the joys of motherhood have lessened her attendance somewhat, but she still does the London ones, oh yes.

But with Sarah my fondest memory (well, apart from the time she went to Londis next to our house in Canning Town wearing her pyjamas) is probably when Jesus Underground Band did a gig in a pub in Peterborough. As with most bands we had our circle of close friends who seemed to make it to every gig, but nobody got to this one (in fact we only just made it ourselves). Nobody that is except for Sarah. Okay, it wasn't too far for her to drive over from Milton Keynes, but she made it, and none of our other friends did. The boys in the band were delighted and kept telling me all night how special Sarinka (their Slovak pet name for her) was.

As we had a bit of quiet time together prior to JUB creating mayhem in such a nice pub I said to Sarah, 'Well, you made it and no-one else did. You don't realise how comforting that is for us playing a gig somewhere like this.'

'Well, I couldn't let you down,' she smiled.

Rinks, I love you now as much as I did the day I first met you, and you know for a fact that I always will. x x x

* * * *

Annette and trouble at Tesco

Now Annette was pretty unique too, in more ways than one, not least because she was my first foreign girlfriend, her being of German birth. But for the purposes of this book her uniqueness sprung from the fact that she was the only girlfriend of mine to strike up a conversation with me because of the Cardiacs t-shirt I was sporting when we first met. Let me explain…

By autumn 1997 I was still slaving away as a Night Manager for Tesco, and if ever I had a Friday night off I was determined to do something with it. On this occasion however all my usual routes were closed off, despite making numerous phone calls. Ian was off somewhere with his then-girlfriend Maggie, Sarah was stuck in Milton Keynes, and Clayre (Claire – I'll explain elsewhere) was off to Hinton-in-the-Hedges with her then-bloke.

Well, I was still determined to do something with the evening so wolfed down a Tesco Thai Curry ready meal, realised this wouldn't make me attractive to the opposite sex, swilled my mouth out with Listerine, accidentally swallowed some, nearly threw up, held it off (there was no way I'd be going out if I'd chucked up, trust me), then headed off to the Locomotive in Brackley, looking a bit of an odd mix what with my jacket and ripped jeans with Fish *Outpatient* tracksuit bottoms showing through underneath. But the real eye-catcher was my Cardiacs YOUsletter Members Only t-shirt which featured a giant 'Little Man And A House' logo with the words, "I am in it". At this time I still had my mop of curly hair, so goodness knows what I must've looked like, but as with most stages in my life I really wasn't that bothered.

The Loco that night was rammed, with enough Tesco colleagues in there for me to get by without looking like Billy No-Mates, but what really caught my eye were three girls sat at the end of the pool table. Brackley being Brackley (a rather small, boring town) everyone knew everyone else, and I knew these girls were from out of town. What's more, they intrigued me, especially the little one with the dyed-copper-hair, nose piercing, stripy Doc Marten's (them again) and stripy trousers to match – girls like this just didn't exist in Brackley. I had to introduce myself, but how? I pondered asking her where she got her stripy Doc Marten's from but for some reason couldn't summon up the courage. Whilst I pondered I propped myself up on the slot machine and watched the game of pool taking place, and then noticed that Stripy Doc Marten Girl was looking at me in a puzzled way (contrary to popular belief, it doesn't happen that much), so I smiled at her.

She smiled back and asked in a foreign accent that immediately set my heart a-flutter, 'Can I ask you a question?'

'Fire away!' I replied, trying to appear cool and calm.

'What does "I am in it" mean?' she asked.

'Oh, it's a rock band, Cardiacs, and I'm in their fanclub if you like, so this is my t-shirt telling everyone that I'm in that fanclub, hence "I am in it",' I rambled.

She gave a look that suggested she'd perhaps asked for more than she could handle, but then shrugged and said, 'Oh, I thought it might be a religious cult or something…'

'Well…' I started, then thought better of it and changed the subject.

She was from Germany (Bavaria) and was over here for the best part of a year doing voluntary work at the nearby home for the mentally handicapped, Evenley Hall. Her name was Annette (pronounced Ann-ette-a), and she left the pub that night with my phone number, whilst I left with a very broad grin…

By October 1997 we were a couple, but a very independent couple. We both had rather full social lives so the pattern was that whilst I was up in Sheffield she'd be down in London, and when I was down in London at a gig, she'd probably be up in Leeds visiting her sister, but it didn't matter because once or twice a week we'd both be in Brackley and we'd both be happy to see each other. And so it was that I found myself on my own down in London on Saturday 18th October for a Katherine In A Cupboard gig at the Red Eye in Islington, Annette presumably gadding around somewhere else in the country.

Katherine In A Cupboard featured the mighty Bob Leith from Cardiacs (though not on drums this time, but vocals instead) so there was quite a Cardiacs presence in attendance that evening. Now, 1997 was Cardiacs 20th anniversary year, but all had been incredibly quiet on the Cardiacs front until the announcement of a tour supporting Hawkwind. Blimey, as a massive Hawkfan and a member of Cardiacs' YOUsletter family this was one to get really excited about. Unfortunately Cardiacs then pulled out of the tour, but for some reason they couldn't wriggle out of the gig at Stoke's Trentham Gardens, scheduled for the Saturday after the Katherine In A Cupboard gig, October 25th (Jon Anderson's birthday actually).

As my rota had me down for working that Saturday I was resigned to missing it, especially as my fellow Night Manager refused to swap his shift. I then tried asking every manager in the store if they fancied covering it (oh yeah, they were all going to be really happy to cover a Saturday night) but no-one was playing ball, not even when I brought up the subject of cash-in-hand. So Katherine In A Cupboard would have to make do as a consolation.

Still, as consolations go it was not a bad one, and of course Katherine In A Cupboard served up their usual delightful dish of Sleepy People/early-Genesis deliciousness.

By the end, word had got out that I wouldn't be able to attend the only gig of Cardiacs' 20th anniversary year the following weekend due to work commitments, and as I leaned up against the railings outside the venue afterwards, a familiar voice was heard to whisper, 'Pull a sickie!'

'I've never pulled a sickie in my life,' I sighed.

'Then it's about time you started,' fired back the voice with unquestionable logic before disappearing into the night.

I wrestled with my conscience for a few days, but by the middle of the week numerous phone calls culminated in a plan that meant I was somewhat committed, whether I wanted to go or not. Previous-girlfriend Sarah agreed to drive up there with friend Lisa, and we reckoned that we could fit current-girlfriend Annette in the car even if she dragged along her visiting-from-Germany male-friend Andreas (oh yes, these relationships were never straightforward).

Saturday arrived with the end of my Friday all-night shift, and I made sure I mentioned throughout the night my worsening headache. That Saturday morning I went straight from work to the doctor where I complained about my persistent headaches. Oh yes, this was an elaborate plot all right...

When I got home and headed for bed I turned the heating up full (sleeping in a warm room usually brings on a crashing headache for me), then just for good measure I banged my head on the wall three times (those that don't know me may doubt the truthfulness of this, those that do will know it to be sad but all too true).

And guess what? When I woke up in the afternoon I had the clearest head ever. The German delegation turned up, so with fingers to lips I made the call to Tesco, putting on that voice that you do even when you are genuinely ill.

I felt guilty straight away because the Personnel Manager was so nice about it: 'You just stop at home and take it easy, Adrian…'

Next up was the taxi to Milton Keynes. Brackley being what it is, and just in case any of my colleagues should be out and about, I undertook the whole journey wearing shades, shades which eventually came off when Sarah's little motor hit the M6…

The gig itself was as memorable as you'd expect Hawkwind and Cardiacs on the same bill to be, even if Mr Murder, Cardiacs sound engineer, did get rushed to hospital suffering an allergic reaction to nuts and Tim's guitar packed up completely during "Is This The Life", thus allowing Jon Poole to steal the limelight by playing the guitar solo (erm, it actually sounded pretty good you know).

And Hawkwind were as magic as ever, even though I found myself bemoaning the absence of Nik Turner.

Meanwhile, it seemed that Annette and Andreas preferred Hawkwind to Cardiacs, Cardiacs having left them scratching their heads a little. Well, I wasn't too worried what Andreas thought, and I'd worry about converting Annette later, because for now I had more important things to worry about, like greasing my way around the Return to Work interview back at Tesco the next day…

My fellow Night Manager, the senior out of the two of us, eyed me suspiciously across the table and cast doubt on my integrity. 'What's the problem?' I asked.

'The problem,' he scowled, 'is that you asked EVERY SINGLE ONE OF YOUR COLLEAGUES to cover for you, and then when they all said no, you phoned in sick. Can you say in all honesty that you didn't pull a sickie?'

Now this is where I put on my acting hat, fixing him with an unflickering stare and saying with a perfectly straight, serious face, 'Do you really think I'd be that stupid?'

His back-down was swift and complete. He apologised profusely and offered support if the headaches were being caused by the pressures of the job. I thanked him for his understanding then retreated to the toilet for a much-needed chill…

If Sarah and I had lasted eight months, then Annette and I managed an even-less-impressive six, but we managed to make the same amount of Cardiacs gigs as a couple – two. But just like in October 1997, Tesco were threatening to get in the way again for this next one on January 22nd 1998 at the Bull & Gate, Kentish Town, London. The selling point for this gig was that it was a bit of a secret one, and only the great and the good and the privileged would be in attendance. It was not as if I really needed to prove my Cardiacs Credentials; after all, at that point my Cardiacs Gig Count was sitting on 60, but I felt I *had* to attend. Trouble was, it wasn't falling on a night off, and after the last time I wasn't about to start messing around asking colleagues to swap shifts. Instead I decided I could make it down to London on the Oxford Tube, go to the gig, then come straight back via the same service and be at work for 1am(ish). The senior Night Manager was on a night off and I decided this was an advantage – what he didn't know about wouldn't hurt. Instead I had a quiet word with our Options Management Trainee on the night-shift, instructing him to get in at 8pm, take the handover from the Duty Manager, tell them I had a "personal problem" to attend to, and that I'd be in later, like around 11 o'clock. (As I write this, and knowing Tesco as I do now, I can't believe I really thought this would all go off without question)

As it was, Annette and I bussed it off to Oxford then London and I felt all very relaxed about everything, only starting to worry a little when we got held up on the Tube and I began to fret about missing the gig, or at least it selling out before we got there. As it was, we were the last two in before the Bull & Gate put the "HOUSE FULL" signs up.

Amongst the familiar crowd was Ian, along with his ex Tara, and of course Sarah was there. Annette confided in Tara that she wasn't too happy about Sarah and I being best mates but she was prepared to accept it as she herself had plenty of male friends. It must have been true love.

As is often the case with Cardiacs they came across much better in the more intimate atmosphere of the smaller B&G than the hangar-like hall that was Trentham Gardens, and Annette admitted afterwards that she much preferred them this time round. Of course, when it was all over we should have been speeding off so I could get to work, but I love to socialise and with all these Cardiacs fan buddies around, I just wanted to chat and chat and chat…

Even with a cab picking me up from Oxford I didn't make it in to work until gone 3 o'clock, but I probably never worked harder than I did that night just to ensure that everything was done. I was rather puzzled that in the morning no-one asked where I'd been the night before, so I shrugged my shoulders and went off to the Time and Attendance book to manually clock myself in. Now, this was where I went wrong because I felt that as I'd told the Options Trainee to pass on that I'd be struggling in for about 11 o'clock, that's what I'd better clock myself in for. I'm still not sure why I bothered, because more often than not I never clocked in, manually or otherwise, and my wages always came out right. But there I was physically writing in that I'd started work at 23:00.

Well, I *say* this is where I went wrong, but I also went wrong elsewhere by telling the Options Trainee where I was really going that night. Options Trainees are ambitious. Options Trainees are keen to impress. Options Trainees can conceivably be after someone's job…

The gig had been on the Thursday night, and the whole of the following weekend passed off without any mention of anything so I really began to think I'd got away with it. Silly old naïve me had forgotten that Sunday nights at Tesco Superstores run from 4pm store closing until store reopening Monday morning at 8.30, and nobody wants to cover all that. What's more, no Night Manager wants to work from 4pm to 8am, so the usual split shift arrangements were followed that Sunday with me doing the later shift.

But they were waiting for me at 8 o'clock on Monday morning. Why, the Night Manager (senior) had even grabbed a few hours sleep at home before coming back to deal with me, along with the Personnel Manager to take notes.

Where had I been on Thursday? Why, I had a personal problem to resolve, and I made it in for 11 o'clock.

'Adrian, we know you didn't start at 11 o'clock.'

'But…'

'We've studied the CCTV, and it quite clearly shows you entering the store at gone 3 o'clock.'

Oh, erm, hmmmm…that'll be me entering the store at 3 o'clock wearing my psychedelic trousers and Cardiacs t-shirt, just the sort of thing you wear when resolving a personal issue. The game was up, but I gave it one last shot when they asked me where I'd been.

'My brother had an issue to resolve, and he lives in London so I…'

'Adrian, we know you went to London to see Cardiacs. Why don't you just admit it?'

'Erm, okay – I went to see Cardiacs, at the Bull & Gate, and it was, erm, really good.'

The Night Manager's eyes lit up a little and he said, 'Of course, we've suspected that you've tried this before, last October…'

'I called in sick that time and I think you'll find the records say as much, and if you want to check with my GP, I did pay the Health Centre a visit that day,' I prickled, sort-of defiant to the end.

They then adjourned the meeting and gave me a nice little letter suspending me on full pay which also invited me to return in 24 hours for a disciplinary hearing with my good mate (splutter) the Store Manager. It seemed the primary charge was one of Falsifying

Company Documents, something to do with that ridiculous manual clocking.

That Monday evening I spent a miserable night in Morgan's Bar, Brackley, with Annette, bemoaning my lot and drowning my sorrows in Britvic. I thought I was doomed, but Annette kept saying, 'Don't worry, at least you've still got me!'

'No offence, Annette me dear, but you can't pay my wages,' I replied dryly.

'We'll work something out,' she said, but I only half believed her.

So, the next morning there I was in the store, wearing my suit. All the staff were saying, 'Oh hello Adrian, what are you doing in at this time of day? Why are you looking so smart...?' At this point the smiles would fade from their faces as they put two and two together...

I nervously hauled myself off to the Store Manager's Office where the Union Rep I'd requested was waiting for me. The Store Manager left me with a huge disciplinary manual and suggested I look up "Falsifying Company Documents" in it until he came back. I did as he said and cheerfully read about how the maximum punishment was dismissal. When he came back he wanted to know why he shouldn't sack me.

My answers were something about my previous good record, them needing me to work for the rest of the week (even faced with the gallows the humour comes out), how I was genuinely sorry, how I'd never worked harder than I did that night...

Well, he seemed to be in agreement because they issued me with a Final Written Warning which would stay on my file for six months, and what's more, they wanted me back in that very evening. Nice.

As I prepared to leave the office the Store Manager asked me, 'Why did you do it?'

'Sometimes I have to do everything,' I replied, 'and I can't bear to miss certain events. This was one such event and I felt I would be prepared to do anything to get there. So I did.'

'Was it worth it?' he asked.

'Providing I behave myself for the next six months, yes,' I said with a smile. No wonder we never quite hit it off.

* * * *

Katrina and Jitka – Tottenham against the Czech Republic (with a little bit of Leeds versus Canada thrown in)

Of course, mine and Annette's free-spirited relationship was far too good to last, and without going into the gory details, let's just say that when France played Brazil in the 1998 World Cup Final I was the only person in the pub who wanted Brazil to lose. Within a year of the break-up I'd moved from Brackley to London, Annette had gone back to Germany having split with her samba lover, and then came to visit me for a week in Canning Town where we kissed and made up, exorcising a few ghosts along the way (and we finally got to do the proper goodbye at Victoria Coach Station – how romantic). We're still in touch to this day, but I haven't seen her since a rather lively visit to Berlin in 2002, but that's a story for another time, another book…

Before leaving Brackley for London I embarked on a few ill-advised, short-lived relationships. All I will say is that at this stage in life I seemed to have perfected my knack for attracting girls (and women) who were, shall we say, a little bonkers. Big bracket coming up: (I started this habit in the aftermath of my split from Sarah. A word of warning then; when a crazy hippie chick thirteen years your senior says she wants nothing serious and will allow you to roam no-strings-attached, don't believe her. And a word of advice; it's perfectly acceptable under the circumstances to plead with Tesco to do a night of overtime then leave a message on a crazy hippie chick's answer machine saying Tesco begged you to go in so you can't make that evening's date. What I wouldn't advise is getting up in the middle of the afternoon following a night shift in order to watch England v Scotland at Euro '96, because when you open the curtains there may well be a crazy hippie chick coming up your garden path, so you may have to dive behind the sofa then crawl to the doormat in order to read the note she's just posted telling you how disappointed in you she is, and then you'll have to watch the match with the curtains closed in case she comes back.)

So yes, May 1998 and I'd attracted another note-poster (working nights was great – you could always pretend to be asleep when people rang your doorbell), except these notes always seemed to be written in red ink on red paper. When hints of a rival's murderous state of mind were dropped into conversation, moving to a communal madhouse in Canning Town didn't seem such a bad idea, so in August 1998 off I went, leaving Brackley behind.

My first relationship in London was with the beautiful Andrea, a Czech au-pair who tried to do her shopping in Tesco Pinner Green but was hindered somewhat by a bloke from Sheffield telling her about his Slovak band all the time. Our relationship was, shall we say, tempestuous to say the least. However, she avoided the Cardiacs thing altogether, her interest being more centred around her near-neighbours the Jesus Underground Band.

But hey, if it's tempestuousness you want, then Katrina is your girl. Well she wasn't really tempestuous, but put her in a Tesco Metro at Bishopsgate alongside me and things certainly went that way. Indeed, I still go in that store today and the long-serving staff always ask me two things: 'How are Sheffield United doing?' and, 'Do you still see Katrina?' But of course, much of the Me and Katrina thing is recorded in *Fever Hitch* so there's no need for details here, except to say that when I meet people who have read that first book, they only ask the *one* thing: 'Do you still see Katrina?' No I don't, okay?

Katrina's only Cardiacs involvement in those early days was that I once loaned her my Cardiacs woolly hat when it was raining and she never gave it back (what was I thinking?). But it was maybe my next girlfriend Jitka's enthusiasm for Cardiacs that spurred Katrina to investigate further. But hang on a minute, you'll have to forgive me slipping out of chronological order here, because really Jitka's part in all this Cardiacs business is best left to the end to wrap up all these tales of love and anguish.

So back to Katrina, who fell either side of Jitka. Almost exactly a year after I'd last taken Jitka to see Cardiacs at the Astoria in 2001, I was taking Katrina to see them at the same venue, November 15th 2002. Katrina had accompanied me to a couple of gigs before, one being Hawkwind's all-nighter at Brixton Academy in 2000 for the Hawkestra clash of egos, and the other was to see the Naked Goat at the Fountain in Seven Sisters, the Naked Goat featuring Ben Golomstock out of Miranda Sex Garden and Endre from Cheese Cake Truck, a band I was working for at the time. That Naked Goat gig led Katrina (just a matter of weeks into our relationship) to pronounce that 'I'm learning more and more about you and I'm not sure that I like it.' Therefore I decided it was perhaps sensible not to take her to any further gigs. So I didn't. But then Katrina was a very strange creature, and an unpredictable one at that. Even though our relationship was over, barring Just Good Friends, by autumn 2001 she seemed to take an awful lot of interest in what Jitka and I were up to in *that* fledgling relationship. Katrina was especially interested in how we'd got on when I'd taken Jitka to see Cardiacs, firstly at Whitchurch Progressive Rock Festival, then secondly at the Astoria in London. She also seemed morbidly happy when Jitka and I split up, and even more so when Jitka returned to the Czech Republic late on that same year. Unsurprisingly, once Jitka was gone Katrina lost interest again, and I began to rue the day that I'd ever treated Jitka so badly.

One thing remained though, and I was highly delighted that Katrina seemed genuinely interested in attending a Cardiacs gig with me. It turned out to be a long-held promise because, like I said, it was nearly a year before they played again, in November 2002. Even though I'd splashed out on the tickets myself, I wouldn't believe that Katrina would attend until she was in that venue and Cardiacs were onstage, a feeling not helped by Ian saying, 'I bet she doesn't show up.' Cheers mate.

Before the gig, to take my mind off things I went for a wander round an exhibition of Roger Dean artwork somewhere on (or near) Oxford Street. And of course, Katrina being a good old girl really, she did show up, and she did enter the venue with me largely, as she put it, 'to see what all the fuss is about.' Well, as it happened I don't think she *did* get what all the fuss was about because she came out of the gig saying that she thought she preferred the support band Oceansize, so I was at pains to explain that Oceansize all hero-worshipped at the shrine of Cardiacs, a statement borne out by the fact that during Cardiacs' set Oceansize stormed the stage and thundered through a version of the *Sing To God* stormer "Eat It Up Worm's Hero".

At one point during the gig she'd wandered off and returned to report that she'd climbed up next to the PA speaker to have a look at us all "dancing" (as it were) to "R.E.S." or some such. 'You all liked quite funny actually,' she said.

Her assessment afterwards was, 'They're not very Rock and Roll really, are they.' I tried to explain that they are and they aren't and…just what constitutes Rock and Roll anyway? At least she'd got going to see Cardiacs out of her system, and I'd deduced that converting her to the ways of the Alphabet Business Concern was as unlikely (and pointless) as trying to change her from being a part-time Tottenham fan to being a part-time Sheffield United fan – it just wasn't going to happen.

If I thought Katrina was difficult, she was nothing compared to Debbie, a girl from Leeds who found herself crossing my radar at Tesco Bishopsgate as my reign there was coming to an end in spring 2004. Debbie had a friend who possessed a couple of Cardiacs albums, and in conversation it transpired that Debbie had never really warmed to them. Indeed, on the occasion of our first date Debbie announced that she'd tried to listen to her friend's albums that day 'but I'm afraid I just don't like them – in fact I find them unlistenable.' Oh, all right then.

As our fraught relationship stumbled on Debbie became ever more scathing of Cardiacs and their music with it becoming apparent that what she actually felt for them was all-out hatred. After we'd gone our separate ways later on that year, it got to the point where when Cardiacs were supporting Wildhearts at the Astoria in December I felt the need to text her informing her that if she liked the Wild-hearts (she did like her music, did Debbie) she'd be better off turn-ing up late in order to not be "disturbed beyond the point of all reasonability" by the support band. Well, it turned out she didn't like the Wildhearts either…

Of course, there was a bit of a postscript to the Debbie story, and once again it involved the Astoria. By now it was November 10th 2006 and once again Cardiacs were treading the boards at that fa-mous old venue. In the previous year I'd met a fantastically eccen-tric Canadian girl called Serena, a Rock singer herself, and a Mormon with pagan sympathies (only I could meet a girl like that).

As that gig approached I'd developed tonsillitis, but despite my absence from work this was a Cardiacs gig, so attendance was compulsory. It remains unique in the annals as being the only Car-diacs gig where I've worn a Sheffield United woolly hat and scarf throughout whilst slumped up against the front of the stage feeling very very ill (Serena meanwhile loved it, and whooped and hollered all the way through – why didn't I marry this girl?).

But anyway, before all that, Serena being Serena she was run-ning a bit late so I decided to wait for her in The Angel pre-gig, and as I entered the pub looking all ill and pathetic, I saw Debbie com-ing out. I don't know if she saw me or not, but I chose to pass her by without a word, and that for me with any of my old flames (or even quick flickers) is extremely rare. That sort of reflected the tension of our fall-out two years previously, and I dare say she would have re-acted in exactly the same way if she'd looked up at the fascia above the Astoria that night and seen the name "CARDIACS" emblazoned against the night – feeling of dread, head down, walk straight past. Jitka would never have behaved like that…

Ah yes, Jitka. Going all the way back to 2001, as I was sweating over the final proofs for *Fever Hitch*, and with Katrina now just my Best Friend (I'm good at that with my ex-girlfriends), I struck up a relationship with Jitka, a bit of a hippie chick from the Czech Re-public, and quite possibly a bit of a crazy one, but endearingly so. By now the Jesus Underground Band had ceased to exist, but some of the remaining entourage had moved to another communal madhouse, this time in Stratford, East London (although to be honest the vibe was never as good as at Canning Town), myself included. Less Slovaks, more Czechs, but still the same amount of friendly, beautiful girls from the London Czech community popping in to visit. Jitka was one such, and we immediately hit it off when I found out she liked Yes. She gasped in wonder at the size of my record collection, and marvelled at the fact that not only did I like Yes, but early Genesis also, and Pink Floyd, not to mention King Crimson...

As ever though, Jitka heard no end about Cardiacs from me and was intrigued. She adopted the policy that if I liked Yes *and* Cardiacs then Cardiacs must be good. Quite right Jitka...

So on August 3rd 2001 Jitka accompanied me to see Cardiacs at Whitchurch Progressive Rock Festival and stood there enthralled throughout the gig. At least, it *seemed* like she was enthralled. It was just that it was hard to tell because she wouldn't say anything. When the gig was over I asked her if she'd enjoyed it and she just looked at me and sort of smiled in an exasperated way. The next day as we hitched back to London I asked her again and she told me not to ask her anymore because she was finding it hard to put into words what she'd experienced, but when she'd found the words she'd tell me.

In the end those words came in the form of an email when she was briefly back in Czech Republic; "Cardiacs – the coolinst (sic) band in the world." So, she liked them then.

Knowing that Jitka was now on board made it so much easier to drag her along to the Astoria on November 23rd 2001 to see, yep you guessed it, Cardiacs again. There was certainly excitement in the air before this gig. Sean from *The Organ* said that he was barely able to contain his excitement, knowing what was coming that night. This in turn meant that I could barely contain mine either, and I *didn't* know what was coming that night.

As it happened Cardiacs turned in a pretty special gig, but the best bit was saved for the final encore. A couple of keyboards were dragged on by the roadies, behind which were positioned Jon Poole and long-since-departed Tim Quy. Meanwhile Dominic Luckman perched behind the drumkit for the first time in many years, and with Jim astride his bass the opening chords to "The Whole World Window" shone forth. None other than Bob Leith stepped up to the microphone and sang the words whilst Timmy was nowhere to be seen. All I could think was that this was the first time I'd heard them play this live since that first date with Annie thirteen years earlier, and it's fair to say that it brought a tear to the eye.

When the Consultant, Miss Swift and Timmy all entered the stage for the grand finale and balloons and flowers were cast everywhere and the confetti cannons exploded, the tear in the eye became a bit of a steady flow. With the band now departed and with stray confetti gently falling from above, the lights came up and Jitka looked at me saying, 'You're crying!' and then she gave a sweet little chuckle.

I looked around for support and saw Andy Thompson nearby also in tears. His female companion for the night, Susie, was also chuckling and she nudged Jitka saying, 'Look at these two, eh?'

Well, I didn't mind. I wasn't ashamed or embarrassed in the slightest, because to me this song had such huge personal significance, whether it be from my first experience of Cardiacs at Reading Festival 1986, or from that first date with Annie in 1988, or even just from the only other two times I'd seen them perform it live when they'd brought the house down at the Hammersmith Clarendon Hotel Ballroom in June 1988 and the Town and Country Club in November of the same year.

Of course, Jitka was soon off back to the Czech Republic, our relationship having already stumbled to a halt, but we stayed in touch and I read her emails with interest as she went off to live and work in Spain. By 2004 she was back in England for a week or so and we met up. It just so happened that she was around for Cardiacs' annual jamboree at the Astoria and she even went off and bought two tickets from the box office. Two tickets? Ah yes, the second one was for her new Spanish boyfriend who was flying in that day to meet her for the rest of her holiday. I knew she must truly be in love when she didn't make the gig and texted me instead to say that her boyfriend had been really tired and didn't feel like going out, and she'd wanted to be with him. Nope, not even the "coolinst band in the world" could separate them, and I reflected that this was probably where I'd always gone wrong, because I'd have just gone to the gig regardless and left the wiped-out other half to be miserable on their own…

* * * *

Postscript

The Brit Awards had just taken place and some ghastly "anthem" which I can't even bring myself to mention within these pages had won an award for being the Best Song Ever In the History of Everything, or something. Anita Anand on Radio 5Live's late night show (compulsive listening for me) had decided that her listeners wouldn't agree with this award and invited them to text in their own nominations. But she didn't just want the texts to remain at an artist and a title; she wanted an explanation as to why it was the best, and the best entry would win CDs by all the Brit winners.

Well, I wasn't bothered about the CDs, but as a regular 5Live texter I *was* bothered about inflicting my opinions on the nation, so I fired off a heartfelt text stating the case for "The Whole World Window".

I was delighted to hear that my text was judged the best, and I later had the pleasure of telling the researcher that rather than some rubbishy Brits CDs, they could just send me a couple of DVDs; *Ripping Yarns* and *Pink Floyd Live At Pompeii*.

Meanwhile, I received a warm glow from hearing my text read out at the show's climax at 00:59 hours (as the music faded up to bring in the news):

"The best song ever is Cardiacs' epic "The Whole World Window", last performed live in 2001 when it was seen to make grown men cry. It climbs deep into your soul, tugs at your heart, then rips it right out, making you yearn for every single ex-girlfriend you ever let slip through your fingers…"

Amen to that.

My first Cardiacs photo,
Tim at the Leadmill, Sheffield,
April 23rd 1988

Sheffield Star,
April 23rd 1988

in town

WHETHER The Cardiacs were playing at The Leadmill tonight remained a mystery for quite a time. The venue said yeah, the record company said nay, but then changed their mind. The dirt says hot, the label says not, but the Man From Del Monte he say yes . . .

Anyway, assuming there are no other alterations, this is your chance to see the band described by one rag as the ultimate entertainers, and by another as the worst group in the world. Ever.

Only having heard the album, a grotesque, but reasonably listenable mixture of musics, and seen about ten seconds of their horrendous Tube video, I'll reserve judgement, but any band with a fan called Belch can't be bad.

They've been going for over a decade and are so ugly that even this page isn't printing a photo of them. And that <u>takes some</u> doing.

Jim Smith looking miserable at the Leadmill, April '88

The first of many best-gig-ever nights - Tim at the Hammersmith Clarendon Ballroom, June 23rd 1988

Tim at the end of "Goosegash", Clarendon June '88

Sarah Smith's sax all sparkly, Clarendon June '88

A pensive Tim at the Clarendon, June '88

Tim in reflective mood at the climax of "The Whole World Window", Clarendon June '88

Tim Smith and
Tim Quy,
Leeds Uni,
Nov 8th 1988

Tim in pain, possibly
Leeds Nov '88

Jim nearly smiling,
Huddersfield, Nov 9th 1988

Tim sits down after a bit of a slog,
Manchester Uni, Nov 16th 1988

Tim before or after
nearly causing a riot
at Keele Uni,
Nov 23rd 1988

William D Drake in Rick
Wakeman pose, Rayleigh Pink
Toothbrush, Nov 24th 1988

Tim getting close to the audience, Rayleigh Nov '88

Tim Quy hijacks the pipe organ, Aylesbury Civic Centre. June 23rd 1989

Tim gets a shock, Birmingham Foundry, May 25th 1995

THE PITZ

DATE 24-5-95
CONCERT CARDIACS
ACCESS THEATRE

GUEST

A backstage pass that was the key to Sarah's heart, Milton Keynes Woughton Centre, May 24th 1995

Bob Leith doing a "Los Endos",
Wolverhampton Civic Centre,
June 18th 1996

Jim, the day England beat
Holland, Wolves June '96

Jon Poole auditioning for Kiss, Wolves June '96

Jon explaining some chords to Jim, Chelmsford, Army & Navy, June 27th 1996

Jon in shorts, Pete looks on as guitar tech, Glastonbury, June 23rd 2001

Tim looking a bit like he did in 1984, London Astoria, Nov 16th 2007

Jim, Sheffield Boardwalk,
Nov 19th 2007

Cathy not avoiding my
camera, Stoke, Sugarmill,
Nov 20th 2007

Tim, the day England lost to Croatia,
Manchester, Carling Academy,
Nov 21st 2007

Belch glowsticked up by Pete,
Clare and the Dogstands,
Cardiff, Clwb Ifor Bach,
Nov 23rd 2007

Jim on a wonderful night in Leeds,
Woodhouse Liberal Club,
Nov 24th 2007

Tim on the last of
many best-ever-gig
nights, Leeds Nov '07

Kavus Torabi plugged in, Leeds Nov '07

My last Cardiacs photo, Kavus and Tim, Leeds Nov '07

Chapter Thirteen
"Affectionate Friends"
Little Trophy at Notting Hill Arts Centre and North Sea Radio Orchestra at Chalk Farm Roundhouse, November 17th 2007

"Affectionate Friends"
Little Trophy at Notting Hill Arts Centre and North Sea Radio Orchestra at Chalk Farm Roundhouse, November 17th 2007

There was only one place for any self-respecting Gong fan to be over the weekend of November 3rd, 4th and 5th 2006; the Melkweg, Amsterdam, for the Gong Family UnConventional Gathering. As a Gonghead of over 25 years standing, this was the culmination of everything I'd ever hoped for from the inhabitants of the luminous green planet. Believe you me, when Sewer and I were battling against the trendy masses to get Gong on the turntable at 6th Form parties in 1983/84, and suffering a load of grief I might add when we hustled "Zero the Hero and the Witch's Spell" (the best version, the one off *Gong Live Etc*) on and then guarded the record player jealously until the thing was finished, a whole weekend of this Gongitude seemed a long way off. And what was it that made it so special? Well, apart from just about every Gong-related band and solo artiste imaginable, the whole weekend would climax with a performance by the nearest it was possible to get to the classic Trilogy line-up, with THE Gong guitar hero, Steve Hillage, back in their ranks for the first time since 1977.

My only regret was that Sewer himself couldn't get out there. But me, I was going to do everything necessary to make sure I spent that weekend in Amsterdam and I wasn't disappointed. But it wasn't just the performance by Trilogy Gong that made it; it was the whole weekend. I said to Chris, the beautiful Russian girl I met there, as events went this was on a par with Stonehenge Free Festival 1984 for good vibes and downright wonderfulness, high also in spirituality. No band in the world can evoke feelings of spirituality like Gong, and just like whenever you visit Stonehenge, there was magick in the air that weekend. Every performance was worth seeing (even Mother Gong were blistering), some totally and utterly unique, off the scale even. Acid Mothers Gong almost blew the roof off the place with their improvisational Sonic Attack, and the Glissando Guitar Orchestrae was an event of aural bliss the like of which had never been seen or heard before, perhaps never to be repeated either (must get the

DVD). What's more, Steve Hillage blitzed through a solo set for the first time in donkey's. As for Gong, they were just…*sigh*; "Master Builder" with Mr Hillside-Village soloing into oblivion is perhaps one of the finest moments of my life.

On the inside of the DVD of Gong's set from that weekend there is a quote from one Steve Lake in an article for the *Süddeutsche Zeitung*: "At the Amsterdam 'Uncon', Daevid Allen was able to see his influence reflected back at him in the work of more than a dozen bands: Gong as a school of thought almost, or at least an attitude, as much as a series of musical processes."

Indeed, no band can claim such a widespread family of successful solo ex-members (Hillage, Tim Blake), new projects (Gliss Orchestrae), bands with Gong in the name somewhere (Mother Gong, Planet Gong, Acid Mothers Gong), bands heavily influenced by Gong (Here & Now), or even the many, many projects featuring Daevid Allen himself (Sacred Geometry, Stroking the Tail of the Bird, University of Errors). But there is one band that might get close, given time. Nope, not Yes, not King Crimson (although they both have something of a thriving family, granted), but Cardiacs, with Tim Smith fulfilling the role of the Daevid Allen-type father-figure. Yes, if ever they have a Cardiacs Fest in the future, Timmy will be "able to see his influence reflected back at him."

Quite wonderfully, slap bang in the middle of the Cardiacs 2007 tour, on the Saturday after their performance at the London Astoria, there were two gigs that perfectly summed up what Cardiacs and their influence are all about; firstly Little Trophy at Notting Hill Arts Centre, a band who wear their love of Cardiacs very prominently on their sleeve, and secondly North Sea Radio Orchestra at the Roundhouse in Chalk Farm, a collective with more than one direct link to the Alphabet Business Concern, not least via the presence of Kavus Torabi and William D. Drake in their expanded ensemble. Even more wonderfully, the timings of the gigs and the brilliance of London Transport enabled me to attend both, thereby allowing me to write about Cardiacs and their wider family generally – lucky or what?

* * * *

I first became aware of a Cardiacs offshoot at an early stage in my obsession, when I attended that second gig at the Leadmill in Sheffield in April 1988. On my spending blitz, I saw a cassette simply titled *Mr And Mrs Smith And Mr Drake*. I knew enough back then to work out that this was most likely Tim and Sarah Smith along with William D. Drake. I was also quick enough on the uptake to deduce that this was going to be well worth buying, so in my shopping trolley it went. I wasn't disappointed; upon listening to the tape I discovered a treasure-trove of tinkling, gentle beauty, like a stripped down, almost-pastoral Cardiacs, although actually nothing like Cardiacs really, but undoubtedly bearing the hallmarks of, well, Mr and Mrs Smith and Mr Drake. The day I picked up a CD copy to replace my in-danger-of-wearing-out cassette was indeed a happy one (and I've only just realised the happy coincidence that that day was the very next time I saw Cardiacs at the Leadmill, a whole 17 years later, on the Wildhearts support tour).

I remember feeling somewhat intrigued when I read in a Cardiacs *YOUsletter* around the autumn of 1991 that Mr And Mrs Smith And Mr Drake had changed their name to The Sea Nymphs and that another cassette album would soon be available. For those that couldn't wait, there was a free Sea Nymphs seven-inch ("Appealing to Venus"/"Tree Tops High") with the new Cardiacs twelve-inch ("Day Is Gone"), of course duly snaffled up by myself.

I was supremely impressed by The Sea Nymphs single, especially the 'a' side, it coming across as something of a 60s pastiche to these ears, not unlike the whimsy of the Dukes Of Stratosphear. The sound was much lusher than that first tape and the production fuller, meaning that I couldn't wait for the whole album, even if it was a tape.

But wait I had to, almost a year as it turned out, when in the autumn of 1992 The Sea Nymphs were announced as support to All About Eve, the first gig being at Nottingham Rock City. Annie and I drove up, and I was delighted to see that copies of the new cassette album were finally on sale, so my money headed over to the other side of the Alphabet Business Concern Sales Desk once again.

The gig was a real nugget. I'm not sure what the All About Eve fans made of it, but there was a significant Cardiacs contingent in attendance, ensuring that there was a good reaction to their delicate but somehow powerful performance (Bill's keyboards had a lot to do with this). One thing we were all intrigued to see was how Tim would play it as a frontman, and the bizarre thing was, he acted very much like he did with Cardiacs (he even squirted the audience with water, albeit over his head with his back to us), which seemed slightly out of place, but in a way added to the surreal effect of the whole gig (interesting to note that when The Sea Nymphs reformed for a few gigs in 1998/99, Tim played it in an entirely opposite way, sitting down with his guitar or bass and not saying a thing between songs).

One song in particular struck a chord in my heart, a song we discovered was called "Lilywhite's Party" as Annie and I played the tape in her car on the way home to Brackley. It had a haunting simplicity, but with such an atmosphere about it, Tim putting so much feeling into his singing, that one couldn't help thinking this song meant a heck of a lot to him. Of course, Tim never explains what his songs are about, which in this instance was a good thing because it enabled me to interpret it *my* way, and it became a song with massive personal meaning for me, guaranteed to bring a tear (yes, another one) to that old Belch eye…

After that initial tour with All About Eve in 1992, Sea Nymphs gigs were few and far between, making it a shame that I'd only managed to get to one gig on the tour (although I'd made valiant attempts by failing in a three-way hitch with Ian and Tom for the London gig, and hitchhiking all the way to Norwich and the University of East Anglia only to find that the gig there was cancelled), made even more of a shame by the announcement that William D. Drake had left. Jon Poole sat in instead for the next two gigs, a magical night at the Islington Powerhaus, and an *Organ* special at the Monarch in Chalk Farm. It was *The Organ* who came to our rescue again by mounting something of a Sea Nymphs revival in 1998, putting them on at the Camden Falcon, complete with Mr Drake reinstated behind his stack of keyboards (and I believe this was the one where a youthful Joe Cole tried to sneak in). By this time the Alphabet Business Concern had saved all our tape copies of the Sea Nymphs album, simply titled *The Sea Nymphs*, from disintegration by releasing it on CD – tinkling beauty never sounded so powerful.

The Sea Nymphs supporting Cardiacs at the Falcon in January 1999 should have been one of the greatest nights ever, and I'm sure it was, but for some reason I was late in arriving, stumbling through the door just as The Sea Nymphs were playing their last couple of songs. As far as I'm aware this was the last ever Sea Nymphs gig; the long-awaited is-it-or-isn't-it-recorded follow-up album has yet to see the light of day – "The Sea Ritual" is the song I'm looking forward to most...

Around the same time that the Alphabet Business Concern put out the Sea Nymphs album on CD, they also issued to a grateful world a Tim Smith solo album entitled *Tim Smith's Extra Special Oceanland World*, "recorded in bits ages ago ('89-'90ish)", not forgetting that the songs were "Recorded alone (by way of penance) onto eight tracks blah, blah..." The result was a rather splendid collection of catchy-but-quirky-and-slightly-complex pop tunes.

The nearest we got to a follow up was in the form of Spratleys Japs, a project where Tim worked with musicians from his new base in the New Forest, the resulting album being almost exactly somewhere in the middle of *The Sea Nymphs* and *Oceanland World*. The album saw the light of day at the end of the century thanks to the good grace and generosity of one Clive Hutton, aka Big Ship Iron.

There never were any Spratleys Japs live performances, but a rare treat in the early 21st Century was the opportunity to see Tim Smith play a handful of solo sets armed with just his guitar, voice, whistle and box-of-tricks; oh and that toy ball/apple thing that makes the jingly sound at the very start of *Sing To God*. I managed to witness a couple of these rarities, one supporting Naught, Upstairs At The Garage, and one on his own at a pub in Brixton (and actually there may have been another supporting Miranda Sex Garden, again Upstairs At The Garage – spot the person who doesn't keep such a rigid listing of non-Cardiacs gigs). There was one more Tim solo gig for me when he toured as support to Ginger & The Sonic Circus in 2006, the one I caught being at the Islington Carling Academy. In order to stop him from getting bottled off by Wildhearts fans, Jon Poole and Ginger stood behind him throughout with guitars, joining in for a bit of added "beef" when the need arose.

William D. Drake hasn't remained idle since departing Cardiacs in 1991, for besides being a Sea Nymph from time to time, Mr Drake also saw fit to play in a band called Nervous for a while (I caught them at Glastonbury in 1997) as well as unleashing three solo albums for eager devotees to devour, and it is these that are of most interest to fans of Cardiacs. The eponymous debut album was produced by a certain Tim Smith and featured a whole bunch of delightful ditties, some light-hearted, nay, even humorous, everything making sense when you realise that Bill is a fan of Ivor Cutler. In 2006 we were treated to an album of solo piano, *Yew's Paw*, but the real masterpiece was the album released at more or less the same time, *Briny Hooves*. This wonderful piece of Progressive-Serious-World-Jazz-Pop notched everything up to a new level, what with a full band and all, and deserved to make Drakey a household name.

The live gigs that followed the release of *Briny Hooves* really were something to behold, especially the Bush Hall event, featuring the full band (including Bob Leith on drums and starring special-guest Sarah Jones, once known as Sarah Smith) playing the album in running-order from start to finish. "Melancholy World" is always guaranteed to bring a lump to the throat and a tear to the eye, but as well as it being "melancholy", it somehow induces feelings of happiness too – don't ask me why, it just does, right? I filmed him playing it once at a gig in Dulwich somewhere, the results available for viewing on YouTube.

Prior to *Briny Hooves*, William D. Drake gigs were either proper solo affairs, or featured a little help from the Larcombe brothers, Richard and James, and/or Terence Pitt on trumpet, and all had been splendid nights leaving all present glad of heart and high in spirit.

Talking of Terence Pitt, he once gave me one of my finest "witty-riposte" opportunities when he was doing a spot of stand-up at an *Organ* night at the Camden Falcon. Huge Baby were the head-liners, but support were Shrubbies, giving us a massive Cardiacs connection what with Dominic on drums and Sarah on sax, also introducing us to Craig Fortnam on guitar, and Sharron Saddington (eventually Sharron Fortnam) vocalising. Terry appeared before Shrubbies I think, and his brand of comedy was…different, to say the least, bizarrely funny in its own special way. He demanded participation from the audience intermittently-but-directly, so would wander amongst us with a microphone asking seemingly random (possibly stream-of-consciousness) questions, only to be met more often than not with bemused silence or an equally-nonsensical answer. My opportunity arose when he approached me and asked, 'If Jesus were here today, if he went outside what would be the first thing he'd see that was red and white?'

I looked at him incredulously and said in a slightly well-what-do-you-think tone, 'Sheffield United…' To my eternal pleasure the audience laughed, whilst Terry looked a bit peeved and walked off without saying a word. I eventually wiped the silly grin off my face about half way through Shrubbies' set. However, I'm glad to announce that the sound engineer chuckled long and hard, it being particularly gratifying because that sound engineer is, in my opinion, the best in the business.

I sought Terry out afterwards to apologise and explain that when you've been brought up in a certain half of Sheffield you automatically associate the words "red and white" with "Sheffield United", so I didn't even have to think about my answer. But Terry wouldn't accept my apology, insisting that 'it was the perfect answer, which is why I couldn't say anything to follow it.'

Shrubbies meanwhile thundered through an incredibly powerful set, incredible considering the delicacy of the music, but then it was only to be expected with Tim Smith adjusting the sound levels and Dominic thumping the tubs. When I'd first seen Shrubbies (then known as Shrubby Veronica) supporting Cardiacs at the Point in Oxford in June 1996, they hadn't featured a drummer, and although I'd enjoyed their set I felt it was lacking something. Subsequent gigs with Dominic resolved this issue, blowing me away every time. But why oh why have I never got round to buying the Shrubbies album…? (Don't worry folks, I've got it now.)

When I found out Bob had his own band called Katherine In A Cupboard I assumed he was the drummer, maybe allowing himself to do a spot of Phil-Collins-with-Genesis-on-Top-of-the-Pops singing from behind the kit. But no, Bob was up front alongside his then-other-half Yvette, the two of them sharing vocal duties like I'm sure they did household chores. If you ever had the chance to wake up in the morning on Bob's sofa and study his record collection, you'd notice a proliferation of Genesis releases as well as all of what little output there had been from Sleepy People, and that is magically what Katherine In A Cupboard sounded like, a cross between those two, something you'd be able to hear if you could ever get hold of their tape which they briefly had on sale at gigs in 1997.

That year of 1997 I went and put on a gig at Brackley Cricket Club using the excuse that it was my 31st birthday. As it was a party I couldn't justify charging for entrance so let everyone in for free (can you see why my career as a promoter never quite took off?). Katherine In A Cupboard were first on the bill, followed by Magnilda. Magnilda provided another Cardiacs connection in that vital-member-of-the-crew Captain John Hook was their drummer. They also had a bassist called Iain Lee who went on to do *The 11 O'clock Show* which made some bloke called Ali G famous and made me fancy Daisy Donovan (oh Daisy, where are you now?). Iain currently does a load of radio programmes, but I know for a fact that he's never forgotten that night at Brackley Cricket Club…

You see, he ended up presenting *RI:SE*, Channel 4's not-very-successful breakfast show, and after Sheffield United lost to Arsenal in the FA Cup semi-final of 2003 (curses on you, Graham Poll), a group of us London Blades were invited along to the studio to "add a bit of atmosphere" (so why when we tried to add this atmosphere did fussy media graduates with clipboards keep threatening us with ejection unless we quietened down?). I cornered Iain in the green room (just what you need when you're trying to relax, a manic Belch in a Sheffield United shirt) and asked him if he remembered the glorious occasion of my 31st birthday party. 'I'll never forget it,' he replied, 'because it was the last night before I went to Pakistan for six months.'

That Magnilda performance was my first introduction to Richard Larcombe as he sang and guitared his way through the set. Two years later I was delighted to see him supporting Cardiacs at ULU with his brother James as the duo Stars In Battledress. At the time I was a mature student at the University of Greenwich so as part of my course I wrote a review of the whole event for my own website, a piece that included what the Larcombe brothers still proudly (?) proclaim was the first ever Stars In Battledress review. I was suitably impressed by that gig, and have been by every performance ever since. Again, their sound depends on a delicate beauty similar in feel to that of The Sea Nymphs and early William D. Drake solo work, the sparseness of the sound only highlighting how intricate their interactions are. Their album *Secrets And Signals* is the most beautifully-crafted of works, providing as it does the intensely spine-tingling climax to "Doing Well", a mesmerising swirl of brilliance created with the help of master-producer Tim Smith. Essential, trust me.

As well as Katherine In A Cupboard and Magnilda, the other stars of Belch's Birthday Binge were the Monsoon Bassoon, their set climaxing with that unforgettable smoke-machine moment mentioned elsewhere. Suffice to say, securing the services of the Monsoon Bassoon back in 1997 was quite something because they seemed on the brink of making it big, what with favourable reviews of their gigs and singles in the music press. A large chunk of the band had been part of Plymouth Death-Metallers Die Laughing, but had moved to London to seek their fortune, and it was at this point that I first stumbled across them. In fact I'd first encountered Kavus at a Cardiacs gig at the Camden Palace back in the days when he still had dreads. He was down the front, quite happy to join in with mine and Pete's slightly optimistic shouts for Yes songs. The other thing that stood out was when the DJ announced Cardiacs as 'the best band in the country', Kavus shouted, 'Not the country, the world!' Bless…

Afterwards Andy Thompson gave me and new-found friend Al Gittens a lift to the station, as well as driving Kavus wherever he needed to get to. It was the start of many friendships, leading to Andy driving vans for just about every Kavus-project since, and Al borrowing my idea by getting the Bassoon to play his birthday party later in 1997. The night of Belch's Birthday Binge, Andy drove the Bassoon up and I'm proud to say that just like that Camden Palace night of 1994, all of us were present as Al had driven down from Runcorn especially for the gig.

The first time I saw the Monsoon Bassoon was at the *Organ* night mentioned in the *Organ* chapter when they were on the same bill as David Cross and Pop-a-Cat-a-Petal. I remember when the Bassoon took to the stage I excitedly pointed out to Ian that one of the guitarists sharing the vocals was 'that bloke I met at the Camden Palace, except he's shaved his dreads off…'

It's safe to say that during that mid-to-late 90s period the Monsoon Bassoon were just about the hottest property around live, and some of the gigs I saw them playing in venues such as the Camden Dublin Castle and the Falcon were right up there with the best of Cardiacs. Ian and I were regular travellers down to London, and I believe I even attended one Bassoon gig whilst off work with stress and tension in 1998. There was always a heavy Alphabet Business Concern and Little Family of Fish presence at their gigs, appealing to the harsher, heavier side of a Cardiacs audience, hardly surprising when you consider the Bassoon's Die Laughing roots combined with a Cardiacs-style complexity – their heavy bits really were bone-crushing.

And yet by the time their debut album, the caustic, toxic, sonic masterpiece *I Dig Your Voodoo*, surfaced in 1999, it was seemingly over for them. I'm not quite sure what did for the Bassoons, probably the usual band-internal-strife thing, but they faded away with a whimper, not a bang, and the world was a worse place for it. In recent years Authority provided the nearest one could get to the

Monsoon Bassoon, hardly surprising considering they featured original Bassoons Kavus Torabi, Dan Chudley (guitar/vocals) and Jamie Keddie (drums), as well as one-time Shrubby Craig Fortnam on bass. Now, just where is their debut album…? (Lost forever I think, as indeed Authority appear to be, but at least we've had the delights of Kavus' project Knifeworld and their self-titled debut album.)

Ring and Zag And The Coloured Beads were two bands interconnected via personnel and a desire to play squat parties in the 80s. They were also massively influenced by Cardiacs, so it was no surprise when post-Ring, guitarist Bic turned up in Cardiacs as a replacement for Sarah's sax in 1989. By 1991 he'd also joined Levitation, teaming up with ex-House of Love Terry Bickers (guitar/vocals) and former Ring bandmate Bob White (keyboards). When it became apparent that Levitation were to be The Next Big Thing thanks to their wonderfully dark and dense Alternative Indie Rock, Bic had to leave Cardiacs which was a shame as he'd just recorded *Heaven Born And Ever Bright* with them. But every cloud and all that… Levitation toured twice with Cardiacs in 1992, and despite my initial misgivings, by Nottingham I was won over, and their fabulous album *Need For Not* gave all us Cardiacs fans a joyous excuse to own a top-notch "Indie" album, as well as the chance to marvel at the wonderful production of expert-knob-twizzler Tim Smith.

Sadly, Levitation World Domination was denied when Terry Bickers left unexpectedly. They struggled on, recruiting a new singer, but for whatever reasons new album *Meanwhile Gardens* was only ever available in Australia, although you could pick it up on import at HMV (and I advise you to get hold of a copy if you still can). Levitation subsequently knocked it on the head, only to re-emerge a few years later in the reduced form of a three-piece featuring original Levitationers Bic on guitar and vocals, Dave Francolini on drums (a more energetic drummer you'll never see) and Laurence O'Keefe on bass, complete with a new name, Dark Star.

Armed with a deal (good old Prog-Rock standard bearers Harvest Records) and a new album, *Twenty Twenty Sound*, they looked set for wonderful things (why, they even appeared on *Later*

With Jools Holland), but sadly it was not to be, although Dragons seem to feature a few Dark Star chaps, and apparently Bic's Mikrokosmos albums are a must (so why haven't I yet?).

Linked to Levitation, one band I wished I'd seen live were Panixsphere, featuring as they did Tim Smith and Jon Poole from Cardiacs and Bic and Dave Francolini from Levitation. I believe they only ever existed in live form, and surfaced (or possibly resurfaced) when The Sea Nymphs were unable to support The Enid. According to the review in *The Organ* it combined the heaviest and punkiest elements of both parent bands, and from the sounds of it those that witnessed the fastest, wildest version of "To Go Off And Things" will still be in a state of shock now, over 15-or-so years on.

Dominic Luckman briefly flirted with a bit of Alternative-Indie-Power-Pop when drumming with Flinch in the mid-90s, but the best thing he ever did for me was drum for Here & Now in 1991. You see, this enabled me to link Cardiacs into the giant Rock Family Tree I have in my head (and which I sometimes commit to paper). This mass of wiggly lines usually starts with Yes and has as its key Bill Bruford, for it is he who not only drummed with Yes, but also with King Crimson, Genesis and Gong, so four of my favourite bands in the whole world can be linked forever, and all because of a posh drummer from Kent.

Sadly though, I could never work Cardiacs into this maze, largely because they operated in a different era and weren't exactly big on sending out ex-members to play with some of Prog's giants. But then in 1991 Dominic went and joined up with Here & Now, presumably because Keith le Missile, their erstwhile bassist, was a huge fan of Cardiacs. Of course, back in 1977 Here & Now had formed part of Daevid Allen's post-Gong Punk project, Planet Gong, and just to make sure there was no doubting the Cardiacs-Here-&-Now-Gong connection, in 1991 Here & Now managed to do a few gigs with Daevid Allen again as Planet Gong, with Dominic on drums (I grabbed them at that chaotic all-dayer at West Bromwich Town Hall). Joy unbounded, my Family Tree now including all Belch's Top Five (order dependant on how I'm feeling): Yes, Gong, Cardiacs, Genesis,

King Crimson, and all thanks to two drummers, one called William, one called Dominic…

Sidi Bou Said were a band I'd read about in the music press and who had particularly impressed with an interview in a fanzine called *Tea And Biscuits* (I wrote a couple of reviews for them), so when I saw they were supporting Cardiacs on their "comeback" tour of 1995 I was keen to check them out. If I'm honest, I wasn't bowled over straight away, but I recognised well-crafted songs when I heard them, and an all-girl-trio playing music of this adventure was always going to create interest eventually. Besides, I saw them supporting Cardiacs so many times (and if I'm honest again, I'm really not sure how many times, but it was a lot) I grew to love them in time.

I believe I'm right in saying that neither bands were particularly familiar with each other's work at the start of that 1995 tour, but by the end Cardiacs and Sidi Bou Said had built up a mutual respect, so much so that Tim produced the Sidis' next album, *Bodies*, and Jon Poole produced the one after, *Obsessive*. Both albums are giant slabs of Alt-Indie-Rock, but in a blindfolded taste-test you would be able to tell which was which by the differing styles of the producers – no offence Jon, but *Bodies* just shades it for me… The Cardiacs connection to Sidi Bou Said was made unbreakable when Claire Lemmon (Sidis' vocals and guitar) and Melanie Woods (drummist) sang backing vocals live with The Alphabet Business Concern, Mel still chorusing and banging things right up to this very 2007 tour.

Goodness me, I seem to have been writing for hours, and yet I can't help feeling I've barely scratched the surface. For not only are there bands who feature former and current members of Cardiacs, there are bands who are most definitely influenced by them, some better known than others. Perhaps top of the fame tree are Blur, with Damon Albarn particularly keen on Cardiacs, and all of Faith No More who apparently once cancelled a signing session at the Phoenix Festival because it coincided with Cardiacs' set. Mike Patton is perhaps the most vocal of Faith No More in his admiration of Cardiacs, anyone who has listened to a Mr Bungle or Fantomas album surely able to vouch for this.

Then there's the whole Sleepy People/Pop-a-Cat-a-Petal/Ultrasound thing. Sleepy People were undoubted fans of Cardiacs, again just one listen confirming this, but they did have that big-Prog thing going on too, setting them apart from the Punky-elements of Cardiacs' sound. Pop-a-Cat-a-Petal were the half of Sleepy People that left the North East and headed to London to seek the Fame Thing (and fortune), and they nearly succeeded when they morphed into Ultrasound, having a couple of minor hit singles and a bit-of-a-hit album, *Everything Picture*, a gloriously pumped-up Prog-Indie-Alternative effort spread over two discs. And there on the messy cover, included as a bit of a nod-in-the-direction-of, was a Cardiacs Big Flower badge...

Then there were bands like the People's Friend who were around in that wonderful late-90s period when there'd always be a decent band on at the Dublin Castle. The first time we saw them, singer Jake's in-between-song banter bore a certain resemblance to someone: 'He's seen Cardiacs,' smiled Ian. Again though, they had a different take on it, flushing out the epic moments and building them up into these fantastic song-pictures all about life as it appeared to us all in 1998, Jake relating rather than singing the words. Where on earth did the People's Friend go...? (I still see Jake at Cardiacs gigs though.)

Wizards Of Twiddly's mere name suggested they jazzed-up a similar storm to Cardiacs, so it was no surprise to see Tim Smith given a "thank-you" on their debut album *Independent Legs*, but perhaps my favourites were Poisoned Electrick Head, a band who first grabbed my attention in Cholderton Woods, Summer Solstice 1988, just outside the four-mile exclusion zone around Stonehenge. They wouldn't let us in the Stone Circle you see, so as there was no Glastonbury that year there was something like 5,000 of us camped in those woods. Someone had a generator and a stage was set up under a tarpaulin. After a site meeting my attention was grabbed by the large amount of musicians setting up under the tarps. Keyboards and *two* guitars? They had to be Proggy...

I hung around to investigate and wasn't disappointed. They were a seven-piece, and besides the afore-mentioned keyboards and guitars, they naturally had bass and drums, but unnaturally (and magnificently) had *TWO* vocalists whose boundless energy saw them groove from start to finish. Not wanting to be outdone, I stayed at the front and bopped away in the dust, stopping only to get my breath back in between songs. 'A cross between Cardiacs and Gong,' I explained to Tim Quy when I saw him a few days later.

'Poisoned Electrick Head?' he replied, 'I think they sent us a tape.' Ah yes, that'd make sense.

By the next time I saw them, at that West Bromwich Town Hall mega-event again in 1991, they'd taken to wearing black boiler-suits and alien death masks, fashion accessories most welcome to my mind. I picked them up live as much as possible from then on, their eponymous debut album and superior follow up, *The Big Eye Am*, both getting played to death. I know not so many appreciated their later *The Hanged Man* album, but I rather enjoyed it, and their "Hanging By A Thread" song became something of an anthem in my head whenever I thought of mine and Katrina's strained relationship; you know, the "No matter how you look at it, no two minds can agree" line.

Perhaps my favourite PEH gig was at Stamford Quayhole Kate's on December 3rd 1992 when I arrived after an improbable hitch from Brackley. The venue was packed with students and the Leckie Heads had the place rocking, despite the frequent falling-onto-the-stage of the audience (it was one of those stages that was on the same level as the punters, so not really a stage at all). The set-closer of "Pendulum" was at the most mind-blowing I'd ever heard it played (that guitar solo!), its epic length taking them beyond the curfew. When they returned and started to play an encore of "Out Of Order" the venue were having none of it and pulled the plug on the PA. There was nearly a riot, but the fact that singers Pee and Andy attempted to finish the song unaccompanied satisfied the throng, and everyone went off into the night sporting big stupid grins. I rated that one as Belch's Gig of the Year, even beating anything Cardiacs could come up with – praise indeed.

So there you have it, Cardiacs and Affectionate Friends; like I said, I've definitely missed some out, but then if I'm not careful we'll be up all night.

Of course I've missed some out, two at least, Little Trophy and North Sea Radio Orchestra, but then that's what the next bit's all about…

* * * *

Two gigs in one day can be pushing it a bit, especially when those two gigs are slap bang in the middle of a fortnight of almost wall-to-wall live concert performances, but never one to shy away from a challenge, I was up for this one. Besides, I'd done it twice before (that I remember anyway); I once caught Katherine In A Cupboard first on the bill Upstairs At The Garage before Ian and I legged it on the Victoria Line to King's Cross to see Miranda Sex Garden at Splash Club @ the Water Rats, and another time I did Cardiacs at the Astoria before strolling down Oxford Street to mellow out to Nik Turner's Space Ritual. One thing this latter example taught me was never to follow up Cardiacs with anything, because no matter how much you love Nik Turner, the mayhem of a Cardiacs gig cannot really be bettered. But this night in 2007 was no problem because for the first time in five nights Cardiacs were NOT on the bill – instead we had two bands who owed a lot to the organisation known as the Alphabet Business Concern; Little Trophy and North Sea Radio Orchestra.

What made this double-gig possible was the wonderful fact that Little Trophy were being put on by *The Organ* at Notting Hill Arts Centre at teatime, so I even had the luxury of a decent day's rest, made all the better by Sheffield United not having a game that weekend. Even so, it was Saturday so I felt it only right to wear my vintage Sheffield United shirt, only to be stopped in my tracks by the bouncer on the door of the Arts Centre informing me that he was 'sorry, no football shirts allowed.'

I tried telling him that as it was a Blades shirt of 1971 vintage all it would do was inspire feelings of love and peace, but he was having none of it. He was obviously a decent sort though because he let me keep it on providing I did my coat up and kept it so (you see, I *can* compromise). Down the stairs and into the venue, Sean was manning the decks and in tribute to my shirt-strife he played a punked-up version of "Annie's Song" (for the uninitiated, the Sheffield United fans' signature tune, "The Greasy Chip Butty Song" is belted out to the tune of "Annie's Song").

Already present were a number of Cardiacs aficionados including Duffy, Pies and Max. I asked Max if he was making the trip across town for the North Sea Radio Orchestra but alas he had to dash off to board his flight back to the States – still, you've got to hand it to someone who's brave enough to risk London transport by attending an event a matter of hours before flying. Max may not have been able to do both gigs, but Duffy was definitely up for it, and what's more, Duffy was feeling generous. He thoughtfully bought me Little Trophy's demo CD without realising I'd bought it myself just ten minutes earlier. The thing was, he'd already bought one for himself then broken it so had gone back to the sales desk and purchased *another* along with the one for me, so he'd kind of wasted his money twice but not twice if you see what I mean. Anyway, he insisted I keep the spare, so I still have two copies of Little Trophy's demo – I may be able to cash in if Little Trophy ever make it mega-huge…

Ah, but *will* they make it mega-huge…? This was my first viewing of them, and mighty impressive they were too, so if there's any justice in the world, they'll make it all right. But then we all know there ain't no justice in the world, otherwise Cardiacs would have been bigger than Blur or Radiohead, so I guess Little Trophy will just have to take pot-luck. Encouragingly, one of the bands they reminded me of, Sleepy People, split in two and the half that evolved into Ultrasound briefly flirted with success and *NME* rave-reviews, so there is hope.

When a band is endorsed by *The Organ* via their Cardiacs MySpace page, then you already feel a certain amount of confidence, but as with Old Fruit, just one look at a band as they take to the stage can boost that confidence even higher, and as Little Trophy took up their instruments I was transported back to that Ring gig in 1987, both in sound and vision. A bowler-hatted bass-player called Munch, a spiky drummer named Malc (no relation), a dark-but-colourful lady, Charley, on the ivories, Russell-Brand-alike Nick on guitar and vocals, and the incredibly beautiful Emily in a flowing skirt picking out tricky chords on her guitar – all they needed were some fire-jugglers and it really could have been the Hammersmith Clarendon Hotel Ballroom all over again.

The fact that I'd first met Nick and Emily at a Cardiacs gig at the Astoria suggested that their influences may exist somewhere around the Alphabet Business Concern, and the music bore this out – lots of prickly little tunes bouncing around with niceness, compact to the point of brevity but dicing with danger every time. I can't even be sure that they've heard any Ring or Sleepy People, but folks, if you like those two bands, then check out Little Trophy, and if by the time you read this they've made it to the top of the pop charts, I have a rare demo that may interest you…

Following Little Trophy were Imperial Leisure so Duffy and I stopped for a couple of their tunes, and to be honest, so enjoyable and lively were they that I half-considered staying, but North Sea Radio Orchestra at the Roundhouse, Chalk Farm, were a must. Besides, I needed to get above ground to obtain a mobile-phone signal in order to check the score between Israel and Russia. You see, Israel and Russia were both in England's European Championship qualifying group, and in order for England to stand a chance of qualifying ahead of Russia, we had to rely on Israel. If Israel drew with Russia then we had to beat Croatia the following Wednesday to qualify, and if Israel won then all we needed was a draw. If Russia won then we were as good as out, barring a miracle win for Andorra over Russia on that same Wednesday we'd be taking on Croatia…

To my delight, via the wonders of Vodafone Live, I saw that Israel were leading 1-0 before Duffy and I disappeared underground again, this time onto the tube. I'm a little unclear as to why we emerged at Euston (possibly a line-closure – it's a wonder Max made his check-in), but as soon as we did I was straight back to the football and continued to refresh all the way to the Roundhouse as the Duffster and I got there on foot and bus. By the time we entered the venue and were seated with the great and the good in the café there, Russia had equalised so I started to panic. 'I need to find a telly so I can keep an eye on things,' I announced, suddenly not feeling so trustworthy of Vodafone Live.

'Well you'd better go and find a bar with it on,' advised Moke, 'because you know none of us care and that'll only start to annoy and frustrate you even more.' So off I went across the road to Studio 88 to watch the last 15 minutes.

For those 15 minutes I went through hell as Israel did their very best to allow Russia in, but after some incredibly close scrapes, including a toe-poke against the post, Israel broke away and knocked one in, leading to wild celebrations and a high-five with the dude behind the bar. The scorer, someone called Golan, would be guaranteed a place in English footballing folklore, if only England could do the business the following Wednesday... Well, at least Golan could look forward to the four days of over-the-top coverage he'd get in the English Press telling us all how he deserved the freedom of the country and such like... There was time to worry about England against Croatia later, but for now I was one happy Belch as I re-entered the Roundhouse and settled down in the FreeDM Theatre for North Sea Radio Orchestra.

How best to describe the North Sea Radio Orchestra? Probably by referring back to a conversation I had with my eldest sister Fiona (the piano teacher one) and her learned musician friends at her 50th birthday party. That was in May 2007 and in an attempt to prove to her that I was quite sophisticated musically you know, I'd threatened her with a trip to see NSRO in concert as a birthday treat the following Friday, something I'd hinted at via text.

'What have you got planned for next Friday?' asked a worried Fiona.

'Well, I know you always laugh when I say their name, but North Sea Radio Orchestra are performing at the Roundhouse (same venue, different date).'

'And just who ARE the North Sea Radio Orchestra?' she enquired further.

Conscious of the fact that I'd got the attention of a bunch of professional musicians into the bargain, I went a little bit pink in the face and said, 'Well, they're a small chamber orchestra (good so far) with Cardiacs connections…' (d'oh! Mistake!)

'You're losing me!' snapped Fiona, confirming what I'd already guessed (I'd once taken her daughter, my niece Jessamyn, then aged 15, to see Cardiacs at the Army And Navy in Chelmsford in 1996, and whilst Jessamyn enjoyed it, I'm not sure her description of it would have created a brilliant impression on her mum).

Deep sigh 'Let me start again. Craig Fortnam used to be in a band that featured two ex-Cardiacs (Shrubbies), and now he's formed a small chamber orchestra with his wife Sharron, and they do stuff like setting poems by Yeats and Tennyson to music…'

Short pause then, 'Hmmm – that sounds quite interesting actually.'

Ah, I was through at last. More so, one of the professional musicians perked up a bit here and asked, 'Who composes the music?'

'Craig mostly,' I replied, 'although Bill Drake writes a bit – he's Cardiacs' former keyboard player…'

'You're mentioning the C-word again,' warned Fiona.

'No no no!' I agitated. 'Bill's a proper piano player who plays a real piano and everything…'

Well, I had her interest, but as it turned out she was busy that Friday so had to make do with the eponymous North Sea Radio Orchestra CD instead. And now nearly six months on we were all gathered back at the Roundhouse for another dose of NSRO, except this time I'd forgotten to mention it to Big Sis…

The conversation with my sister and her muso friends, nicked from a blog I wrote at the time on MySpace, may well have described who NSRO were and what they did, but not how they sounded. In order to do that I might as well also nick all the descriptive phrases I used in that very same blog – besides, I rather liked some of them.

Rare beauty – that's what the music of North Sea Radio Orchestra is. If the word hadn't been ruined in a way by the Fat Slags in *Viz*, I'd describe them as lush; well, maybe luxuriant would be better, even lustrous, like a musical version of a full head of hair. Pastoral, quintessentially English, heightened by the words of the poems that they set to chamber music – what could be more British, nay, ENGLISH, than good old Alfred Lord...? But it's not just chamber – it's folksie in places, hymnal in others, and all in all an aural feast that sets your ears peacefully rejoicing. Even the more funereal moments make you feel happy and warm inside.

All of the above came to light once more as NSRO provided a night of delicacy and wonder at the Roundhouse, with the wildness of a Cardiacs gig seemingly a million miles away, and yet Cardiacs' influence was writ large all over the place, not least because of the presence of Kavus Torabi and Bill Drake in the NSRO chorus, alongside Tim's lovely lady Suzy, not forgetting Craig's Alphabet Business Concern pedigree, and Sharron's fantastic live appearances with Cardiacs in 2005 when she would stride on and rattle off "Will Bleed Amen" with sexy, sassy aplomb.

Afterwards as I chatted with some of the overseas nutters who put my Cardiacs gig-hopping well in the shade, namely Maarten of Cardiacs Online Museum and Frostbyte both from Holland, and Schlep from the USA, Schlep confessed to shedding a few tears of joy as the pastoral beauty of the orchestral music swept all before it. I felt a few tears welling up myself as I headed home on London Transport – it could have been the wonder of the music, but then it could have been the fact that I felt a spot of toothache coming on, and my usual tried-and-tested method of healing (I'm not telling you what it is – you'll only get annoyed like my Mum) only succeeded in making it worse.

In the absence of any toothache-tincture I had to make do with a different type of soothing – a luxuriant blast of NSRO on the iPod Nano all the way home; "Mimnermus in Church" and "Kingstanding" – guaranteed to ease any dental pain...

Chapter Fourteen
"As Cold As Can Be In an English Sea"
Those Overseas Enthusiasts

ALPHABET
Business Concern

A WORD FROM MR. VALMESLEY

Hi kids!! Wasn't it a great week out in Holland!!... not to mention that Brilliant Party in Belgium... but I'm terribly sorry about the police interference on that occasion, for as you know, tragically fatal accidents must be reported to the proper authorities. Therefore on behalf of myself, the *Alphabet Business Concern*, and CARDIACS, I thank you all unreservedly for behaving with the moral commonsense that we have promoted throughout our careers, and thoroughly look forward to our next continental extravaganza.

We at the *Alphabet Business Concern* have had to insist that, in order to fill their lackadaisical days, CARDIACS begin to record their second Long-Playing record, although on their rest days we have allowed the following Live Concert Performances:-

June 9	SCUNTHORPE Baths Hall
June 11	GUILDFORD Surrey University Students Union
June 21	NEWCASTLE Riverside
June 23	HAMMERSMITH Clarendon
June 24	MAIDSTONE Kent Hall

ALWAYS CHECK VENUES FOR CONFIRMATION

There may be more dates added soon, so check music press for details.

RECORD NEWS

"A Little Man And A House And The Whole World Window" Compact Disc is now available, and can be ordered from any reputable record store. (Cat. No. ALPH CD007, distributed by Pinnacle).

"A Little Man And A House And The Whole World Window" Cassette is available from record shops (Cat. No. ALPH MC007, distributed by Pinnacle). The first thousand include a FREE "Rude Bootleg" cassette album (CARDIACS live at Reading Festival 1986).

A compilation cassette album entitled "State Of Independence Volume 4" including tracks by Cardiacs, The Smiths, The Wedding Present, The Primitives, Pop Will Eat Itself, Wire, and many more, is available by mail order from the following address:

> Melody Maker Special Offer
> A.A.V. Harcourt
> Halesfield 14
> Telford
> TF7 4QR

The cost is £2.99 + 50p post & packing (£1.00 abroad); cheques or postal orders payable to I.P.C. Magazines LTD.

ALPHABET, PO Box 202, Kingston Upon Thames, Surrey, KT1 2QG

"As Cold As Can Be In an English Sea"
Those Overseas Enthusiasts

On May 6th 2005 Van der Graaf Generator performed their first concert since 1976, taking over the Royal Festival Hall in London's South Bank complex for the occasion, and what an occasion it was. People had come from all over the world, making my bus trip from Hackney seem positively dull. Why, even Al journeying down from Runcorn was considered small beer compared to those who had flown in from mainland-Europe (Italy especially) and the United States of America. At the time I didn't possess a VdGG t-shirt so I decided to adopt Ian's policy of wearing the merchandise of another band in an attempt to stimulate comment and conversation. Except whenever I adopt this policy I almost always without fail choose to wear a Cardiacs t-shirt, and this gig was no exception as I could be seen floating around the lobby area modelling a 'Little Man And A House' logo long-sleeved shirt sporting a back-print emblazoned with the word "CARDIACS".

As I stood at the bottom of some escalators chatting to Andy Thompson, I heard a voice behind me exclaim, 'I don't believe it! There's a guy in a Cardiacs t-shirt!' Not only had I stimulated comment, I'd seemingly flushed out a Cardiacs devotee from across the pond as the voice had an unmistakeable transatlantic drawl to it. I turned round to see a bearded hippie-type sporting a tie-dyed Gong t-shirt – blimey, they would have all on getting me into the gig if I struck up a conversation with this one.

Ah, but it would be rude not to. 'Blimey, I didn't know Americans had discovered Cardiacs,' I beamed.

'Oh we have...well, I have anyway; I'm trying to spread the word back home,' he replied.

'Fantastic!'

'What are the chances of them ever playing in LA?' he continued.

'Slim,' I frowned, letting him down gently.

'Gee, looks like I'll have to do what I've done for Van der Graaf Generator and fly over to London to see Cardiacs then,' he sighed. 'The trouble is, I've used up my entire budget on this trip, but it would be worth it to see the other of my two favourite bands,' he carried on. Now that was truly impressive; Cardiacs getting recognition from fans of the mighty VdGG – Progressive Rock fans weren't so po-faced after all.

At that point the "bing-bong" went to announce VdGG's imminent arrival onstage so our LA-buddy scuttled off to take his place whilst I hung around a bit longer, getting all agitated with the latest Belch-waiting-for-Ian-because-I've-got-his-ticket-and-he's-late episode, and we'd never even had the chance to discuss LA Guy's Gong t-shirt...

Of course, I already knew Cardiacs' message had spread abroad because by then I was aware of a number of American fans on The List, even though I still couldn't get on it myself, so had to receive odd snippets of information from Ian. Also back in the late-80s Cardiacs tours always included mainland-Europe, especially Holland (one of my biggest regrets in life is that I never got it together enough to venture abroad on any of those specially-arranged Mark Walmsley Charabangalangs to see Cardiacs in Amsterdam and Belgium and the like). Indeed, in 1988 I'd been introduced to a gentleman called Martin Roest who had come over from Holland for the December 21st Marquee gig, Martin subsequently making the trip over relatively frequently for Cardiacs gigs, including this current 2007 tour.

As the years progressed, to add to the Dutch fanbase of Martin, Maarten (no relation) of Cardiacs Online Museum and Frostbyte among others, it was a joy to discover Cardiacs had an expanding following in Italy (hence William D. Drake doing gigs in Venice) (hello Carlo) and Israel, where apparently some crazed radio DJ once did a whole show devoted to them. And when I met the beautiful Gong-Princess Chris from Moscow at Gong's UnConvention in Amsterdam, and told her that at the end of the week I'd be seeing Cardiacs at the Astoria, she sighed and said, 'I'd love to see Cardiacs live...'

Of course, a lot of this word-spreading was to do with the

World Wide Web, meaning that even those who lived in countries where Cardiacs had never toured (like Russia and the USA) could stumble across their fantastical sounds via cardiacs.com and hope that one day the Alphabet Business Concern would pop the band on an aeroplane. Failing that, any new fans from foreign climes could always jump on a 'plane themselves, and gosh golly, quite a lot of them were doing so; thus, it is those that have flown over from the States that really do earn my unstinting respect, considering that even a hardened traveller such as I has only ever ventured abroad to see England stuff Germany 5-1 and Slovakia 2-1, as well as a nightmare coach-trip to Amsterdam for that Gong thing, and my first ever flight in order to see Magma and Guapo (featuring our very own Kavus Torabi) in Carmaux, France (and in case you're wondering, the nearest Sheffield United have ever got to meaningful football "abroad" is Wales).

The other wonder of the Internet is that it enables all those lovely Cardiacs fans from all over the world to talk to each other, hence it was possible for Ian to obtain a *Curb Your Enthusiasm* t-shirt for my 40th birthday by instructing a Cardiacs Email Chat Listee to pop into the Stateside HBO shop and purchase one before bunging it in the post. And it meant I could receive wonderful emails via MySpace, like the following one from a certain Schlep:

"Hi, I've just had a look around your very entertaining My-Space/blog – I like a bit of Gong, Yes, auld P.G. (Peter Gabriel) Genesis (and all sorts of other weird things) myself, and last year, at the tender age of 46, first heard of this peculiar band 'Cardiacs'…imagine that! I live in the States, where Cardiacs are almost completely obscure. They completely changed my perspective on music, certainly.

"I spend quite a bit of time online with the loverly people at the Mare's Nest forum, as Schlep… Just wanted to say hello, and I really enjoy your writing.

"Best wishes – Steve aka Schlep"

Apart from the bit about really enjoying my writing, the stand-out thing for me here was Schlep's discovery of Cardiacs "at the tender age of 46". The fact that he was then prepared to fly over from Wisconsin and trek over to Bristol for the Thekla gig before heading back to London for the Astoria showcase was indeed worthy of laudation. Schlep's blog on the trip makes essential reading as it brings out the joy of not only discovering some truly brilliant music, but also of witnessing a band whilst in a strange country for the first time, a band who even when Schlep was initially swept along by the wonders of Cardiacs probably doubted he'd ever get the chance to see in the flesh. Of the whole adventure he says, "Honestly I was prepared for some degree of disappointment – that maybe the concerts would be not-that-special, the people in the audience not-that-wonderful, the weather dismal, the accommodations grim, the whole thing a huge waste of money and effort…but NO, everything was super fantastic (though the weather was *a little* dismal, but par for the course)!"

Of the Thekla gig, Schlep blogged: "The melee at the front of the stage is difficult to describe – a moshpit of grinning baldy men who hopped up and down and thrashed all around during the set…a wonder to behold."

More importantly, he says of the music, "The sound was LOUD but clear, and immense – I was vibrating from it for many hours afterwards. Something about this music – it's very harmonically dense and rich; it hits you on all kinds of levels. The added sonic presence of the Girls on vocals was quite surprising, very beyond what you hear on recordings."

Musing on Cardiacs' music in general, Schlep blogs, "I've decided that this Tim Smith and his musical creations have at least one big shiny shoe in the realm of Art and of Spiritual Things, though it is made all up of Pop Music, of humble elements, drum-kits and loud guitars and shouting at microphones, in smelly rock clubs. Because you can walk around it in all directions describing what you see and hear forever, but never get to the essence of what it REALLY IS, the music maintains its mystery and integrity and just is what it is, which is beautiful and moving, and which resonates very deeply for certain people who, for whatever reason, are happily able to take the experience on board."

You know what, Schlep my old pal, if I'd not heard Cardiacs but read this, you can be sure that I'd *want* to hear them straight away...

And just in case you remain doubtful as to Schlep's conversion, he says of "Dirty Boy" at the Astoria, "When the Girls opened their mouths to sing the ultimate final note (continuous for some three minutes, has to be heard to be believed), I thought my head might come off. The ultimate Cardiacs anthem, in the ultimate context..."

Jesse Vecchione was another of our American converts, and I'm sure it was 2005 (may even have been 2004) when we met in a pub around the corner from the Astoria (although he reckons it was 2006 – all I remember about 2006 is having tonsillitis and not wanting to talk to *anyone* pre-gig). Sadly Jesse couldn't be around for 2007, but as it was his suggestion that I do a chapter on Overseas Educated Dedicated Supporters (big prize to anyone who can tell me where I nicked that from), then it is only fair that he has his say, so I got him to email the tale of his conversion. This is it:

"I learned about Cardiacs when I was DJ-ing at my college radio station in Vermont. I had a website in conjunction with my radio show on audigalaxy.com called *Testing The Limits*, which basically was a multi-genre share site for audiophiles like me.

"At the time, I would travel every other weekend to my hometown on Cape Cod and regularly make mix-tapes of whatever was being shared at the time on *Testing The Limits* to listen to on the road (it was a 3.5 hour trip through the mountains and down into the coastal plain).

"One week, the tape I put together happened to have "Fiery Gun Hand" on it. On first listen I was horrified, it just sounded like a mess to me. However, even at first listen it was clear to me that the band had an undeniable uniqueness to it – I just loathed it initially. I remember thinking that it sounded like a gaggle of murderous Muppets covering a Pet Shop Boys song at breakneck speed. Since then I can make better estimations of what Cardiacs sound like of course (oh I dunno Jesse, I rather like that description, especially the bit about "murderous Muppets").

"Over the next few weeks, I found myself thinking about "Fiery Gun Hand" and what set it aside from other songs. I have a personal philosophy about music I refer to as "The Kryptonite Theory". In *Superman II*, Richard Pryor's character was beset with the challenge of synthesising Kryptonite in his lab. All of the chemical elements of Kryptonite were known by him, except for a small percentage of some "unknown material". I think about music in the same way in the fact that every song (or band) can be broken down into previous influences or styles. In unique, creative bands, there is always this "unknown" where it just sounds like nothing else that has been made before. It's always a percentage, and in the most creative, most inventive bands, the percentage can be quite high. For example, I'd rate an average Zappa song 40% or so. On the other end of the spectrum your run-of-the-mill Pop song can range from 0-2%. Over the first few listens of Cardiacs, it was clear that they would rank high on the Kryptonite Rating.

"When I was in the process of determining the extent of their uniqueness was when what I refer to as the "Holy Itch" occurred. At the time, I was mainly into American Post Rock, Post Punk and Glam Rock, so my ears were not necessarily primed to hear the dense Thrash-Psychedelia that is *Sing To God*. But over a few listens, I began to become obsessed at getting to the bottom of what it was this band was all about. To me, listening to a Cardiacs song initially was like a riddle I needed to solve. But, once I learned a song in my head and could anticipate the changes, it was more like an amusement park ride. It provided a feeling unlike anything I had heard before (and since).

"I acquired as much of their material as I could and began playing it on my radio show. After a few months, I would play at least one Cardiacs song every show. Some of my regular listeners became fans and I made them mix-tapes of my favourite songs. Also around this time I began inundating all of my old musician friends with Cardiacs any time we would be together. Some people loved it, some didn't, but that's usually the case with Cardiacs. I carried some of their material with me wherever I traveled (sic) which qualifies me as some sort of Cardiacs missionary in the USA.

"I moved to Oklahoma for work but brought my enthusiasm about the band with me and made some converts over here. In 2006 (I think) I finally made the pilgrimage to the London Astoria to see the band live. I was treated like a celebrity by the die-hard fans as we had long-since all made friends on the Internet chat-lists, and even got to meet a few former members." (I seem to remember Tim Quy sitting in the pub actually, Jesse, and there were one or two others kicking around.) (And Jesse, it was 2005, but you know that now!)

So there you have it. Proof that the Cardiacs Family is truly worldwide, and that sometimes the things that need working at a bit bring the greatest satisfaction in the long-run – "murderous Muppets" indeed…

* * * *

What makes the inclusion of our American brethren in this book all the more interesting is that it brings in a slightly different slant on the "musical influences" part of my research (although it must be pointed out, Schlep's liking for Gong, Yes and early-Genesis has a bit of Belchness about it), Max Crowe being a fantastic example of all this, and as he flew in from the States for the Bristol gig in seven hours whilst I spent eleven hitching it from Kettering, he is worthy of further investigation, so I'd better get on with telling you all about him…

It could be said that music, for those of us who care, is with us from the cradle to the grave, and in Max's case this seems to be extra-specially true as his first musical recollection is almost beyond recollection, if you see what I mean (except thankfully he's not reached the grave yet). 'A difficult one, this,' he says, 'but I'm pretty sure my earliest music-related memory was being in my bedroom as a very small child, possibly even in a crib, and hearing Devo's "Jocko Homo" playing on a stereo.' Oh my word! That's some introduction, certainly putting my "Two Little Boys" in the shade. What's more,

Tim and Jim Smith both went on record on BBC6 Music's *Brain Surgery* declaring their love of Devo.

Records also seem to have been around for ever in Max's life, making it very difficult to pinpoint exactly what the first one to make its way into his possession was, but he's settling on The B-52s and their self-titled album, '…one of the gifts at my fifth birthday party.'

Once again, the first record Max purchased is a little hazy, but 'the first memory I have of picking out a record in a store and buying it is a purchase of Devo's *New Traditionalists*, bundled with a 45 of "Workin' In A Coal Mine".

All this cool, adventurous music at such an early age – surely parents had something to do with this (heck, what would I have been like if my Mum and Dad had been 1960s Flower Children?) (for the record, they're as far removed from this as it is possible to imagine)? 'Yep – my Dad played me things like Devo, The Residents, some Frank Zappa, and the avant-garde stuff he likes; and my Mom played me things like The B-52s, Elvis Costello, and other new wave.' Wow, you can already start to see how all this lot thrown together would emerge with a liking for Cardiacs…

Dad's influence possibly weighed a bit heavier however, because the first band Max was really passionate about was Devo, unsurprisingly: 'Are you picking up a pattern here yet?' he asks. Yup.

When Michael of Circulus saw Cardiacs at the Astoria he was most impressed by how they brought a "West End slickness to music of such complexity", and presumably this "showy" side of Cardiacs has always appealed to Max too, because the first gig he went to was 'Weird Al' Yankovic, 'and let me tell you, that man knows how to put on a good show,' he says.

After that rather fantastic introduction in life to music, the sounds that influenced young Max until Cardiacs came wandering along should come as no surprise to those of a certain vintage. 'I wouldn't say I came from any one specific genre; it was more like strange and interesting music in general: Frank Zappa, Devo and Mr Bungle were probably at the top of my list at the time, and of course all of these are groups/artists for whom Cardiacs themselves have professed admiration.' And as with all good music lovers, Max kept on liking all the stuff he was already into whilst expanding his taste and record collection, to the point where these days he considers himself 'very much a fan of Area, The Bad Plus, Captain Beefheart, Call Me Lightning, Miles Davis, Kool Keith, King Crimson, The Mars Volta, Oingo Boingo, The Police, Sparks, STNNNG, Talking Heads, Béla Bartók, Charles Ives, Igor Stravinsky, and Edward Varès.' Not forgetting Cardiacs of course...

Okay, so when did Cardiacs first come into the equation? 'I was 21-years-old, and a junior at the University of Iowa. I had, and still have, a band called Genital Hercules, and the singer at the time was a guy I had recently met named Les Ohlhauser. He is the type of guy who is always on the lookout for good music that he hasn't heard before. One day he came for rehearsal, and before we started, he said, "Dude, you have got to go and download a song called "Angleworm Angel" by this band Cardiacs *right now*." So I did, and I think I probably resembled the guy in the old Maxell advertisement when it started playing, me being blown back in my chair and everything. I couldn't believe what I was hearing – the constant key changes, the relentless turmoil, the soaring chorus, and the nuclear meltdown tempo. It was perfect. I had been waiting my whole life to hear music like this. I asked Les how he found it, and he said he and a friend just happened upon it while surfing the web. I immediately downloaded, via the now-sadly defunct Audiogalaxy, the next song that came up, which turned out to be "A Bus For A Bus On The Bus". Being a big Frank Zappa fan I immediately recognised the reference to "A Pound For A Brown On The Bus". I could tell it was much older and cruder but I heard the same spark of brilliance that I heard in "Angleworm Angel". This was the beginning of a long time spent scouring the Internet for any recorded Cardiacs material I could find.

'The first Cardiacs recorded work that I managed to get my hands on, apart from a few mp3s downloaded here and there, was *Sing To God*. I listened to it very loudly every day for about two weeks after I got it.' You and me alike, Max...

Hailing from the States, Max's first Cardiacs gig was always going to be a bit more interesting than just a little hitch down the motorway to stumble across them at Reading Festival:

'I spent the first semester of my senior year at university studying abroad in Alcalá de Henares, Spain, near Madrid. At this point I had managed to get my hands on *Sing To God* and *Guns* thanks to Amazon.com, at great expense. I was hooked, but as I recall I wasn't really yet aware of just how great Cardiacs were. I checked their website one day and saw that a gig was scheduled for November 15th 2002 at the Astoria Theatre, which was about a month or two away. Right away I booked my passage to London. When the travel date arrived, I almost didn't make it; due to a combination of naiveté and poorly allocated timing, I didn't get to the airport until just before the scheduled departure time, and I had to frantically talk my way on board. Fortunately I managed it, and was in the United Kingdom for the first time in my life within a couple of hours.

'The first thing I did after unloading my bags at the hostel was to visit every record store in the vicinity of Oxford Circus and buy every Cardiacs disc I could find. Since I had actually arrived on the afternoon of the 15th I didn't have a lot of time to spare, so I zipped back to my hostel to drop off my purchases and listen to a few selected tracks, something I was glad of because several of them turned up in the performance later and it was nice to have a little preparation. Shortly thereafter I was queued up at the Astoria, which was apparently undergoing some renovations (to be honest Max, it always looked about ready to fall down) and I saw a sign reading "Crowe Scaffolding". I figured that seeing my last name in these circumstances must constitute an omen...

'The first act was Claire Lemmon and Melanie Wood performing as a duo – I quite liked them, and I did eventually become a fan of Sidi Bou Said. The second act was Oceansize, of whom I have also remained a fan. In between songs the singer mentioned what an honour it was to be performing in front of the Alphabet Business Concern banner, and got a big cheer.

'While waiting for Cardiacs to come on, I chatted with a few of the attendees, and upon hearing that it was my first Cardiacs gig, one of them warned me that where I was standing, right in front of the stage, approximately where Tim Smith was about to appear, was about to become "a pit of danger". He was right. The excitement built around me as the ABC chimes played over the PA system, and I soon found myself pressed in by a wild-eyed English crowd. My eyes were pretty wild themselves as the band took the stage and launched into the first song, "The Alphabet Business Concern (Home of Fadeless Splendour)". I had listened to this song for the first time in my hostel bunk-bed just a few hours previous, so I was able to sing along to the first two lines, and no more. The second song in the set was "Arnald", which ignited a frenzy of moshing and heaving that did not let up for the next ninety minutes. Suffice to say, I left that gig transformed into a total fanatic.'

So, just how many times has that fanaticism led to Max Crowe getting all adventurous and trekking over land and sea to see Cardiacs in total? 'I suppose it depends whether you count the 2003 Garage gigs as three or one (oh, three, definitely, otherwise I'm left high and dry on 99 gigs). Counting them as three, I've seen them eight times now – not bad for a Yank!' Indeed – could that be a record for a non-UK-based American? Place your orders everyone...

In amongst all this joy and discovery, it can sometimes be difficult to pick out things that you consider to be more favourite than others. 'There's no way I can single out an individual album as a favourite, much less a song. As for favourite gigs, I think it's a toss-up between that first one in 2002 and the Oxford gig in 2007. I have a few favourite moments...seeing Ian Taft bounce up and down to "Big Ship" in 2003 was pretty fantastic, as was suddenly finding my mouth covered by Marina (*The Organ*) Anthony's hand during "Dirty Boy" in 2005 just during the "hold his mouth and stop him breathing" part. I also felt like I had really arrived when, during the 2007 Bristol gig, Jon Poole bumped into me and we pretended to get angry at each other.'

Yes indeed, a pretend argument with a former-representative of the Alphabet Business Concern – a badge to be worn with honour, all the way on the flight home to the USA for sure...

Chapter Fifteen
"There's Too Many Irons In the Fire"
The Boardwalk, Sheffield,
November 19th 2007

"There's Too Many Irons In the Fire"
The Boardwalk, Sheffield, November 19th 2007

Gigs in Sheffield are not exactly rare in my life. This obviously has something to do with the fact that I spent the first 22 years of my existence living there, aided further by frequent visits since then to watch Sheffield United (the guarantee of a bed for the night at my Mum and Dad's always far too good to turn down). Ah yes, the combination of football and music, something I'll be going into in more detail in later chapters, but for now you might like to know that Fish has featured twice in this doubling of "pleasure", firstly in November 1989 when performing a gig at Sheffield University after a rather fortuitous 1-1 draw for the Blades against Leicester City, and secondly in October 1993 at the Leadmill after I'd watched us struggle in overcoming Blackpool 2-0 in the second leg of a Coca Cola Cup match, the downside of this being that Blackpool had stuffed us 3-0 at Bloomfield Road in the first leg, so on aggregate out we went. The Leadmill thus provided a touch of solace that night, although a bit of a stand-off with the bouncer about my Sheffield United badge had things looking shaky for a while (for those of you familiar with "Chaingate" at Charlton Athletic away November 2008, you'll be glad to know that on this Fishy occasion I removed my badge, but not before I'd made it quite clear how daft and petty I felt they were being).

One thing I wore that night *did* provoke a positive response however. Upon entering the venue I discovered that I knew the promoter, Barbara again, she formerly of Push And Plug, and she arranged for me to go backstage after the gig in order to meet the great man. I was proudly sporting my "CARDIACS respectfully remind you All That Glitters is a MARE'S NEST" t-shirt (before the sleeves were removed), a t-shirt that drew the attention of Fish.

'Cardiacs!' he exclaimed. 'Are they still going?'

It had been well-documented in the 80s that Fish was a big Cardiacs fan, so much so that he'd got Cardiacs a support slot on a Marillion tour in 1984. I was however now rather disappointed to find out that nine years on, our scaly friend had lost track of the Alphabet Business Concern's activities, so ever faithful, I was happy to update him about the current four-piece and the relatively recent *Heaven Born And Ever Bright*. 'They're just as exciting and brilliant as ever live,' I enthused, but it has to be said, I've not noticed Fishykins at any Cardiacs gigs since. Perhaps he didn't believe me…

So yes, far too many gigs in Sheffield to rave about all of them here, apart from perhaps any Cardiacs gigs along the way (which is after all the point of this book). The first one at the Leadmill in April 1988 has been mentioned before, and was memorable for being my first Cardiacs gig since the obsession took hold, but the second in June 1989 at the Take Two club in the lovely Sheffield suburb of Attercliffe (ho hum) was just as memorable in its own way, largely due to the extreme heat. It was one of those hot summer days that don't quite make it to "gorgeous" status due to the muggy nature of the air. Just what you need on such a stuffy evening, a small venue packed solid with insane Cardiacs fans. I knew they were insane due to the fact that many of them moshed as if it was a cold February evening in the open air. Sane old me sat on the ledge by an open window with Annie, aware of a thunderstorm outside but more fascinated with the fireworks going on inside. Jim, the only band-member still dressed in full bandsman regalia, barely moved an inch all night but still had sweat pouring off him throughout. Tim meanwhile was obviously keen to keep up with the nutters in the audience and was as manic as ever onstage (at least he didn't wear his big coat back then). Apparently he kept blacking out mid-song, thus making it even more remarkable that the whole band turned in a magnificent performance, all keeping perfectly in line and in time.

For whatever reasons I missed Cardiacs' next visit to Sheffield in 1995 on the Chumbawamba support tour when they graced the stage of the Octagon Centre at Sheffield University, so I had to wait over 15 years for my next hometown gig when Cardiacs returned to my favourite venue of the Leadmill on December 11th 2004 whilst touring as support for the Wildhearts. This also provided me with another opportunity to combine football with Cardiacs. Normally Sheffield United playing away would pose a problem, but a trip to neighbouring Rotherham was a godsend. But what was this? Sky nipped in and moved the kick-off to 5.30, thus making it a little tight for time. Not a problem (just a bit of a worry) – a sharp exit would be necessary, followed by a prompt train to Sheffield, then a quick jog from the station to the Leadmill (the not-a-problem bit), all whilst not knowing what time Cardiacs were onstage (the bit-of-worry bit).

Of course, Sheffield United messed up a good day by chucking away a two-goal half-time lead to draw 2-2, but a perfectly executed dash back to Sheffield led to an entrance into the venue just in time to see Captain John moving Cardiacs' gear into place. And then as we waited at the front there seemed to be a constant stream of Sheffield Cardiacs fans willing to tell me they had waited a heck of a long time to see their heroes on home turf.

None of us were disappointed as those representatives of the Alphabet Business Concern did what they seemed to do all through that tour; play without pressure, satisfy the faithful, puzzle the watching Wildhearts fans (those that weren't in the bar), and subsequently make a few new fans.

Amongst those faithful were three most welcome old faces, Mr and Mrs Quy, and Richard Jackson, my old hitchhiking-to-Cardiacs-gigs mate from 1988/89. Tim Quy was apparently working on secondment in the Steel City, whereas Richard had returned as a resident long since that brief spell in Oxford. Both were impressed by what they saw and heard that night, especially Richard who'd not ventured out to see Cardiacs since one of those New Cross Venue gigs in 1994. Most remarkable to him as a drummer was how on earth anyone could come up with a click-track for Cardiacs. 'Well, that's Tim for you,' said Tim Quy.

Afterwards we stood out on the street and watched in amusement all the scantily-clad maidens queuing up to get in to the after-gig nightclub, braving the cold December Sheffield night-air and shivering uncontrollably as a result. I was reminded of a bloke who'd given me a lift once telling me he'd always thought it'd be a good idea to turn up outside a nightclub wearing a big pair of massively fluffy gloves, then offer to warm-up girls legs and shoulders in exchange for cash – enterprising chap that one, if only he'd ever been brave enough to actually try it. As it was, I had no massively fluffy gloves so I headed off for a late-night curry before taxi-ing parentwards.

And now bringing us up to date, at last Cardiacs were about to headline in Sheffield for the first time in 18 years. However a gig in Sheffield has always seemed slightly incomplete when Sewer hasn't been there, and for the preceding 19 years Sewer had consistently remained resistant to the attraction of Cardiacs, but was all that about to change…?

* * * *

Back in 1982 I befriended a new chap in the sixth form of High Storrs School, Sheffield, who rejoiced in the name of Sewer. We sat next to each other in Geography and instead of studying Hydro-Electricity in the Upper Volta (or something), we discussed music. I detected a glimpse of good taste in him upon discovering that he liked the Electric Light Orchestra, so recommended Gentle Giant to him (well, they did have a violin and a cello).

He was converted, and from then on everything I put his way got the thumbs up – Gong, Yes, Genesis, King Crimson, ELP... Sewer and Belch became a fixture at just about every Prog-Rock gig in Sheffield, be it the Leadmill, Sheffield Uni, Sheffield Poly, or humbler venues like the Hallamshire, so thus we discovered Haze, Solstice, IQ, Pallas, The Enid and so on and so forth.

By 1988 we had been chums for six years and flatmates for three. Thanks to the sighting at Reading in 1986 and those hearings on Garry Davies' Radio One show, my Cardiacs obsession was taking hold. This time however, I met with resistance from Sewer. He just couldn't get his head round them at all. In fact, it wasn't just that – he seemingly HATED them. With a passion. When challenged by me, his main objection seemed to be the overly-contrived complexity, something I always found a little surprising coming from someone who liked Frank Zappa more than I did and had all the Yes and King Crimson albums. But not to worry – I ploughed headlong on into the world of the Alphabet Business Concern whilst Sewer declined my invitations to attend those Cardiacs concert performances at the Leadmill in April 1988 and the Take Two in June 1989.

By summer 1989 I was long gone from Sheffield, so Sewer was spared any more conversion attempts. All that remained for him was his knowledge that he hated them and sad-deluded-me loved them...

Then just prior to the 2007 Cardiacs tour I texted Sewer to inform him that Cardiacs were playing at the Boardwalk in Sheffield on November 19th and he should therefore attend. This was the unexpected text I got in reply:

"Strange you should mention this. I've been meaning to call you. They've finally got into my brain after twenty-odd years and I can't get them out! It's sending me potty. Is there any cure? Seriously. I will call Dr Belch tomorrow..."

I texted him the quick answer – there is no known cure, but a listen to Stars In Battledress might calm things down a little.

That call "tomorrow" eventually took place the next week (all my fault, and Tesco didn't help either), but finally a full confession was heard.

It turns out Mr Sewer spied *A Little Man And A House And The Whole World Window* second-hand somewhere and picked it up for next to nothing, because if nothing else he remembered liking the opening sax-salvo of "The Whole World Window". Upon listening to the whole album though, he was glad to realise that yes, he still hated Cardiacs.

But when you're driving for three hours a day with only a CD player for company strange things can happen, and the poor lad was compelled to listen to the thing again. This time he was struck by the production values, and so on the CD went a third time. By now the earworms were at work, and despite thinking he still hated the music, a few weeks on he found the tunes were in his head, and they wouldn't go away. Doomed...

It was around now that the childhood imagery started messing with his brain – all plinky-plonky xylophones and nursery rhymes. He really was a goner now, as with trembling hands he found himself visiting cardiacs.com and ordering *Songs For Ships And Irons* and *Heaven Born And Ever Bright*. He was almost relieved to find he hated these two, but once again those little wormies got to work and before he knew it he was hauled well and truly in: 'I'm not kidding Belch, I must have listened to those three albums a hundred times each!' Blimey – he was a worse case than me...

More visits to the Internet produced orders for *The Seaside, On Land And In The Sea, Sing To God Parts One and Two* and *Guns*, and working through them sequentially he found that yes, he hated them on first listening, but ended up addicted after around three listens. 'I'm on *Sing To God Part Two* now, and I hate it. But I know what's coming. I've not listened to *Guns* yet...'

'You'll hate it,' I advised, 'but you know what's coming...'

'I don't know if I'm unique...' he mused.

'Nope,' I reassured, 'many people hated Cardiacs on first hearing but grew to love them, not least Marillion fans when Cardiacs supported them in 1984. It's just most of them didn't spend around twenty years coming round...'

So now the possible last-piece-of-the-jigsaw of a live viewing was about to be put in place at the Boardwalk in Sheffield, although lucky old Sewer already had an idea of what to expect; 'I may not have seen them live,' he explained, 'but when listening to the songs I can imagine what the performances are like because I remember you cavorting around the living room with your air guitar back in '88...' Me, behave like that? Never…

After I shared this sorry tale with the Internet Community, Sewer posted this little reply just to shed a touch more light on things: "God help me. It's the honest truth and there is no cure. I even find at night that I'm possessed by little Cardiac tunelets that glue themselves together into brand new bits of cod-Cardiacs of my own undirected confection. I don't know if this is a profound vision, or some sort of psychosis. I don't even know if there is a difference. God help me. It's the honest truth…and there is no cure."

* * * *

So, we were about to have a continuation of the common occurrence of Belch attending a gig in Sheffield, and even more exciting, a reunion of the Sewer/Belch partnership was on the cards. Another common theme was about to be played out too; me turning up to a gig feeling a bit rough. Having already done Nottingham feeling somewhat under the weather, Sheffield was shaping up to be even worse as the slight toothache that had sneaked up after the North Sea Radio Orchestra recital on Saturday was now a raging menace threatening to shatter all my plans the night before the Cardiacs gig at Sheffield's Boardwalk. I'd spent most of Sunday afternoon traipsing around Ashford buying a bewildering array of painkillers and gels in an effort to calm things down, but a sleepless night suggested nothing was working.

If you remember, somewhere at the start of all this book business I'd been planning to hitchhike to ALL the gigs on the tour, but thus far I'd managed to drag the old thumb out for one, Bristol. The idea was to get the hitching back on track with this Sheffield gig, as a hitch from London to Sheffield had become such a regular activity for me it was almost like catching the bus. However with searing toothache and a glance in the mirror which convinced me my face was swollen hideously as a result of the pain, the last thing I needed was a cold November wind blustering down a slip-road and into my gnashers. Besides, with no sleep all night what I really needed was a trip where I might be able to grab forty winks, so rather than it being almost like catching the bus, that's exactly what it was, the Megabus no less.

There was a board-game called Test Match back in the 1970s advertised by Fred Trueman (you know the game, the one where the bat resembled a vacuum cleaner) in which Fiery Fred said, "If they'd had this when I was a lad, I might not have bothered with the real thing." By the same token, if they'd had the Megabus back in 1984, I might not have bothered with the "real thing" of student/unemployed travelling, hitchhiking, in which case instead of *Fever Hitch*, you'd probably have had a scintillating tome all about squashing up in a rickety bus with either the heating on way above "reasonable" level, or not on at all so everyone was of a shivering heap, with perhaps a tale or two chucked in about going to a niece's wedding and being daft enough to get a Megabus from London to Aberdeen, then suffering as it breaks down twice and the whole miserable, cramped journey takes 16 hours from start to finish. But hey, it never happened like that, so you got all the mundane stuff about service stations, all-night vigils on the M40, and snatched Burger King suppers before dashing off for another lift with a potential murderer.

Anyway, all unpleasant Megabus memories of 16-hour nightmares to Aberdeen were pushed to one side by the severe pain in my tooth and the cheapness of a trip on said bus-service, aided by a guaranteed arrival time well in advance of gig-start-time (i.e. plenty of time for grub at Mum and Dad's). At least the gig was on for me, and believe you me, the way I'd felt the night before there was a distinct possibility of me wimping out. But then had I not attended a Cardiacs gig at the Astoria with tonsillitis in 2006? Indeed I had, so a silly old toothache wasn't going to stop me, I decided. Just in case, I armed myself with the phone number for the Charles Clifford Dental Hospital in Sheffield (a place I knew very well from the traumas of regular visits as a teenager – hard though it is to believe, my mouth was too small for all the teeth it had to accommodate) and all those painkillers and gels.

The result was that by the time I arrived in Sheffield, and after a bit of a kip on the bus, I was feeling quite mellow, the pain having subsided considerably, meaning eating food at my Mum and Dad's was so very easy. Another luxury was being able to drop my rucksack off there, thus avoiding any disputes with cloakroom officials at the venue. And just to top it all off, there was the wonder of getting a bus 200 yards from the front door all the way to the venue, the very fabulous number 85, which didn't exist when I were a lad. Of course, I was there ridiculously early so ended up sitting on the steps outside the Boardwalk listening to a sparkling Cardiacs soundcheck whilst waiting for Sewer and Lil Malc to respond to texts.

Malc was first off the mark, similar to Brighton, so as he was in a hotel just down the way near the canal basin he quickly joined me outside the venue, and with the arrival of Pete we were soon sat in Burger King (them again, just like *Fever Hitch*) building up the carbs for that night's excesses. As we sat in there putting the world to rights, one of the employees came up to us and asked, 'Are you a bunch of Death-Metallers then?'

I laughed, Malc smirked, and Pete snapped, 'No!' We then tried to explain to him the wonders of Cardiacs music, but he'd obviously made his mind up that we were big-time rockers of some description, hence why he asked us, 'Have you heard about Lemmy?'

The tone of his voice suggested the worst. Pete looked the most worried, one of his many tattoos being that rather scary Motörhead armoured-tusky-skull thing, but as someone with a fair smattering of Motörhead albums myself (including gold-vinyl *No Sleep 'til Hammersmith*) and a card-carrying Hawkwind fan, my heart sank also. Could it be that old Gravel-Voice himself had finally overdone it and popped off?

'He's got done for smoking onstage at t'Arena,' bombshell-dropped our BK-employee friend.

A collective sigh of relief followed by, 'I thought you were going to tell us he was dead!' was sufficient to let him know how much upset he'd caused us.

As the evening progressed our group got bigger and bigger, and by the time we settled in the Banker's Draft pub we'd commandeered a couple of tables, including Big Ship Iron, Sewer, Nige (an old school mate and something of a Haze gig veteran) and, most excitingly for me, Paul Hope and Tiny, both of Sleepy People. Paul happily told me that he was now running the Sky Apple Café in Newcastle, the card he gave me proudly describing him as a "VEGETARIAN CHEF".

Eventually we all decamped to the venue where I re-acquainted myself with Chris the promoter. You see, of the bands I'd worked for in the past, Jesus Underground Band (Slovakia), Human Oddities (Israel), and Cheese Cake Truck (Norway), all had got gigs at the Boardwalk through my efforts, and all had gone down really well, especially Jesus Underground Band who Chris absolutely loved (a rarity with a promoter this), so much so that on one occasion on a Sunday when we'd been delayed (as ever) and the gig looked like going well over the curfew and long after the buses stopped, Chris dimmed as many lights as he dared, locked the doors, and offered to pay taxi fares for anyone who missed their last bus – like I suggested, a rare promoter.

Chris had always told me it was his ambition to put Cardiacs on, so he was very excited before the start. I never got the chance to catch up with him afterwards, so I've no idea if it had met his expectations, but I can only guess that it had as he rebooked them for the following year, until unforeseen circumstances intervened...

Also in the venue that night, not surprisingly, were Richard (no need to wait eleven years between Cardiacs gigs this time) and Haze sound engineer Warren. The audience in general seemed a little older on average than recent gigs, whether in Sheffield or elsewhere, and this was reflected in the slightly more sedate reaction from the Pond at the start. However, "As Cold As Can Be In An English Sea" certainly livened things up, especially in my case. During this foot-tapping number I always feel it essential to maintain my wild cavorting throughout, so that manic bit at the end is a real test of endurance. If they were to play this every night, I would be very fit indeed.

* * * *

At the end of the night, in order to cool down, and with one or two people calling me the Elephant Man due to my perceived tooth/face swelling ('Can't see any difference,' said someone who shall remain nameless, either being honest or very cheeky), Sewer, Richard, Nige and I were all stood outside discussing the evening's entertainment. Richard needed no conversion, but Nige was undecided (as Sewer proved, it's not always an instantaneous thing with Cardiacs). Sewer on the other hand, as the most recently-obsessed convert, was most impressed, and re-emphasised it later with a text stating simply, "Loved it!"

A late-night back at Nige's for me and Sewer saw me sharing many shoplifter Tesco King's Cross tales with them, as if to prove that there wasn't much of the peace-loving soft-touch hippy left in me. But overwhelmingly, as Sewer gave me a lift home, my feeling was one of satisfaction as I congratulated myself on finally helping Sewer to appreciate the wonders that Cardiacs provide. Well, that's what friends are for, surely.

Chapter Sixteen
"Pip as Uncle Dick but
Peter Spoiled It"
Thrupty and Clare

"Pip As Uncle Dick But Peter Spoiled It"
Pete "Thrupty" Davis and Clare Kelly

Pete "Thrupty" Davis (sometimes known as "Skitzo Pete") is certainly a familiar face at Cardiacs gigs; well, familiar *and* memorable – more of a presence really. During those early-90s four-piece-Cardiacs concert performances, Pete was quite a boisterous character in the Pond, so if you hadn't already noticed his piercings, shaved head and tattoos, you'd certainly become aware of him if he made physical contact with you. As I'm a reasonable sort, I can safely say Pete always plays fair in the Pond, making sure that he keeps those elbows in, and if he engages you in playful joshing, he's operating on the understanding that you look like you want to join in (and let's be honest, if you are in the Pond, you are usually up for it) – trouble is, if he nudges you a bit hard, you're usually the one to go over, such is his strength. But like I said, he plays fair, and believe you me, if he sends someone a-tumbling, he's the first to worry and attempt to drag you back to your feet; more than once I've been hauled back up by Pete, and I'm sure many more can say the same. In that Cardiacs gig melee, providing the audience *do* keep those elbows in, all the damage inflicted is by, and to, the upper-body, just like in rugby, thus meaning there are less injuries than you'd expect, that area of the human body being far more resilient than down round the shins and ankles (thereby supporting the theory that I drag out when non-football fans moan that rugby players don't roll about in agony like girly-footballers do – they would do if they got kicked on the shins a bit more, trust me). This is why it was such bad sport when some unidentified rotter singled Pete out at the Leeds gig in 2007 and chopped him off at the knee – a good old fashioned shoulder-charge would have been game, but this was just not on.

So yes, I'd seen Pete around at many a gig, but as far as I recall the first time we ever chatted properly was at the Camden Palace, March 15th 1994, one of many Cardiacs triumphs at the old Feet First Club. On this occasion I was squashed up at the front with a be-dreaded Kavus to my left and Pete to my right. For some reason we started shouting for Yes songs (where this came from I have no idea, but I suspect I may have been the instigator) (I wasn't the instigator; I now know the answer – it was Pete's usual response to seeing Tim take up his acoustic before "March"). I was delighted to discover that Pete was as enthused about Yes as me, judging by his shouts for "Wonderous Stories" and his passable impression of Jon Anderson doing "I've Seen All Good People". Now, I can't be sure, but this falsetto Northern accent that Pete was putting on may just have prompted Kavus to tell me about the song he (or a band mate) had once written called something like "Jon Anderson Sounds Like A Farmer".

Pete reached his century long before I did, his 100th Cardiacs gig being at Portsmouth Wedgewood Rooms on November 7th 2005, a night where Tim singled Pete out for special attention: 'This **** has seen us one-hundred times!' he announced from the stage. Not only was he now a centurion, his gig canon included one or two appearances as stand-in guitar tech for Cardiacs where he could be seen all togged up at the side of the stage, singing all the words to his heart's content in between running on and changing Tim's broken strings. Also, a lift to or from a Cardiacs gig in Pete's car is always an eye-opener in that it makes you aware of just how bewilderingly wide his taste in music is. He's also pretty adept at pointing out that not only do Marillion owe a lot to Gabriel-era Genesis, they've also made a nod or two in the direction of the post-Gabriel stuff, as the hitherto-unnoticed-by-me similarity between Genesis' "All In A Mouse's Night" from *Wind And Wuthering* and Marillion's *Fugazi* lead-off single "Punch And Judy" proved.

An obsession with Cardiacs, a love of Genesis and Yes, a familiarity with Marillion, a massive Motörhead tattoo; all this points to an interesting musical-upbringing, so let's explore…

* * * *

It's surely no coincidence that many of the Cardiacs lovers studied here have come from families with a passion for music. Pete is no exception, his earliest musical recollections dating back to, well, as early as possible: 'I was exposed to mostly classical music from age zero, bizarre stuff from my Dad's old 78s, although it was probably

Borodin's "Prince Igor" that grabbed my fancy first, or maybe "Night On Bare Mountain" by Mussorgsky. I was also heavily drawn to TV music, certain theme tunes I just sat transfixed, listening intently, then getting upset when they finished. I was probably about two-to-three years old.'

As usual when an infant shows an interest in music, the gifts that can shape a life soon follow, and when Pete was aged around four, he was given use of his parents' old record player, proving that a taste for vinyl was developing already. The first record he was given 'was possibly the soundtrack to *Dougal And The Blue Cat* (from the *Magic Roundabout* for those that aren't aware; those crazy Belgians have obviously freaked out any number of us 1970s kids with their wigged-out animations) for my birthday, followed shortly after, and completely by accident, with "Forbidden City" by John Buck & The Blazers that my Mum got on holiday in the 1960s and donated to me after I showed an interest in pop music. It is now apparently quite a cult track; Lux Interior of The Cramps played it in his *Purple Knif* radio show a few years back, and it features on a couple of *Ultra Rare Surf-Volume 19* kind of compilations. Also "Wichita Lineman" by Glenn Campbell was in there somewhere, for the guitar solo and the Morse code bits.'

Of course, being given a record is somewhat different to venturing out to buy one with your own pennies, as this is when the budding music lover shows signs of developing their own tastes, thus possibly defining their musical path a little. Relates Pete, 'The first record I actually went out with the "express intention" of buying for myself would have been "St Valentine's Day Massacre" by Motör-head & Girlschool, who called themselves Headgirl for the occasion. That record changed, even damaged, ha ha, my life irrevocably. I was ten, and I had discovered Metal! The main track, "Please Don't Touch", is one of my all-time favourite songs, as is Elvis Presley's 1956 recording of "Hound Dog" – they spoke volumes to me, real in your face music with loud guitars.'

Pete's emphasis on "express intention" suggests that there was a disc somewhere before that he maybe didn't really mean to buy: 'I just happened across it at a jumble sale when I was about nine; *The Ripoffs Play A Golden Age Of Rock 'n' Roll*. I bought it because it had Fats Domino on it. When I got home, I discovered it was a terrible Rock 'n Roll covers album by some session musicians, probably for K-Tel or Pickwick or some such crapola label. There was one standout track though, "Off My Blue Suede Shoes", an instrumental with a really piercing, scary guitar sound on it. Can you see a pattern forming…?'

A love of Rock 'n' Roll is one which thus far has lain untouched with regard to the Cardiacs aficionados studied in this book, therefore making it all the more intriguing. This unexpected development is perhaps due to Pete's uncle: 'He lived and breathed Rockabilly and used to do me compilation tapes; he started with Jerry Lee Lewis and Carl Perkins, then started to dig deeper. He was the "wild one" of the family and he played the electric guitar, therefore appearing dangerous and cool to my six-year-old mind, like the Fonz, but from High Wycombe.'

All this Rock 'n' Roll and Rockabilly led to a first gig for Pete of Danny Wild & The Wildcats 'in some hotel in Dorset around 1978 – I was transfixed!' However, it was Progressive Rock that gave Pete his first real passion for a particular band, and he sounds almost embarrassed about this: 'It was probably Marillion (nothing to be embarrassed about Pete, I've still got a soft spot for Fish-era Marillion, even after discovering that he got even more ideas from Peter Hammill and Van der Graaf Generator than he did Peter Gabriel and Genesis). By 1984 I was branching out from the Metal path and had discovered *90125*-era Yes, so this bunch of clean-cut rock types with their musicianly leanings, but looking back, such horrid 80s styling, production and Genesis mimicry, fitted a niche I had discovered. I have to admit a lot of it subsequently left me cold, but I know that amazing Mark Wilkinson artwork had a LOT to do with liking the band. Most of my peers at the time were also unaware of the Genesis-thievery going on, so we just ignored the thirty-somethings who were slating them. It didn't last long though – I've never been keen on limiting myself to one genre, and the same year saw the glimmerings of a lifelong love for two distinctly different styles, namely Psychobilly and Thrash Metal, uncomfortable bedfellows at the best of times. But Marillion *were* responsible for my first Cardiacs experience…'

Coming to Cardiacs from what Pete describes as 'a horrid concoction of Metal, Psychobilly, Prog, and 1970s TV theme music' may be quite unique, but discovering Cardiacs as a result of going to see Marillion in 1984 is not, as we have seen already with Paul Ashby. But before that fateful tour, Pete was already familiar with the name "Cardiacs" due to scouring the *Hounslow Informer*, and *Sounds* (when he could afford it) 'and other papers for gig dates that *Kerrang!* didn't have, so I was aware of the name at least, through adverts for the Clarendon, King's Head, Marquee, Brentford Red Lion etc. I used to read the music pages over and over and over, digesting information and working out where the venues were so I could sneak off to gigs without my Dad finding out.'

And then there was *that* tour, Cardiacs supporting Marillion on the 1984 *Real To Reel* tour, where, like Paul Ashby, Pete had his first Cardiacs live experience at the Hammersmith Odeon. 'Nobody would go with me, so I was on my own. This was probably a good thing in retrospect, as I had mentioned the support band in passing to a couple of 6th-formers at my school who knew about these matters and who subsequently advised me to arrive late because the support band were "rubbish".

'Back then it was polite to be in the hall to see the support, and I was sitting there looking forward to Marillion playing stuff from the recent *Fugazi* album, when there was this bizarre intro tape and lots of green light, then this bunch of what I could only have described as "dishevelled students" crashed the stage, and from the first impression I thought, "Oh no, this is going to be crap – have I got enough to buy a drink before the interval as well as during it?" The set got under way and I was struck by this mix of different musical styles, the lurching, mocking, bespectacled singer with his horrid bright green guitar, the fact they had a dedicated percussionist, the odd clown makeup they were all wearing; it was like a nightmare set in the *Play School* studio. There was Rock, there was Prog, there was Ska, there was this bizarre fairground music like that Mobiles band who bothered the charts in the early 1980s, and some Toy Dolls style childishness thrown in for good measure. It was like when you were a kid and you mixed all your Plasticine up; all the yellows, greens, reds, blues, and it became this disgusting swirly brown mess – THAT was Cardiacs.

'Being young and foolish (13) I stuck with it, and was surprised, then later quite worried to see my first negative gig experience. People were booing Cardiacs and starting to throw things. This was equally exciting and scary, as this was about my tenth gig ever, and up till now they had all been pleasant affairs with no trouble. It got to a point where the crowd were shouting, "Off! Off! Off!" and I was further surprised to see none other than Fish, Marillion's 6'5" vocalist, storm on stage, grab the microphone and actually have a go at the crowd. His exact words are lost in the mists of time, but he made a point about how Marillion had to struggle to get where they were now, and the crowd should be supporting this band, who he himself had invited on the tour. "Wow," I thought, "they come with Marillion's approval? There must be something in it then…"

'"If you don't like it, then go to the bar!" boomed the giant Scotsman. To my horror, people started to get up and leave the auditorium. I was faced with a dilemma – "Do I follow the crowd and have a half-pint now, or shall I stay and have a proper pint in the interval, even though people seem to be glaring at me for not leaving?" I stayed.'

Well, the wheels were in motion now, and Pete's first Cardiacs recorded work was 'a dodgy copy of *The Seaside* taped off a mate.' Twenty-three years on and his latest was the CD single "Ditzy Scene", with 115 gigs along the way and a whole plethora of favourites and happy memories. On the subject of those 115 gigs, Pete says, 'I know it sounds a lot, but I am aware of a handful of people who have seen them over 200 times, then there is John Daniel who must be approaching 500, although the last 400 of them he was their tour manager…'

As for Pete's Cardiacs chart-toppers, his favourite album is *On Land And In The Sea*, an album that contains his favourite song, "The Duck And Roger The Horse", which would explain why whenever that thrashy guitar bit that sounds a bit like the heavy bit from "Return Of The Giant Hogweed" by Genesis approaches, Pete taps me on the shoulder and asks, "Are we going for it?" We always are…

His favourite live shows see the trio of Camden Falcon gigs in January 1999 hitting the spot for Pete, doubtless helped by the fact that he removed the sleeves off my t-shirt in order to show-off my tattoo at one of them. But the favourite "moment" as such is one of those gloriously unique personal moments: 'I was driving home from a Chelmsford Army And Navy gig with Tim Smith in the front and my mate Carl in the back. I had Devo's *Duty Now For The Future* very loud on the stereo, and we were all grooving along, *Wayne's World* style. As "Wibbly World" started, Tim and I simultaneously reached for the same invisible synthesiser control on the dashboard to make the "Spbwbwfftttteeeowww!" noise, then made it, realised what we just did and burst out laughing. I nearly crashed the car.'

After a near-musical-lifetime of following Cardiacs, Pete is in the fantastic position now of living in a house where Big Flowers and Cardiacs clocks can go unchallenged, because Pete's partner, the lovely Clare, is a devotee of the Alphabet Business Concern too, an enviable position, and of course it is well worth seeing how Clare got to that position to see how things compare and contrast when Whole World Windows collide…

* * * *

Clare Kelly was another familiar face at Cardiacs gigs, from the mid-to-late 90s period onwards, it seemed to me. It also seemed that she was from the faction that belonged to and had been converted by the connection with Sidi Bou Said, an astute observation as it turned out. But before the Sidis and Cardiacs arrived on the scene, there was a musical pedigree chart in Clare's lineage almost every bit as varied as Pete's…

Clare's first recollection of anything musical was of sitting under the table aged about five when "All Around My Hat" by Steeleye Span came on the radio. 'My parents and brother, seven years older than me, all began to dance to it. I've a memory of watching dancing legs from my limited viewpoint and being surprised by the spontaneity of the whole thing.' A story to make Rose Kemp smile if she should ever read this... 'Other than that I must have sung in school and stuff, I just don't remember it.'

Peter And The Wolf comes sneaking along again here, as it was the first record Clare was ever given, '...as narrated by Peter Ustinov. There was a *Young Persons' Guide To The Orchestra* on the other side – unsurprisingly I never requested that side to be put on for me.' Branching out slightly, "Super Trouper" by Abba was the first record she bought for herself when she was ten-years-old. However, the earliest signs of musical obtuseness were showing here as 'I preferred the 'b' side – a slightly folksy number about the Pied Piper.'

Meanwhile, Dad and big brother were slugging it out to influence the impressionable young Clare. 'I think on balance my brother has the edge, because whilst my Dad shaped my adolescent preferences, Queen, ELO, the Beatles, my brother had more of a lasting effect, not least by introducing me to the Pixies, New Order, The Art Of Noise and other delights.' Dad seems to have had the first knockings though, as Clare's admission that Queen proved to be her first passionate-about band shows. However, presumably big brother's more Alternative-Indie promptings had some say in Clare's first gig attended, 'The Waterboys at the Kilburn National Ballroom in 1989 – 19 years of age makes me something of a late starter I guess.'

First becoming aware of Cardiacs doesn't seem to be too fuzzy a memory for most people, but Clare finds this a bit tricky. 'The first I can actually remember to this day would have been around the time they toured with the Sidis, seeing as how I was living with their manager. Gayl (Sidi Bou Said's bassist) was pretty evangelical in telling me how amazing they were.'

Hmmm, seems to be pretty straightforward. Well, no actually, because the question of first Cardiacs gigs sticks a big fly in the ointment. 'This really is a vexed question,' puzzles Clare, 'because I don't actually know when my first Cardiacs gig was. An old friend once told me I saw them with him in about 1991 or 1992, but didn't like them – now there's a surprise! Problem is I have no memory of this. Looking at my clever-old boyfriend's comprehensive gig list (Pete's pride and joy), I'm pretty sure it would have been one of the (mid-90s) shows at the Venue (in New Cross).'

As for that first Cardiacs recorded work, Clare got her hands on a bona-fide collectors' item without having to try or even pay a penny (expect a very big offer coming up from Big Ship Iron any day soon, Clare): 'It was *Guns*, the first time I helped them out with the artwork. The promo copies had turned up the day of one of the 1999 London gigs, which must have been at the Garage, and Tim gave me my copy then. The CD and all the printed inserts were all bunged together in a crappy plastic CD envelope. That's how my copy of it still is, but I listened to it loads, I really did!'

Of course, the finished product ended up looking far better than something "bunged together in a plastic CD envelope", thanks largely to a zesty, very together Tim, full of ideas and letting Clare know exactly what he was after. Indeed, it was around this time that I felt Cardiacs really got to grips with aesthetically-pleasing CD design, and *Guns*, *Cardiacs Greatest Hits*, and *The Special Garage Concerts Volume I* and *Volume II* all have a certain uniform look, and in my opinion, the actual CDs themselves look splendid on all four.

Obviously not as particular about noting down all her Cardiacs gigs as Pete, Clare can only hazard a guess that she's seen them 'closing on thirty-ish' times, but the joy of camping with the band and seeing them at Glastonbury in 1999 seems clear and pretty special. What's more, Clare's somewhat precise about the day she met Pete:

'It was Bob Leith's wedding to lovely Liz, 3rd September 2006. I'd known of Pete and seen him around at gigs for at least a decade but had never spoken to him – he's not terribly approachable-looking to be fair. Nevertheless, I found him sitting next to me on my picnic blanket chatting to Jane (Ordinary Shop Girl). I thought I'd be friendly and introduce myself, which I did with the deathless words, "You're Pete, aren't you? I'm Clare…"'

Pete goes into more detail: 'I had been invited to Bob Leith's wedding. It was on a Sunday and I nearly didn't make it, as this was at the end of a bit of a three-day bender. I got to the wedding on time after finally getting to sleep at 7 o'clock on the Sunday morning all bleary-eyed.

'It was really weird at first; Bob likes Daleks so there were several full-size ones careering round the car-park of the venue, barking orders to the guests (ah yes, we have one of those at our family occasions, but I've been advised by my legal team to mention no names) and having their photos taken. I bumped into Duffy, Moke and a few other friends, and shared something out of a hipflask before we were ordered round to the other side of Dalek HQ to see the wedding. It went well, and they had chosen great music for their ceremony, "Good News For The Pus Pickers" by the Danielson Famile, and "I Know What I Like (In Your Wardrobe)" by Genesis, which perked me up a bit. We cheered the bride and groom, then went out into the fields to a special area set aside for the guests with a lovely open-air picnic.

'It was at this point that Bill Drake and friends arrived after missing their train, so I got talking to Gayl and (other half) Peter who I hadn't seen for ages. I spotted Jane a few feet away and there was a space on the picnic blanket so I plonked myself down and started chatting to her, becoming increasingly aware that there was a really gorgeous girl sitting next to me. "You're Pete aren't you?" she asked. We chatted for a while, then a while longer, and realised we had both been around Cardiacs for years, and we shared some of the same friends, but had never actually met properly. She was in the pub after the wedding had finished, so we talked some more and seemed to be getting on really well, and I tentatively asked her for her number.

'I invited her to a Cardiacs Chatlist booze-up in the West End a few days later and the rest is history…'

Indeed it is, and evidence of how one chap coming from Metal, Psychobilly, Prog and 1970s TV theme music, and one girl who unashamedly describes herself as 'Indie Kid through and through' can come together with a joyful Cardiacs noise is there for all to see, as well as coexistence of Pete's current listening habits of Yellow Magic Orchestra, ELP, Motörhead, Mr Oizo, Egg, The Cramps and early-Genesis, and Clare's of Elbow.

I know this because I witnessed it first hand when I developed a rather evil stomach bug whilst attending a social function round at Pete and Clare's place. Pete put me gently to bed and was the perfect host (I wouldn't have minded, but as ever I was the only one not drinking), but before, during and after my violent illness, all around was perfect harmony and Big Flowers.

Chapter Seventeen
"Two Civilians Scrap"
The Sugarmill, Stoke-on-Trent,
November 20ᵗʰ 2007

"Two Civilians Scrap"
The Sugarmill, Stoke-on-Trent, November 20th 2007

Considering the, erm, lively style of the music and the rather frenzied nature of the audiences, there has been remarkably little trouble at Cardiacs gigs. Other than the odd accidental stray elbow and as a result the subsequent seeking of retribution, not forgetting Tim having to stop a gig mid-song in Oxford to calm everybody down, most of the time it's been abundant love and peace all the way. Apart from, that is, two gigs in Stoke; one at Keele University in November 1988, and now the first hint of trouble on this current 2007 tour, at the Sugarmill in Hanley.

Coincidence? In the interests of fairness I should point out that it's not a 100% representation of Stoke-on-Trent Cardiacs gigs; don't forget, the one at Trentham Gardens when I played hooky from Tesco was in the immediate vicinity, and there was no hint of trouble then, although that could have been something to do with Hawkwind also being on the bill, making it total love and peace that night. On the other hand, some of the most spectacular fights I've seen break out have been at Stoke City's Britannia Stadium, most famously the two times I've seen Sheffield United equalise in the last minute to make it 2-2, firstly Brian Deane with a looping header Boxing Day 1998, and secondly a Jack Lester penalty in the 2003/04 season, a goal that really got the locals whipped up into something of a frenzy.

But to be fair to Stoke-on-Trent, nothing prepared me for the aggro of this night at the Sugarmill, and it was only afterwards when discussing the events of the evening with those lovely Cardiacs Email Chatlist Listees that I remembered the previous aggravation which had taken place at nearby Keele University almost exactly nineteen years earlier…

* * * *

It was November 23rd 1988 and if I remember rightly the reason I was cutting things a bit fine was because I'd set off hitching straight from work in Brackley, Northants. This was to be my tenth Cardiacs gig so there was a small wave of excitement coming over me, along with a large wave of determination to get there. There was an added dose of adrenalin brought about by the fact that the M6 was largely uncharted territory for me.

As with most of November that year it was a misty but relatively dry night, and as I found myself at Hilton Park Services with the evening ticking by, I began to fear that I'd never make it for the start of the gig, if at all. However, there was a huge truck sitting on the hard-shoulder of the slip-road and as the driver wandered back to his cab he asked me where I was going. When I told him Keele University he told me to hop in as Keele Services was right by the University and he was trundling straight past.

And so it was that I arrived at Keele Services with time running short, or so I thought, what with it rapidly approaching 10 o'clock. But I was here now, so even if I only caught a bit of the gig it'd be worth it. The only thing was I still had to work out how to get from the services to the venue even if it was smack bang next door, so into the shop I went for directions. Just as I was about to ask, I noticed a group of likely-looking punters all wearing Big Flower t-shirts and the like, and a huge surge of relief came over me (and I'm pretty sure one of them was the North Sea Radio Orchestra songstress now known to us as Sharron Fortnam) (it was her – I asked).

'You look like you're going to the same place as me,' I beamed. They were, but like me they were unsure of how to get there. One shop-assistant-with-directions later and I'd got myself a lift the few hundred yards up the back of the services into the university with my new-found friends. Further relief came when we entered the venue and a representative of the Alphabet Business Concern told us Cardiacs were going onstage at 11 o'clock, not for another hour or so; good job I had no work the next day…

As with all the gigs on that November 1988 *Cardiacs Live* tour, it was an absolute stormer. I don't want to make people who didn't see them back then envious, but this really was the classic six-piece at the peak of their powers, Tim being at his liveliest and most entertaining throughout, especially this particular night. I'd secured pole position underneath his microphone stand so was able to watch events unfold at very close quarters, including the usual water-squirting and physical abuse of Jim.

Now, it was a recent conversation on The List which enabled me to discover that on that night the rugby club (or society or whatever they call them at university) had been having a beer promotion, which would indeed explain the way things transpired during the gig, especially as the bloke standing next to me was a bit of a chinless wonder, and there was something definitely affecting his behaviour, whether it be alcohol or drugs.

In between songs he started to shake Tim's microphone stand quite violently, so Tim just shook his head, squarely and deliberately, all with a fixed, rather stern expression. The chinless wonder shook it even harder, and after a few songs of this you could tell Tim was getting very annoyed, so after a bit more ignored head-shaking and stern looking, Tim started to remonstrate with him.

The chinless wonder started shouting, 'You think you're so ****ing hard don't you!' Tim got down on his haunches (it was a high stage) so he was closer to eye-level with his tormentor and started to beat his chest ferociously with attendant gorilla noises for added effect.

'Oh, sooo hard. You think you're the ****ing Sex Pistols,' shouted the chinless wonder.

Tim got really close-up now and looked right into his eyes, saying, 'The lights are on but there's nobody at home. There's nobody at home!'

At this Mr. Chinless Wonder gave the "come on" signal with his hands, at which point Little Hicky of Cardiacs Crew appeared on the stage and took him up on the offer by jumping into the crowd. I think Hicky was a little surprised by the size of the bloke when he was down there next to him, but he was in too far to back out now, and so a brief but lively scuffle broke out which resulted in Hicky getting his lovely *Cardiacs Live* Doggy t-shirt ripped and Mr. Chinless Wonder getting hauled out by the rather belated security. Hicky disappeared off the side looking a little upset but reappeared half way through the next song resplendent in a brand new Doggy t-shirt, beaming in defiance at the friends of Mr. Chinless Wonder who were still down the front giving out a bit of lip (but only a bit).

The gig continued relatively trouble-free after that, but the incident left a nasty taste. Later on Tim was heard to utter the immortal words, 'Why is it this band attracts so many weirdoes?' I wonder...

The trouble didn't end there. In the freezing November air in the early hours of the morning it appeared that the Alphabet Business Concern had misplaced the keys to their mini-coach, and all manner of trickery was required to break in through the sun-roof and then get the thing started. I'm sure they were well and truly sick of the sight of Keele and all attendant Stokery as a result.

* * * *

There was no hint of any forthcoming trouble on the morning of November 20th 2007, but then there wouldn't be as i) it was the morning and ii) I was waking up in the sleepy suburbs of Sheffield. The only whisper of any trouble was when I nipped up to the newsagent to buy a *Daily Mirror* and noticed two different "missing pet" notices on separate lampposts, one for a missing cat and one for a missing parrot – guaranteed to end in tears, that one.

There was talk of snow over the tops and, well, you know where my plans to hitchhike were going. Pete had stayed over at Big Ship Iron's pad in Doncaster so was not a million miles away, and as he was driving over to Stoke-on-Trent he would be passing right by Woodall Services, a convenient 45-minute number-21-bus-ride away from Sheffield city centre. So that's where he picked me up from...

The trip from Sheffield to Stoke has never been an easy one. If you go cross-country it's rather tricky for hitchhikers; my plan had been to go the long way round, M1 down to A50, then across to Stoke-on-Trent from there, but here was Pete to make things a whole lot easier. Through Derbyshire we went, via Tesco in Chesterfield, and witnessed for ourselves the rumoured snow on the tops. It really was the scenic route until we ran out of daylight, but even then we felt it necessary to screech to a halt upon spying a photo opportunity, a sign alerting us to the whereabouts of somewhere called Grin Low. My head went down as Low as it could, my face had a Grin on it as wide as possible, and Pete clicked the camera shutter.

We arrived in plenty of time which was a good job considering the amount of time we spent buzzing round the Hanley one-way system looking for the venue. No wonder it was difficult to find – the Sugarmill was down a very titchy little street, making Cardiacs' tour bus look somewhat incongruous as a result.

My initial Internet appeal for places to stay throughout the tour had served me reasonably well, but much like Brighton there were no offers for Stoke, so my primary concern upon arrival was to track down Malc and Diggy to find out which guest house they were holed up in just to see if there were any vacancies. Thanks to the wonder of mobile phone technology Malc and Diggy met us in the Rockers pub next to the Sugarmill, Malc armed with a phone number for the guest house and directions on how to get there on foot. Malc described it as being 'like something from *The League Of Gentlemen*', but never one to be deterred I gave them a buzz. They'd got vacancies all right, but the proprietor informed me in no uncertain terms that if I came down after the gig I'd be too late to book in, so a traipse across Hanley was to be the order of the evening, but only after a bit of a session in the pub with Pete, Malc and Diggy.

The best thing about this pub was the presence of a massive video screen showing episodes of *Family Guy*. We were so engrossed in the episode about Millennium Eve and the ensuing chaos when all the computers crashed that no-one noticed that Diggy had disappeared. It's unclear how long the Digster had been missing before someone asked, 'Where's Diggy?' but it's safe to say that when he reappeared later he was none too impressed.

'I told you all I was nipping out for a chinese, but nobody responded at all. You were all too busy watching bleedin' *Family Guy*,' he moaned. 'Thanks very much guys,' he added.

Now it was my turn to disappear in order to book myself in to the guest house and drop my gear off at the same time. It was quite a lengthy journey on foot, but armed with Malc's directions I only got lost once – not bad considering my woeful sense of direction.

Upon my return to the venue everyone was in and I'd missed Jon Poole and his God Damn Whores (again). Paul and Karen Helocolin had appeared as well, Paul particularly looking forward to it as it was his home turf. Meanwhile, I got a glimpse of the trouble ahead when I heard someone shouting, 'It's him! It really is him!'

I turned round to see a scruffy-looking gentleman with a haircut similar to mine looking excitedly in my direction. 'Who is him, who is him, he's Jim, he's Jim!' he chanted.

'Er, I'm not Jim,' I denied gently.

A puzzled and slightly disappointed look spread across his face before he turned to his mates, all looking like leftovers from the crusty Brew Crew days of the late-1980s/early-1990s (Karen was less kind in her description on The List: "…absolute dredge out of the bottom of your gene pool, oddballs present, with dredlocks (sic) full of lice…") and said, 'Oh no, he's not Jim!'

Now, there is a rumour that this little group were seen snorting a line off the bar. Rather more certain was that they were all from Walsall (another line of defence for the city of Stoke-on-Trent), not that that's an excuse for the way things turned later. However, the line of coke accusation may well help explain their subsequent behaviour…

Now, I'm all for enjoying myself at any gig, not just a Cardiacs gig, and I'm quite prepared to take the rough and tumble that comes with it. I accept that there are accidental whacks and bashes, and more than once I've gone down in the Pond at Cardiacs gigs, every time being hauled back to my feet by concerned fellow-fishies. Likewise, many times have I hauled others to their feet when they've suffered a similar fate. In the most packed crowds such a frenzy can almost be safer, the Young Gods at the Garage in Islington in the mid-90s perhaps being the best example; it was an incredible crush that night, but nobody was in any danger of going down because the mass of bodies were too squashed-up and held each other up throughout.

The problem with this night at the Sugarmill was that whilst it was well-enough attended, it was by no means packed so there was plenty of space to move about in. This was actually the case at most gigs so far on the tour to be honest, with audiences responding enthusiastically but responsibly. Not so this night however…

Looking around before the start things didn't look too different from normal, it being the usual assortment of young and old, Hippies and Punks, Goths and Metalheads and so on. There was even one bloke called Chris attired in full dress-suit, so much so he could almost have been The Consultant, complete with frilly shirt, red waistcoat, watch and chain, and bow-tie. Koji was there too, having flown half way round the world from Japan. Now, if only I had a contact for him he could (and should) have been in my "Overseas" section. But anyway, as the gig got underway it became obvious that this was going to be a difficult one to control. Our Crusty Crew from Walsall at first seemed intent on wrestling each other to the floor during songs, but then it became noticeable that whenever they got in the way of an innocent bystander they seemed to think it was hilariously funny so went out of their way to do it more, pushing, shoving, tripping, and making a general nuisance of themselves.

Things got worse when it became apparent that others were helping out. One particularly chubby chap who wasn't part of the Crusty Crew was now joining in with their fun and games. The fact that he was rather large made it even worse because when someone of his size starts behaving like an over-excited five-year-old at Christmas and careers around like an out-of-control crazed elephant (think that bit in *Dumbo* when his Mum loses it), it can be quite uncomfortable when he hurtles into you.

Whether Tim could remember his rather trouble-inciting methods of bringing peace to Keele University 19 years ago or not, this time he made a few appeals for calm from the stage whilst not getting too close to the troublemakers. It didn't make any difference as they just carried on unabated, so audience members started seeking retribution. I believe all available permutations of Malc, Diggy, Pete and Paul Helocolin combined to sandwich the perpetrators and bring them to grief, but the problem was that the Crusty Crew seemed to think they were joining in with the fun. Whenever a crusty went down, he'd just grin, dust himself off, get up and carry on, proving that there really is a case for "no sense no feeling".

At one point I was pushed hard into the back of a girl who was leaning up against the front of the stage. Rightfully miffed, she turned round and pushed me back into the melee, something I was less than happy about, so I tapped her on the shoulder and pointed out the error of her ways whilst protesting my innocence; 'It's them behind me you need to be getting upset with,' I politely pointed out. She didn't seem convinced, but I'm glad to say afterwards we had a nice little chat and sorted it all out. Her name was Fiona and I even took a photo of her and her two male friends.

Back to the gig, and perhaps just as annoying as anything else was one of the girls from the Crusty Crew, complete with dreads, who seemed to spend the whole gig shouting at the band. By and large she was shouting stuff such as, 'Do you know what it's like to be homeless? Do you know what it's like to have no money?' Oh yes, you picked a real good target there, love, because everyone knows Cardiacs live a life of luxury. As if.

Despite repeated requests for her to shut up, she just carried on and on and on, and for those of you that don't believe me, put "Cardiacs Sugarmill" into *YouTube* and you'll see what I mean.

Just to cap it all, and to finally make my mind up that I was indeed surrounded by idiots, I received a tap on the shoulder near the end of the gig. One Cardiacs fan with his girlfriend asked me, 'What's that hymn they do? You know, for the Alphabet Business Concern...?'

'You mean "Home Of Fadeless Splendour",' I replied.

'That's it,' he said, and then with a look on his face of uncomprehending indignation carried on, 'they haven't played it. Why not?'

'They've got four different set-lists on the tour, and they've not played it at all this time round,' I explained.

'Yeah, but why haven't they played it?' he continued.

'They don't have to,' I reasoned.

'Well, they should – they always play it,' he moaned.

Yes, yes, of course they do, you muppet. I trust he headed to the promoter at the end and demanded a refund.

* * * *

By the time the dust had settled when the gig was over, there was still a smouldering feeling of discontent. When the tour was done and everyone was let loose on the Internet, the List was already awash with tales of The Battle for Stoke. On the night, all we could do at the end was shrug our shoulders and head back to the pub. There was much debate as to whether they were real fans or not. I pointed out that they must be as it was one of their number who had mistaken me for Jim early on, and only a Cardiacs fan would know the "Who is him..?" phrase, even if I most definitely *wasn't* Jim (I was once walking along the Regents Canal towpath at King's Cross wearing a Cardiacs t-shirt when a female voice from on the deck of a narrow boat shouted, 'Who is him, who is him?' I looked up and saw a punky girl sitting there, so shouted a reply of, 'He's Jim! He's Jim!' She was a fan all right.).

So, they *were* fans – they were just off their heads on something. They were now sat in the same pub as us, but we declined going over for a chat on the grounds that you can't reason with the braindead. When I started getting amorous advances from the halfwit drunken Rock-chick-Carpenters-fan on the same table as us, Diggy, Malc and I decided to head off to our *League Of Gentleman* guest house. Even now our adventures weren't over as we stopped off at a chinese take-away along the way. Whilst waiting for our supper two lovely young ladies called Katie-Jane and Jane-Katie (well, that's what we christened them) started questioning us about our night out and our Cardiacs t-shirts, as well as about our jobs. When Diggy told them he was a club singer they didn't believe him, so by way of evidence he treated them to a club-singer-stylee version of "Tarred And Feathered", a rendition that had to be heard to be believed, and reduced all present, including the take-away employees, into helpless fits of laughter.

After that excitement it was back to the guest house, and to be honest it seemed quite luxurious to me, as well as the owners being friendly, but I suppose as in *The League Of Gentlemen*, the big test would be whether we'd be able to escape in the morning. Heaven forbid we'd have to spend the rest of our lives trapped in Stoke-on-Trent.

Chapter Eighteen
"If You Wanted to Catch One You Would Have to Take a Car"
Andy Hossain, Diggy, Lil Malc

"If You Wanted to Catch One You Would Have to Take a Car"
Andy Hossain, Diggy, Lil Malc

Hitchhiking really did take a bit of a backseat on this 2007 tour, did it not? I've already trotted out all the excuses (all pretty valid I think) about feeling off-colour and so on and so forth, but then a lot of it was probably down to fear, fear brought on by that eleven-hour nightmare reaching Bristol. The prospect of missing one or even, heaven forbid, two of the gigs filled me with dread. If I missed two, I'd be stuck on 99 not out at the end of the tour, and the whole idea of the book would be somewhat redundant (although I'm sure I would still have thought of a way round it). So it was that offers of lifts proved too tempting, and the added warmth of a car meant I was less likely to retire hurt. Two cars that took an extra-special hammering were Andy Hossain's and especially Lil Malc's. As more-often-than-not Diggy was Malc's passenger, the three of us got to know each other very well over the fortnight, especially on that long drawn-out trip from Manchester to Portsmouth.

But Andy got the ball rolling with his offer of a cheating lift back on the very first night of the tour, all the way back in Brighton, so it is to Andy we shall go first...

* * * *

I think The List has provided Andy Hossain with a New Age of Discovery when it comes to music. Obviously, he'd already discovered Cardiacs otherwise he wouldn't be here, but as you doubtless know by now, the Listees have wide and varied tastes, and this can prove a boon for anyone wanting to know what a certain band or artist is like – someone out there will have heard them somewhere along the line. So, if it's a Canterbury Scene band you want to know about, Nick Loebner is your man; if Morris-dancing Punk intrigues you, then Chris Luxford can usually point you in the right direction; Malc can advise you on Folk, Roy Harper and cricket (okay, not strictly music this one, but surely a Michael Vaughan cover-drive is as beautiful as any well-played Celtic harp); and just about everyone on The List can tell you how brilliant Gong are. Yes, it's fair to say that other than Cardiacs, the inhabitants of that luminous green planet are possibly the most popular band on The List, so much so that Andy needed to see what all the fuss was about himself.

Rather than go out and buy any albums, in order to indoctrinate himself Andy's first experience of anything from the Gong Family was to attend the Here & Now/Planet Gong gig at Camden Dingwalls, Spring 2007, a gig that I described as "Gig of the Year by a mile" on MySpace (well, it was until Cardiacs came along in November). Andy was suitably impressed, so post-gig he splashed out further by sampling from the merchandise desk whilst I congratulated Steve Hillage on the wonder that is *Rainbow Dome Musick* (I'd had a dream years ago where I did this very thing and Mr Hillside-Village had said, 'Oh, you don't like that rubbish do you?' so I was a bit nervous about broaching the subject; standing nearby was an American chap who said, 'I think this guy needs to know about *Motivation Radio*,' but much to my delight, Submarine Captain Spillage said, 'No, I think *Rainbow Dome Musick* is where it's at...')

A year later, in June 2008, Andy, a certain Belch, and what seemed like hundreds of representatives of the Alphabet Business Concern were all there at the Forum in Kentish Town to see Gong themselves, this time with Hillage onstage as opposed to just fielding compliments from some over-excited idiot in a Cardiacs t-shirt by the merchandise desk. Whereas Planet Gong at Dingwalls had been an explosive Punk/Rock spectacular, this night of wonder at the Forum was a spiritual feast of such gargantuan proportions that "Master Builder" alone quite possibly constructed a thousand temples in the minds of those there. Andy bought a t-shirt this time, but had to ask me where the featured Gong Mandala had originated from (it's from the back cover of *You*, the few of you that aren't familiar with this album of albums).

It all seems a million miles away from Andy first hearing David Bowie's "Space Oddity" as a kid (or is it? Bowie and Gong both played at Glastonbury in 1971): 'I have memories of hearing lyrics of Major Tom floating in his tin can,' says Andy. 'I wanted to do that. Still do actually. I must have been young anyway. I looked it up on Wikipedia and it says that it was released in 1969 and I was born May 6th 1967…'

However, it wasn't until the onslaught of Punk that music took a bit of an upturn in Andy's life: 'One Christmas I got the X-Ray Spex album *Germ Free Adolescents*, it would have been 1978. I recall listening to it at my Nana's house in Scotland with great big headphones, all holiday; I wasn't allowed to play it out loud. I've just seen they're playing the Roundhouse in September – hmmm.'

There was plenty of sibling-influence coming Andy's way too, and in time-honoured tradition he let big-brother Jon do all the record-buying, although he admits, 'I did buy a Siouxsie & The Banshees twelve-inch single in the early 80s.' His elder brother in turn had been influenced by their cousin Riaz, and things moved on in a Punky/Ska way, adding to a first gig of The Clash at the Brixton Academy: 'It was on the *Combat Rock* tour in about 1983, although I'd better look it up to be sure. I was baby-sat by Jon. I remember before trying to learn the Spanish bits to "Spanish Bombs".'

As for passions, the nearest Andy got to one particular band was 'a period when we saw King Kurt almost weekly, but I suppose less for the music – it was more of a social event.' Now that sounds familiar…

Indie started to move in on Andy's liking for Punk and Ska, and this inevitably led to an introduction to Cardiacs, this time via another cousin or two: 'I first heard of Cardiacs from my cousin Jack Healy. His brother David is a Cardiacs fan too and is on *Emmerdale* now – he uses the stage name Matt Healy as there was already a David Healy registered with the actors' union, Equity. He plays the part of Matthew King in *Emmerdale* (and he wore a Cardiacs t-shirt on *Celebrity Stars In Their Eyes* if I remember a certain thread on The List correctly (author's note)). He has told of battles with the wardrobe people at *Emmerdale* trying to get Alphabet Business Concern apparel on the show. I think he did manage to get a 'Little Man And A House' polo-shirt on when his character was playing golf. Anyway, I can thank my cousins for introducing me to the best band in the world. Jack has known Cardiacs from way back at the Stonehenge Festivals.'

My Cardiacs gig list did a bit of a job for Andy in determining when it was he first spied Cardiacs live (makes a change from me having to look it up for everyone else via Pete's list): 'It was Sunday 31st January 1999 in Camden, wasn't it? (Yep, the Falcon) I was taken there by Jack – he lives in Dublin and travels over for Cardiacs. I thought I should go and see this band that he makes all this effort to see, see if it was all worth it. Well, I know the answer now. Anyway, looking at Pete's list (hey Andy, don't make *my* list feel jealous!), Cardiacs played so many times around South London in the 1980s, I fear I may have seen them back then and not noticed.' Hmmm, slapdash make-up, bandsmen's uniforms, Tim snogging Sarah, Jim's hangdog look – nah, I think you'd have remembered them, Andy…

Normally the preserve of blokes trying to impress their new girlfriends, cousin Jack fell back on a time-honoured tradition in order to advance Andy's musical education, albeit using more-modern methods than the humble C90: 'He made me a compilation CD, but my first Alphabet Business Concern purchases would have been at the Astoria gigs in the early 21st Century – I'm thinking *Guns*, *Greatest Hits*, *…Mare's Nest*, *Heaven Born And Ever Bright*…not such a good selection at times.' Oh I dunno Andy; it just makes it all the more wondrous when you finally hit upon *A Little Man And A House And The Whole World Window*, *On Land And In The Sea* and *Sing To God*…

As for Desert Island Cardiacs, like many others Andy finds it difficult to be selective: 'It's impossible to say. Anyway, I'd better not tell you my favourite songs because I might give away some log-in passwords of mine, but then again you'd probably not be interested in logging on to arsenal.com for tickets (correct). Gig-wise, I reckon I've done 15 or so now, but the whole 2007 tour and the last weekend of Cardiff and Leeds especially were very special – I can't imagine it getting any better than that, and I've heard many say it doesn't. The one song that they did not play that I would really like to hear live is "Loosefish Scapegrace".' It sounded great at the Leadmill in 1988, Andy; not to make you feel jealous, but in that big long drawn-out chord in the middle, they did all the swirling-confetti-in-the-wind-machines stuff…

Andy has taken the Cardiacs thing even further now, in that most of the stuff he's currently listening to is either related-to or influenced-by in one way or another. When asked what currently floats his boat he says, 'It's got to be those Silvery boys – I've got to spread the word, and buy the album myself (me too, Andy). And a special mention must go to Zag And The Coloured Beads – I really have enjoyed their recent gigs. Other stuff I'm listening to has even more of a Cardiacs connection, you know, William D. Drake, North Sea Radio Orchestra and so on. Then there's a bit of Gong thrown in recently, but then I am looking forward to Killing Joke in October.'

Ah yes, Andy, don't forget those Punky/New Wave roots; starting with Punk in the 70s and ending up listening to über-hippies Gong in 2008 isn't how it's supposed to work you know. But then, it could be argued that Daevid Allen and his Gong community were closer to the Punk ethic than many a spiky-haired youth; now there's a debate to get them going on the Cardiacs Chat List…

* * * *

They like a good debate on the Cardiacs Chat List, they do. In a way, it reminds me of the old Sheffield United Independent Shareholders Association *Viewpoints* messageboard that featured so heavily when I was writing *Fever Hitch*, except there was a lot more confrontation on SUISA than there is on The List; the only time we get really uptight about things on The List is over the odd political issue, or when some of the Listees feel the subject has strayed just a bit *too* "off-topic". The only tactics that are called into question are Cardiacs' lack of gigs up North (surely laid to rest after 2007), oh, and Piesy not liking "Dirty Boy". But despite the good vibes, there are still debates aplenty, and two major contributors just happen to be the gentlemen I was doing an awful lot of travelling with in November 2007, Diggy and Malc.

One of the joys of The List is the proliferation of "off-list" emails on topics that wouldn't interest the whole List (although it can be quite funny – and embarrassing – when someone thinks they are "off-list" but just happens to have declared undying love for someone in view of all of us). Two such prized off-list emails came my way from Diggy, one being my opinion and help on his own literary aspirations (humbled, but freely given), and another commenting on my MySpace profile. In that one he said he'd never come across anyone with quite so many similarities to himself, not just on my massive list of favourite bands (too many to list here, but IQ figured somewhere, and most of the others get mentioned elsewhere within these covers), but regarding my favourite television programmes and films also. Thus it was that we were able to email each other back and forth about the joys of *The Prisoner*, *Jam*, *A Clockwork Orange* and *The Wicker Man*, amongst others.

Thanks to contributions to The List, I was already aware that Diggy was another of the lucky souls who first saw Cardiacs supporting Marillion in 1984, and like many others, although he'd not seen or heard of Cardiacs up to that point, he was both shocked and intrigued. Further delving had unearthed that Diggy had got into Prog-Rock prior to that Marillion gig via (in reverse order please), American Rock (thanks to a friend's obsessed brother), a first gig of Kiss at Wembley in 1980, a youthful passion for Ian Dury & The Blockheads, and a first-record-purchased of *A Tonic For The Troops* by the Boomtown Rats. Not too shabby a charge-sheet when you consider that he could have been put off music for life by once being given the *Grease* soundtrack, and a first musical recollection of getting a ticking off from his Dad after hearing "Knock Three Times On The Ceiling" and thinking it was an instruction, so duly got the broom before his Dad told him to stop in case he cracked the plaster (now, where else would you hear a story like that, eh?).

Cardiacs, after seeing them supporting Marillion, were something of a slow-burner for Diggy (better than a no-burner mind you), but eventually hard-earned cash was parted with in exchange for a copy of *Rude Bootleg*, and from then on there was no looking back, what with fifty-plus gigs attended and a most-special album of *Sing To God*. "A Horse's Tail" and "Dead Mouse" fight it out for "best-song" supremacy, but undoubtedly his favourite moment was meeting Tim Smith himself at the New Cross Venue in 1990.

As I sat in the back of Malc's car listening to Diggy, I was bewildered by the vast knowledge of the man. I could just about hold my own on Prog of all vintages, but his almost-encyclopaedic erudition on almost any genre had me beaten hands down, especially on 1970s Rock (Leafhound?) and 1980s Metal. As for his instant-recall facts on films and movies, I just had to sit in the back listening to him and Malc and hope that they'd mention *The Wicker Man* again, or switch back to 70s telly.

Undoubtedly one of the highlights of the 2007 tour was Diggy's rendition, club-singer stylee, of "Tarred And Feathered" in a Stoke Chinese take-away, and it's worth mentioning again that when it comes to this sort of entertainment, Diggy is a pro. Many's the time he has shared tales with us on The List of slipping little Cardiacs phrases or riffs into a run-of-the-mill pub gig, every so often flushing out a devotee in the audience or stationed at the mixing desk.

However, it was a posting on The List that perhaps best summed Diggy up for me, and also led to one of those List-defining posts from Malc. Diggy: "One for Malcy here... I just took a job six hours a day driving prescriptions round people's houses for a pittance... I love it, am I weird?"

This led to the Luxford replying, "Not weird at all Digster. You have the warm glow of knowing that you are doing good for people..." I'll leave Malc's response until the end of the chapter, as it sums things up rather nicely, I think...

But Malcy responding? Well, it's not unknown... Alongside the Helocolins and Jill, Malc's name appears the most in the Cardiacs Chat List in-box, largely because he has an opinion on just about everything, and he's pretty funny with it too...

Well, you'd expect someone to be amusing when their first encounter with music was stock-film of the Beach Boys on the television in Germany, the humour-capital of the world, in the early-70s, and their first gifted-record was an Alvin & The Chipmunks album. Mind you, a first purchase of "Angel Eyes" by Roxy Music is pretty hard to quantify.

One thing that always amazed me about Malc was despite championing Folk Music, and Roy Harper especially (I know, I know, he's not really Folk, but his roots were there), his knowledge of Prog-Rock was always pretty deep, especially Yes. Indeed, he once admitted to being able to recite all the lyrics from Yes' *Going For The One* album, a fact that was always going to impress me (I once got chatting to a tramp on the tube after he offered me a bit of his pizza – I declined – and after we got onto the subject of music, he made the big mistake of asking me, 'Have you ever heard of a band called Yes…?'). Well, the reason for Malc's Prog tendencies was unearthed by Belch's Question Sheet: 'The biggest influence on my early musical development was the dead brother of my best mate at school, Keith Butler. We would raid his cassette collection and listen to Prog and Folky stuff.' This might also explain why his first big passion was Led Zeppelin, with an eventual debut gig of The Firm (that's Jimmy Page, not "Star Trekkin'") at the Birmingham N.E.C. in the mid-80s.

The Proggier side to Malc also helps explain why he was able to come up with one of my favourite ever List postings after I'd told a story about Ian sending his little sister to me and asking me to sing any melody played on a harpsichord, and, not knowing that I was being tested as to my predictability, just as Ian forecast, I immediately sang Rick Wakeman's harpsichord break from "Siberian Khatru". I even added to the email the tune in word-form, something like, "Diddle diddle diddle diddle diddle dt der der dert dt der dert…" etc.

Malc immediately followed this up with the following:

"Baap….bapp..dur dar dur dar
Baap…bapp..dur dar dur dar dur dar
Badda dup..dap..dup..doobee.dee..da..doo.bee.dabooo"
That's "Siberian Khatru" that is, the chanty bit near the end.
"Doodle-a, doodle-a.doodle-a, de-doodle-a-boom"
That's the start of "Going For The One".
"Bink….bink…. bink… bink, bonk…, bonk…..bonk…., bonk"
That's those dabby keyboard bits in "Close To The Edge",
you know with the dripping tap in the background before he
sings

"In her white lace".
"AWAKEN GENTLE MASS TOUCH"
That's Anderson singing 'Awaken, Gentle, Mass, Touch"
"Art ov mi fekkin wigh"
That's Trevor Rabin telling someone to move.

Only a true Yes fan would be able to write that (and only a true Yes fan would find it funny).

It would seem that the majority of, shall we say, older Cardiacs fans stumbled across them either when they supported Marillion in 1984, or when they saw them on *The Tube*. Malc falls into the latter category, presumably scarred for life seeing the classic line-up in full bandsmen/face-paint regalia plundering through "Tarred And Feathered". It took another four years for him to see Cardiacs live, at U.L.U. in 1991, but at least the Janice Long session *Night Tracks* EP was picked up along the way.

Malc obviously keeps a rigid record of his Cardiacs gigs because he was quite definite in his assertion that Portsmouth on the 2007 tour was his 50th, meaning that by the time we all crept home and went for a big long sleep when the tour ended he was on an impressive 52. He's fairly definite about his chart-toppers too, stating quite boldly that *Sing To God* is top album and "The Everso Closely Guarded Line" is his most-loved song, with the secret Bull & Gate gigs of 2005 coming out ahead of the other 50 concerts, and a favourite moment of 'the whole of the last (2007) tour'.

When it comes to current listening pleasures, unsurprisingly Malc has an opinion: 'Fleet Foxes – they are a great example of how mainstream music came about in the first place by being original, beautiful and universal, like the Beatles. Great mainstream music is worth more to me than tired experimental music.'

And just to sum up his feelings for Cardiacs, Malc says, 'I like the fact that good art which stands the test of time depends on the observer as much as the artist; it's a meeting of minds and as the observer's mind develops, so they are able to reinterpret or newly re-enjoy the old material as well as the new material that the artist creates as their minds develop in turn. Cardiacs music is very like that for me; you can visit the old stuff and find new points of interest, and you can be given a totally new perspective by the new stuff. It also explains for me why people who have little to bring to the party don't get the enjoyment out of it that they should.'

But I've tried to keep my main focus in this chapter on The List and the joys it can bring to its individuals, so going back to Diggy telling us that he was delivering prescriptions, and the Luxford pointing out he'd have a warm glow, here is Malc following up both by expounding the joys and positive effects of contributing to The List:

"Well, Piesy was down on chaps (no cheap jokes) and she got a nice beardy fellow. Lol was just down and she got job offers (and a happy nod of the head from this patronising old sod). It's the power of The List. I like The List.

"I like The List because when you're on a downer about y'self, you can help people with advice or share knowledge or a joke or an experience or you can take the piss because that's what friends do, and you can give y'self a pat on the back that you were fortunate enough to love Cardiacs.

"Like Chris said, it's the warm glow of being better than you have to be and remembering that you're all right really. I think I'd like that job too, but then I like my job most days (nearly wrote 'Dave' then, Diggy; that seems very wrong somehow)...

"...I love Cardiacs. All of it."

That goes for all of us, Malc.

Chapter Nineteen
"Hopeless"
Academy 3, Manchester,
November 21ˢᵗ 2007

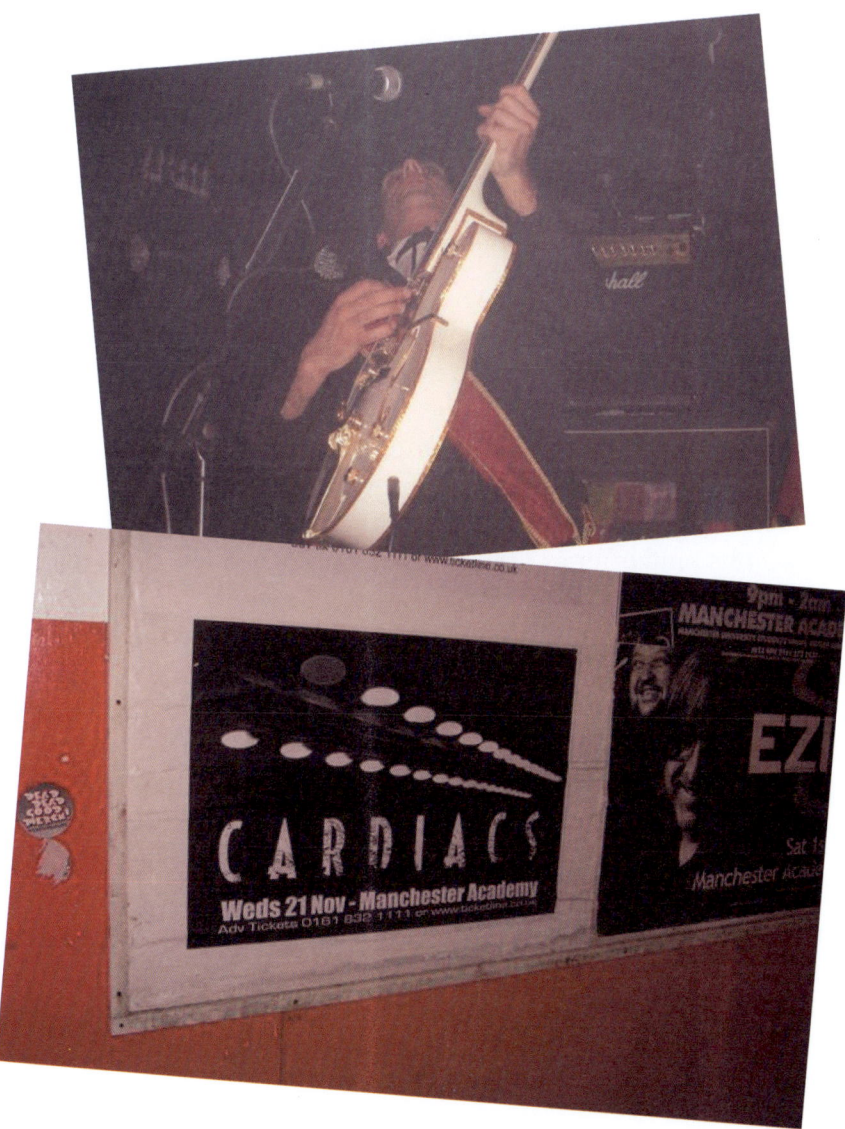

"Hopeless"
Academy 3, Manchester, November 21st 2007

'What's it going to be then, eh?'

Whether it be football or music has been a constant battle in my head as to which is the more important. The truth is, I still can't pinpoint the winner. Sometimes football is top of the league, other times music hits number one. And sometimes there's an honourable draw, usually brought about by the wonder of television in pubs. One thing's for sure, whichever wins, the other is never far behind. Hence in the days before mobile phones (well, a long time before I had one anyway), I'd find myself wandering through, say, Leeds in the early hours of the morning after a Cardiacs gig at the University in November 1988 wondering how on earth Sheffield United had got on away at Aldershot, only to find out upon breaking off from my dash to the bus station to buy a newspaper that they'd lost 1-0.

Fever Hitch was littered with examples of helping out at Cheese Cake Truck gigs of an evening, then hitching off through the night in order to make some Sheffield United match the next day, but it was Cheese Cake Truck themselves who offered me a chance to allow football to come out on top when they told me they were off to do some gigs in LA and would I like to fly out with them? I turned down this kind offer as I felt it would impinge on the book too much; heaven forbid I'd probably miss a match, two at tops. As daft decisions go, this one ranks right up there near the top of the tree – a freebie to LA, and I turned it down for my beloved Blades. *sigh* Still, music was able to strike a blow back that season when Cardiacs were due to play the LA2 (no, not that place again, but the London Astoria 2 before it became the Mean Fiddler) on the same day Sheffield United played away at Burnley. I'd agonised long and hard about how on earth I was going to fit both in, but then a bout of debilitating flu sorted that one out – on the morning of the match I was feeling better, but nowhere near well enough to hitch up to Lancashire. Instead I spent all day in bed, and then raised myself to go and see Cardiacs in the evening despite still feeling rough.

Now, it's fair to say that Ian of the Skinner variety is no lover of football. Indeed, until his Czech wife Veronika probably forced him to watch her Republic's progress to the Euro 2004 semi-finals, the only football he'd ever watched had been as a result of having to sit in a pub with me to observe England crash out of some tournament or other somewhere around the globe. And so the famous Graham Taylor "do I not like that" match against Holland in 1993 was watched in a pub in Carterton, Oxon, as Ian's band Strangeland prepared to do a gig in that self-same drinking establishment. Then England's exit on penalties from the World Cup in 1998 at the hands of Argentina was watched by the two of us (and a supportive Debbie aka Little Ming Mong) in the Sussex, Islington, as Jesus Underground Band waited to take the stage at the rather bizarre Klinker Club in an adjoining room. Euro 2000 saw England eliminated by a last-minute penalty in a 3-2 defeat to Romania on Solstice Eve, Ian and I viewing it from the safety of the Bell in Amesbury before walking up to Stonehenge for the first Solstice celebration open to the public since the troubles of the 80s and 90s, affording me the pleasure of discussing England's shortcomings with Dave Brock and Richard Chadwick of Hawkwind whilst standing in the middle of a very soggy stone circle.

Notice a theme here? England disasters are plentiful of course, examples of Ian watching football are not, but just to prove that he can't always carry the blame, it's worth pointing out that World Cup 1986 and the Hand of God exit was confirmed via a radio whilst sitting round a fire at a Stonehenge Pilgrims' campsite in Kings Somborne, Hampshire, with not a Skinner in sight (I didn't even know the lucky chap at this point), and when England crashed out of Japan and South Korea 2002 thanks to Ronaldhino's spawny-get of a free kick, I was trying to stay awake in the George, Amesbury, having been up all night at Stonehenge waiting for the sunrise with ex-girlfriend Annette from Germany. And just to get Ian completely off the hook, he *was* present when I witnessed one of England's greatest triumphs of modern times. What's more, there was some Cardiacs involvement too which, for the purposes of this book, is something of a good job, especially as all this is serving as a build-up to Cardiacs' Manchester gig of November 21st 2007 when on the same evening, all England needed to do was draw with Croatia to make it to Euro 2008. But for now, we must travel back in time to June 18th 1996 and a Cardiacs Concert Performance at Wolverhampton Civic Centre taking place on the same day that England took on the might of Holland at Wembley in Euro '96...

* * * *

On that June morning in 1996 Ian and I had woken up in a park somewhere in Birmingham after discovery stowing away on Cardiacs' minibus the night before, thus finding ourselves ejected before we'd left the city boundaries. That previous night Cardiacs had played at the Foundry in England's second city, and a rather traveller-friendly itinerary meant that it was just a short bus-ride to Wolverhampton for the next stop-off on the tour. One thing was for sure, we had plenty of time to get there as when you're kipping in a park in Birmingham you don't really want to lie around too long in a ditch. As it was we had a fair number of dogs sniffing around us in the early hours, so before we were reported as dead bodies (by the way, handy tip – if you don't want to find a dead body, don't go walking your dog first thing in the morning) we got up and moved off. After a bit of breakfast and a public convenience wash-and-brush-up (you haven't lived until you've had one of these), we were on a bus to Wolverhampton, arriving well before lunch. By about still-well-before-lunch we'd exhausted everything there was to do in Wolverhampton, meaning the only form of entertainment was Ian listening to me whinge about my sore finger which was swelling up to cartoon-Tom-and-Jerry proportions.

Bored, we found the venue and decided it'd be a good idea to sneak in and see if we could stay in there until the gig started. This led to us watching in amazement as hundreds of pensioners took part in a tea dance in the main hall (the main hall not being where Cardiacs were playing that night, I might add). On this massive stage was sitting a bloke right in the middle with just a single keyboard on spindly legs, making him look all tiny and lonely, whilst on the dance-floor his audience danced their ageing legs off. And there at the other end of the hall, like a glimpse of far-off fairies in a glade, could be seen a group of Big-Flower-tee-shirted individuals joining hands and dancing to the music in a mad, out of control circle, pretty much like an insane Cardiacs version of "Ring-a-Ring o' Roses". Meanwhile talk between the old folk in the foyer was all of flirtations and who'd asked who to dance – gives me something to look forward to I suppose.

The hours passed by and kick-off for England v Holland approached, presenting me with a difficult decision. Did I leave the venue and pass up my guaranteed stow-away free entry in search of a pub showing the game, or did I carry on mooching around the venue in the hope of finding a telly? I'm sure Ian preferred the pub option, but for me I just had to do whatever would enable me to watch the game. Just as I was giving up hope I heard the sound of a television coming from behind a closed door. The only trouble was, a sign on the door read "CARDIACS DRESSING ROOM – ADMITTANCE STRICTLY RESTRICTED TO REPRESENTATIVES OF THE ALPHABET BUSINESS CONCERN". I tentatively opened the door anyway, Ian and I looking around at the sight that greeted us: a totally abandoned dressing room, but one with recent signs of occupation – half-empty bottles of water and cups of fresh orange juice, still-warm slices of pizza, a discarded 'Little Man And A House' t-shirt, a television blaring out loudly to no-one, a curtain flapping in the open window… It certainly had the look of a hasty exit, but I decided it was worth the risk that nobody would come back until the match was over.

And so it was that Ian and I settled down to watch England take on Holland, a match that was vitally important because England needed a win to secure a place in the knock-out stages of a tournament we were hosting. I dare say that Ian didn't really give a monkey's about the result, but I'm sure he derived great amusement from watching my antics as I got all excited with England turning in one of their greatest ever performances of any era, storming to a four-goal lead over a Dutch side that was considered by many to be almost the equal of the great Total Football side of the 1970s. As an added touch, late in the game England went and let Holland get a goal back to make it 4-1, a result that would ensure Scotland didn't qualify, whereas if it had stayed at 4-0 Scotland would have scraped through (sorry to mention this, friends from North of the Border, but it *was* quite funny at the time, especially as the watching Scots in the BBC studio were convinced England had done it deliberately).

The only interruptions throughout the 90 minutes were from Big John Daniel himself who, as a regular at Queens Park Rangers, wanted regular updates on the score. Whenever I'd update him with a 'two-nil' or whatever, he'd ask, 'What does that mean?' as in where did it leave us as regards qualification.

Ian would reply with a cheeky, 'It means England have scored two and Holland haven't scored any,' but then I'd come to the rescue by letting John know that whilst ever England were winning, we were going through to the next stage, and let's not worry about Scotland.

The most relieving thing was John's acceptance that we were supposed to be in there. It must have been the Big Flower t-shirts that made us look like we were representing the Alphabet Business Concern.

Well, with a fine victory under our belts Ian was safe from accusations of being a bit of a hex on England, at least for a few years anyway. Meanwhile, the band had all been down the pub where they'd met the Helocolins, and yet another opportunity to meet that esteemed couple long before we finally did had gone begging. After such a fine showing by England on the football pitch, Cardiacs had quite an act to follow, but of course it's impossible to compare – like comparing apples to bananas or something. All I can say is that despite the strange decision by the venue to leave the house lights on all evening (at least it meant I got some very clear, very wonderful photos), and a rather sparse crowd (people obviously unaware that the game would be available on a dressing room TV), Cardiacs triumphed again, and as Ian and I were thrown out of a moving minibus once more, this time alongside a playing-field on the outskirts of Wolverhampton, I had a warm glow that was doubled up this time, the kind of warm glow that only a history-making win at football and a brilliant gig by the best band ever can bring about.

* * * *

As opposed to waking up in a ditch in a park in Birmingham, eleven years later I was coming-to in the relative comfort of a bed and breakfast in Stoke-on-Trent. Despite Malc's concerns that it was like something out of *The League Of Gentlemen*, breakfast was all very full and very English, and most importantly we were able to leave. As Malc and Diggy were heading off in Malc's car to Manchester for the next scheduled gig, you can guess where my plans to hitchhike were heading. There are still one or two Sheffield United supporters, most notably (and most appropriately) justoutsidestoke blade, who refer to me as The Cheating Thumb due to my tendency every now and again in *Fever Hitch* to arrange lifts via mobile phone mid-journey (and also due to the fact that they know how much calling me this winds me up). Well, on this tour I really was proving myself to be the biggest cheat of all – sorry guys.

Stoke to Manchester isn't too far as the crow flies, or even as the Malc drives, and before long we were driving into the centre and looking for Malc and Diggy's hotel. I was hoping not to have to shell out for another night's accommodation as I'd arranged to borrow a scrap of floor at the home of nearby friend Livo, but there was just that niggle at the back of my mind that I'd left home for Sheffield on Monday not quite having confirmed anything. From the outside it looked like a reasonable hotel so maybe a stop there wouldn't have been too much of a bind, but once we got in it was distinctly…shabby. If the boys had thought the one in Stoke had been *League Of Gentlemen*, then this one was more *Fawlty Towers* (come on Belch, surely you can think of something better than this) (I couldn't). Malc and Diggy were suitably unimpressed, and I started to hope Livo really would come up trumps.

A walk through town led to a pub lunch, followed by an elongated sit in said pub before heading back to the hotel to wait whilst Diggy went through his incredibly long-winded gig-readying routine. Whilst Malc and I sat in the bar for what seemed like an eternity, what looked like a beach-volleyball team walked in, except it was November so they must have been hockey players. (Actually they might have been a netball team.) Still, sporty, fit girls – I was just thinking of inviting them *en masse* to come to the gig with us when Diggy appeared and spared me the embarrassment of rejection.

Now, there was one thing troubling me, and in a way it still is. The venue was billed as Manchester Carling Academy 3, which someone reliably informed me was attached to the University of Manchester complex, and indeed made up part of the building where gigs used to be played at the university back in the day. You see, I'd seen Cardiacs at Manchester University way back on November 16th 1988 and now I was left puzzling over whether this was the exact same venue or not, and I still can't be sure one way or the other. But as the number three in the venue name suggests, it was a series of venues stacked up one on top of another, so for the sake of the Great Belch Gig List they just go down as venues with different names 19 years apart, and…and… I'll leave others to work out exactly which bit the first gig took place in. Look, these things are important – to me anyway.

It turned out the Carling Academy 3 was at the top of a load of winding stairs, but before I even thought about venturing up there I had to establish if there was a telly for watching England v Croatia elsewhere. There was – downstairs in the ground-floor bar. What's more, there were plenty of screens so whichever way you turned, you weren't going to miss the action. Now I needed to find out what time Cardiacs were due onstage, and once again John Daniel was on the scene to help out. Bit of a worry here though – Cardiacs were due to go on when there would still be half-an-hour of the match to go. I just hoped that as usual the gig would start late (has anyone ever been to a gig that started on time?) and that by then England would be out of sight, meaning missing a bit wasn't going to upset the applecart too much. If only…

The bar began to fill up with faces both familiar and otherwise. Simon, a veteran of well over 100 Cardiacs gigs (he stopped counting after he'd reached his ton) and a Millwall fan for his sins, called me over and asked if I was going to watch the game. 'Of course,' I replied.

I then spied Al and his missus Carol along with Livo, and was mighty relieved to hear Livo say that even though he thought I didn't need somewhere to kip for the night anymore, I was still welcome 'but we won't be able to hang around afterwards.' Well, beggars can't be choosers… Now Simon was calling me back over and introducing me to a girl called Caroline who, he informed me, was a Sheffield United fan. We had a good old moan about losing to Wigan and getting relegated on the last day of the 2006/2007 season, and had a compulsory whinge about Carloz Tevez and West Ham before I remembered what I was wearing underneath my trousers.

'Here, you'll love this,' I said, undoing my belt before realising just how dodgy those words followed by that action may have appeared. I'm sure Caroline was as relieved as everyone in the building when all I revealed were my Sheffield United combat-shorts, ready for another hot and sweaty gig.

As kick-off at Wembley Stadium was fast-approaching, I glanced up at the screen to look at the team news and noticed that England's tactical genius of a manager, Steve McLaren, had selected Scott Carson in goal. I had feelings reminiscent to when in October 2000 against Germany Kevin Keegan selected Gareth Southgate in midfield; you know, initial thoughts of, "Brave – he'll be hailed as a mastermind if it comes off," followed almost immediately by, "No, no! Don't do it, you idiot! Change it! Change it! Injure him in the warm-up! Bomb scare! Abandon the match!" But when you're sat in a bar in Manchester there's not a lot you can do to change things at a rather rainy, distant Wembley. All you can do is watch and pray. Besides, we only had to draw, and we *were* at home…

As the match got underway I was back with Al and entourage having one of those conversations where you don't look at anyone or anything apart from the TV screen. Despite not removing my gaze from the telly, I found it hard to believe what I'd actually just seen. 'Did I really see that happen?' I bellowed to Al, just as the replay confirmed that I had indeed seen Scott Carson let an innocuous shot slip through his gloves and over his shoulder into the net with barely ten minutes on the clock.

I'd just gone back to Simon's table to let off steam in time to watch in horror as the England defence all stood still waving their arms in the air for an offside that never came, whilst the Croatians waltzed through the defence, rounded the goalkeeper and went 2-0 up. Time to sit down, head in hands, and time for me and Simon to discuss what we would do when it came to gig-starting time. Providing England weren't out of sight (the wrong-way-round out-of-sight this time) by then, we decided that as we'd seen every gig on the tour (well, Simon most of), we'd miss the beginning and stick with England to the bitter end, a decision made easier when Big John Daniel appeared again and said the commencement of Cardiacs' performance had been put back by 15 minutes. Still, an England recovery hardly looked on the cards as they did a pretty convincing impression of clueless idiots, all whilst McLaren watched impassively from the sidelines underneath an umbrella – yes, an umbrella. Oh dear.

As the second half got underway a lot of people had headed upstairs, presumably to check out the God Damn Whores, but there was still quite a crowd in the bar to watch what was now developing into an England comeback. McLaren brought David Beckham on at half-time and the improvement was noticeable. We got a penalty which Frank Lampard, showing nerves of steel, stuck away to bring us back into it. Then Beckham played in a perfect cross which Peter Crouch chested down before drilling home. Simon and I jumped up and hugged each other, doing a little dance around the table, because at 2-2, England were going to Euro 2008. Never can a Sheffield United and Millwall fan have been seen together in such perfect harmony. Crouch meanwhile was probably blissfully unaware of his impending appearance in *both* my books after his 'Freeeeeaaaak!' torment at the hands of the Sheffield United supporters in *Fever Hitch*.

The one wonderful thing about following England is that it allows supporters of the likes of Manchester United and Arsenal, you know, successful teams that get all upset if they go a whole season without winning anything, the opportunity of knowing what it feels like for the rest of us. For a Sheffield United or Millwall supporter there is a certain familiarity about the dread feeling of realising your team is suddenly sitting deep, having done the hard bit of clawing back a two-goal deficit, and are now looking in danger of chucking it all away. Such a caring sharing moment to know that fans of other teams are going to experience this for themselves, and all because we *all* have this shared passion for England. And there it was, unfolding before our very eyes – England think they've done enough, Croatia start sneaking forward, Croatia bang in a belter of a goal from well outside the area with 15 minutes to go. 3-2 down, and England are going out as Simon and I watch the last rites in a rapidly emptying room. Inside we both feel as miserable as the torrential rain at Wembley looks when the final whistle goes. Dismal, absolutely dismal.

We dragged ourselves up the stairs and as I took a quick call from Big Ship Iron, Simon nipped into the venue most hastily. Meanwhile the sounds of the climax of "Tarred And Feathered" came wafting through the door, and as Cardiacs belted out in unison, 'As they who to the sea go down, And in the waters ply their toil, Are lifted on the surges crown, And plunged where seething eddies boil,' the words came tumbling down the stairway towards me, sounding almost hymnal, like I was standing outside a church listening to the choir within. This had a most comforting effect on me, as did yet another storming gig, but every time there was a lull, that feeling of disappointment washed over me, and I knew that no matter how cheerful I might be on leaving the venue at the end, I'd wake up in the morning feeling as miserable as only a ridiculous defeat at international level can make you feel.

At least Ian hadn't been there to take the blame.

Chapter Twenty
"Wind and Rains Is Cold"
Al "Little Squirrel Feet" Gittens, Andy Thompson, and Livo

"Wind And Rains Is Cold"
Al "Little Squirrel Feet" Gittens, Andy Thompson, and Livo

The trouble with hitchhiking is more often than not you either arrive way too early or way too late. The good thing is, because the sensible hitchhiker normally takes this into consideration, you do the early thing more often than the late thing, and this can often lead to chance encounters that would have been missed if you had arrived ten minutes before "doors", queued up and just gone in. That oft-mentioned Camden Palace gig of March 15th 1994 was one such example, it being a night when life-long bonds were formed, and all because of some band called Cardiacs.

Well, actually it wasn't just because of Cardiacs; Poisoned Electrick Head had a lot to do with it too. Although I don't remember for certain, I figure I must have booked some time off from my exciting job working for a tele-marketing agency in Banbury (I'd spend all day on the phone booking appointments, conducting questionnaires, selling advertising space in Post Offices, and avoiding calls about Gulf Oil) because it was a midweek gig, and to arrive there when I did, about 6pm, I must have set off rather early. Knowing that the whole Feet First Club thing wouldn't kick-off for at least three hours, and that Cardiacs wouldn't be onstage until around midnight, I still did that sensible thing of checking out the venue first, even though I'd been there plenty of times before. There's a good chance that my early arrival had been in order to see who was hanging around and to see if I could scavenge my way onto the guest list, but as I walked around the corner the place was spookily deserted. Deserted that is except for one solitary figure sitting on the steps, a soul who was sporting dreadlocks and a Poisoned Electrick Head t-shirt. This was Al, and that shirt led me to (rightly) believe that here was a kindred spirit…

Alastair Gittens considers himself a late-comer to Cardiacs: 'I saw my first Cardiacs gig in 1994 and purchased my first record, *Heaven Born And Ever Bright*, as late as 1993 or 1994, but I had seen the 1987 film for "Tarred And Feathered" on *The Tube* when it was broadcast, which left me disturbed (as it did many, Al), but impressed and in need of further enlightenment.'

That enlightenment came around 1991 'as I got to know local psychedelic heroes Poisoned Electrick Head (we're talking St Helens and Runcorn here). Our paths crossed regularly with me playing the Chapman Stick in bands like The Titus Groan Experience and The Vent Set. '"Lecky 'Ead" were always raving about Cardiacs and were obviously influenced by Tim and the Gang. Eventually I made it down to London for my first Cardiacs gig in 1994, and it was amazing.'

Yep, this is where I came in, wandering round the corner and immediately spying that Poisoned Electrick Head t-shirt. The wearing of this t-shirt made it obvious to me that this chap was here to see Cardiacs, so I skipped that bit by way of introduction and immediately commented on the PEH t-shirt instead. I was most impressed to discover that Al was from up the same way as PEH, and was close personal friends with both them and other local heroes Wizards Of Twiddly. This was music to my ears, and so we were off. As the evening progressed, as Al puts it, 'We talked the hind leg off the Prog donkey all evening, and we haven't really stopped since.'

You see, as we talked we discovered that not only were our tastes in music mirrored when it came to Alternative Underground Pronk, it was pretty much the same when it came to everything else; mainly everything else from the Prog Canon anyway, including Yes, early-Genesis, King Crimson, Gentle Giant, The Enid etc etc.

Al continues: 'Once we were inside the gig, I met my second new friend, Andy "Mr Mellotron" Thompson, who immediately added his considerable knowledge of Progressive music to the weighty discussion…a bond was formed.'

The excitement of meeting new Prog-heads wasn't over for Al yet though: 'The enthusiasm of this trinity must have been contagious because we were suddenly joined by future-Cardiacs member Kavus Torabi, then having just formed the band that would become the Monsoon Bassoon, and a then-Cardiac, Mr Jon Poole, who took one look at me with my big beard and woolly hat and screamed,

"Bundles of fivers!", a line from "Robbery Assault And Battery" by Genesis, because he thought I looked a bit like Phil Collins circa 1976 (think of him drumming for Brand X, Al, it might make you feel better about it). "You can actually hear the beard," said Jon, referring to Phil's vocals from that era.'

That night in the Camden Palace, phone numbers were swapped, but back in the days before any of us had access to mobiles and emails, staying in contact wasn't as easy as it is today, what with us all living in different parts of the country, possibly only one or two phone-calls taking place between Al and me over the next couple of years. The next time I actually saw Al was an unexpected occasion at the Band Chapel in Derby for The Gig That Never Was.

It was June 13th 1996 and Cardiacs were due to play the second date of their tour at said venue in Derby. The night before they'd opened the tour at the Alleycat Live in Reading, and after kipping the night on Reading station, Ian had cleared off somewhere else, so on a whim I decided to train it from Oxford to Derby for the next gig. Again, I arrived stupidly early, so after a mooch round town, I sniffed out the venue and parked myself in the pub next door, finding a nice selection of Big-Flower-shirted people to chat with, including a lovely couple from Bristol (the bloke was called Dave and he had a Big Flower tattoo) (and it turns out the Helocolins were there too).

It happened the pub landlord also ran the Band Chapel next door, and he came up to us with the worrying news that Cardiacs hadn't arrived yet due to their van breaking down. However, he still seemed hopeful, as well as being very proud of his venue, so much so that he took us through for a sneak preview. I was most impressed by the stage, sitting as it did on top of some kind of altar (the venue was actually an old church), so high up that even if I'd have been sitting on someone else's shoulders, I'd only have been able to tickle Tim's feet. I was looking forward to seeing Tim ham it up on this stage, that's for sure, but only if they made it up the motorway.

Sadly though, the landlord delivered the inevitable bad news that Cardiacs had abandoned ship and had had to cancel. Seeing that

Dave and his lady and I had travelled fair distances to get there, he felt a touch of sympathy, so offered his spare room above the pub for the night, an offer we gladly accepted. As we were now in no hurry to get off, we settled in for an evening of glorious Cardiacs chat with those others that had made the fruitless trip. At this point I spotted a large chap across the pub in a Big Flower t-shirt, and with reference to his size said to Dave, 'I don't fancy telling him the gig's off,' only to realise that as he got closer and caught his eye it was Al. After a big hug we settled down to carry on talking the hind leg of that Prog donkey again. To this day I still refer to that night as "the best gig I never attended".

Later on that year, on Cardiacs' second tour in support of *Sing To God*, November 5th 1996 saw Cardiacs playing the Manchester Roadhouse on the occasion of Al's 29th birthday. The night before they had played at the Crown & Cushion in Bolton which I'd felt duty bound to attend, but as the wind and rains really were cold that night, whilst all bona-fide representatives of the Alphabet Business Concern snoozed in a Travelodge, this Belch somehow managed to tiptoe into their van and spent a sheltered night in there. It was natural therefore that I make the short journey the next day to Manchester, and there once again was Al, all happy and celebrating the fact that it was his 29th. Little was he to know that he was about to be gifted a new name that very night…

Al obviously wanted those that mattered to know that it was his birthday, so between songs he saw his chance and went for it. 'I drunkenly marched to the stage,' he explains, 'interrupted Tim, told him it was my birthday and asked if he could dedicate the next song to me. After a stern telling off, and after Jon Poole said I was "just a big curly bear", Tim named me "Little Squirrel Feet", presumably because of the dreadlocks I had at the back of my head I think. He then put my new character into the lyrics of the next song, "The Duck And Roger The Horse".'

In November 2005 on the train from London to the latest Cardiacs triumph in Oxford, I got chatting to a Cardiacs fan (it was the t-shirts again) and somehow we got onto that 1996 Manchester gig, and much to Al's delight when I related this tale to him later, this guy could remember the whole Little Squirrel Feet thing as if it were yesterday. Al obviously can remember it clearly too; as he says, 'What a fabulous birthday surprise – thank-you Tim!'

Talking of birthday treats, the following February of 1997, Al came down with his mate Batey for Belch's Birthday Binge at Brackley Cricket Club, and Batey proved to be an amazing source of rare recordings by presenting me with a tape of Gnidrolog's *In Spite Of Harry's Toenail*, an album I'd been raving about whilst moaning that I couldn't lay my hands on a copy.

In November 1997, Al nicked my idea and had his own massive birthday blow-out to celebrate his 30th, hiring as I had the Monsoon Bassoon. Like she had for Cardiacs supporting Hawkwind at Trentham Gardens a week or so earlier, Sarah gave Annette and me a lift up for this one, and Annette fearfully confessed that she preferred the Bassoons to Cardiacs…

Since then, mine and Al's paths have crossed so many times it'd be impossible to mention them all here, but highlights include joyfully watching Gong together at Glastonbury 2000, Al making it through the snow for Magma sometime early in the 21st Century, Van der Graaf Generator's magnificent comeback of 2005, and of course, many a Cardiacs gig. What's more, he quite often had company, and so as well as Batey I've befriended a number of his buddies, such as Livo, and the lady in Al's life, Carol. We also managed to bond over football, Al supporting Liverpool. I like to think that Al still credits me with Liverpool's remarkable Champions' League Final comeback in Istanbul, 2005. With Liverpool 3-0 down at half-time, I received a text from Al that cannot be repeated in a family book such as this. I comforted him with a return text stating the ridiculously hopeful (and if I'm honest, not entirely earnest), "It's only half-time – it might be a different game in the second half." One 3-3 draw and victory on penalties later, I received another text from Al, still featuring the same amount of expletives, but this time in a slightly happier context. Thank me later, Liverpool fans…

And finally while we're on with Mr Gittens, he asked me

everso politely to point readers in the direction of his MySpace profile in order to check out what a talented chap he really his. Only too happy Al – readers, please make your way to myspace-music/Ally1967 if you'd be so good…

The idea of staging a massive gig in order to celebrate a birthday wasn't exclusive to me and Al. Andy Thompson got in on the act for his 40th in March 2002. On the same day Sheffield United played West Brom in what became known as the Battle of Bramall Lane, and afterwards I dashed back to London in order to make as much of the party as possible, arriving just in time to see Guapo, Andy's brother Matt's band. Unlike Al, Andy had little or no interest in football, but the events of that day (for the one and only time in English League football history, a match had to be abandoned due to Sheffield United not having enough players left on the pitch) had even filtered through to the likes of Andy: 'Blimey, it all kicked off in Sheffield today, didn't it?' Andy smiled as I breathlessly fell through the door, still wearing my Sheffield United shirt…

Ah yes, Andy Thompson. Myself, I'd first met Andy a year or so before I met Al, after an Enid gig at the Astoria around 1993 when I'd seen him coming down the steps outside wearing a Gentle Giant *In A Glass House* t-shirt. As this was the first (and last) time I'd ever seen someone wearing such attire, I told Ian I was going to have to strike up a conversation, so I did, and yet another bond was formed. You see how good these t-shirts are for informal introductions? From then on, Ian and I saw Andy at just about every Prog-related gig we attended in London, whether it be David Cross at the Kensington Orange or Cardiacs at the Forum. Oh yes, it was a joyous moment to discover that someone as well-versed in serious Prog Rock as Andy was also into Cardiacs. As he was living in London, and up until 1998 I wasn't, Andy's place in North London became an alternative crashing pad for me and Ian when Organ Towers wasn't available. In those mid-90s halcyon days, Andy was driving Genesis tribute band ReGenesis around, and many's the time I spent a night on Andy's sofa with a fox-head for company.

Not only did Andy drive Genesis tribute bands around, but he also did a pretty good job of doing it for me, and a whole host of others too. Just about every time I've moved house since (and including) moving to London, Andy has done the honours, and there was a time when he seemed to be Kavus' personal roadie, especially in the days of the Monsoon Bassoon, Andy being the one charged with driving them up to Belch's Birthday Binge at Brackley Cricket Club in an old rattle-trap of a van owned by Sidi Bou Said. Andy also came to the rescue in 1999 when Jesus Underground Band scared the heebies out of Banbury Mill Theatre's Miller's Bar. The rest of the band had come up in their van ("Tranny"), but for some reason "singer" Martin couldn't escape early enough, so he was personally whisked up by Andy in that lovely white Escort-sized van of his. It's worth mentioning that Jesus Underground Band were where mine and Andy's musical tastes divided a touch. Andy couldn't quite get a grasp of them at the Bull & Gate in 1997, and things hadn't altered much two years on, but he was alert enough to notice that for this particular Banbury gig Martin bore a striking resemblance to Fish of Marillion, choosing as he did on this occasion to wear red face-paint (Martin that is, not Andy). One thing Martin did that Fish possibly wouldn't have done is punch a hole in the (temptingly low) ceiling of the Miller's Bar, something that led to my usual post-gig apology to the venue promoter, but unlike many promoters (I'm thinking of the time we set the smoke alarms off at the Trinity in Harrow and when our water machine flooded the cellar of the Red Eye in Islington), this one was happy to write it off as 'all part of the show'.

Not only does Andy help out with his driving, but his Mellotron has done its fair share of coming to the rescue too, including one night when Focus borrowed it for a gig at the Astoria (that's the 21st Century version of Focus by the way). I'll never forget the look of horror on Andy's face as he walked into the venue to see a monitor perched on top of his beloved 'Tron. It's also a safe bet that if there's a Mellotron on any Cardiacs-related recording in recent years, then it's Andy's device that has done the honours; Spratleys Japs sent it back all broken.

Sometimes he even got to play it himself, especially when he was a member of Hawkwind sound-alikes Litmus. Andy's position in Litmus was sealed for a time because of his ownership of not only the Mellotron, but also a Moog, and one of my greatest privileges was to act as Mellotron-and-Moog Roadie when Litmus supported Julian Cope at the Leadmill a few years back.

Perhaps Andy's greatest work is his remarkable *Planet Mellotron* website where he attempts to not only list every recorded appearance of said instrument, but also review them all. Thus I'm aware that Andy doesn't have much time for Marillion or *Tales From Topographic Oceans* by Yes, but his love of King Crimson, Cardiacs and early-Genesis is unbounded (but then to be honest, this was rather obvious to me anyway). His unstinting research for *Planet Mellotron* has led to much correspondence with keyboard wizards young and old, and every now and again the poor chap will receive a text from me saying, "I think I heard a Mellotron on (fill in names of numerous albums here)," leading to Andy periodically turning up at my house and borrowing potential 'Tron-ish recordings. I'm always left astonished by how on earth he can tell the difference between a sampled Mellotron and a real one, but if anyone can, Andy can.

One fantastic bit of genealogical research has led to Andy working out that his Mellotron was once possibly owned by King Crimson in 1974, and one year later found itself in the hands of Gryphon, in time for it to appear on their *Raindance* album. If I'd known this when I was humping it up the slope at the Leadmill, I'd probably have asked it for its autograph...

Andy's path to Cardiacs had started in the late-70s with his first love, the New Wave of British heavy Metal. This transmuted into Prog Rock sometime in the 80s, and eventually Cardiacs around 1986/87 thanks to brother Matt, the very same Matt Thompson who was the original creative force behind Guapo. When Ian worked at HMV on Oxford Street, he stuck on Guapo's name-plate, half-way down where you wouldn't see it unless you wanted to, "Andy Thompson's brother's band".

Not having attended many "away" gigs (i.e. outside of London), Andy was not at the Manchester gig of 2007, but as the nearest Cardiacs got to Runcorn and Warrington and the likes, Al, Carol and Livo most definitely were. Livo had kindly agreed to put me up for the night, Al telling me to look after him as he was 'a national treasure.' And as promised, all those who helped me out on the tour would get profiled. Not having as much information about Livo swimming around in my head as I did for Al and Andy, I had to get my question sheet out again, and once again, the results were fascinating...

* * * *

When you come into the world at a gig then there's a pretty good chance music will be in your veins. 'My Mum went into labour with me at a Four Tops gig,' explains Mike "Livo" Livesley, 'which must have been a bit of a shock because she didn't even know she was pregnant. Hard to believe she wouldn't know a big lad like me was in there.'

Still, as he didn't have much of a say in this, Livo can hardly count it as his first ever gig. Instead that band Poisoned Electrick Head are awarded this privilege 'if we're talking "bought the ticket and walked to the venue on my own two feet". They were at the Queen's Hall, Widnes and I must've been about 14-years-old.'

A bit like myself then, in that my first gig of Rick Wakeman at the Sheffield City Hall in 1980 took place when I was 14, and like myself there was a considerable amount of build-up and influence in the years leading up...

'The first band I was passionate about were the Bay City Rollers,' confesses Livo with no hint of embarrassment; 'Hard to believe, but I was about two at the time. I remember watching their TV show in my wee tartan trousers.'

TV spin-offs obviously featured strongly as the first record Livo received was "Rupert The Bear" by Jackie Lee, whereas the first one he bought with his own dosh was "Don't Give Up On Us Baby" by David Soul: 'I must have been about four – I was a huge

Starsky And Hutch fan.'

Meanwhile, it's no surprise his first live concert "attendance" was the Four Tops, aged zero, because his Mum, his biggest musical influence as a youngster, was a massive Motown fan, as well as a huge lover of T Rex. As Cardiacs loomed on the horizon in this musical development, Livo couldn't bracket himself with any one particular musical genre or youth sub-culture: 'I've always had an enormously eclectic taste, which has infuriated a lot of my "purist" friends. Aside from digging the occasional thing, I guess mainly it's been Indie, Prog, Folk, Lounge Jazz, Canterbury Scene, and as I can't fit him into any category, Viv Stanshall. My taste changes from day to day sometimes, but I always have my "constants", which definitely includes Cardiacs.'

Yep, here they come again, God bless them. When Cardiacs steam into your life, they don't often drift off elsewhere. Much like Al, Livo first became aware of Cardiacs thanks to the presence of Poisoned Electrick Head: 'Through following PEH around I met Al Gittens, or "Little Squirrel Feet" as Tim christened him. Al played me *A Little Man And A House And The Whole World Window* on his Walkman one morning in the canteen at college, and it literally blew my mind. He told me they were playing at The Citadel in St Helens that Saturday and he wanted me to go check them out – what a night!'

Extensive research (a quick look at Pete's all-inclusive all-consuming Cardiacs Gig List) confirms this first Livo-Live-Cardiacs-Experience as being May 27th 1995, as he says 'we went to the one the night after at the Boardwalk in Manchester (again confirmed by Pete's list) where I interviewed Tim for my radio show. A bunch of us ended up going down to London to see the end of the tour – I just couldn't get enough!' Aye, they can grab you like that, Livo…

Inevitably, hard-earned money soon started to be parted with in exchange for Cardiacs phonographic recordings, but after the obvious initial purchase of *A Little Man And A House And The Whole World Window*, Livo picked up what he described as 'the best bargain of my life' when he discovered Cardiacs' 1984 cassette *The Seaside* in a second-hand shop 'purely by chance for 50p. I then tracked down all the albums and listened to nothing but Cardiacs for about six months straight. I would kill to be able to hear them now as I did for the first time – heaven…'

Livo's a little unsure just how many times he's seen Cardiacs live now, 'especially as they had a patch of not playing the North for some years, and having to hold down a tedious IT manager's job, before I quit to be a skint musician, so I had to fit them in "as and when". I'd put it as between ten and twenty, but then it might be thirty… Sorry, the last 15 years are quite a blur.'

He's a bit more certain of his favourite album though: '*A Little Man And A House And The Whole World Window*, no question,' he says, going with the policy I often adopt that the first one you hear is the most special (and so it is that if push comes to shove, that's my fave album too). As for top songs though, there's two battling it out for number one: 'I can only narrow it down to two, "R.E.S." and "In A City Lining" – both bliss…'

Special gigs brings to mind another Belch Favourite, in the form of the Friday night of the 2003 Garage Concerts: 'Such a special night – I hadn't seen them in years and it was great to catch up with old friends, people like you Belchy.'

His favourite moment is rather familiar too: 'On Al's birthday in 1996 in Manchester, Tim told Al and me that we were "all snowy in the Pond". We were very "snowy in the Pond" – we'd been drinking for about eight hours. Oh, and then there was when Jon Poole told me that Genesis didn't sound anywhere as good after Phil Collins shaved off his beard. He assured me that if you listened to everything he did prior to exposing his chin to the world, you could "hear the beard". I still laugh out loud at that.' And at least we know that Jon Poole is consistent…

Added to the constant of Cardiacs, Livo now finds himself drawn to foreign parts (after winding me up with a little joke about listening to Coldplay; 'Aren't they fabulous?' You know my answer to that one, Livo…): 'Aside from the evergreen classics, my attention has been drawn toward Scandinavia for the last six years or so; bands like Dungen (ah, I suspect Al drew you towards them, as he brought them to my attention too), Anekdoten, Hitten, and The Lionheart Brothers all play the music that really does it for me at the moment. I have also been hearing more North American stuff, like the Mars Volta and a band in Vancouver called Black Mountain (ooh yes, I think *The Organ* mentioned them). The only British band worth a listen are Circulus, whom I like a lot.' Too right, Livo, and we all know who Belch is currently doing a spot of work for...

That night after the 2007 Manchester gig, despite my anger at England's miserable failure, Livo and I sat up until the early hours chatting about everything and anything, including quite an extensive theological discussion, what with me being a member of the Church of Jesus Christ of Latter Day Saints and Livo having studied theology. He also proved he is indeed "a national treasure" by running me off a CD copy of an old long-unavailable Poisoned Electrick Head cassette, *Drink Me*. He also happily posed for a photo in front of his musical gear, and showed off his collection of annuals, including an old *Beezer* annual that I'd once possessed but had long-since lost, enabling me to get all misty-eyed about "The Numbskulls" and "Smiffy" amongst others. It really was a miracle that we both got up in reasonable time the following morning...

Since putting me up for the night, Livo has left these shores and emigrated from England to Canada, settling in Vancouver. He sent me an email just to fill in a few gaps: "I originally went to Art College where I trained as a Graphic Designer and Photographer, but by definition I would describe myself as a Musician.

"I came to Vancouver because I was offered a chance to live in a beautiful city in the sunshine in another country and decided to go for it as life is too short."

He then signs off with a heartfelt plea: "Jim, could you fix it for Cardiacs to come and play over here in Canada?" Somehow, I can't see it Livo – we'll just have to send Circulus out there for you instead.

Well, of course this here book took so long to get out that there is a Livo postscript, in that he's back here in England now, doing (amongst other things) live solo performances of Vivian Stanshall's play *Sir Henry At Rawlinson End* and the like. As Al said, Livo – a national treasure…

Chapter Twenty-One
"The Seaside"
Wedgewood Rooms, Portsmouth,
November 22nd 2007

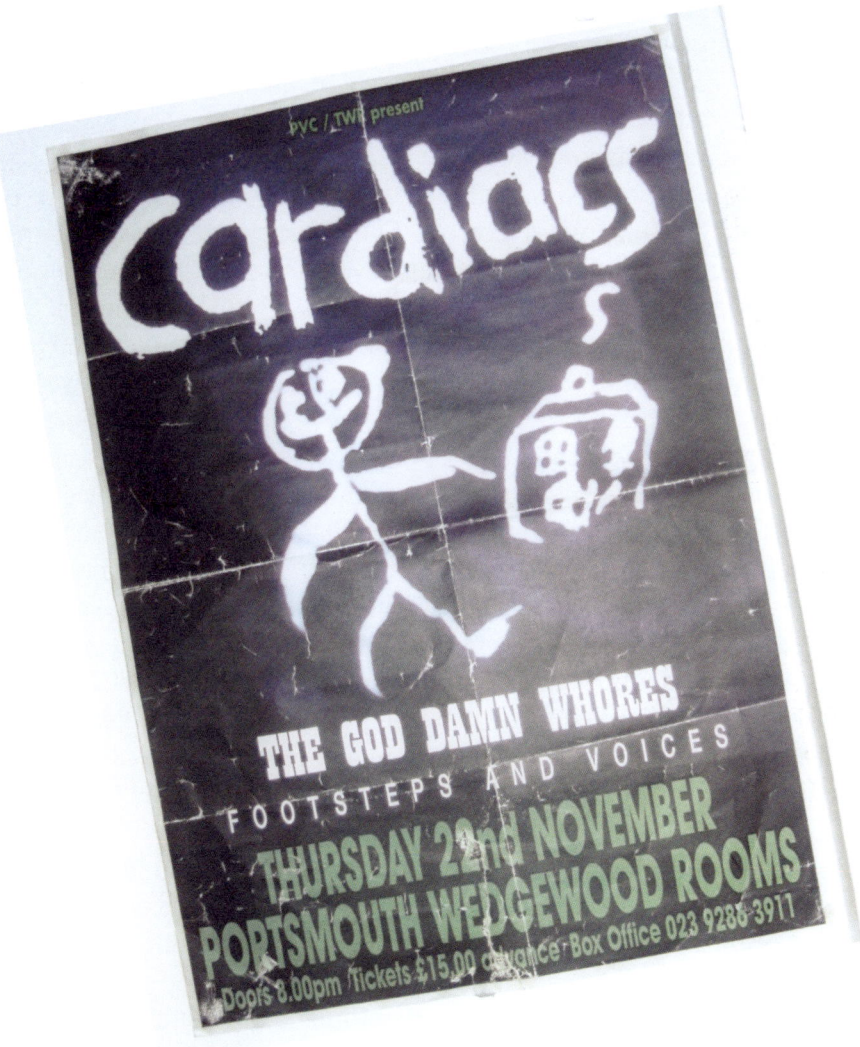

"The Seaside"
Wedgewood Rooms, Portsmouth, November 22nd 2007

In *Fever Hitch*, a book I may have mentioned before, I described Portsmouth as being like the Barnsley of the south. Now, I don't know who'd be most offended by this, and if I felt the need to apologise to the inhabitants of either settlement, I'm not sure which lot I should be directing my apology at. But I was possibly wrong, if only because Barnsley is nowhere near the sea, whereas Portsmouth most definitely is, especially the venue for the next Cardiacs gig (Belch Cardiacs Gig #99), the Wedgewood Rooms, which just happens to be situated in the locale of Southsea, the place where you can get a hovercraft over to the Isle of Wight if you so wish.

So, if Barnsley isn't the Portsmouth of the north, where is? Ladies and gentlemen, I give you… Scunthorpe! Not because Scunny is a seaside resort in any way whatsoever, and I doubt you can get a hovercraft from there to anywhere, but it is a bit nearer the sea than Barnsley (well, the River Humber if you go due north, and the North Sea if you keep going east, after you've encountered the mouth of the Humber – Geography lesson over). No, I compare Scunthorpe to Portsmouth largely because i) I've only ever been to one previous gig by anyone (Cardiacs, of course) in Portsmouth, so have few tales to tell (apart from Pete's 100th gig which is dealt with elsewhere), and ii) I had rather a good time when venturing away from Sheffield to Scunthorpe to see Cardiacs at the Baths Hall (made famous by Jasper Carrot) in June 1988. What's more, I actually hitchhiked to that gig, and as you can no doubt guess, my trip from Manchester to Portsmouth in 2007 was not going to involve thumbing-it at all. Besides, I used up any stories I may have about Portsmouth in that other book of mine, so I'd better get on with telling you all about Scunthorpe instead.

* * * *

By June 9th 1988 I'd joined the ranks of the unemployed thanks to the generosity of H. Turner and Son Ltd who decided that after nearly three years of unstinting loyalty, including a final three months of employment working in Barnsley for their wholesale news operation, I was surplus to requirements. Well, as an optimistic kind of chap I decided to take the positives out of the situation and figured that at least work wasn't going to get in the way of any gigs I might want to attend, no matter where they were in the country. Okay, paying for entry may be an issue when money became a bit tight, but even back then I was operating on the principle that getting there was the biggest concern, and if indeed you arrived outside the venue well before the event started, even if your pockets were empty you were going to get in one way or another.

Richard was also claiming unemployment benefit like me, and we'd already done Cardiacs at the Roadmender in Northampton on May 27th 1988. Compared to that, Scunthorpe was positively local so when our eagerly awaited *YOUsletter* told us about the gig at Scunthorpe Baths Hall we didn't need to work too hard at persuading each other to make the effort.

Even though it was in the summer months, and that gig in Northampton two weeks earlier had been accompanied by gorgeous sunshine, come the day of the Scunthorpe concert it was grey and drizzly with no sign of clearing up. Not to be put off, Richard and I met in our usual watering-hole, the Old Queen's Head by Pond Street Bus Station in Sheffield and planned our route: bus to Woodall, walk across field to Woodall Services on the M1, cross footbridge to north-bound carriageway, hitch towards-and-up the M18, sharp right after Doncaster onto the M180, stick with it all the way to Scunthorpe – that should do us. Simple enough, so it seemed, even with a persistent drizzle...

Well, the bus ride to Woodall *was* simple enough (still is actually – quite possibly the most wonderful bus in the whole history of the hitchhiking world, the number 21 from Sheffield to Rotherham via Woodall village). After that though, it all got a bit tricky – well, not so much tricky as incredibly slow...and wet. Back then my policy of not carrying a sign displaying our destination in case it put drivers off who weren't going all the way was backfiring hopelessly (it took me about another ten years before this policy was abandoned) as everyone who stopped was going straight up the M1. Nobody seemed interested in the M18 or indeed Scunthorpe, something that was hard to fathom. Not only was it drizzly, but it was cold as well, so a lift anywhere, providing it was up the M18, was going to be good enough, or so we thought. At last, one such lift came along and we were on our way, just not very far up the M18…

An hour of waiting for the next lift saw the drizzle worsen, but eventually an RAF bloke came to our rescue and dropped us at the source of the M180. Scunthorpe was not only a matter of miles away, but it was all in a straight line, or so we thought. Our next lift was indeed going all the way along the M180, but actually to Grimsby, not Scunthorpe. Our benefactors were two young lads who informed us that if we wanted to get into Scunny we'd have to branch off up the M181. It really was only a short distance, they reassured, and as everyone going up there was going into Scunthorpe, we'd be fine. What we didn't know, and to be fair they probably didn't realise, was that the M181 unmerged (blimey, it *is* a word because Word didn't underline it in red) straight off the M180 with not a roundabout or slip-road in sight. So, not only were they stopping illegally when they chucked us out on the hard-shoulder, we would be hitchhiking even more illegally, and rather impossibly judging by the speed of the traffic. To counter this, mainly because we could see some big industrial-looking cranes up ahead presumably marking the Gateway to Scunthorpe (and they *did* look agonisingly close), we decided to illegally walk along the motorway and hope we made it before the police spotted us.

Having been told off (and made to turn round) by coppers before for walking on a motorway (the M5 on the way to Stonehenge Free Festival in 1984), I didn't fancy this again so I suggested we scramble down the embankment at the side of the M181, hop into the neighbouring field, and walk to Scunthorpe legally (notwithstanding the possibility of trespass or a farmer's shotgun up our backsides). Richard refused point-blank, largely due to the anticipated dampness of the field (it was still persisting-it down), so I suggested a compromise of walking along the bottom of the embankment on the grass verge. As far as I was aware we'd still be illegal, but if we stayed down the bottom we'd be out of view of any nosy police-cars. At least Richard was prepared to give it a go this time, but after only a few-hundred yards he decided his feet were getting too wet in the grass so back up the bank he scrambled to continue the walk to Scunthorpe in the relative dry of the hard-shoulder.

We then had a bit of a barney with me protesting that he'd get nicked up there, but Richard was not coming down, so for a while we continued in silence, me wading through wet grass at the foot of the slope, Richard stomping along tarmac at the top. Five minutes of this arrangement gave me a little time to think, and I soon realised the futility of it all. If the police saw Richard breaking the law and pulled up on the hard-shoulder to tick him off, they wouldn't have far to look to spot me also breaking the law down below. So as my feet were getting a thorough soaking in the grass, I figured I might as well join Richard up the top and allow my socks to at least not get any wetter. If we got spotted by the coppers then we'd get spotted together, and we'd possibly get arrested together, just Richard with drier feet.

After about five minutes of this, and with us both expecting any second the proverbial tap on the shoulder from a Highway Patrol car pulling up behind us, lights flashing, on the hard-shoulder, we got interrupted by a different kind of vehicle. A honk on the hooter suggested we should get out of the way of something, and then a builders' tipper-truck pulled up in front of us. Had they stopped to pick us up? Had they stopped to ask us if we wanted our hard-shoulder tarmacking over? Well, it didn't look like they were offering us a lift as the cab was full with three of them in there, but the window was winding down and the one nearest us was saying, 'Quick, get in the back because if the police see you on the motorway, they'll nick you, but keep down.' He then asked where we were going, and when we said Scunthorpe Baths Hall he said they were going right past it.

So, we clambered over the side and into the tipper-bit of the truck where we undertook the remainder of our journey lying flat on our backs in amongst all the spades and sand. And it was still raining. Not the most luxurious of lifts then, but up until that point in my life, the coolest one ever, one that has possibly only ever been equalled when sometime in the mid-90s Ian and I were hitching back from London through the night after a Wizards Of Twiddly gig at the Camden

Monarch. On that occasion an almost identical tipper-truck pulled up at Staples Corner at the bottom of the M1 and I said to Ian, 'Don't know why they've stopped, there's already three of them in there.'

Again the window went down and we were addressed by the nearest builder: 'I don't know why we stopped because we can't fit you in, but (slight pause) you can always get in the back with the spades.'

'Done it before, so no problem,' I replied, so after establishing that they'd take us as far as Scratchwood Services (now London Gateway, those under the age of 20), in we clambered. The difference this time was that firstly, it was the middle of the night, and secondly, it wasn't raining. However, instead of dropping us off at the services as agreed, they drove straight past Scratchwood and motored on up the M1. Nevertheless, whilst fearing abduction by Gay Builders From Watford, Ian and I rather enjoyed ourselves as every time a lorry went past we'd give a little wave to the astonished driver from our prone position in amongst all them spades and shovels again. As it turned out, we were dropped off at the Watford junction of the M1, junction 6. 'Those services looked closed,' said Chief Builder, 'so we thought we could either drop you off here, or you could come back to Watford with us, stop the night, then do a day's work for us tomorrow.'

'Erm, no, well we need to get back home tonight in order to go to work tomorrow,' I replied. To be honest I was a little bit cheesed off that they'd decided to speed past the agreed point of dropping-off without even bothering to pull off and consult us, and possibly even more so that they assumed as hitchhikers we were unemployed layabouts. It was a long hitch back through the night in the end, and a day at work without any sleep the following day, but at least I wasn't a slave to some dodgy builders.

Back to June 1988, and I *was* of course unemployed, but not a layabout I like to think. Well, I was lying about in the back of a grubby truck, and as Richard and I got dropped off right outside Scunthorpe Baths Hall we both looked a bit of a scruffy mess, what with all that sand and sludge getting everywhere. The only disappointment was that the builders didn't tip us out onto the road, but even so, I doubt very much that anyone has ever arrived at a Cardiacs gig in such style…

Of course, as often happens with hitchhiking, our arrival was ridiculously early, but at least this enabled us to wander into the venue unchallenged, secure guest-list slots by being a little cheeky, and dry ourselves off in the Gents. The gig itself was something of a special one in that the set-list threw up quite a different running order to the previous three times I'd seen them (yes, it's quite hard to believe that this Scunthorpe Baths Hall gig was only my fourth ever Cardiacs gig). Long before the band took to the stage, I was leaning on the monitors chatting to a Cardiacs fan from Leeds when I did that thing that I always try to avoid doing – I glanced at the set-list. Once I'd glanced, there was no going back. For a start, rather than the set-opener being listed as "Icing On The World", my eye was caught by the word "Burn" at the top of the list, which I assumed meant "Burn Your House Brown" was going to get things underway, which seemed to make sense when I thought of all the sonic mayhem and beating drums at the start.

So of course, with my eye now caught I had to look down the rest of the list, and I was rather attracted to see that there seemed to be a group of male names in the middle somewhere. How quaint, I thought, they've got pet names for all their songs. I saw a "Robert", a "Roger" and an "Arnald" all scribbled down on the set-list (later discovered to be "Fast Robert", "The Duck And Roger The Horse" and "Arnald", naturally). I went back to Richard and informed him that we could be in for one or two surprises in the set. We weren't disappointed.

Indeed, I was right in my assumption that "Burn Your House Brown" was going to open proceedings, but from then on there was very little material that was familiar as Cardiacs played one new song after another. It later turned out that this was the night they'd chosen to premier most of the songs that would eventually end up on the next Cardiacs album, *On Land And In The Sea*, the result of five days intensive practice apparently. Why they chose Scunthorpe I have no idea, but I was rather glad that I'd chosen to make the effort to attend as Cardiacs seemed to be in an inspired mood, almost as if the extra concentration they were having to put in to get the new songs right was making them play at the absolute top of their game. Tim was so pleased with how "I Hold My Love In My Arms" turned out that he got the band to play it three times, one after another. 'That was brilliant!' he exclaimed, and we all had to agree. Just in case we weren't sure how brilliant everything was, they wound the set up with "Big Ship" and "Is This The Life?" before they returned for encores of "In A City Lining" and "I'm Eating In Bed". My journal entry from the time (ah yes, that explains how I remembered so much about it, eh?) states that "I shed many pounds as I grooved the night away." As if I needed to lose any weight back then, skinny, curly-mopped thing that I was – ahhh, them were t'days…

After the gig a bizarre bit of detective work by me deduced that Tim, whilst sound-engineering for Here & Now at Sheffield University earlier in the year, had been wearing a Pathetic Sharks *Viz* t-shirt. As Richard said at the time, if I went on *Mastermind*, my specialist subject would be "Useless Crap 1972-1988". A little unfair I felt – I knew an awful lot of useless crap from 1966-1971 too.

Whatever my specialist subject back then or even now, one thing I was getting very good at, perfected in later years, was stowing away in vans belonging to bands, and thus it was that Richard and I found ourselves breakfasting in the early hours of the morning at Woodall Services whilst puzzled representatives of the Alphabet Business Concern probably wondered how on earth we'd got there. We then found ourselves sleeping in an alcove at the bottom of the stairs of the service station footbridge, an alcove that usually only housed a firehose-reel. Well, now it had a Richard and a Belch to look after, and as we were abused by passing teenagers at 7 o'clock in the morning with taunts of 'Vagrants!', and I reflected on a bit of a World Premier gig after an arrival in the back of a tipper-truck, I wondered if in fact it would ever get any better than this…

* * * *

There were no alcoves housing firehose-reels present or youths calling me a vagrant when I woke up in Livo's living room on the morning of November 22nd 2007. Instead there was Livo hurrying me along because he was going to drop me off at Burtonwood Services on the M62 on his way to work. I was feeling a bit groggy, not unlike the morning after England had lost to Argentina in the 1998 World Cup on penalties. That time I'd spent the night in Jesus Underground Band's squat in Upton Park, and the first feeling I got upon waking was one of dismay when remembering England's unfortunate exit the night before. Well, Livo's place was considerably more upmarket than a squat, but the feeling of gloom was just the same for England's terrible capitulation against Croatia the previous evening. I say the feeling was the same, but this time there was possibly more anger as I thought of Steve McLaren and THAT umbrella...

I also had a slight sense of guilt over a late-night text message I'd sent to Cath, Cardiacs' percussionist and backing-singer. In an effort to cheer myself up I sent her a text telling her that my digital camera seemed naturally drawn to her beauty, something evidenced by the amount of photos I'd taken of her onstage. I wasn't feeling guilty about what I said, but more about the fact that when you're all living together on a tour bus as Cardiacs were, there's not much that remains hidden. Actually, guilt probably wasn't the right word. Fear, that was more like it; fear that by the time I reached Portsmouth there wouldn't be many people who didn't know about my late-night texting activities.

Anyway, Livo proved that he was indeed a national treasure as Al had said by dropping me off at the aforementioned services, and here as I sat feasting on breakfast, thanks to Big Ship Iron's funding, and reading the doom and gloom of the football reports in the *Daily Mirror*, I fired off a text to Malc letting him and Diggy know where I'd be situated (what a big girl; I really could have hitched to this one now that the cold had gone and the toothache was but a painful memory, but for some reason the spirit of adventure had been totally and utterly extinguished – I think I was just scared stiff that I'd miss a gig and thus miss my target of 101 by the end of the week).

And so it was that Diggy and Malc moved themselves even further up the Wonderful Persons List by venturing slightly out of their way to pick me up from Burtonwood Services. I'd breakfasted on the eastbound side, but in order to make sure I caught those two at the earliest opportunity I ventured over to the westbound side and was rather shocked to observe the tumbleweed and shabbiness of a service station that had obviously closed down. Very odd, but with the petrol station still operating, at least strangers weren't driven out of town by pitch-fork-wielding locals, so Diggy and Malc were able to locate me easily enough sitting on my rucksack in the middle of an almost-empty car-park.

As the journey unravelled it became obvious why I'd not hitched – it was a heck of a long way from Manchester to Portsmouth. However, with such entertaining company as Diggy and Malc it was never going to be dull. Just in case it did get dull we had Diggy's CD that came free with *Classic Rock*, a compilation made up of early-70s Heavy Rock; that is, Heavy Rock that wasn't Black Sabbath and from well before Motörhead defined (in my controversial but humble opinion) the genre – in other words, Heavy Rock that wasn't very good. One track in particular, all full of suicidal angst, had the car in uproar, but so as not to cause offence I'd better not mention who the song was by (which means that I've forgotten, and never quite got round to emailing Malc or Diggy as to who it was before deadline).

Eventually we arrived in Portsmouth and after a bit of confusion and difficulty parking, found the guest house Malc had booked into for the night. Diggy was heading back home after the gig you see, but in the meantime I needed somewhere to crash as Portsmouth had proved as unhelpful as Brighton and Stoke in volunteering to put me up for the night. As it was then, and with that spirit of adventure extinguished remember, the spirit that used to see me turning up at Nik Turner gigs in London without the foggiest notion of where I was going to spend the night, hoping instead that it would all work out (and if it didn't I'd just sleep rough), I took no chances and booked myself into that self-same B&B.

The good news was that Malc was very clever at booking places to stay, and this was no exception as he'd booked within walking distance of the venue. Despite having attended the venue myself two years earlier, I couldn't quite remember which way we should have been going, and a bit of aimless wandering up and down the street was undertaken before finding the Wedgewood Rooms, a hunt largely helped by deciding to look for the rather big Cardiacs tour bus instead.

On the recommendation of the Alphabet Business Concern, the three of us visited a local curry house that was rather obligingly having a happy hour. We followed this up by hitting the pub on the corner, wherein were seen many representatives of the Alphabet Business Concern, including Jon Poole who told everyone how he'd once gone into Tesco King's Cross only to see me filling the milk. I'd summoned a guy called Joe who worked for me over and said, 'Remember that band you said you really hated? Well, he (pointing at Mr Poole) was in them…' Playing Cardiacs over the store tannoy before opening-time has never been popular…

Jon also told me some stories about a mutual acquaintance that could possibly be libellous (hence why I'm wussing out and not naming them in here), then berated me for missing the God Damn Whores every night, especially as he was slipping a bit of a Pink Floyd reference into every performance. Well, sorry Jon but there was Staines Town against Stockport County in the FA Cup on the telly in the pub, and Staines (almost my local team) were winning. However, before a win could be confirmed I had to leave the pub to head for the venue – missing the start of a Cardiacs gig for England was one thing, but for Staines Town, well, it was never going to happen.

And so there we all were again, gathered together waiting for the start of a Cardiacs gig. After the ugliness of Stoke and my post-football misery of Manchester, it was nice to see everyone (me included) in good heart for this one. I got an especially big hug from Meesha who, as a resident of Portsmouth, was going to enjoy his hometown gig to the absolute max. Why, even those entering the stage seemed in high spirits, especially as Jim turned to Cath with a wry smile and mimed taking a photo – ah yes, everyone DID know about my text of the previous night.

The Wedgewood Rooms was the only venue on the tour (apart from the Astoria) with a big barrier between us and the stage, meaning the photographers had plenty of room to mooch around getting their shots, but despite the slight presence of security, we managed to enjoy ourselves, Malc celebrating his 50th Cardiacs gig by leading the way with both the yo-ho-ho-and-a-bottle-of-rum-style sailor dance (most appropriate for a gig in Portsmouth) during the instrumental ending of "The Breakfast Line", and the patting-head-rubbing-stomach interlude during the REALLY complicated bit of "R.E.S.".

Afterwards we were a happy crowd standing out on the street, Pete and I joining the Mother Of Dapper in belting out Gabriel-era Genesis songs whilst Marina from *The Organ* filmed us. Ah, but just who is Dapper I hear you ask? Dapper is a very beautiful young lady (16 at the time of the gig) who proudly showed me the word "CAR-DIACS" scratched into the back of her hand (oooh painful); crazy kids – certainly made my tattoo seem a bit light by comparison (but still very impressive). Just to add to my joy, Cath was happy to talk to me proving that a late-night Belch text doesn't put everyone off.

Eventually the venue security (obviously worried that our rendition of "Dancing With The Moonlit Knight" was upsetting the neighbours) shooed us all off. Cardiacs' big tour bus drove off into the night, Diggy hopped into Pete's car and headed north, Dapper went off with her mum perhaps to dab TCP on her hand, and Malc and I strolled happily back to the guest house via some chips from a kebab shop.

Malc and I were sharing a room, and as a bit of a snorer I did the decent thing and let Malc fall asleep before me, not that I had to wait long. I looked across the room and saw that Malc had indeed nodded off mid-text, sitting up in bed like the dead Mr Leeman in "The Kipper And The Corpse" episode of *Fawlty Towers*. Late night texting? That's a dangerous pastime, Malcy. At least I'd learned my lesson now and kept my mobile well out of the way. My main concern was, unlike Mr Leeman, making it through the night without dying just to make sure that I got to my 100th Cardiacs gig the next day in Cardiff. There were times over the preceding ten years or so when I thought I'd never get anywhere near 100 gigs, especially in 1997 when all was very quiet, but now it was in touching distance, and I really had to make sure I didn't miss out for any reason whatsoever.

Chapter Twenty-Two
"Ideal"
The Dogstands and the Howards

"Ideal"
The Dogstands and the Howards

When I made the editorial decision to include profiles in this book, I was especially interested in what I termed "Cardiacs Couples", partially because my original plan to only do profiles on those that put me up for the night was looking like leaving me a bit short, as featured guest houses in Stoke and Portsmouth wouldn't hold much interest for the discerning Cardiacs fan. So off I went in search of loving Cardiacs Couples, except I didn't really have to search at all, because as well as the already-featured Helocolins and Pete and Clare, I knew of four perfect subjects who were happily joined together in holy matrimony (not all four together in some bizarre Alphabet Business Concern arrangement, you understand, but two couples made up of four individuals). Not only were Graeme and Carli Dogstand and Jill and Paul Howard already known to all via their frequent contributions to The List, but what's more, they all featured heavily on this 2007 tour, making them, ahem, Ideal.

I first met the Dogstands for proper at a North Sea Radio Orchestra recital at St Martin-in-the-Fields church just off Trafalgar Square early in 2007. They'd seen me on Sky Television's oft repeated *Football's Hardest Away Days* when I'd featured hitchhiking to Plymouth in the snow just to watch Sheffield United lose 3-0. The thing that stood out for all Cardiacs fans who accidentally caught it was me wearing a big 'Little Man and a House' logo t-shirt whilst being interviewed in my kitchen, and shots of a Big Flower t-shirt on the wall as well as my Cardiacs mug on a shelf when I was seen packing my stuff (nobody's mentioned the copy of *Xitintoday* by Nik Turner's Sphynx propped up at the end of my bed yet though). The Dogstands congratulated me on my "subtle" plugging of everyone's favourite band and as we shook hands and headed off to the pub, I realised that both were familiar faces, especially Carli who seemed to have been around for years at Cardiacs-and-related gigs. In fact, the more I thought about it, the more I suspected it may well have been Carli who I'd spotted at the front for the Special Garage Concerts waving her arms aloft in time to the gentle ending of "A Balloon For Bertie's Party".

By the end of the 2007 tour, and after several Cardiacs-related gigs and social functions prior to that, it felt like I'd known them for years, especially as they contributed freely to The List, especially Carli. However, in order to gather a few facts that would otherwise have eluded me, out came that Belch Question Sheet once again…

Carli is a rarity in that the first band she ever became passionate about were our beloved subjects of this tome, Cardiacs, but as ever there was a bit of a way to go before they exploded into her life. With a father who played the guitar, there was always music in the house, and with a mummy willing to sit the infant Carli on a stool in the kitchen and teach her to sing "Once In Royal David's City", a lifetime of song was always on the cards. The first possession that really set things on the way was the gift of a toy which was accompanied by a record, *Sammy Sound With The Tomtom Tummy*, closely followed by a Wombles record. Ah yes, those little furry litter-pickers from Wimbledon Common again – I think we need to reassess their place in Cardiacs folklore…

A debut record purchase was next up as Carli and her sister spent time 'umm-ing and ahh-ing, trying to choose between "Agadoo" by Black Lace and "Hole In My Shoe" by Neil – I'm so embarrassed,' she confesses. No need to be embarrassed Carli, it was okay back in the days of *The Young Ones* to laugh at the post-modern irony of Neil the Hippy – why, he even name-checked Steve Hillage in one episode; but hang on, let me reassess – hmmm, yes, maybe you've got a point about feeling embarrassed over Black Lace… Perhaps it was this acute embarrassment that held Carli back for a while: 'I didn't buy another record until I was 15 or 16 when I purchased *Life's Too Good* by the Sugarcubes – I loved that.'

Live music was introduced into Carli's life via Roberta Flack at Lewisham Concert Halls, a gig she attended with her Mum. 'After that,' she continues, 'it was Trouble Funk at the Brixton Academy (she seems a little coy about this too, but I'm put firmly in my place with a terse 'Don't ask!'), then I finally found myself and saw Butthole

Surfers also at the Academy; when I finally got to see Cardiacs I felt like I'd come home.'

Good old Cardiacs, coming along just in time for Carli's first proper obsession: 'Cardiacs were played incessantly by my boyfriend at the time and his flatmate. I don't remember exactly when I first heard them, they just seeped into my consciousness and before long I knew the words to all the songs. The first time I saw them was Woolwich Tramshed in 1988 (actually Carli, I've done my usual of looking it up on Pete's Gig List, and I reckon it was June 9th 1989). I've yet to meet someone else who was there, apart from the people I went with.'

Coming into Cardiacs for that late-80s period saw *A Little Man And A House And The Whole World Window* as Carli's initial Cardiacs acquisition, but she has a bit of a late-80s/late-90s conflict over which her favourite album is: 'It changes often and usually flits between *Guns* and *On Land And In The Sea*. If I had to choose it would be *On Land And In The Sea* as it followed me around the world, appropriately enough.' Likewise, the choice of favourite song is difficult to pinpoint: 'It changes a lot, but I always come back to "Everything Is Easy"'.

As for Champion Gigs, Carli plumps for the secret Bull & Gate gigs of December 2005. Ah yes, these have been mentioned elsewhere, and should perhaps have been brought up by myself at the end of the chapter on The Special Garage Concerts, but I felt I'd waffled on enough at that point, so perhaps a little bit of background is justified here instead. The CDs to commemorate those glorious 2003 concerts finally emerged in October 2005, and after Cardiacs had completed a short tour in November, it was announced to Listees only that they would be indulging in two concert performances at the Bull & Gate on December 21st and December 22nd. Tickets would only be available via the Internet (as I'd still not got my Hotmail account past the stringent red-tape of the List administrators back then, I had to rely on Ian to do the honours for me), and on the first night they'd be playing the songs from *The Special Garage Concerts Volume I* CD in the exact running order that they appeared on the album. Unsurprisingly, the second night would feature exactly the same idea, but from *Volume II* this time. The nights were, of course, wild and brilliant, but for me not *quite* as special as those initial Garage Concerts, due to the lack of surprise and shock, mainly because by then I'd absolutely played the two CDs to death so knew the running order and the less-well-known songs backwards…

From what Carli describes as 'lots' of gigs ('but not as many as you, Belch,' she adds), there are many memories, both happy and poignant: 'I threw my bra at Jon Poole onstage at the Grand in Clapham once, but the funniest moment was kneeling on the stage at the Venue in New Cross and absent-mindedly saying to my "new-best-friend" Lucy, "Bugger, my leg's fallen off in my tights."' At this point, it should be mentioned that Carli has a false leg, but carries it off with such aplomb and humour that it neither seems important or indeed noticeable, apart from the use of a stick at times.

'For me,' Carli continues, 'the nicest moment was crying during "Is This The Life" in November 2005 during filming. Tim looks down at me after the song and I say, "That made me cry". He tells the audience it was one of the nicest things anyone's said to him and proceeds to go off and things, sorry, to go off on one.' He does that quite a lot, does our Tim…

If you haven't got the message already, Carli's final words confirm that Cardiacs can indeed change lives: 'I was in a musical no-man's-land until I found Cardiacs, and Cardiacs have helped me appreciate LOADS of other stuff since, like Misty's Big Adventure and Polysics who are currently floating my boat.'

Yep, Cardiacs can change lives, and bring people together, as Graeme, Carli Dogstand's other half, proves…

* * * *

Graeme Dogstand found himself getting all emotional over music (a good sign) at a very early age when he was 'moved almost to tears by the beauty of Keith West's "Excerpt From A Teenage Opera" when I was about six-years-old.' Ah yes Graeme, but don't you realise all that "Grocer Jack" stuff caused chaos on the Underground Alternative scene of the late-60s? Keith West's solo-success led to a spot of jealousy amongst his bandmates in Tomorrow, subsequently resulting in their break-up, Steve Howe eventually going off and defining Progressive Rock with Yes – see what Keith West started there…?

Long before Peter Kay gave Tony Christie a bit of an Indian Summer in recent years, Graeme's dear old Nan was buying him the Sheffield crooner's hit single "Is This The Way To Amarillo?" in 1971 (another Belch aside: when I was about eight, I regularly used to cross the River Porter and Endcliffe Park in Sheffield in order to gaze through the gates of Tony Christie's mansion – not because I liked his music, but because his Rolls Royce invoked feelings of great wonder in me, mainly because the registration plate was "TON10").

The first evidence of anything remotely Progressive emerged when Graeme bought his first ever disc, Argent's "Hold Your Head Up" in 1972. However, it wasn't really Prog that became prominent, but another 70s phenomenon, Glam Rock: 'I lived with my Aunt Audrey when my Mum was in hospital for a prolonged spell, and her son, my cousin Billy, was fanatical about music. Billy got me into T Rex – I was a huge Bolan fan.'

The first gig Graeme attended is possibly the reason why he developed quite a broad taste in music, and also hinted at possible political leanings: 'It was the People's Jubilee at Ally Pally in 1977, a Communist Party-organised counter-celebration to the Queen's Silver Jubilee. The bands featured were Shakin' Stevens & the Sunsets, Soft Machine and Aswad – quite an eclectic mix!' I'll say, and Shakin' Stevens a commie, eh? *Viz* never picked up on that.

Cardiacs were still a long way off in Graeme's life (although of course 1977 saw our boys mutating from The Filth to Cardiac Arrest), but a trek through all sorts of musical styles saw him heading in one heck of an interesting direction: 'Boys Wonder, Kinks, Buzzcocks, Stranglers, Punk, Pop, Psychedelia, Pulp, Brel, Bowie, Walker… In short, melody, melody, melody, power, light and shade – I think that sums up Cardiacs quite well too…' All this continued to the present day with Graeme currently wrapping his ears in Misty's Big Adventure, David Devant, Cats In Paris and the Divine Comedy.

By 1984 at least Cardiacs had crossed Graeme's radar: 'They were supporting Nick Cave and I was due to attend but had to call off at the last minute to my disappointment. In 1987 I caught their *Tube* appearance and put them on my "must see" list, and managed to ignore them for about 15 years. My band BUM! were dropped from the supporting line-up at one of the New Cross Venue gigs too – another near-miss – we were drafted in to support Guana Batz at a later date instead.'

So it was left to Carli to finally do the business and bring Cardiacs into Graeme's existence in the late-90s: 'Not only had I discovered early on that Mrs Dogstand had the same love of Half Man Half Biscuit as me, but she had music by a band that had supported my band at the Marquee. She had seen Homage Freaks supporting Ad Nauseam (Jon Poole and Bob Leith's pre-Cardiacs band), and whilst relaying this story got on to the all-important subject of her love of all things Cardiacs. She was just surprised that I had even heard of them, let alone failing on numerous occasions to get along to see them, and even coming close to opening one of the Venue gigs for them. It did seem as though the gods of wonky pop music had sent her to me to rectify my lack of live attendances.'

And rectified it was with a first gig 'at the Astoria around 1999 or 2000 (it was probably the London Astoria 2 on November 11th 2000), but I had already seen Timmy on his own at the Camden Barfly though.'

As for record buying, Graeme has a bit of a confession to make when it comes to Cardiacs: 'I have never purchased anything; there, I admit it! Carli buys the vibes in this household, and I just sponge up the spare music with my little pink ears.'

Despite this, he's still allowed his favourites: '"Fave album" changes all the time, but much of *Sing To God Parts One & Two* find that little spot in my brain Keith West discovered in the sixties, the innocence of childhood in a f****d-up world. "Fave song" is "Stoneage Dinosaurs" – more childhood folly. "Fave moment" was definitely the letting down of what little hair there is left at the end of the last (2007) tour. That Leeds gig still makes me come over all smiley – I think Tim enjoyed that one…' Presumably that makes it a contender for "fave gig" too, but as Graeme admits, 'I should probably have been a lot more, but I've probably seen Cardiacs more than a dozen times anyway.'

Outside of any gig though, there's one of those t-shirt moments we've all had, with what Graeme refers to as his "finest-meeting-someone-in-a-Cardiacs-t-shirt moment": 'The best one was the bloke I saw when I was talking to Eugene from the Rezillos: "Excuse me, Eugene – Heyyyyyyyy!...Cardiacs!...Yeeeeeeeaaaaaaah!"'

Not sure that I've ever broken off from talking to a 70s Punk icon, but we all know what you mean, Graeme, we all know what you mean...

* * * *

Zag And The Coloured Beads and Ring have already been mentioned quite a lot in here, especially in that chapter on London and the tale of seeing Ring at the Hammersmith Clarendon Hotel Ballroom in 1987, but before venturing on, it's worth mentioning once more that Jill was indeed present at that gig, flogging Ring t-shirts from behind their merchandise desk, and that Paul was/is the bass-player (with a little bit of guitar) in the Ring-related Zag And The Coloured Beads. What's more, Jill was also at the Stonehenge Free Festival of 1984, that life-defining event for this-here Belch, so my interest was always going to be at a peak for these two and their Cardiacs adventure. I wasn't disappointed...

Paul Howard's early life was surrounded by music, once again thanks to parents, although unlike most, this was a combination of both "popular" and "classical" music. His earliest recollection of anything musical was 'probably listening to the strains of "I Am A Rock" by Paul Simon, coming from my Dad's reel-to-reel tape recorder as he redecorated the bathroom. There was also music from *Sgt Pepper's*...and Bob Dylan – well, it WAS the Sixties.'

So that's the pop, what about the classical? 'My parents were always playing stuff on a Sunday whilst the roast was cooking – Mahler, Brahms, Sibelius and Debussy. They also loved Gershwin, "Rhapsody In Blue", and Holst, *The Planets*. Then there was a record called *The Jazz Influence* which was jazzy classical pieces by Bernstein, Copeland etc.'

This introduction to all things classical led to a birthday present of a first record unlike any other unearthed by this research: '*The Rite Of Spring* by Stravinsky – I had to have it after seeing *Fantasia*. I was moved by watching all those dinosaurs dying out…' Blimey, nothing too heavy for a young mind to be getting into then. At least the balance was redressed somewhat with the first record Paul purchased with real money, "Money, Money, Money" by Abba.

A few years later, 1979 actually, Paul's first fixation was just around the corner, provided in the form of Public Image Ltd's *Metal Box*: 'I couldn't find anything comparable to it. It blinkered my vision for ages and stopped my appreciating other bands.'

Bit of a Belch-sidetrack coming up here: I've gotta say Paul, this isn't too bad an album to get fixated with – I myself remember when "Death Disco" came out as a single (listed as "Swan Lake" on the album) I was totally enthralled by John Lydon's caterwauling on *Top of the Pops*, as well as Jah Wobble's eerie smile that displayed his lack of front teeth. I was also fascinated by Radio Hallam's seeming censorship by their refusal to play it (believe it or not I even phoned Martin Kelner up about this during an ad-break – I was amazed to hear Mr Kelner himself answer the phone, and even more amazed to hear him tell me that he felt PIL had lost it somewhat with this latest release; there you have it, confessions of a teenage Prog fan – I probably hadn't realised at that tender age that Mr Lydon had supposedly killed off the music I was just getting into with his Punk Rock). I was also taken with the idea that Public Image Ltd released *Metal Box* in, erm, a metal box, spread over three 12-inch 45rpm discs. I should have bought it then, but probably chickened out in favour of a Yes solo album – as it was, I had to settle for buying it on CD in the 90s, delightfully packaged in, yep, you guessed it, a metal box. Belch-sidetrack over…

So, erm, yes Paul, a decent enough obsession if I may say so. Warning – more Shakin' Stevens coming up; and Shaky, something you didn't see coming either. Paul happily points out that his first gig was to see Shakin' Stevens, but quickly points out that he had a free ticket: 'A girl threw her knickers at him. He picked them up and wiped the sweat from his forehead with them. It seemed cool at the time…'

Shockingly, *Viz* never picked up on this either.

With a love of *Fantasia* alongside Punk and Indie stuff, and a little bit of Jazz on the side, it was no wonder Cardiacs weren't long in appearing on the horizon. Paul, mixing with fellow musicians, was always going to hear about them as the Eighties progressed: 'All our group of friends/musicians began to talk about them. I remember Bob (White, keyboard player with both Ring and Zag And The Coloured Beads, and later with Levitation) telling me about this incredible band he'd seen, probably at Stonehenge. No-one was able to pin down for me exactly what they were like, which was frustrating. I was one of the last of us to get to see them.'

This was eventually sorted out when Paul finally got to see them at a college gig in London, 'sometime in 1984, but I'm not sure which – was it ULU, or the Imperial…?' Well, Paul, thanks to Pete's Gig List (again), I reckon it was the Imperial, actually on February 8th 1985. Whatever the venue and the date, this first Cardiacs live encounter made quite an impression: 'Seeing them play live for the first time was my most intense, and quite disturbing/amusing, live experience to date.'

Back in the mid-80s there wasn't exactly a mass of Cardiacs product flooding the market, so inevitably Paul's first Cardiacs-related purchase was the cassette of *The Seaside*: 'That's all there was then, apart from seventh-generation cassette copies of *Toy World* and the other one.' (That'll be *The Obvious Identity* then, accredited to Cardiac Arrest of course.) Later product didn't establish any particular preferences: 'I don't have a favourite album or song – there's too much variety.' There is a little confession however: 'When it comes to seeing them live, I reckon I'm somewhere in the forties – I didn't see them for a very long time, after the "classic" line-up began to disintegrate.'

Last, but by no means least, Jill came on the scene, but Paul seemingly leaves her to fill in much of the detail about this, saying only, 'We quickly found out we both liked Cardiacs; she'd seen them before me though, drat!' A minor irritation this though, I'm sure, as Jill's influence seems to loom strong even now, as Paul claims "this week" to be listening to Steve Hillage and Gong, as well as Kate Bush, and Jill is a self-confessed worshipper of all things Planet Gong, and also admits to bearing a resemblance to Kate Bush when she first met Paul in the 1980s. You'll see what I mean when she has her say, coming up right now…

* * * *

Big sisters haven't featured very heavily in these Cardiacs fan in-depths, but with time running out, up comes Jill to squeeze one home, for instead of parents and big brothers, or cousins and "wild" uncles, it was indeed Jill's Big Sis who put her on the road to a life entwined with music: 'My earliest recollection is being very naughty and playing my big sister's copy of David Bowie's *Hunky Dory* on her darling little portable battery-operated Phillips tape recorder. She was most likely attending to her Saturday job in Carnaby Street whilst I was pretending I was working in a bar in Benidorm, selecting my sounds,'

But it wasn't just Big Sis though: 'My uncle, a cab driver in Beckenham, used to regularly pick up David Bowie, and I gave him a portrait I'd painted of him with an inscription declaring my love; "from Jill aged 7" it said, because I didn't want Angie or Zowie to feel unsettled by my feelings.' Such thoughtfulness, so rare in youngsters in this day and age.

As for *Hunky Dory*, Jill says, 'My hero Mick Ronson (Bowie's guitarist) is all over this album, and before Cardiacs completely clicked for me, it was the Mick-Ronsonesque chord changes played by Sarah Smith, heard during "The Whole World Window" at a performance by them at a free festival in Oxford 1986, that got my ears pricking.' Well, here's a little-known fact then, Jill; my brother officiated at Mick Ronson's funeral, Mick being a member of the Church of Jesus Christ of Latter Day Saints, and my brother being Bishop of Hyde Park Ward at the time.

A familiar record crops up for Jill's first-bought: 'It was "Tiger Feet" by Mud. Armed with a 45p record token, I marched off down to Diamond Records in Catford, aged eight. Most likely I was sporting a nylon blouse over a polyester skinny polo-neck, as was the fashion that month, tucked into an A-line skirt from Marks & Sparks – Sparks, they were another favourite band of mine from around that time,' adds

Jill, getting sidetracked, before returning to the description of her infant-self, 'knee-high socks, Clark's shoes, dodgy teeth, bunches…'

Around this time, Big Sister's influence was now starting to weigh quite heavily: 'She had what would have then been considered a massive record collection for her age. Being ten years older she was the embodiment of cool in her Chelsea Girl hotpants, Mary Quant make-up, and Ravel platforms. Amongst the vinyl laying around the Boots record-deck were the *Tighten Up* reggae series of albuls (sic – Cardiacs fans in-joke), plenty of Motown, flirtings with Prog, like ELP and Yes, along with Deep Purple and Quo, not to mention all the C90s. In particular, I loved my sister's compilations, each one an Aladdin's Cave packed with jewels such as Barry White and Mr Bloe. Status Quo and Deep Purple were definitely "Down The Dustpipe" as far as I was concerned back in those days. For me, the Kings of Pop were 10cc; all those sudden changes of tempo – now, what other band is good at that…?'

To return to a previous theme though, there was a cousin providing some inspiration eventually: 'Nearly a third of my life later, I was standing outside Diamond Records this time – I wasn't allowed in. I was waiting for my brilliant cousin, a year older than me. We had just been to see *Bambi* at the Catford ABC and he wanted to purchase a copy of the latest band on everyone's lips, "Pretty Vacant" by The Sex Pistols of course. Not long after, he was spraying black car-paint in his hair, spiking it up with soap and water (so that's how they did it); I used sugar myself, far more effective, and he was off to see bands at the Hope & Anchor in Islington,' then getting side-tracked again, 'my husband's playing there soon.' I know Jill, I went – I was particularly impressed with the Steve Hillage *Motivation Radio*-pastiche Zag And The Coloured Beads flyer…

Anyway, back to the 1970s: 'Through my cousin I was aware of so much good stuff that my girl-friends at school had never heard of such as Crass, Slaughter & the Dogs, Poison Girls, Patti Smith, The Ruts, Vice Squad, and in particular Adam & the Ants' *Dirk Wears White Socks*, Cardiacs aside probably my most favourite albul of all times along with *Hunky Dory*.'

This introduction to things Punky and New Wave led to Jill's first real passion, Blondie: 'Completely obsessed I was. I devoured any magazine article about Debbie Harry. Her looks still blow me away; such a true star. I can't believe one person could be blessed with such beauty, style and talent. I sang along to complete albums whilst looking at myself in the mirror, hairbrush for mike. I badly fancied keyboard player Jimmy Destri which gave me an ear for Roland synthesisers and the like. When I look back now I think all the blokes were really handsome; 60s Punk fusion written in the 70s – can it get any better?'

But wait, it wasn't all Punk and New Wave. In February 1982 Jill attended her first gig, Black Sabbath: 'My big sister's dosage of Quo and Deep Purple started kicking in.' Then by 1984 Jill had developed a love of Psychedelia and intense, exciting guitar licks. As Jill points out, 'It has become obvious to me that Cardiacs like that stuff too,' so you'd expect that when Jill ventured off to Stonehenge Free Festival that summer of '84 and came across Cardiacs, they'd have hit it off immediately. However, it didn't quite work out like that, as Jill explains:

'I had just turned 18, and my then-boyfriend Pete was a lovely-looking gothy hippy. He was my first true love, not the love of my life – that's Paul of course. Six years older than me, Pete had done a lot of travelling and hitchhiking and had attended many free festivals in the company of The Convoy. He completely opened my eyes to this new world of illegal festivals, travellers and hitching, and also opened my ears to the sounds of Gong, Here & Now and Steve Hillage. So after a very hot, happy day of shopping for alternative clothes along the King's Road, we bought our tickets to Amesbury from Victoria Coach Station and the following morning set off to 'Enge.

'There I found myself in this magical village set up in a field, Punks pacing the site, their "bum-flaps" (oh my goodness, I'd forgotten all about "bum-flaps") doubling as advertising hoardings for all manner of things. I was having a thoroughly lovely time this particular summer's night, waiting for Hawkwind or Here & Now to get on stage, and then Cardiacs came on stage instead and spoilt it all – uncomfortable viewing. Like unloved children with learning difficulties let out from their institution into the whole wide world with a set of instruments – continuous juxtaposed noise, me unable to follow the rhythm (actually Jill, this is pretty much how it sounded to me as I tried to get to sleep in my tent). Tweaked, twitched, wrenched, yanked I was, through a relentless unforgiving tunnel of horror and abuse. Then The Enid came on – or was it before Cardiacs? (it was before) – completely freaking me out again with their perverted rendition of "Wild Thing". Along with the legendary cesspit, The Hawks and Here & Now were not to be witnessed by me at this 1984 summer festival.' Well Jill, if it's any consolation, I witnessed both of Hawkwind's "Earth Ritual" sets, and Here & Now, but missed Cardiacs. At least we both saw The Enid…

1986 saw the Oxford Free Festival, and back up in Sheffield this little Belch so wanted to go, but no-one was willing to hitch with him, so I abandoned plans and did something far less rewarding instead, but Jill was a little luckier, even though Cardiacs were on the bill: 'Well, Cardiacs were a band I certainly never wanted to see again, I can tell you, no siree! So it was with great trepidation that I allowed myself to watch them a couple of years later at the Oxford Free Festival. Exceedingly vulnerable and anxious having recently being dumped by Pete, I was in no state to see Cardiacs again. Still, my then-best-friend Sue looked upon them, hating it, Sue shouting out an accusation of "Sloane Rangers!" as if they would be defeated by such a remark. But then a funny thing happened at the end of their set. I heard "The Whole World Window" and felt my heart being tugged by Sarah's saxophone – prior to this she'd scared the living daylight out of me by giving me a stare.

'A few months later my new boyfriend, the first one since Pete, dragged me along to Dingwalls to watch Cardiacs again. I didn't want to go, but he enthused and he made me happy so off I went. It was all rather sweetened by the fact that Keith The Bass, my all time hero from Here & Now, was at the door and he kissed my hand. So in I went expecting to be bored, made to feel uncomfortable and miserable for the next hour or so. But instead, do you know what happened?

It clicked! I dug those tricky little time-signature changes, and I was blown away by the heights that the more accessible tunes of "Is This The Life?" and "Big Ship" soared me up to. I felt happy, watching other people being happy dancing around in top hats, stripy tops and the like, to this most idiosyncratic of bands. I was at the beginning of a love affair that has so far lasted over half a lifetime with the most wonderful of groups, its members being the most wonderful of people, its fanbase being the most wonderful of people.'

Jill's eventual conversion led to a first acquisition of Cardiacs product in the form of the *Rude Bootleg* vinyl, followed by around fifty gigs over the years, although a favourite album is again hard to pick out: 'I haven't got one as they all have fantastic, good, and not quite-so-good moments for me.'

One song does stand out though: '"In A City Lining", *Rude Bootleg*-stylee.' Ah yes, that version I have often described as the definitive Cardiacs song, what with its mix of the epic, the thrashy, Ska, Punk and out and OUT Prog (and if you've not heard it, that description should go someway to describing just how many times it stops and starts and speeds up and slows down).

And just to prove that not everyone who saw them in the 80s reckons they were much better then than now, a contender for Jill's bestest gig of all time is one of the most recent it is possible to have: 'Possibly Cardiff 2007. I loved the intimate venue, the whole excitement of staying in a city with other members of The Pond nearby, the setlist, the people at the gig, the joyous pleasure of knowledge that it was all going to happen again the following night at Leeds.'

This gig also brought about one of those special moments you can only appreciate if you get yourself right down the front: 'I was standing in front of Jim at Cardiff, saying loudly to my husband, "Jim's wearing spats!", Jim giving me the most scariest of looks before looking away and breaking into an amused little smile.'

Oh yes, we must not forget hubby Paul in amongst all this Cardiacs love: 'The best thing about boys, especially boyfriends, is that if they are half decent they turn you onto good music. I had good musical breeding and found Cardiacs by myself. Paul is and was everything when I met him. I was completely in awe; middle-class, hippy-folky parents, he'd opened and lived in a squat; an extremely talented artist, possibly the most dishiest, slinkiest man I'd ever set eyes on who kept me dangling on a string. I yearned for him bad, he treated me bad, then realised "I" was the only one, and we have been solid ever since.

'So we came to each other both having discovered and loving Cardiacs already. However, Paul turned me on and still does turn me on to some really good sounds, such as Leonard Bernstein, Ivor Cutler, Pere Ubu, Scritti Polliti – he used to play me "The Sweetest Girl" – Can, Luke Vibert… Whereas I'm responsible for his sudden interest in Steve Hillage, Gong, Kate Bush, who I used to bear a remarkable similarity to when we met, a bit of decent Metal, and loads of other stuff. Oh, and I forgot to mention that back when I met him and nowadays, Paul plays with the brilliant Zag And The Coloured Beads (don't worry Jill, I mentioned it already), individual and wonderful, the pool that they have drawn from is not dissimilar to all my own musical-taste-development pinpointers.'

* * * *

So, there you have it, two totally wonderful and beautiful Cardiacs Couples. I consider it a privilege and a pleasure to have become friends with all of them, as individuals and in their partnerships, and it is with eternal delight that I can state they were all present at my 100th gig at Cardiff. What's more, they were all there for that final gig in Leeds too, and just to prove how deep their love runs, both Carli and Jill chose to wear their wedding dresses on that night, and both looked totally and utterly stunning.

I'll leave the last word to Jill when it comes to Cardiacs the band and Cardiacs the fans: 'Of course, the obvious advantage of loving Cardiacs is the wonderful fanbase it has put me in touch with "brain-to-brain", too long to mention everyone's name but they are the Icing on the Wonderful, Fun, Intelligent, Astounding World that is Cardiacs. Being a fan has brought me nothing but joy, pleasure and love, and for all the fantastic things that darling man Tim Smith has given me, I send back to him a trillion times over…'

Chapter Twenty-Three
"A Time for Rejoicing"
Clwb Ifor Bach, Cardiff,
November 23rd 2007

"A Time For Rejoicing"
Clwb Ifor Bach, Cardiff, November 23rd 2007

Cardiff is a pretty cool city. I obviously wasn't in a position to pick and choose the venue for my 100th Cardiacs gig, but if I could have chosen, somewhere as beautiful and historic as Cardiff would probably have been as good as any. Having said that, I'd never been to a gig in Cardiff by anyone, never mind Cardiacs. Instead, my visits to the capital city of Wales had been for ex-flatmate Liz's wedding in 1994, and not surprisingly for some mixed football results; a Play-off Final defeat in 2003 at the Millennium Stadium, a midday FA Cup 3rd Round win at Ninian Park in 2004, and a promotion-clinching win at the same venue on Good Friday in 2006.

But no gigs at all, which in a way made the prospect of Belch Cardiacs Gig #100 taking place in Cardiff even more special, I reckoned. What's more, Liz was going to attend, as was the Original Checkout Chick from Tesco Brackley, Claire, who had recently moved back to the town of her birth, and who when she featured in chapter 29 of *Fever Hitch* was spelling her name Clayre. However, as this was a bit of a school-girly quirk, and as it wasn't as her name appeared on her birth certificate, with the onset of maturity she'd reverted to the proper spelling of "Claire" (if truth be known, when she'd told me "Clayre" was a made-up thing I was slightly disappointed as I've always loved a bit of quirkiness).

Liz and Claire were no strangers to attending gigs with me of course. As mentioned in Chapter 12, Liz was a loyal supporter of mine and Sewer's gig-going antics, coming along with us to many a Haze gig in Sheffield as well as the odd Marillion concert, and a rather special performance by Hawkwind at Sheffield University Octagon Centre in 1984, back when Nik Turner was entering the stage in a roadie-borne coffin and dividing opinion with his front-man antics (I loved it of course, but many die-hard Hawkfans resented his presence).

Claire meanwhile had done her fair share of Belch-humouring by accompanying me to see whichever band I was currently ranting and raving about, most notably the People's Friend at the Dublin

Castle in Camden (I even bought her a t-shirt), and more than one Industrial Hardcore Jazz night of mayhem courtesy of the Jesus Underground Band, including my personal favourite at the Fountain in Seven Sisters for a Battle of the Bands contest, when Ian kindly gave up his seat in the band's minibus to allow Claire the opportunity of coming back to Canning Town for the post-gig party x x (Ian never did make it back).

Neither Liz nor Claire had seen Cardiacs though. By the time my Cardiacs obsession took hold in 1988, Liz had long since moved out of the house she shared with me and Sewer in Sheffield, whilst Claire had spent the twelve years we'd known each other (in Brackley and in London when she was attending university in Kingston) listening to me nagging her to come and see the best band of the lot. Well, now they were both about to witness the top dogs, and as special occasions go, this was going to be a pretty good one to attend. My only regret was that Sarah wasn't going to be there, but two out of three ain't bad.

* * * *

There are two things I love about stopping in a bed and breakfast; the bed, followed by the breakfast. If I was to choose my favourite out of the two though, I'd probably go for the breakfast, mainly because when I make my booking I'm only really thinking about the immediacy of the bed, so it's always nice to wake up in the morning and remember that included in the bill is a hearty breakfast. The Abbey Lodge Guest House in Portsmouth was up there with the best, and Malc and I took full advantage Hoovering up as much brekkie as we possibly could. An added bonus was the genial host who engaged us in conversation, largely about the pack of yappy little dogs he had running amok in the out-of-bounds bit of the guest house. Fascinating though this was, we soon had to be on our way, as the tenth gig of the tour lay all of 138 miles west.

With no Diggy onboard we had to make our own entertainment, which largely involved Malc telling me that when he'd given Lawrence a lift, and his SatNav had said, "Bear right," Lawrence had shouted, 'There's a bear on the right!' every single time, and me pointing out to Malc all the spots along the route where I'd found myself hitchhiking down the years. In between all this, I reminisced on a few of the previous 99 Cardiacs gigs. I've not really much recollection of which gig-tales I regaled Malc with, but there's a good chance that amongst them were many of the stories already related in this very book. There's a pretty good chance that one or two gigs not mentioned thus far featured prominently also, so as a milestone gig is always going to be heavy on nostalgia, now seems as good a time as any for those lesser-known Cardiacs-gig moments to take a bow in the form of a few well-earned awards.

* * * *

So, here they are – the Belch Best-of-the-Rest Cardiacs Gig Awards. First up, the award for **Most Audacious Gatecrash** goes to London's ULU on October 22nd 1999. What I really like about doing things in a slightly different way is that sometimes you get a repeat, just when people are possibly believing that it maybe hadn't even happened once; for example, not only do I get a lift to a gig in the back of a builders' tipper-truck on the way to Scunthorpe in 1988, six years later I get an identical lift coming back from a Wizards Of Twiddly gig in London. And so just to prove that I really can make myself invisible from time to time, following on from being overlooked by strict security at the Hammersmith Clarendon Hotel Ballroom in 1988, I went and did it all again eleven years later. On this occasion, the reason was much the same in that the fact that it was a London gig meant that the guest list was most full-up, and once again I was skint. In 1988 it was due to unemployment, but by 1999 I was a mature-student at the University of Greenwich waiting for problems with my student loan to sort themselves out; the only way I was going to see this gig was by bunking it. The trouble was, I'd been warned that security were every bit as keen as those at the Clarendon, and so it was that whilst security were checking band member partners and Stars In Battledress girlfriends, I sat there reading a newspaper, not daring to look up. When I did pluck up the courage to look over the top of the 'paper, all security had disappeared and I was in, except I had to spend the rest of the night hiding in the toilets until Stars In

Battledress took to the stage as first support.

A related award is that for **Most Illegal Entry** which must go to Glastonbury Festival 2000. Officially there were 100,000 in attendance that year, but anyone who was there will tell you that there were massively more people present than that. Some reckoned it was double; I'm more inclined to think it was treble judging by the claustrophobic mass of people *everywhere* you went. When you talked to people, most had a tale of how they'd got in, and just from looking around it really did seem like only one in three had wristbands on. Doubtless some of it was bravado, but there were many genuine cases, myself included. My desire to gain entry by any means (except the means of shelling out one-hundred quid) was heightened by Cardiacs' presence on the bill, albeit on one of the sub-stages in a big tent somewhere. I'd hitched there, my final lift being in a van with a load of festival-goers, but the traffic was so bad the closer we got to Worthy Farm that we spent hours (and I mean hours) at a standstill, me snoozing in the back. We eventually parked up at 4am and I surveyed the prospects. Over to the left was the entrance, with a steady stream flowing through under the watchful eye of a number of stewards. About 100 yards to the right was an even steadier stream going over the fence, whilst the stewards chose to look the other way. This looked good enough to me and my new-found friends, who were all going in legally, agreed to meet me on the other side of the fence. I got in line and was amused to find that the gang charging a fiver to give people a leg-up to the half-way point of the chicken-wire fence at an angle to the main fence were all from Liverpool. The other part of their service was to chuck your luggage over the fence, and I watched with slight concern as my rucksack was flung high over the top, leaving me to think that there was no going back now. There then broke out an argument between a leg-upper and a would-be scramble-overer, and I began to worry that by the time I got over myself, my rucksack would be long gone. Eventually, one leg-up later I was on the chicken-wire and hauling myself up onto the top of the main fence. As I peered over in the dark I was pleased to see my baggage was still lying there, and impressed to see my new pals were still waiting for me despite the lengthy delay. 'Oh, he IS coming over,' one of them said. Well, I'm glad they were certain of it because I wasn't, even now. I sat on the fence (not like me), and looking down it seemed one heck of a long drop. To be honest, I didn't really fancy it, but as I looked back on the outside of the fence, those below shouted, 'Hurry up – there's others waiting to come over,' so I launched myself off the edge. After all that excitement, it was doubtful as to whether Cardiacs could match up, but they did, even if it was a bizarre three-piece line-up with Jim absent and Jon on bass. It was quite a crush down the front, so Leah and Debbie, my female companions for the evening, stepped back a bit and watched from a safe distance, but were impressed enough to ask me if Cardiacs were always this good. 'They're even better, trust me,' I beamed.

It was another festival that threw up the next award, **Worst Headache Suffered At A Gig**. This time it was the Phoenix Festival at Long Marston Airfield near Stratford-upon-Avon on July 17th 1993, and once again I found myself getting a lift in the back of a van, this time with Tom and Ian in attendance, as well as a large number of would-be revellers. Quite possibly this back-of-van-which-is-going-quite-fast-round-bends scenario caused my later *mal á la tete*, but at least during the journey I was allowed the chance to show my shining wit when one of those already in the van asked us if hitch-hiking worried us. 'I mean, what would you say if we told you we were all devil-worshippers and we were going to rape you and kill you?' he asked. 'I'd say we have a lot in common,' I fired back, to much laughter. Once we arrived (we only had day-tickets), Ian, Tom and I spent most of the afternoon in the tent housing the *Lime Lizard* (short-lived alternative-music mag) Stage where, amongst others, we saw Mint 400 who were most impressive. However, as the afternoon wore on my headache worsened to the point where I felt I had to do something or else I wouldn't enjoy Cardiacs, so instead of watching Senser, I wandered off to the medical tent where they plied me with water and paracetamols before returning me to the stage to watch Cardiacs, but heck, I was still in agony. Afterwards we bumped into the sax player from Wizards Of Twiddly who, upon hearing of my plight, said, 'Yeah, that's just what you need to do when you've got a headache – go to see Cardiacs.' He had a point. That was also the day when Cardiacs were doing their signing session with Tim signing anything that was given him. Someone gave him a plate, so he signed it, "Plate Timmy". Someone else gave him a serviette, so he asked, 'How do you spell serviette?' Waiting patiently nearby I said, 'S-E-R-V-I-E-T-T-E.' Tim looked up and without saying a word leaned over and scribbled something on my forehead with his marker-pen. Jon Poole then added something else under my nose. 'What've they done?' I asked, turning to Ian and Tom, but they just spluttered and laughed, as did everyone else in the immediate vicinity. I instinctively started to frantically rub my forehead and upper-lip, eventually Ian telling me I'd been sporting a Hitler-moustache accompanied by a swastika on the forehead. Judging by the large number of people distributing anti-Nazi literature around the festival, it was probably a good job this marker-pen was less than permanent…

On the subject of gigs spent in agony, the award for **Most Swollen Finger** goes to Bristol Fleece & Firkin on June 19th 1996. Always one for biting my nails (I blame Sheffield United), every now and again I'd go a bit far and give myself a whitlow. The night before Cardiacs' gig at the Foundry in Birmingham was one such occasion, but this time I feared it was much worse than normal. The Birmingham gig was accompanied by some discomfort, Wolverhampton by great distress (the pain lessened slightly by England's magnificent win over Holland), and Bristol the next night by total agony, not to mention a finger that had swollen to twice its normal size. Not only that, it had turned a rather fetching yellow colour with red swirly bits mixed in, it giving the impression of throbbing like on a cartoon. The problem was, I was taking great pleasure in freaking people out by showing it to them, something I was still doing three days later at a wedding in Sheffield when gangrene had set in (my brother Alex lost patience at this point and whisked me away from said wedding to A&E to get it sorted). The wonderful thing is, I no longer feel the pain, but just by playing *Sing To God* I can recreate all the wonderful feelings of those splendorous gigs, including a very lively night in Bristol.

The pain and suffering of that gig meant that I was kept up all night afterwards, and of course sleepless nights were nothing new for me when it came to Cardiacs. However, most were due to travelling home in the hope of getting to work the next day, but out of all these one arguably stands out from all the rest, thus **Best Trip Back Through The Night** goes to Rayleigh Pink Toothbrush, November 24th 1988. The two Bills (Drake and Hiles) gave me a lift back to London, and we visited an all-night bagel bar upon arrival. For months afterwards I had pleasant dreams about the hot smoked-salmon sandwich I had that night. Bill dropped me off somewhere up the A1 (might have been near Archway, but then possibly not) and as I walked up the hill in what I hoped was the vague direction of the M1, the police, who were having a bit of a row with an Indian take-away proprietor (they weren't going to be bribed with a free curry, even though he'd trayed it all up for them), turned their attentions to me, hardly surprising as it was gone 3am. I must've given them all the right answers though because they let me carry on. In the end I spied a black-cab so flagged it down and got it to take me to 'the beginning of the M1 please.' There was me expecting what I now know as Staples Corner, but instead I got junction 2 and Fiveways Corner. Well, it was now nearly 4 o'clock in the morning and I wasn't walking another yard, so I stuck my thumb out and hoped for the best. A lorry did the honours, dropping me at Northampton, and in so doing gave me the chance to pick up one of my favourite ever lifts, in a milk float. Admittedly, it was a petrol (or diesel) vehicle, not an electric one, but it was still quite a thrill to go on his rounds with him as he delivered to remote country houses around Northants in the mist. It was another lorry that fitted the final piece of this bit-of-a-jigsaw trip home to Brackley, but Brackley by 6am is Brackley in time for work, even affording me the luxury of my old trick of nipping up the stairs of Circle K (my place of work remember) for a bit of a kip in the stock-room.

Another sleepless night came about after the Harlow Square

gig of June 9th 1999, a gig thereby deserving of the award for **Most Legendary Moment According To My Family**. This was another gig attended with Ian, surprisingly the only one we managed to get to on the initial *Guns* tour. We'd got the train to Harlow from Liverpool Street Station and had vague ideas about missing the last train back in order to hang out with buddies etc. Of course, when a good dose of ligging is in the offing, Ian and I can never resist, and thus it was we strolled along to Harlow Station in the early hours to find only a bit of tumbleweed and an urban fox sniffing around. Decisions were made then changed, and rather than sleeping on the station we opted for a walk to the M11 and a hitch back into London. However, it seemed the tumbleweed had followed us there, and after a miserable half-hour of next-to-no vehicles whatsoever, we turned our attentions to the adjoining garden centre on the roundabout. The weather had been glorious during the day, and it was still clear by night, albeit a little chilly. We decided a night sleeping in the relative privacy of the garden centre was the best way forward, so off we went to explore. Over a fence we went, only to realise that yes, it was cold, and we had no sleeping bags or even coats to protect us from the chill. But there just beyond another fence and a lovely wooden door was a pallet of Fisons covered in plastic sheeting, enough plastic to make two makeshift blankets. Ian was first to go over the wooden door, and as I watched him struggle to haul himself up, I noticed there was a nice gap underneath (I was a skinny, long thing back then) so under I went, grinning broadly as I watched Ian nearly breaking his neck whilst flinging himself over the door to join me on my side. Oh, how he laughed... Large chunks of plastic were duly hacked off the pallet of fertiliser and a corner of the garden centre was found to sleep the rest of the night away. The trouble was, despite the plastic sheeting, it was still rather cold, and even more annoyingly, Ian got to sleep first and his snoring was keeping me awake. After an hour or so lying awake wondering why on earth I was trying to sleep in a Harlow garden centre when there was a warm station platform a few miles away, I decided that if I couldn't get to sleep then Ian should suffer too, so I did that thing that only best-

friends are allowed to do and woke him up. He was ever so pleased…
After another hour or two of sitting around shivering wrapped in our
"blankets", we decided that the first train to Liverpool Street was
probably due, a decision possibly aided by the fear that the early shift
at the garden centre may arrive any moment to prune the roses, so
back out we scrambled, and one brisk early-morning walk to the station later we were waiting patiently amongst the early-bird com-
muters. So where does the family legend come in? Well, my sister
Fiona lives close by in Chelmsford, and so whenever she or any of
her family drive past that garden centre, they always feel the need to
say out loud (sometimes to no-one in particular), 'That's the garden
centre where Uncle Adrian spent the night…'

And finally we come to the prestige award, that for **Best Gig
That Is Not One Of THE Gigs**, an award that goes to Windsor Old
Trout, May 13th 1995. I'm not sure what it was that made this gig so
special really, it just was, and Diggy must agree with me because he
selected it as his Special Limited Edition Hardback Book gig. Maybe
it was because it was close to the start of that bit-of-a-comeback tour
of May and June 1995, so the novelty was still strong. It also fitted
neatly in with my theory that Cardiacs come across better in the more
intimate venues. It was one of those nights where they rocked in their
offbeat way whilst remaining note-perfect throughout, and everyone
both onstage and off it seemed to be enjoying it to the max. I remember seeing this young teenage girl grooving away from start to
finish, and when I asked her afterwards if she'd enjoyed it, she
replied in a German accent that 'it was the best concert I've ever been
to!' She said she had no idea who Cardiacs were beforehand, but
goodness me, she knew now. Back at the station (I was living in Banbury back then and the train was the easy option) I saw these teenage
Indie-kids all wearing Cardiacs t-shirts so struck up a conversation.
'We'd never heard of Cardiacs before – we came to see Pura Vida
(support band),' said one of them, 'but Cardiacs blew us away. I can't
believe we weren't aware of a band so brilliant. And the t-shirts (they
were 'Little Man and a House' ones) are the coolest things ever, so
we bought some.' The Windsor Old Trout closed soon after, but I

can't imagine they had many better nights than when Cardiacs shredded the paint off the back wall with their unique brand of sonic attack.

* * * *

So many happy memories, and yet potentially the best was still to come. Over the years I've read in books and magazines about many a super-fan, you know, a Yes fan who has seen them over 30 times, a Rush obsessive who has been to 40-odd gigs all over North America, a Hawkwind fan who has travelled from Europe to see them 25 times, that sort of thing. Now, don't get me wrong, I'd love to have achieved all those things (especially the Yes one – my Yes count currently stands at a meagre six, plus one Anderson Bruford Wakeman & Howe), but here was I on the brink of a century of Cardiacs gigs, and yet I still considered myself to be a mere babe-in-arms. Countless others had done it before me, including, as we've already seen, Pete with his 100th, clocked up at Portsmouth in 2005, and John Daniel who made it to 300 at Milton Keynes Woughton Centre in May 1995 (so goodness knows how many he's been to now as he seems to have been at every gig since). Not only that, but Simon the Millwall fan told me years ago that once he'd got to 100 he'd stopped counting, so he must be well on his way to at least 150. Add to that the amount of Cardiacs fans that have tapped me on the shoulder at gigs and told me that they've been following them since the era of Cardiac Arrest or since the mid-80s halcyon days, and you realise that there's plenty more where I came from – maybe perhaps they don't always keep count of their gigs – and plenty more fans have doubtless achieved many more than me. It's just that the Belch way is to shout it loudly from the rooftops whenever a milestone or achievement is made, and don't you just know, that is the way it will always be…

* * * *

So, there Malc and I were in Cardiff by mid-afternoon, unloading Malc's gear into his hotel room, me crossing every road with so much caution it's a wonder I wasn't stuck looking right and left and right again in perpetuity, thus missing the gig completely. In order to erase any possibility of an unfortunate road accident, I found a pub opposite the venue, Cardiff's wonderful Clwb Ifor Bach, and sat in there until close to kick-off. I could see Cardiacs' big tour bus through the window unfeasibly parked down the incredibly narrow street, and as I sipped my j2o in the pub, people came and people went, stopping for a quick chat and a pat on the back before disappearing into the night.

Claire texted me to say she was on her way, so I duly dispatched her on a detour to buy some batteries for my digital camera. Liz texted me to say she was on her way too, and that she was bringing a work-colleague who'd not seen Cardiacs since he'd seen them at Stonehenge Free Festival in 1984. This got me to thinking about how that very festival 23 years earlier could well have been my first ever Cardiacs gig, if only I'd not crawled off to my tent to grab a bit of sleep between The Enid and Hawkwind's dawn Earth Ritual. Sometimes I wish I'd stayed up all night for Cardiacs, but then who's to say that the 1984 Belch would have been receptive to the Alphabet Business Concern back then? I could have been put off for life, and as a consequence may have ensured that when they were first band onstage on the Sunday at Reading Festival in 1986, I would have been seeking out a Japanese food-stall somewhere instead. Besides, if Stonehenge 1984 had been gig number one, then Portsmouth would have been 100, with Cardiff relegated to 101, and in all honesty I preferred it this way, with Cardiff winning the ton-up.

Finally paying heed to Jon Poole's moans from the night before, I figured I'd better move across the road to the venue to watch the God Damn Whores, and as you'd expect where Mr Poole was concerned, entertainment was never far away. Their opening rendition of an unaccompanied "Another Brick In The Wall part 2" was hilariously masterful, as was the quick blast of Genesis' "Musical Box" that I possibly imagined was in there later in the set. "Physical Training" provided another amusing interlude, and their version of "Silvery" shredded wallpaper.

But as ever, we were here for Cardiacs, and in the meantime Claire and Liz had both arrived. It was quite a weird feeling as I felt like I'd been transported back in time to both the mid-80s of gig-going with Liz in Sheffield and the late-90s of those Camden nights with Claire. As we waited for Cardiacs to take the stage, I got a couple of congratulatory texts. There was one from the Helocolins saying, "Air Guitar (that's Lawrence) has a new babe and is happy. Wish we were there. Happy hundredth you old git." Then there was one from Sewer saying, "HAPPY HUNDREDTH! If you see Tim tell him my sad tale (his very long-winded conversion) and say 'hello'".

Well, there was Tim bouncing onto the stage with the rest of the band, ready to start Belch Gig 100. As well as the afore-mentioned Claire and Liz, also present were Jill and Paul Howard, the Dogstands, Pete and Clare, Malc (of course), Duffy (possibly with recording equipment concealed), Lol, Tim Jackson, and finally, after missing three gigs on the trot, Big Ship Iron. Forget my 100th, we were all anticipating a gig in one of those intimate venues I was so fond of, a gig kicked off with "The Duck And Roger The Horse". One "Buds And Spawn" later we were into the twice-played "Aukomacic". And then it happened.

Tim gave me a big beam and announced, 'Adrian Bell has seen us one-hundred times!' at which point I was pushed to the front by Pete. Tim was just saying something about if I made it to 200 they might all start believing when Pete and Clare proceeded to stick glow-sticks into every part of my face, ably abetted by the Dogstands and indeed anyone close enough to Pete to grab some of those glow-sticks. I kept my head bowed in humbleness, all whilst Tim, Jim, Bob and Kavus played this messy little jam in my honour, to the accompaniment of laughter from the audience (Rose Kemp, she of the incredible voice and wonderful *Unholy Majesty* album, was in attendance it turned out, and she told me almost a year later that it was one of the funniest things she'd ever seen at a gig). At the end, Tim smiled, 'We love you Belchy, and I bet you never thought that would ever happen in a million years!' He was right. It seemed appropriate that "Tarred And Feathered" should follow on from that, except this time it could have been renamed "Glow-sticked And Honoured".

On this night of all nights we were treated to Set D, the one that delved deeply into the really early stuff such as "Dead Mouse", "Scratching Crawling Scrawling" (where I became a Cardiacs lyric for the night, Tim inserting a quick 'Belch!' and 'Adrian Bell!' in those micro-gaps), and "An Ant", at the beginning of which Tim tried to engage Jon Poole in the pre-song banter heard on *The Special Garage Concerts* CDs. However, Jon was absent, so Tim gave me the chance to fill in, but I blew it. You see, Tim wanted me to carry on from the middle of the exchange, whereas I wanted to start from the beginning. Tim's the boss, hence his admonishment of, 'No, it's TWO ANTS, Belch, not one!' and my latest big moment was gone. Ah well – if you've not been lambasted by Tim from the stage, you haven't lived...

Even without all the century-of-gigs nonsense, this would have been up there amongst the best of them (but possibly not Top Ten material), as an enthusiastic audience moshed and freaked as only a Cardiacs audience can. I expended so much energy I wondered that if I dropped dead part-way through the gig, would I be allowed to count it as 100 gigs or only 99-and-a-bit? As it was, I survived to the end, which was a good job as they finished with a splendid final encore of "The Everso Closely Guarded Line" which (depending on what day it is) is Belch Number One Cardiacs Song.

Afterwards Liz said, 'Well, I've seen better and I've seen worse!' but her colleague who'd seen them at 'Henge 1984 was more impressed. 'They've not changed a bit,' he grinned, 'just as brilliant as they were back then.'

'I slept through that gig,' I confessed, 'but they sounded good as they kept me awake.'

Claire had thoroughly enjoyed it too, and was full of congratulations afterwards. Meanwhile, Big Ship Iron shouted, 'Belchy, get yerself over here,' and as I did so he chucked a long-sleeved tour t-shirt in my direction. The front was covered in badges, but on the back were all the signatures of the entire Cardiacs-and-crew, reminiscent of when I'd done a similar thing for Sarah on the *Sing To God* tour of 1996 (Sarah still cherishes it as her favourite ever present). Duffy took a photo of me sheepishly burying my nose in the neck of the t-shirt, and the shirt itself has pride of place on my wall, along with a framed set-list from the gig.

Sarah Smith (now Jones actually), formerly of sax in Cardiacs, was then spied, so I got her to add her signature to the shirt, and clutching it happily, a gang of us wandered off into the night to grab a curry in the trendy bit of Cardiff. We were led by a mate of Pete's, and fine food was consumed by all, that is myself, Claire, Pete and Clare, the Dogstands, Andy Hossain, Tim Jackson, Malc, Lol and Big Ship Iron. Mr Iron had to leave early to rescue his car from a car-park but failed miserably, and so had to return via phoned-instructions from Pete's very useful local friend before booking into a hotel for the night.

When After Eights had been consumed and hot-towels brandished (and placed on heads for comic effect), we all headed out into the night and went our separate ways. Claire was putting me up for the night in her spare room, and despite a relatively early start to get the train to Sheffield following on from a very late night, I slept soundly and happily, but not before I hung that t-shirt on a coat-hanger on the wall and looked at it for half-an-hour or so. Tim's comment inked onto the shirt stood out; "Your 100th Night of Rotten-ness," he'd written. Ah Tim, you do yourself a disservice, you really do. One-hundred gigs, and every single one of them a winner, for even the ones that didn't quite hit the mark, like Brighton (twice), had been fantastic social occasions, but most of all, the huge majority had been brilliant nights the like of which you couldn't experience with any other band anywhere in the world. Not a hint of anything rotten, Tim, not a hint.

SET D

DUCK
BUDS
AUK X ? + TARRED
DEAD MOUSE
ANYTHING CANT EAT
MADE ALL UP
BURN

LIFE
IDEAL
AN ANT
GEN
(SCRATCHING
ARNALD
DITZY

JIBBER
DIRDY BOY

C_____BE CLOSED

Cardiacs
+ GOD DAMN WHORES

TACHWEDD 23 NOV · £15 · 8PM
CLWB IFOR BACH · CAERDYDD
myspace.com/cardiacs

Chapter Twenty-Four
"Look Out Everybody…"
Clive "Big Ship Iron" Hutton

"Look Out Everybody…"
Clive "Big Ship Iron" Hutton

It was a lovely Sunday summer's afternoon in 2007 and I was sitting nervously in the bar of The Cherry Tree on Carter Knowle Road, just round the back from my Mum and Dad's in Sheffield. I was nervous for a number of reasons, not least because as usual in that area I was in a bit of a mobile-phone-signal black-zone, so if the person I was meeting was late, I didn't have my usual safety valve of an agitated text. Perhaps it was for the best though, as the person I was meeting was quite possibly *the* most important ever, and a bit of a controversial character to boot, which maybe explains all the other reasons for my nervousness – really not the kind of person you'd want to agitate with a silly text.

At around the five-minutes-late mark I was shifting uncomfortably when I noticed everyone in the pub was looking outside at the car-park, and it soon became obvious why, for there reversing into a space was a gleaming Jaguar sporty-job convertible, roof down so we could all see the driver resplendent in his shades, spiky blond highlights glinting in the sun. I noted the registration: HUT10N – look out everybody, the Big Ship Iron was here.

Now everybody in the pub was looking my way as the scruff in the Stonehenge t-shirt got up, wandered out into the car-park and shook this apparent superstar by the hand. As I did, my mobile suddenly woke up and I received a text saying, "Belchy, I'm here!" Yep, I'd spotted that…

* * * *

Clive "Big Ship Iron" Hutton had something of a reputation on that there Cardiacs email Chatlist, and it wasn't always a good one. Ian subscribed to The List long before I did, and he once told me of a South Yorkshire businessman with an Internet alias of Big Ship Iron who had upset a few of the Listees by buying up all Cardiacs' rarities (and indeed anything at all, rare or not) on eBay. A penny dropped when Ian mentioned this, and I worked out that this was the same gentleman who'd helped out financially when Tim came to doing the rather splendid Spratley's Japs album, a certain Clive Hutton. Without Clive Hutton, *Pony* wouldn't exist, and the sleeve-notes on said Japs album stated as much. I thereby deduced that Mr Big Ship Iron couldn't be all that bad, but by the time I was able to sign-up to The List, the vitriol was still flying around, usually when something nice and juicy appeared on eBay. I kept out of it by not bothering to bid on anything, instead choosing to buy up loads of silly Yes singles from New Zealand and the like.

One thing I did notice though; Big Ship Iron never seemed to come on The List to put his case himself, and only one Listee seemed to step forward in defence, that being Pete of the Thrupty variety (someone later told me Jill did also). It appeared that Pete was the only Listee to have knowingly met Big Ship Iron, and from what he said, he'd witnessed first hand the legendary collection. I seem to remember Pete said he understood Big Ship Iron's motivation but struggled to put it into words. Well, I was going to get a chance to do that myself as it turned out…

Not long after I'd had my *Eureka!* moment about the idea for this book (go back to my introduction if you've forgotten) and posted it excitedly on The List, I received an email from Big Ship Iron saying simply, "If you need any help with your Cardiacs book, let me know."

Being a bit cagey I replied, "Erm, are we talking financially here?" to which the reply was positive, so I got all excited (and grateful). A few emails later and a phone-call, and we were on for that first meeting in the Cherry Tree, Sheffield.

That first meeting went some way to helping me understand what Big Ship Iron was all about. He didn't need to tell me he was a generous person – the very existence of the Spratley's Japs album evidenced that – but he told me anyway, going on to explain that if people emailed him asking him to hold off the bidding when a desired item came up on eBay, then he would either do so, or if he'd already bid silly money, he'd go ahead and buy it anyway then send it on to the person that really wanted it. More than one person can vouch for this, I know…

As for not defending himself when the email fisticuffs started, Big Ship Iron was happy to explain that he wasn't very good with words: 'Being a businessman, numbers are more my thing. I'm not very comfortable writing emails – if you want to contact me, you're better off just picking up the phone and letting it ring.' He wasn't wrong there, but you might want to let it ring quite a few times on one of his busier days…

When we'd finished discussing all things Cardiacs and my plan for this very book, Clive asked me if I wanted a lift back to my Mum and Dad's. It was only a matter of a few hundred yards, but I wasn't about to turn down a lift in this fantastic convertible, so in I hopped, spotting both Zag And The Coloured Beads CDRs as I did so. Turning up in style outside my parents' abode certainly got the curtains twitching, and my Dad was fielding questions over the following week as to who on earth it had been dropping their idiot son off this time. My Dad was only too happy to tell them, as Clive had made quite an impression when he'd popped in. We needed a pen, you see, so I could sign his copy of *Fever Hitch* – well, I say 'copy', it was one of seven that he'd amassed (more than me; in fact I don't have any copies right now, as I sold my last one when funds ran out recently – must check on eBay), a fact that gave me another insight into what makes him tick, but just in case I wasn't sure, he'd pointed it out for me; 'I'm a bit of a compulsive collector…'

So anyway, we popped in for a pen, Clive referring to my Mum and Dad as 'Mr and Mrs Belch' which made them smile. He was also quite happy to take his shoes off before being asked to, him realising almost immediately my Mum's strict no-footwear-in-the-house policy (there must have been something in the way I swiftly removed my boots). My Dad being a retired steelworks engineering manager, they were quite happy to discuss business (Clive's business is power tools you see) and it turned out they knew one or two of the same local Master Cutlers.

He'd made an impression all right, and I felt I'd got a little closer to understanding what Big Ship Iron was all about. Over a number of further meetings regarding the book, and on the tour itself, and then with regards to Circulus, who Clive offered a bit of a helping hand financially, I learned a little more, but I still felt I'd not quite cracked it yet. For that I'd have to wait for the interview from which I'd glean most of the information for the Big Ship Iron chapter in this very book.

Well, I've done it. However, I still might not have all the answers, so you'll just have to read it for yourself and see if you can fathom it all out…

* * * *

Mr Big Ship Iron made it quite clear to me that I was wasting my time emailing him the questionnaire I'd sent to most of the other subjects featured herein as it'd never get filled in, never mind sent back. No, for this one I was going to have to do a proper journalistic thingy on it and sit there across a table with my digital voice recorder switched on. It was, after all, the very reason why Clive had bought me the digital voice recorder in the first place.

The problem was finding a time that was mutually convenient for both of us, but eventually a very small window of opportunity opened up sometime rather longer after the 2007 Cardiacs tour than I'd hoped for, but it was a window nevertheless. Basically, I had to be in Doncaster, where Clive is based, for around 9.30 in the morning on my day off in the middle of the week. This involved finishing work on the Tuesday evening and heading straight off to Victoria Coach Station in order to board the last Megabus to Sheffield of the evening. I then ended up walking from the drop-off point of Meadowhall to my Mum and Dad's in the early hours (a two-hour-plus hike if you must know) where I grabbed an hour of sleep before heading to Donny via bus and train. I'd been told to text when I hit Doncaster station, upon which one of Clive's employees was sent out in a rather striking CH Power Tools van to collect me.

'How will I know what he looks like?' the CHPT employee apparently asked Clive.

'He'll be wearing a Cardiacs t-shirt of course,' Clive had replied. For the record, it was the long-sleeved 1995 tour shirt…

It was a small window all right; as I sat down across Clive's desk, voice recorder switched on, I was told I'd got just over an hour. Blimey, better use that hour wisely…

* * * *

As with all the subjects in this book, one chapter alone is not sufficient to go into every detail of their lives, and Clive Hutton is no exception. For all the wonderful stories he's told me about becoming successful in business, and for what he was a champion at in his youth, you'll have to wait for *Big Ship Iron: The Biography*. Here, we are largely concerned with how music came into his life, and in particular where Cardiacs came in and how indeed they became an obsession, like they have become an obsession for all of us within these covers. And in Clive's case, there was a very early inkling as to where Cardiacs may later come in with his first recollection of music, going back as far as he can remember: 'It would be fairground music, the tooting. I've always liked the erratic-music sort of thing…'

Well yes, the erratic thing is certainly there in Cardiacs and their sound, as is the fairground-music thing, "fairground" perhaps being the element most people think to mention when trying to describe Cardiacs' sound when they don't want to mention the words "Progressive" and "Punk" together. So, it's no surprise that someone should mention that their earliest musical memory is the tooting of a fairground organ, and when you add to that a *Thunderbirds* album, Clive's first record received 'aged about 6, possibly 7', you can already see the young Clive's musical future being mapped out. 'There's been a *Magic Roundabout* in there, and *Captain Pugwash*,' he goes on. Yep, all classic signs of impending Cardiacs Adoration.

However, the first record that Clive went out and bought with his own money showed a distinct steering in the direction of Punk: 'Believe it or not, it was Sid Vicious and "My Way". I liked it because it started all dramatic, instrumental-dramatic, orchestra-dramatic, then it just came down to some strange singing that nobody got; a lot of people didn't "get" the "My Way" record for some strange reason. For me, it was the showmanship, the bright lights, the stage, acting towards the video, the whole *Great Rock And Roll*

Swindle as such, and as a part of that, the theatricality of it all, the full stage show, for what it was… It wasn't raw, not in your face, not Thrash Metal, but a big presence; there was a big presence walking down them stairs, with the lights, the glamour – well done, probably one of the best. Not the best record by any means, but it all comes to the collective as a whole…' And as I've noticed, Clive still collects the clothes from that era today. 'I'm into music visuals,' he adds.

And as ever, there's a big musical influence of a figure on the way just when one's at one's most formative, musically, in Clive's case not a big brother or a kindly uncle, but a school-friend, 'a guy called Neville Howe – fantastic musician, really old Punk Rock sort of thing, with a massive music collection, you know, old Stranglers, Fall, "Fiery Jack" and all that. He was a year younger than me, we're talking about me being about 12 or 13-years-old at that time, but music became really essential for me when I was 11-years-old. You see, all the seven-inchers that people were collecting then, XTC, Plasmatics, stuff like that, it all became collectible – we're talking about 1980, everything came to vinyl, so you got your picture discs, and coloured vinyl was really coming in then, so the marketing tool was one single you could buy in six or seven formats, box-set, the lot.

'The biggest impression at that time would have been The Cramps, *The Smell Of Female* and all their old records, they were all made very collectible, and as you know I'm a very avid collector…' (there then followed a bit of chat about different formats and how when a band release a single on green vinyl and yellow vinyl, you have to buy both, as well as the CD single – look, some of us are just made like that, right?). So we can look to late-70s/early-80s record company marketing of Punk and New Wave as being the reason why Clive got the collecting bug.

So, what about passion then? 'I've not been as passionate about anyone else as I have been Cardiacs, but as an 11-and-12-year-old, it was The Cramps, just them, then I fell right into Cardiacs. For "passion", the all-time greatest high for me was listening to

"R.E.S." played on a Saturday afternoon on Radio 1. It was when it was first released (on *A Little Man And A House And The Whole World Window*), on a lunchtime. I'd love to find out exactly when, because having to have the LP with the needle and drop it on the record at that time, and then all of a sudden just to hear it on the radio…'

So, was this the first time you heard Cardiacs?

'No, that was back in '84 or '85, but this was in 1988, …*The Whole World Window*, the actual album got a mention on the radio…'

But we've got a bit ahead of ourselves... We've had Sid Vicious, then The Cramps – how about the first gig attended? 'It was t'Angelic Upstarts in Doncaster. They played a festival, Hyde Park I think (all towns must have their own Hyde Park – in Sheffield it's a horrible block of flats). It must have been around '82, '83… '82 I think. Around that time I tried to sneak in to see t'Damned at Rotters – couldn't get in there, too young for t'pub. I thought about putting an eyeliner moustache on myself, but I had second thoughts when I'd seen what it looked like…'

Around the age of 12 or 13, young Clive wasn't just fighting a losing battle with trying to sneak into gigs; it felt like he was fighting a losing battle with all those around him and their musical taste too. 'At that age, you're trying to get where you need to be, but everybody at that time, every single friend I had, every single person I knew was wearing Rolling Stones "Lips" t-shirts or Whitesnake t-shirts. School youth-clubs were dominated by "Angus! Angus!"; AC/DC, Whitesnake, they were playing that all the time. ELO were having to take a back-step to some of this raunchier stuff. Although the Stones had been out there for ages, it was really cool for an 11/12-year-old kid to wear a "Lips" t-shirt, when I've got a Cramps *Off The Bone* t-shirt or a UK Subs t-shirt on. There was only me used to like The Cramps.

'I thought to myself, "Why don't they like it?" I always play my music and can't understand why other people don't like it – "Can't you see the brilliance of it?" Like *The Smell Of Female*, I just couldn't understand why one person liked it and a thousand people didn't – they were wrong!' I know that feeling all right, Clive – they're all wrong and I'm right!

So, just when was that first hearing of Cardiacs, and how did it come about? 'It came on a small compilation tape,' Clive explains, 'from one of the guys out of a band called Kitchens Of Distinction, just a normal old TDK 90. They were really young people, Kitchens Of Distinction and Popinjays, and before they really came to those bands they were experimenting themselves, getting hold of live recordings and recordings off people, and on this tape that one of them gave to me was an old Cardiacs "Jibber And Twitch". I've still got the tape somewhere – it might have been *Obvious Identity* era.'

It was love at first sight, or hearing, for Clive: 'What really appealed to me was putting notes in where they shouldn't belong. A classic example is towards the end of "R.E.S."; you're expecting that beat to be there but it skips a bit, I'll not sing it (he then *does* try to sing it, with limited success, because, well, it's nigh on impossible to sing – goodness knows how Cardiacs play it, especially as Tim has now stuck in that extra bit presumably because it was becoming too "easy"; better off describing it really Clive); then it stops, then you're expecting that beat to come back in, and it goes… *silence* Another good example is the instrumental bit in "Eating In Bed" (sings again). All the beats are in the wrong place, which then questions it, then you go along, you can bring it in and recognise that beat, but you don't go to 4/4 time or 8 time or 10, 16 time – you know, you're tapping (taps on desk), and you're actually (taps extra unexpected beat on desk), it's sort of…well, THAT'S when you can understand the music. And a lot of people don't understand that…' he ends with a glorious touch of irony.

That first hearing of Cardiacs made such an impression on the teen-Clive that he went to extraordinary lengths to find out more about the band. "No Internet back then remember, so you had to go and find it. Nothing in the *NME* either (well, they've never liked Cardiacs), so how would you find a group that's got a following of something like 40 people? But that's when it started, when it became obsessive. You look round, you ask record people: "Have you heard of a band called Cardiacs?" "No, but we'll find out for you." Angie's Records would come back and say "No," but then you'd turn round and say, "I'll do you a tape," so you do a tape for Guy that works in Angie's Records in Doncaster, Guy starts doing some research, then he turns round and tells you they're a little group from Kingston... You see what I mean...?' Blimey, yes! Good old fashioned networking, like what Sean from *The Organ* has always advocated.

'I got another fanatic on music to give it a listen,' Clive continues, 'and they said, "Well, I don't *mind* it; I'll find out something for you..."' So, they knew the little clubs in London like Nag Nag Nag, expecting Cardiacs to have played there, or to have talked to someone who knew Cardiacs. Nowadays, with the Internet, I could just look up clubs in London and straight away you'd come to the Garage, and then you'd make the call. But I had to do it this way back then. I'd phone the Garage and say, "Have you ever heard of a band called Cardiacs?" and they'd say, "No, but I'll ask my booking agent." You'd then get through to the booking agent (does ringing tone), and, "Yep, we've heard of Cardiacs." "Have you got a manager's contact name for 'em?" And that's how it all started, which led me to Mark (then-manager) Walmsley...' Stunned, I must say. Clive's efforts put the teenage-Belch and his search for all-things-Yes-related around the same 80s period to shame...

It's a shame that Clive isn't as meticulous about his personal-Cardiacs-event logging as the likes of Pete or me, because he's slightly unsure about the date of his first ever Cardiacs gig. The Marquee Club in July 1985 is the most probable, but 'I've got to confirm that – map it back with my photos.' He's got photos? Oh heck, one day we're going to have one heck of a trawl through the archives... As for how many times he's seen Cardiacs, well, 'I'd like to think it's about 60 or 70 now, but I really don't know. I don't think it's up to 100, but again I could be shocked because when you say '85, and been able to get transport all over freely with friends who were a little older and therefore driving and things back then, going to obscure places where they didn't mind so much that I was 16 but looking 15... So yeah, when you realise that you're talking 25 years ago or so, you think to yourself, well, I've definitely seen 'em at least in one batch four times in each year, five times maybe, and every time they've toured I've seen 'em more than just once or twice... But it really doesn't bother me either way.'

He's a bit more certain about the first physical Cardiacs recording he laid his hands on, however: 'The *Seaside Treats* 12-inch package, with the booklet, the poster, the button.' He made contact with someone via the old Alphabet Business Concern PO Box number, 'possibly the old Ordinary Shop Girl before Bill Hiles, and they sold me Tim Smith's *Seaside Treats*, still with the old brown 12-inch posting envelope, with Tim's writing on it. I paid £50 for it, on my paper-round money...' Yep, the first big-bucks collectors' item!

It had everything with it, the full package, and a letter, but sadly no stick of Cardiacs rock, which it seems is a bit of a Holy Grail. Many people from The List seem to remember seeing a Cardiacs stick of rock around the '85 period, but no-one can be 100% sure that it wasn't just a one-off, or whether it was a regular item sold at gigs. As someone pointed out, if anyone was to have one, it'd be Clive, and he hasn't. Someone else suggested that the food-properties of this wonderful bit of memorabilia rendered it now non-existent and I agreed, chiming in with a tale of how I once had a Sheffield United stick of rock which I vowed to never eat, until one night when I was really, really hungry... But then Ian came along saying he'd still got his Jethro Tull (or was it Fairport?) bottle of beer from 1987, so what do we all know...? One day, someone, somewhere, might find a stick of Cardiacs *Seaside Treats* rock...

So there's a favourite item of merchandise that our Clive would like to possess – a tricky one, that. Instead then, let's try for some favourites from the well-established Cardiacs canon, like albums, songs etc etc. 'Easy-peasy,' says Clive, 'and it's always been so – favourite album is *A Little Man And A House And The Whole World Window*, for all different reasons, not necessarily musically, you know what I mean, just for... everything really; a Cardiacs fan could argue the toss all day long over that one though. Favourite song is "Big Ship" by far – he's singing about me! The most moving record which always leaves a little bit of something in your mind is "Stoneage Dinosaurs", the first time that we know of where he's sung about him and part of his family. But then you never know (Tim famously never talks about his lyrics and their meaning), although I reckon that's the only one where the heart is on the sleeve. Maybe someone should ask him one day what, "Liberace asks for me and all my family," means. His lyrics are for everybody, the songs are for everybody, but they still manage to turn your stomach – we still get butterflies.'

We then get to talking about a Cardiacs gig at Attercliffe's Take Two club in Sheffield in 1989 when one representative of the Alphabet Business Concern was heard in the pub breathlessly trying to explain what the words to "Leader Of The Starry Skies" were all about, and Clive gets all excited: 'I was there, yeah! Red hot that day, absolutely scorching. I remember Tim actually shouted out, "Hot or what!"'

Oh yes, I remember that, Tim repeating, "Is it hot or what; is it hot or what!" It shouldn't have been funny, but somehow it was. It certainly was hot though, as I related back in the chapter on Sheffield. I remember as I observed the nutcases in the pre-Pond Pond, having recognised some of them from Leeds in 1988, and it was perhaps the insanity of those grooving manically in the heat that led to Tim using a phrase that I heard him use before at Keele University also on that November 1988 tour, but which Clive had never before heard in use: 'He pointed at someone and said, "The lights are on but there's nobody home!" That was the first time I'd ever heard that saying. And then this bloke put this papier-mâché horse's head on, and it were absolutely dripping… Then when they were going to come on and do an encore, Little Bic had this little torch and he were swinging it round, shouting and bawling. The rest of 'em came on and did "Nurses Whispering Verses", probably the best version I've ever heard…'

Memories, sweet memories. And always nice to discover

you've been at the same gig as someone from that long ago, although obviously there have been many more. When I met Clive for the first time in the Cherry Tree, his was a face that I recognised, but not one that I "knew" if you know what I mean. Meanwhile, he'd seen me loads of times, but as he kept himself to himself at gigs (more on that later), we'd never got chatting. However, that night in Sheffield in 1989 we figured we must have only been a few paces apart, me perched on the window ledge with Annie, him standing near the back. 'I remember I was jumping around, sweat coming down my shorts, down my legs,' reminisces Clive. We both agree that it was the hottest gig we've ever been to; "Hot or what!"

So right, that's one memorable gig, but what is THE most memorable? 'I'm going to be very anarchic here,' smiles Clive, 'even though every one is different in every way, but my favourite's going to be that last one in Leeds (2007), for all sorts of reasons, especially now...

'I've never had Cardiacs Friends. And now I have you see. I've got to say Leeds because after that one I had three, four Cardiacs fans stop at my house. I got our Keifer (Little Ship Iron) and his friend Lewis Facedown, and all his friends to come. We turned up in a bizarre way (a bit of a fleet, as you'll find out in the next chapter), we turned up in a bizarre place. Then we rocked it, you know, good old fashioned rock. There was nothing put-on or superficial, no blueprint for any Classic Rock... Everything was against us that night, and against everybody to produce a show-of-a-lifetime like that. People were blown away by it, by the size of it all, and it was the end of the tour so we got all the sigh-of-relief thing, and Tim opened up a bit because of that. He wanted to cry, you could see he was full of it – everybody loved it, everybody...

'And Cardiacs Friends. Up until then I'd thought, "Cardiacs are my group and nobody else's, 'cos nobody else likes them." Remember the thousands of people who were wrong. Then all of a sudden there's Pete "Skitzo" (aka "Thrupty") defending me like he did at the time, and then making contact, and all the horrible stuff that was said about me, and all the horrible things that's been done, and me being a ruthless collector. It all started from the times when I could never afford it – I couldn't afford the gear, I wasn't working, and it was my Nana's money that bought me my first t-shirt, paper-round money too. All the things I missed out on as a collector, if I could go back in time now, you'd know what your wish-list would be. Going back in time, I should have bought everything. I should have collected all the flyers, all the gig lists, I should have got taped-interviews from old push-button recorders, I should have followed 'em all over, I should have moved down London, I should have run away from home – followed it all. That's Cardiacs, isn't it...'

Yup, with you all the way Clive. But hang on, could this be where the Big Ship Iron we all know, the "ruthless collector" as he puts it, surfaces and we find out why, what etc? Let's digress from the "Fave gig" question for a minute and concentrate on Big Ship Iron the Collector: 'It's down to the collecting – a lot of people don't understand it. I don't want to justify that, but I'm renowned for it – "Big Ship Iron"... I've never had Cardiacs Friends before, so it's not like I'd go down there and meet up with yourself or Pete, so I've always been in the background for that length of time. Then there was not being able to afford anything until fortunes changed around 1995/'96. And then the collection you have already got, well, there's things you can remember from ten years ago, and you must have them, 'cos they all mean something in different sorts of ways.

'This collection, it's not greed – it's just a statement: "Cardiacs is MY group," because of the thousand people that were into music at that time who didn't like them – there was only me, and there's only ever been me into Cardiacs – there's not been me and Pete or me and Belch. I've had no discussions with anyone about Cardiacs as such. I'm not too strong on the reading and writing, so I didn't discuss things on the Mailing Lists, I don't express my views so nobody knows who I am, what I do or don't do.

'But fortunes change, and there were things that I didn't have the money for years ago, and now I've got them tenfold. So I'll give 'em away, or I HAVE given 'em away, and I DO give bits away...Thing is, I'm not even sure what I've got now so it gets a little hard. I can't necessarily explain the compulsive buying of 20 CDs, but a ticket stub at 99p, someone's forced them to get it out, sell it, so I might as well have it, and it might as well go in great big picture frames, then people will say, "Look at them; yeah, I remember that; oh, I've got one of them." Nobody will ever have the chance again to see it all...' Sounds like an idea for Big Ship Iron's very own real-live Cardiacs Museum, just like the rather fabulous one on the World Wide Web, but this one would be REAL. Who knows, and we can speculate on that later, but meanwhile...

'That Leeds gig though,' Clive says, getting back on track, 'I just think if you were to write it down on paper now and try and sell it as a thing, nobody'd believe you (well Clive, that's what I'll be doing in the next chapter, and I really don't think those that weren't there will ever quite believe it was as special as we all make out, but those that were there, they know – heck, I'm getting goosebumps just writing this).

Clive goes on: 'A working man's club, bingo and pool over the other side; two has-been hippies and Hell's Angels collecting your money on the door, vastly overcharging (tickets were pricey, yes, but I think we all snuck in on the guest list didn't we?); beautiful toilets – we could all have sat on a toilet and talked to each other freely; air-conditioned, curtains, fabric, and all this right in the middle of t'Bronx in Leeds (stop it Clive, tears of mirth about to start).

'One pizza shop across the road; pizzas from the Pizza Nazi – he was a Pizza Nazi 'cos of the prices he was charging. Then there's the girls (Carli and Jill) in their wedding dresses. Then there's seeing Zak Dingle (yes really – it's all in the next chapter folks) and him saying, "Yes, I love it, it's great, I'm a great fan!" We got photos, me and our Keifer with Zak Dingle...' It was a phenomenal night...

'There's nothing that'll ever change my mind, whatever gig it is,' agrees Clive. 'There was another one that might be number two around the time that the *Mare's Nest* video came out in the early 90s when I went down to London on a National Express coach and stopped in somebody's flat – I can't remember whose – but I ended up stuck in London because of the snow everywhere else, all the electric cut off up here and everything. You'll have to find out when it was Belch (well, I've tried but no definitive answers yet). I can't even remember what venue it was… I had to stop an extra two days in London. It was great because I was stuck there in Cardiacsland – London is always Cardiacsland for me.

'But Leeds… even my birthday, I got Cardiacs playing for my 30th birthday at the Leopard in Doncaster in 1998 – I paid for 'em to play and even put limousines on – Leeds even beats that. It even beats my very own personal Cardiacs birthday gig.'

Time is nearly up, but we just have time to touch on the collecting again, and the fact that it was Big Ship Iron himself who funded all that glorious merchandise that appeared towards the end of the last century. 'You can see where the devilment came in there,' he grins, 'that was just sooo terrible! Cardiacs hoodies, record bags. I got one of every single thing, because I went and picked 'em up and paid for 'em, so the scarves, the gloves, the socks, all the kiddies' t-shirts – well, they're all there as you know (see the appendices for the Belch Cardiacs Collection, including some gems from this little lot), and it'll never be done again like that.

'Umbrellas, small, big, large; very silly, it was something that was done silly. I delivered it all down to Mark Walmsley's house myself,' he chuckles.

So *that's* it – if you're a collector, you just pay for a whole load of merchandise to be produced of your favourite band and you're in heaven. It's probably what I'll have to do, because over the years I've had three Cardiacs watches and I've broken every single one of them due to my desire to wear them constantly (not all three at once, you understand…)

As it stands there are 27 boxes of Cardiacs stuff sitting in a unit next to CH Power Tools in Doncaster, because after the floods of 2007 in South Yorkshire, Clive's rather lovely house (previous owner one Mr O. Cromwell) received quite a bit of damage, so the most treasured possessions were scooped up and whisked away, which means that there is a treasure trove of Cardiacs delights, all boxed up and waiting to be sorted and logged. And it's me that's supposed to be going up to Doncaster sometime soon, which should be rather exciting – just got to find another one of those rare windows…

And when it's all recorded and logged, what then for the great Big Ship Iron Cardiacs Collection? Who knows; maybe we *will* see a real Cardiacs Museum, or maybe there'll be lots of little museums all over the place. Whatever happens, with Clive's flair, wit and imagination, it'll be quirky and entertaining, that's for sure…

* * * *

My time was up and it was time to head back to Doncaster station. Little Ship Iron was given a moment's respite from slaving away at a lathe by Big Ship Iron: 'Give Belchy a lift back into town,' he ordered.

Out in the car-park, Little Ship Iron proudly showed me the 'Little Man and a House' logo stencilled by the rear-passenger window. 'I didn't want to be seen in this car until I had that done,' he beamed.

As we drove back to the centre of Donny, we talked about Cardiacs and the ins and outs of the music, and just how good some of those gigs had been, and all the while Gong were playing on the car-stereo. I can thank my Dad for a love of Sheffield United; Little Ship Iron can thank *his* Dad for allowing a little bit of his obsession to rub off onto him. Gong and Cardiacs? It doesn't get too much better than that. Well done Big Ship Iron!

Chapter Twenty Five
"Will Bleed Amen"
Woodhouse Liberal Club, Leeds,
November 24th 2007

"Will Bleed Amen"
Woodhouse Liberal Club, Leeds, November 24th 2007

There are special gigs and there are SPECIAL gigs. Quite often, seemingly-ordinary gigs marking the last night of a tour are promoted to being that bit more special because they become big End-of-Tour parties. One thinks of Reading Alleycat Live on November 16th 1996 for example when almost the entire Cardiacs' audience seemed to be in the dressing room afterwards.

So of course, this last gig at the Woodhouse Liberal Club in Leeds was indeed the last gig of a memorable 2007 tour, a tour when friendships were forged never to be broken, a tour that had seen Cardiacs consistently performing to a level of brilliance that most bands could only dream of, and most people just wouldn't understand. And if ever there was a gig to sum up what Cardiacs were all about, then this was it; a real Gala Concert Performance, from the bonkers wedding-reception feel of the venue, to the be-curtained stage awash with relaxed and happy representatives of the Alphabet Business Concern, taking in an audience from all over the country, with every walk of life and musical sub-culture represented along the way, some of them armed with mini confetti-cannons for added authenticity. Jill and Carli were even wearing their wedding dresses, adding to the surreal atmosphere, and, well, it was quite possibly the most uplifting, splendiferous night of wonder you could ever hope to imagine. It still brings a tear to the eye and a lump to the throat just thinking about it now.

Shall I just end the book here? Nah – I'd better tell you a bit more about it, and in doing so, delve into other triumphs from the past...

* * * *

There's a bit of rivalry between Sheffield and Leeds. It has something to do with certain local news programmes favouring the city in West Yorkshire, hence why those in Sheffield and South Yorkshire refer to *Look North* as *Look Leeds*. It also has an awful lot to do with football, especially in the red-and-white half of Sheffield where we got a bit fed up with seeing our best players traipsing up the M1, players such as Mick Jones, Tony Currie, Alex Sabella, Keith Edwards, and Brian Deane (at least he came back).

However, I have a problem. Like Oxford and Bristol, prior to Woodhouse Liberal Club in 2007, I'd never seen a bad gig in Leeds. What's more, I'd never seen a bad football match there either, although Elland Road was only visited once, when Sheffield United won 4-0 (blimey, that was a night!). Only three gigs, but they were all brilliant. All those happy memories, in the rival city of Leeds; it just wasn't right.

The fact that those three gigs I'd been to in Leeds had all been brilliant was a cause of slight embarrassment to me. Two were in 1996, one being Ian's birthday-Cardiacs gig in June at the Duchess of York, and the other a rather cosmically wonderful night transmitting from the luminous green planet of Gong at Leeds Irish Centre. But perhaps unsurprisingly, it's a Cardiacs gig from that incredible *Cardiacs Live* tour of November 1988 that reigned supreme, at least until Woodhouse Liberal Club came along.

I'm aware that I've probably written just as much about that 1988 tour as I have the 2007 one, for which I make no apologies. Back in November 1988 everything was new for me; I'd left Sheffield for Brackley and had a new job that allowed me to somehow maintain the freedom I'd experienced when unemployed earlier in the year, whilst now possessing a bit more money. Cardiacs were my absolute favourites of the moment, and it's safe to say that they were the best live band around at the time, by a mile. My love of hitchhiking meant that just about any gig was doable and affordable, work permitting. My attitude of not worrying about what time I arrived home afterwards helped this also.

Cardiacs back in 1988 were arguably at the peak of their live-in-concert powers, featuring as they did the considered-by-most classic line-up of Tim Smith, Jim Smith, William D. Drake, Sarah Smith, Dominic Luckman and Tim Quy, and the material they were performing night after night was a mouth-watering combination of old classics and new stuff that was due to surface on the not-yet-released *On Land And In The Sea*. Leeds was to be the first gig of the

1988 *Cardiacs Live* tour I was able to attend, and Richard was up for another trip, especially as it was his birthday. At the time I was doing a pretty good job of keeping a regular journal, and what follows is the story of that Cardiacs Leeds University gig of November 8th 1988, based heavily on what I wrote in joined-up letters all that time ago…

* * * *

Richard didn't take too much persuading that night to come with me to Leeds University to see the wonderful Cardiacs, as what better way is there to celebrate a birthday than by going to see that most wonderful of bands? So that afternoon we met in The Old Queen's Head (haunted by ghosts and me and Richard), and then boarded a luxury coach to Leeds for £1.50. On this coach I bought some hot soup which I was drinking as we went over a level crossing in Barnsley, except it wasn't very level because all the soup ended up on my trousers and on the floor.

Richard and I walked to the University which was huge, but somehow found the venue after stumbling across Cardiacs' tour bus (posh), and Graham Simmonds (Mr Sound Engineer). We wandered into this minute bar and were surprised to see the band setting up their gear in a remarkably small space. We were privileged to witness the soundcheck where they gave an airing to new song "The Duck And Roger The Horse" which sounded ear-numbingly stunning. A group of us then headed to a pub called Favershams, a group consisting of a number of representatives of the Alphabet Business Concern, a Leeds Cardiacs fan called Alan, and another collection of Cardiacs fans from Sheffield who we'd met earlier on the coach. As is often the case, far too long was spent in the pub and it was a bit of a dash to get back to the venue in time for the 10.15 gig kick-off time, and indeed there was the rare sight of some of those due to perform on the stage puffing and panting their way along the back-streets of Leeds.

The gig itself was an absolute stormer, one of the best yet. The crowd were packed round the front of the small stage like sardines and the reaction was superb, with the band responding accordingly, especially Tim who was on top form, leaping up and down on the makeshift stage which was threatening to give way any minute, charging around wielding his guitar in a guitar-hero mickey-take, abusing the audience, hammering Dominic's cymbals, pouring gallons of water over himself and his guitar... brilliant.

They started off with "To Go Off And Things" (not an anticipated or usual set-opener) after the quite superb intro-tape (again, new back then, and the intro that has been used pretty much since), and then played a wonderful mix of old and new stuff, the new stuff sounding really good now, it being quite familiar after Scunthorpe and Hammersmith earlier in the year.

The gig was a tremendous success, and we were rewarded with an encore of "I'm Eating In Bed". Afterwards I managed to make a nuisance of myself and got my entire Cardiacs collection (faithfully hauled up Yorkshire with me) signed by most of those present. Eventually, the venue-manager threw us all out and as the band got in their nice warm tour-bus, Richard and I set off walking through a deserted Leeds in the rain. We got absolutely drenched so sought shelter in a shopping centre. Whilst sitting in there, two boys and three girls came wandering along and sat on a bench next to us. I was taking my jumper off to use it as a towel, so these lads started to sing stripper-type music, influencing me to remove my top shirt, and then off came my Cardiacs shirt, leaving me in just my Pathetic Sharks t-shirt (and jeans of course). I then got shy and stopped. One of the girls was very gorgeous and started being energetic, running around a lot. Eventually she was standing opposite me and she said, 'Let me teach you how to Morris dance,' so she did. She said I was really good at it as I got my knees up, stayed on my toes and swung my arms about correctly. I asked her if she was a professional Morris dancer, but she said it was just a hobby. Just as I had visions of Morris dancing through the night with the girl of my dreams in a Leeds shopping centre, her friends walked off, so she went with them.

With my first and possibly last Morris dancing lesson over, Richard and I decided to get some sleep on our two benches. Richard was asleep in no time, but I found it slightly more difficult. I didn't sleep at all in fact, but when I saw two policemen coming, I woke

Richard up and we quickly disappeared.

We went to the bus station and saw that the next bus was 8am, so disheartened we went to the railway station instead. We'd been here two seconds when an officious BR employee chucked us off, telling us the next train to Sheffield wasn't until 5.40, and 'this station is now closed so would you please wait outside.' For a change, Richard was polite about it and I wasn't.

As we wandered around Leeds, we saw three of the Sheffield Cardiacs fans who'd been in the pub with us. They'd missed their coach, but told us there was another one at 3.15, so we decided to try it. However, the driver wouldn't let us on, even when a tenner was waved in front of his face, the miserable git. So it was back to the railway station…

When we got back there, we saw that Mr Officious BR Employee had put two great big Royal Mail post cages up against the door to keep us out, but a bit of gentle persuasion saw them moving and in we went. The three others were a bit doubtful about this, but faced with the prospect of a night in the rain on the streets of Leeds, Richard and I were going in, so the others followed. After a little exploration, the ticket office looked like the best bet.

So we settled down in the ticket office which was nice and spacious as well as well-lit. We remained undisturbed in here and got some kip. Richard and I, as hardened travellers, found it a bit easier than our new friends did.

At 5am, I was woken up by one of the Sheffield contingent who told me they were going for the next coach. They also pointed out that Richard had vanished. Indeed, where Richard had been there was now just a pair of gloves – mysterious... So while they went off for the coach I mounted a search for Richard, a bit tricky as there was only a fifteen-minute period to locate him then get back to the coach station. Eventually I found him wandering around the station with Mr Officious BR Employee in hot pursuit shouting his head off. Richard had woken up in a mop cupboard which he described as 'nice and warm and smelling of detergent, surrounded by mops and buckets'. He couldn't remember going in, but he assumed he'd been heading for the Gents (which was next door) when he'd found the cupboard.

Anyway, Richard had been rudely awakened from his slumbers by Mr Officious BR Employee who was raving at him, 'You have no right to be in here; you get in trouble with lots of people, the police maybe. I take you to the supervisor's office.' I could hear this commotion coming from round a corner so knew Richard wasn't far away, and sure enough round the corner he came with his agitator close behind. Richard smiled at me, gave a heartfelt two-fingered hand-gesture to Mr Officious BR Employee, and then legged it with me into the night…

So now we headed to the coach station, stopping on the way so I could buy a newspaper (Sheffield United lost 1-0 at Aldershot). Our friends from Sheffield were already there, and this time we were all allowed on the 5.15am coach. This was very welcome, and we slept all the way home. I ended up getting a taxi back to my Mum and Dad's and wandered in through the door at 6.30am, just as my Mum was getting up. Quite some night…

* * * *

Years later, like about 2004, I was in Jack's Records in Sheffield when the gentleman behind the counter commented on my yellow-long-sleeved 'Little Man And A House' t-shirt. Always happy to meet a fellow Cardiacs fan, we got chatting and somehow got onto the subject of Leeds University in 1988. We'd both been there, and it transpired he'd been one of those Sheffield Cardiacs fans Richard and I had met on the coach going to Leeds.

'Blimey, were you one of those who missed the last bus back and spent the night in the station with us?' I asked.

'No, I was the only one who made it back to the bus station in time,' he replied.

'Ah, pity,' I sympathised, 'you missed one heck of a night…'

* * * *

"One heck of a night" would be a pretty good way to describe that last night of the November 2007 tour, but first I had to get there. Cardiff to Leeds is quite a trek, and because I wanted to take in the

Sheffield United match against Plymouth Argyle in Sheffield before travelling on to Leeds, I'd decided long-since not to take any risks, so had booked a train ticket over the Internet well in advance (unlike me to be so organised). Just like 19 years earlier, I found myself in a railway station ticket office in the early hours of the morning, except this time it was as a result of a lift there by the lovely Claire, and it wasn't really that early – it just felt like it after the lateness of the night before.

The wonders of modern technology meant that I could pick up my ticket from a machine just by sticking my debit card in it, and then all I had to do was sit back and let the train do the rest (via a change at Bristol).

Now, there was the small matter of hoping to put to bed a long-held ambition of seeing Sheffield United win on the same day as witnessing Cardiacs in concert. Thus far the Leadmill in 1988 had seen a drab 0-0 draw with West Bromwich Albion earlier in the day, and then the Leadmill again in 2005 had been immediately preceded by a 2-2 draw at Rotherham. And two years prior to that in 2003, in between two of the Special Garage Concerts, the Saturday afternoon had seen a miserable 2-0 defeat at Millwall. I had high hopes for this one in 2007 however, as surely Plymouth Argyle wouldn't present such stiff opposition? Oh, but when will I learn? The less said about that afternoon's "entertainment" the better – suffice to say it was typical of Sheffield United under Bryan Robson, as we petered out to a 0-1 defeat. Grim.

Still, at least I had a gig to cheer myself up, so a hasty exit from the ground was required (thus saving myself the indignity of booing the team off) in order to board a train to Leeds. The thing is, once there I had no idea where the venue was. I had an address yes, but I'd not got around to printing myself a map out for this one. The Woodhouse Liberal Club? Sounded like a working men's club to me...

I looked at the map on Leeds station wall, then checked a bus timetable, and Woodhouse seemed a long way away. A far simpler solution was to give Big Ship Iron a buzz as he was seemingly hiring a fleet of cars to get him and his son Keifer and mates to the gig. 'Wait outside the station, Belchy, and don't move,' he bellowed down the phone.

Meanwhile I received a text from Paul Helocolin saying, "We've found the venue. It's a working men's club!" So it really was then…

When I and the Big Ship Iron entourage arrived, we were awestruck by the venue. Yes, it *really* was a working men's club. Thrupty described it as "another 1960s municipal atrocity, looking for all the world like the club in *Phoenix Nights*." Even better was the function room on the side where the gig was due to take place, it being just the place to hold a wedding reception – a massive hall with lights on the tables and a stage that was swathed in curtains. It was as if it had been set aside specifically for a Cardiacs Gala Concert Performance, so perfect was it for the occasion. The fact that Jill and Carli were wearing their wedding dresses only added to the spectacle, as did the numerous men in various stages of evening dress.

In case it wasn't enough like a wedding already, Big Ship Iron had sneaked in somewhere between a dozen and twenty confetti cannons which he dished out to the privileged. Meanwhile, the crowds kept coming. Not only were both Dogstands there and Jill with hubby Paul, but, almost like a curtain call for the fortnight-ever-presents, Pete (one of those in evening dress) and Malc were also in attendance, as was almost-ever-present Duffy (the only one he missed was Stoke). It was particularly pleasing to see Malc, as due to the late addition of this gig to the tour, he'd already made plans to attend some function with his other half, and had been bemoaning the fact all fortnight. Well, he'd worked his magic on the missus, and here he was.

Talking of other halves, Pete's gorgeous significant other Clare was also there, and behind the Cardiacs merchandise desk, Ordinary Shop Girl Jane was persuading me to buy a new 'Little Man And A House' t-shirt because the venue and occasion merited it. And still they came; Simon the Millwall fan was there, as was Andy Hossain along with his cousin Matt Healy, the one who plays the part of Matthew King in *Emmerdale*, a long-time Cardiacs fan. What's more, the bloke that plays Zak Dingle in the self-same soap was there too, giving Big Ship Iron the opportunity to chat to him and thus fulfil a long-held ambition.

And *still* they came, in their hundreds, all the more adding to the already incredible atmosphere, and the gig hadn't even started yet. The Helocolins were there, and Chris Luxford made it at the very last minute. Amongst the throng Jill and Carli could be seen flitting around in their Gothic wedding dresses, leading Carli to say that Jill looked 'a proper little sexpot' (and who were we to disagree?).

As ever, the God Damn Whores got things off to a start, and "Physical Training" once again brought the house down. But there was no doubt who everyone was here for, and when Cardiacs took to the stage amidst the curtains and smoke, accompanied by that sooo perfect intro tape, everyone cheered until fit to burst.

Not wanting to repeat myself, but this truly wonderful night of incredible entertainment was everything that I'd ever wanted a Cardiacs gig to be; not only a wonderful conclusion to the tour, but a fantastical summing-up of every one of the previous ton of Cardiacs gigs I'd attended. It was almost a shame in a way that this one wasn't my 100th, but then as the 101st it allows it to stand alone, and believe me, this night of wonder deserves to be set aside.

Goodness me, as I'm writing this I'm really struggling because the tears are flowing. Those that were there that night will understand fully; those that weren't there but have had their lives touched by Tim Smith and Cardiacs in some way will have a pretty good grasp of it too. And those that have stumbled on this for whatever reasons who have no idea who Cardiacs are may well find it impossible to understand at all, but if you so much as listened at the door that night, you'd know.

Is it possible to touch and taste the atmosphere when you're at a gig? I swear we could in the Woodhouse Liberal Club. A roomful of joyous people, all celebrating together. Everywhere you looked there were beaming smiles and ecstatic faces, with that peculiar dancing that only fans who know every twist and turn, stop and start of the music can do, and when almost an entire hall is doing it, heck, that's an incredible sight.

What's more, the six musicians on the stage seemed relaxed and happy too, with Tim announcing, to huge cheers, that they were going to play 'for ages tonight.' Pete described Kavus' performance as "pulling out all the stops, gawking, careering round the stage, pulling some great Rockstar poses," adding that "Mel and Cathy broke their stony faces, sticking tongues out at the crowd."

And what a crowd! The Helocolins encouraged Tim to "do the raffle!", Tim informing them they'd got the wrong colour tickets so they'd wasted their money. We were able to do the sailor dance one last time at the end of "The Breakfast Line", and I was given one last chance to wave the peace-signs aloft during the preceding doomy blast of "Master Builder". One more time we struggled to do the rub-belly-pat-head manoeuvre in "R.E.S." and go wild during "To Go Off And Things". It was at this point that the only bad-vibe surfaced when Pete was seemingly singled out by someone who wisely made himself scarce from then on, this someone taking him out in a Roy-Keane-style assassination, thus popping his knee out. Millwall Simon and friend helped him pop it back in, and I swear at least one of them was about to pass out. Pete spent the rest of the gig in agony, but everyone moved aside and let him prop himself up at the front of the stage.

Meanwhile, choreographed confetti-cannon-assaults were planned, so when given the shout from Big Ship Iron, we'd let them off, "Buds And Spawn" particularly benefiting from nostalgic bursts of coloured paper swirling around like it was 1988 all over again. Cardiacs even allowed themselves to pay tribute to Jon Poole with their own version of "Physical Training", and everyone bore a grin as wide as West Yorkshire itself.

"Dirty Boy" wound-up the main set in all its majestic glory, reaching such levels of intensity that even for this tour scaled new heights. The endorphins this produced in Pete were obviously acting as a painkiller, (oh, and apparently Graeme Dogstand kept feeding him brandy, on top of Pete repeatedly chanting a mantra to himself of, "Worry about it tomorrow.") because he could be seen leaning on the stage facing us all wearing a smile of pure ecstasy throughout. And then just when we thought it couldn't get any better, the final final encore was "The Everso Closely Guarded Line", and like I said about Cardiff, if push comes to shove, this is the Belch Fave (depending on the day etc etc), it being a bit of a Prog-tastic epic and all that.

When it was all over, Mel even felt so washed along on a tide of happiness that she got all Rock and Roll and tossed a tambourine into the audience. We bayed for more, but it was well past curfew time, so up came the lights, and for one last time we were able to observe the sweat-soaked happiness that is the Pond post-gig. Despite perspiring bodies, there were embraces all round as people who'd bonded over two weeks, and some who'd bonded over one night, said farewell. Confetti everywhere, I didn't envy the cleaners, but hey, they'd understand that we needed to do what had to be done, surely…

* * * *

Of course, it didn't end there. As luck would have it there was a pub just around the corner with a late-license, so we decamped *en masse*. It seemed that everyone who had been in the Woodhouse Liberal Club was squashed in there, whether they be Cardiacs fans or representatives of the Alphabet Business Concern, and everyone was happily chatting in corners, by bars, or out in the beer garden. The locals seemed slightly puzzled, but enjoyed the spectacle, and good vibes washed over all those present. As Pete said in an email: "Evenings like this are few and far between, and it makes you feel amazing to think this is all down to a bunch of disparates all following the same band. Frank Zappa once said 'Music is the only religion that actually delivers the goods,' and I think the whole Leeds experience sums this up beautifully."

At chucking out time, Big Ship Iron's fleet of cars had returned to sweep us all to our resting places, but not before he'd seemingly bought us all a kebab from the local fast-food emporium, the proprietor doubtless delighted by this incredibly late rush.

Big Ship Iron had booked five of us into a Bed and Breakfast in Doncaster, those five being myself, Pete and Clare, and the Dogstands. Sunday morning, despite the lateness of the night before, I was most impressed to see that Big Ship Iron was indeed there first thing Sunday morning to greet us as we breakfasted, before taking us all back to have a look at his beautiful house, a house that once belonged to Oliver Cromwell no less.

As we sat around reflecting on the Leeds gig and the tour as a whole, and as we discussed the plans to get home (the Dogstands volunteered to give me one last chance not to hitch) I thought about how far we'd all come in that fortnight. Just short of two weeks earlier, the Dogstands were most dismissive of Big Ship Iron and his promise to help me with the book and the tour, and yet now they were all genuinely the best of friends.

That was the strength of this tour; like I said before, friendships forged that will last a lifetime.

* * * *

Carli and Graeme Dogstand proved to be absolute angels by not only whizzing me all the way down the M1, but also round the M25 and then into Ashford (Middlesex) via Staines, right to my front door. After one final embrace from both of them, I opened the door and chucked my rucksack on the floor. There on the doormat was an envelope addressed to me, so I opened it straight away. It contained a letter from the proctologist who'd examined me on the morning of the first gig of the tour, Brighton, to my GP, copied to me of course. After he announced that he'd examined me on Monday 12th November and then gone on to explain exactly what he'd found (I'll spare you the details), the letter went on to say; "He is a music lover and is going on tour with the band the (sic) Cardiacs for the next two weeks, so he will not be around until after then."

Oh yes, this was where the whole fortnight had started, and as if I needed reminding that I was heading back to reality, here it was in black and white. But then it *was* quite funny that the proctologist had seen fit to mention Cardiacs in the letter, so before they drove off, I ran over to the Dogstands' car and read the letter out to them.

'You mean you've had that on your mind throughout the tour?' asked Carli.

'No,' I replied, 'I've barely given it a thought over the last two weeks; been a bit too busy.'

Now, just where *is* that Cardiac Recovery Unit...?

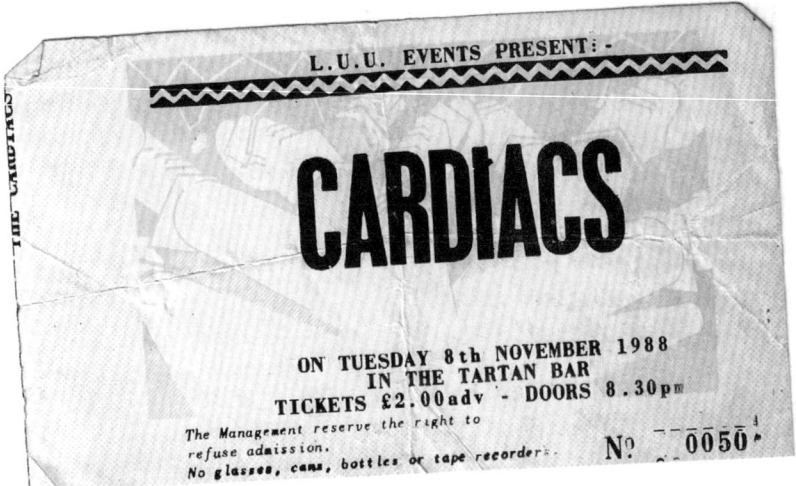

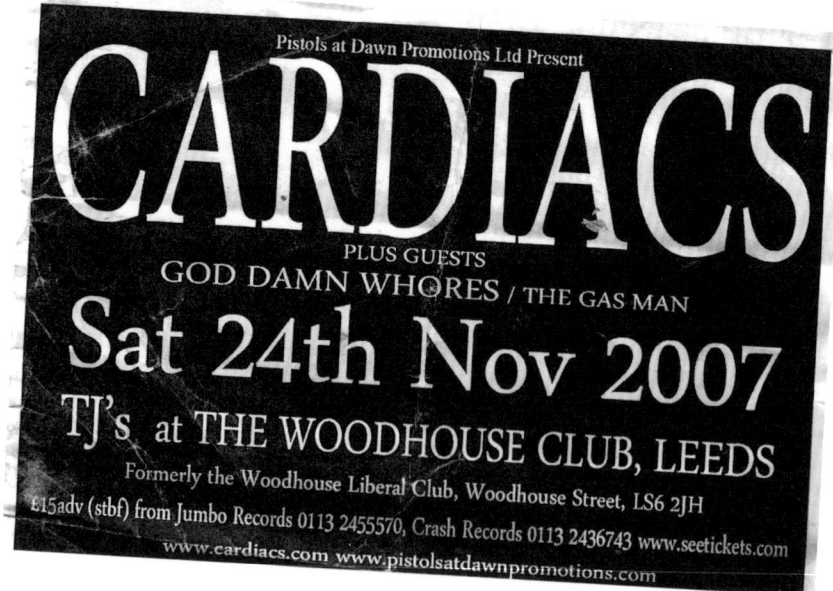

Epilogue
Gong Live At The Forum, Kentish Town, June 15th 2008

Epilogue
Gong Live At The Forum, Kentish Town, June 15th 2008

As mentioned elsewhere, Gong at the Forum in 2008 brought just about every representative of the Alphabet Business Concern out in force, including a huge contingent from The List. Tim Smith was amongst this happy throng, and as one who had gone on record in interviews and such-like as having seen Gong with Steve Hillage in 1974, he was rather excited to be seeing them with said guitarist once again, Hillage having only recently returned to the fold. Before Gong entered the stage, a punky youth was moaning about something of very little significance, Tim was overheard to say, "It doesn't really matter – we're about to see Gong, WITH STEVE HILLAGE!"

And afterwards, all Tim could say was "F***!" A lot of it was probably to do with a rather barnstorming version of "Master Builder" prior to which I'd tapped the punky youth on the shoulder and said, "Better prepare yourself for one of the greatest moments of your life."

One of the joys of living just outside Zone 6 of London Transport, in Ashford (Middx), is that on night's out when everyone else is looking to have fun into the early hours, I have to dash off to get the last train, more so on a Sunday when London closes down unreasonably early. This night was no exception, but being Belch I decided to hang on as long as I dared for that extra bit of socialising. And as a consequence missed the last train from Waterloo, by some distance. I ended up at Clapham Junction and then decided to get the train to Twickenham as this seemed to be the closest I could get to home without having to resort to the dreaded night bus (which wouldn't get me home anyway in case you're wondering, but yes, it would've got me to a better spot than Twickenham, granted).

As I wandered around Twickenham for some reason I felt gloom and sadness, and I had no real idea why, especially as I'd just witnessed the spiritual high of a Gong gig. Possibly it was something to do with the fact that I was worrying that the Belch Fire was being extinguished. Why, had I not spent most of the 1988 *Cardiacs Live* tour hitchhiking all over the place, mostly through the night, and not worrying in the slightest if I had a sleepless night before reporting for work? And had I not spent most of the previous 20 years trying to gatecrash every post-gig party by every band I'd ever seen live, often succeeding? And yet here I was not even bothering to attempt a raid on Gong's dressing room and making a dash home in order to get a decent night's kip so I could be fresh for work the next day. And I'd even failed at that.

In the end I accosted a private cab owner as he attempted to enter a Twickenham kebab shop to get a well-earned feed. Not only did the poor chap have to go without his supper, and not only did I make him break the rules of cabbiedom (although to be fair, I did say I'd call him on my mobile if it'd make things better), the poor chap then had to listen to me ranting and raving about Gong and Cardiacs all the way to Ashford…

The last thing I'd seen just before I headed away from the Forum had been Tim Smith heading up the stairs in order to attend the post-gig party. An evening in the company of Cardiacs and Gong? Could it get much better? Probably not, but off I ran anyway, and my heart soon grew heavy…

Two weeks later, we on the list were made aware of Tim's illness, and this last glimpse of Tim disappearing up them stairs came to mind. Possibly, just possibly, this was why my heart had been so heavy as I wandered aimlessly around Twickenham that night.

Get well soon, Timmy, we really do love you. x x

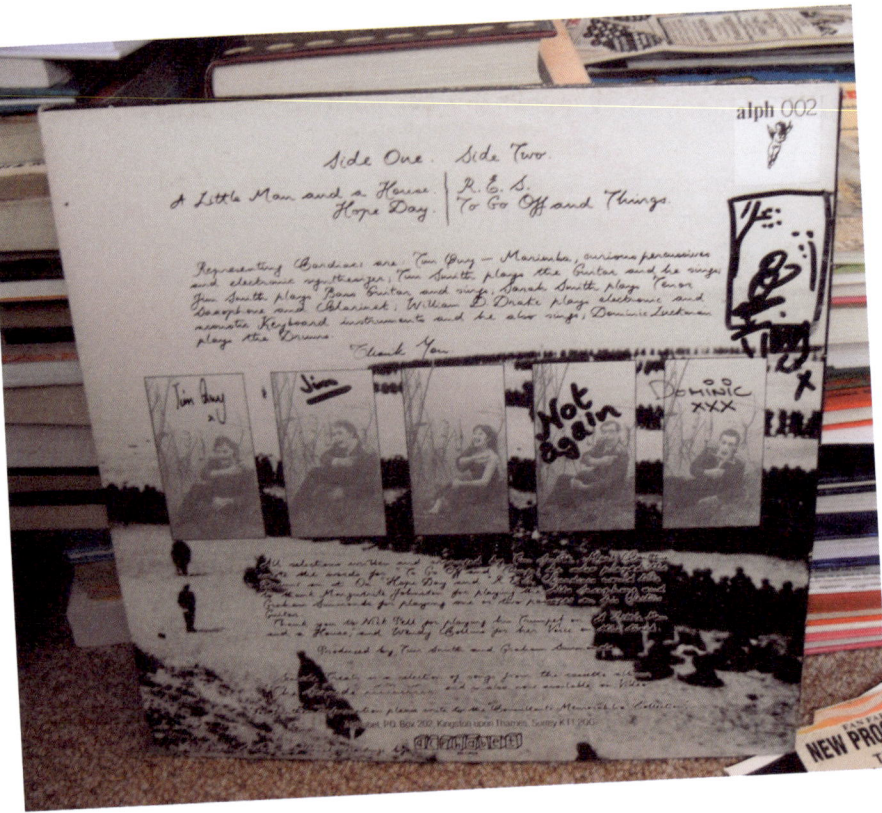

Appendices

Appendices

Top 10 Cardiacs Gigs (in no order other than chronological)

Reading Festival – August 1986

London Hammersmith Clarendon Hotel Ballroom – June 1988

Leeds University – November 1988

London Marquee – December 1988

Aylesbury Civic Centre – June 1989

Oxford Venue – May 1991

Milton Keynes Woughton Centre – May 1995

London Astoria – November 2001

The Special Garage Concerts – October 2003

Leeds Woodhouse Liberal Club – November 2007

Top 5 Cardiacs Songs

As Cold As Can Be In An English Sea

Nurses Whispering Verses

The Whole World Window

The Everso Closely Guarded Line

Dirty Boy

Top 3 Cardiacs Albums

A Little Man and a House and the Whole World Window

On Land and In the Sea

Sing to God

The Belch Cardiacs Collection
7" Singles

A Bus For A Bus On The Bus/A Cake For Bertie's Party/Food On The Wall

Is This The Life?/I'm Eating In Bed

Susannah's Still Alive/Blind In Safety And Leafy In Love

Baby Heart Dirt/I Hold My Love In My Arms

Baby Heart Dirt/I Hold My Love In My Arms (Dutch)

12" Singles

Seaside Treats EP: A Little Man And A House/Hope Day/R.E.S/To

Go Off And Things

There's Too Many Irons In The Fire/All Spectacular/Loosefish Scapegrace

Is This The Life?/Goosegash/I'm Eating In Bed

Is This The Life?/I'm Eating In Bed/There's Too Many Irons In The Fire (Dutch)

Night Tracks EP: R.E.S./Buds And Spawn/In A City Lining/Cameras/Is This The Life?

Susannah's Still Alive/Blind In Safety And Leafy In Love/All His Geese Are Swans!

Susannah's Still Alive/Blind In Safety And Leafy In Love/All His Geese Are Swans! (white label promo)

Baby Heart Dirt/I Hold My Love In My Arms/Horse Head/The Safety Bowl

Day Is Gone/No Bright Side/Ideal/Joining The Plankton

CD Singles

Day Is Gone/No Bright Side/Ideal/Joining The Plankton

Bellyeye/A Horse's Tail/No Gold

Manhoo/Spinney/What Paradise Is Like

Odd Even/Hurricane/Devils

Sleep All Eyes Open/Dirty Boy/Foundling/Insect Hooves On Lassie (instrumental)

Signs/Sang 'All Away Away!'/Dog-Like Sparky (instrumental)

Ditzy Scene/Gen/Made All Up

Cassettes

Archive Cardiacs

The Seaside

Vinyl Albums

Big Ship

Rude Bootleg

A Little Man And A House And The Whole World Window

Cardiacs Live

CD Albums

Archive Cardiacs

The Seaside

Rude Bootleg
A Little Man And A House And The Whole World Window
Cardiacs Live
On Land And In The Sea
Songs For Ships And Irons
Heaven Born And Ever Bright
Sampler
All That Glitters Is A Mare's Nest
Sing To God (double CD)
Sing To God Part One
Sing To God Part Two
Guns
Cardiacs And Affectionate Friends
Cardiacs Greatest Hits
The Special Garage Concerts Volume I
The Special Garage Concerts Volume II

Videos

Seaside Treats (except Sarah's still got it)
All That Glitters Is A Mare's Nest

T-shirts etc (all short-sleeve unless stated)

A Little Man And A House And The Whole World Window album,
Big Flower design
Cardiacs Live tour, Dog-and-Big-Flower design
On Land And In The Sea tour, used to be white, now brown after
washing disaster, with tree, red lettering
A Little Man and a House logo white on black, long-sleeved
A Little Man and a House logo, green on yellow, long-sleeved
"All That Glitters Is A Mare's Nest", now sleeveless (Peter spoiled
it)
A Little Man and a House logo, green on black, long-sleeved
"I Am In It" giant Little Man and a House logo
Heaven Born And Ever Bright with lyric back-print
Big Flower logo, yellow on black, long-sleeved
A Little Man and a House logo on breast pocket, long-sleeved, lots
of holes

A Little Man and a House logo, white on black, 1995 tour dates on rear

A Little Man and a House logo, white on green with a yellow Big Flower too, 1995 tour dates on rear, long sleeved

Sing To God tour

A Little Man and a House logo, black on white, black collar and cuffs, falling to bits

A Little Man and a House logo, black on grey

Guns tour, grey with black collar and cuffs

A Little Man and a House logo, white on black, polo-shirt

Greatest Hits Fish design

Special Garage Concerts Big Flower design

A Little Man and a House giant logo, white on black, Astoria Nov 2004, long-sleeved

A Little Man and a House giant logo, white on black, Wildhearts 2004 tour, long-sleeved

"Extra in Cardiacs Cinematographic Effort" Astoria 2005

A Little Man and a House giant logo, black on grey, 2007 tour, long-sleeved

A Little Man and a House giant logo, black on grey, 2007 tour, long-sleeved, fully signed

A Little Man and a House logo, white on black

"World Tour 1995" tour jacket

A Little Man and a House logo mug, white on black

A Little Man and a House logo alarm clock, black on white

A Little Man and a House logo towel, black on white

A Little Man and a House logo record bag, retired gracefully in bits

Three Little Man and a House logo watches, all broken

Too many badges

A Little Man and a House logo woolly hat, hand-knitted

Cardiacs 2006 line-up mousemat

An Alphabet Business Concern tie (pulled a bit)

Plus:

A Little Man and a House logo black on green t-shirt which Michaela possibly still has, and A Little Man and a House logo woolly hat that Katrina has either binned or taken to the charity shop, or maybe she still has it (but I doubt it).

The Belch Cardiacs Gig List

The Belch Cardiacs Gig List

	DATE	TOWN	VENUE	ROUND TRIP	TOTAL MILES	FEATURED	RESERVED
1	Aug 24th 1986	Reading	National Jazz, Blues & Rock Festival	397.2	397.2	Chapters 2 & 10	Jill Howard
2	Apr 23rd 1988	Sheffield	Leadmill	4	401.2	Chs. 2 & 13	Mark Griffiths
3	May 27th 1988	Northampton	Roadmender	209.6	610.8		Barry Limey-tank
4	Jun 9th 1988	Scunthorpe	Baths Hall	99.2	710	Ch. 21	Carlo aka Windom Earle
5	Jun 23rd 1988	London	Hammersmith Clarendon Hotel Ballroom	603	1313	Ch. 11	Tim Britton
6	Nov 8th 1988	Leeds	University	199.4	1512.4	Ch. 25	Richard Jackson
7	Nov 9th 1988	Huddersfield	Polytechnic	181.5	1693.9		Paul Westwood
8	Nov 10th 1988	Oxford	Polytechnic	78.5	1772.4	Ch. 5	Aaron Miller
9	Nov 16th 1988	Manchester	University	308.7	2081.1		Jesse Schust
10	Nov 23rd 1988	Keele	University	264.7	2345.8	Ch. 17	Neil Ghee
11	Nov 24th 1988	Rayleigh	Pink Toothbrush	164.1	2509.9	Ch. 23	Graham Palmer
12	Nov 27th 1988	London	Kentish Town, Town & Country Club	169	2678.9		Michael "Moke" Chapman
13	Dec 21st 1988	London	Charing Cross Road, Marquee Club	175.8	2854.7	Chs. 4 & 12	Alan Pendleton
14	May 19th 1989	London	Astoria	175.8	3030.5		Kieran Fleck
15	Jun 13th 1989	Sheffield	Take Two	244.2	3274.7	Ch. 15	Clive Hutton
16	Jun 17th 1989	Oxford	Co-op Hall	62.4	3337.1	Ch. 5	Chris Luxford
17	Jun 23rd 1989	Aylesbury	Civic Centre	521.3	3858.4	Ch. 12	Lennaert "Frostbyte" Roomer
18	Oct 23rd 1989	Oxford	Co-op Hall	62.4	3920.8		Gehenna the Horse
19	Feb 24th 1990	Oxford	Co-op Hall	62.4	3983.2		Ady Randell
20	Jun 30th 1990	Salisbury	Arts Centre	557.7	4540.9		Neil Gordon
21	Oct 27th 1990	Oxford	Venue (formerly Co-op Hall)	62.4	4603.3		Dapper
22	May 16th 1991	Oxford	Venue	62.4	4665.7	Ch. 5	Michael Keane
23	Feb 28th 1992	Northampton	Irish Centre	49.4	4715.1	Ch. 9	Paul Helocolin
24	Jun 6th 1992	Nottingham	Trent Polytechnic	160.4	4875.5	Ch. 9	Jesse Vecchione
25	Jun 13th 1992	Milton Keynes	Woughton Centre	53.4	4928.9		Roscoe Brooker

26	Aug 25th 1992	London	Camden Palace	144	5072.9		Andy Prestidge
27	Oct 9th 1992	London	New Cross Venue	155.8	5228.7		Claire Thomas
28	May 2nd 1993	London	New Cross Venue	687.1	5915.8	Chs. 6 & 4	Paul Ashby
29	Jul 3rd 1993	St Helens	Citadel	291	6206.8	Ch. 12	Phil Whalley
30	Jul 17th 1993	Long Marston	Phoenix Festival	89.8	6296.6	Ch. 23	Martin Roest
31	Jul 20th 1993	London	Camden Palace	144	6440.6		Jamie Kelsey-Fry
32	Dec 3rd 1993	London	New Cross Venue	155.8	6596.4		Sean Cooke
33	Mar 15th 1994	London	Camden Palace	144	6740.4	Chs. 13, 16 & 20	Al Gittens
34	May 29th 1994	London	New Cross Venue	175.8	6916.2	Chs. 6 & 4	Brian Carney
35	Dec 10th 1994	London	Astoria 2	153.4	7069.6		Adam Doyle
36	Apr 22nd 1995	London	Kentish Town Forum (formerly Town & Country Club)	158.8	7228.4		Purple Heather
37	May 11th 1995	London	King's Cross Splash Club @ Water Rats	181.7	7410.1	Ch. 4	Karen Helocolin
38	May 13th 1995	Windsor	Old Trout	127	7537.01	Ch. 23	Dave "Diggy" Dawson
39	May 24th 1995	Milton Keynes	Woughton Centre	89	7626.1	Ch. 12	Sarah Hailey
40	May 25th 1995	Birmingham	Foundry	104	7730.1		Stuart Farrow
41	May 29th 1995	Worcester	Northwick Theatre	114.8	7844.9		Darryl Anthony
42	Jul 15th 1995	Long Marston	Phoenix Festival	85.8	7930.7	Ch. 12	Mikey Poole
43	Nov 17th 1995	London	Kentish Town Forum	173	8103.7		Cathy White
44	Jun 12th 1996	Reading	Alleycat Live	267.5	8371.2		Mark Hitchings
45	Jun 17th 1996	Birmingham	Foundry	58.9	8430.1		Pete Moltesen
46	Jun 18th 1996	Wolverhampton	Civic Centre	17.3	8447.4	Ch. 19	Mike Vennart
47	Jun 19th 1996	Bristol	Fleece & Firkin	189.5	8636.9	Ch. 23	Ian Evans
48	Jun 21st 1996	London	Astoria 2	398	9034.9		Dan & Cat Evans
49	Jun 23rd 1996	Northampton	Roadmender	46.6	9081.5	Ch. 6	Kettle
50	Jun 24th 1996	Leeds	Duchess of York	297.6	9379.1	Ch. 6	Ian Skinner
51	Jun 27th 1996	Chelmsford	Army & Navy	234	9613.1		Matt Precey
52	Nov 1st 1996	Oxford	The Point	62.4	9675.5	Ch. 13	Stephen "Schlep" Wilson

53	Nov 2nd 1996	London	Astoria 2	160	9835.5		The Organ
54	Nov 4th 1996	Bolton	Crown & Cushion	154.7	9990.2	Ch. 7	Jon Whitehead
55	Nov 5th 1996	Manchester	Roadhouse	165	10155.2	Ch. 20	Al Gittens and Carol Ryder
56	Nov 7th 1996	Bristol	Fleece & Firkin	243.5	10398.7		Rose Kemp
57	Nov 8th 1996	Brighton	Concorde	232.5	10631.2	Ch. 3	David Sheridon
58	Nov 10th 1996	Southampton	Joiner's Arms	178.2	10809.4		James Orman
59	Nov 16th 1996	Reading	Alleycat Live	103.4	10912.8		Warren Jacques
60	Oct 25th 1997	Stoke-on-Trent	Trentham Gardens	196.2	11109	Ch. 12	Rob Hingley
61	Jan 22nd 1998	London	Kentish Town Bull & Gate	218.4	11327.4	Ch. 12	Jamie Keddie
62	Dec 4th 1998	London	Islington, the Garage	15.6	11343	Ch. 8	Sam Shepherd
63	Jan 29th 1999	London	Camden Barfly @ the Falcon	16.2	11359.2	Ch. 8	Betty Bead
64	Jan 30th 1999	London	Camden Barfly @ the Falcon	16.2	11375.4	Ch. 8	Paul Howard
65	Jan 31st 1999	London	Camden Barfly @ the Falcon	16.2	11391.6	Chs. 8 & 18	Andy Hossain
66	Mar 19th 1999	London	Islington, the Garage	66.5	11458.1	Ch. 16	Jane George
67	Jun 9th 1999	Harlow	The Square	53.6	11511.7	Ch. 23	Richard Crossley
68	Oct 22nd 1999	London	ULU	19.8	11531.5	Ch. 23	William Miers
69	Oct 24th 1999	Brighton	Pressure Point	137.4	11668.9	Ch. 3	Mike Norton
70	Jun 23rd 2000	Shepton Mallet	Glastonbury Festival	323.2	11992.1	Ch. 23	Charlie Bird
71	Aug 5th 2000	Whitchurch	Progressive Rock Festival	313.2	12305.3		Graeme Lockett
72	Nov 11th 2000	London	Astoria 2	14.6	12319.9		Fu & Pet Lamb
73	Aug 3rd 2001	Whitchurch	Progressive Rock Festival	160.2	12480.1	Ch. 12	Ian Taft
74	Nov 23rd 2001	London	Astoria	16.6	12496.7	Ch. 12	Jitka Malkova
75	Nov 15th 2002	London	Astoria	16.6	12513.3	Chs. 12 & 14	Max Crowe
76	Oct 17th 2003	London	Islington, the Garage	14.2	12527.5	Chs. 1 & 20	Lawrence Aegerter
77	Oct 18th 2003	London	Islington, the Garage	14.2	12541.7	Ch. 1	Andy Thompson
78	Oct 19th 2003	London	Islington, the Garage	14.2	12555.9	Ch. 1	Lucy Cooke
79	Nov 12th 2004	London	Astoria	8.6	12564.5	Ch. 12	Andrew "Tat" Tarry
80	Dec 8th 2004	London	Astoria	8.6	12573.1		Sarah Maher

81	Dec 11th 2004	Sheffield	Leadmill	334.6	12907.7	Chs. 13 & 15	Paul Coupe
82	Dec 13th 2004	Cambridge	The Junction	119.2	13026.9		James Larcombe
83	Nov 6th 2005	Brighton	Concorde 2	136.8	13163.7	Ch. 3	Tim Hailley
84	Nov 7th 2005	Portsmouth	Wedgewood Rooms	160.6	13324.3	Ch. 16	Pete "Thrupty" Davis
85	Nov 8th 2005	Oxford	Zodiac (formerly the Venue)	121.7	13446		Benj Heron
86	Nov 9th 2005	Northampton	Soundhaus	183.5	13629.5	Ch. 8	Rob Sim
87	Nov 11th 2005	London	Astoria	9	13638.5	Ch. 22	Patrick Sheehan
88	Dec 21st 2005	London	Kentish Town Bull & Gate	8.8	13647.3	Ch. 22	Nick Loebner
89	Dec 22nd 2005	London	Kentish Town Bull & Gate	8.8	13656.1	Ch. 22	Lynda "Pies" Featherstone
90	Nov 10th 2006	London	Astoria	8.6	13664.7	Ch. 12	Serena Clark
91	Nov 12th 2007	Brighton	Hove, the Old Market	124.8	13789.5	Ch. 3	Helier Bissell-Thomas
92	Nov 13th 2007	Oxford	Carling Academy (formerly the Zodiac)	168.1	13957.6	Ch. 5	Paul Helocolin
93	Nov 14th 2007	Bristol	Thekla Social	278.4	14236	Chs. 7 & 14	Graeme & Carli Dogstand
94	Nov 15th 2007	Nottingham	Rescue Rooms	81.9	14317.9	Ch. 9	Tim Jackson
95	Nov 16th 2007	London	Astoria	156.9	14474.8	Chs. 11 & 14	Maarten Avontuur
96	Nov 19th 2007	Sheffield	Boardwalk	201.6	14676.4	Ch. 13	Simon Wright
97	Nov 20th 2007	Stoke-on-Trent	The Sugarmill	97	14773.4	Ch. 17	Andrew Duffy
98	Nov 21st 2007	Manchester	Academy 3	82.2	14855.6	Chs. 19 & 20	Mike "Livo" Livesey
99	Nov 22nd 2007	Portsmouth	Wedgewood Rooms	245.7	15101.3	Ch. 21	Malcolm Crosby
100	Nov 23rd 2007	Cardiff	Clwb Ifor Bach	164.1	15265.4	Chs.22 & 23	Adrian Bell
101	Nov 24th 2007	Leeds	Woodhouse Liberal Club	452.3	15717.7	Ch. 25	Karen Helocolin

Rules of the Belch-o-meter round trip mileage are as follows:
The round trip is considered to be the total journey from leaving my front door (or work) to returning to that same front door, hence some rather long ones when I took in a Cardiacs gig during a holiday or something, for example Salisbury Arts Centre in 1990 when I took in Devon, Somerset and the New Forest beforehand. However, if there is a sequence of two gigs or more and I don't make it home, then the round trip will end at my resting place for the night, from where the

following round trip will also start. Oh, and don't just trust the bog-standard distance from one place to another as calculated by some travel-planning website, because don't forget, my routes sometimes got a bit convoluted or had extra bits tagged on thanks to my alternative methods of travel. Anyway, it took me ages to do, it's my book, so they're my rules, and that's that.

Home of Fadeless Splendour
Tarred and Feathered
Fast Robert
Hope Day
Eating in Bed

Plane Plane
Burn yo hoose Brown
The Icing on the World

The Breakfast Line
is this the life

Love in Arms
Cold as can Be

Signs
Will Bleed amen
Fiery Gun Hand
Dirty Boy

=========================

Closely Guarded Line

=========================

ABC Bang/To Go Off/Dinosaurs.